THE NEW PERCY GRAINGER COMPANION

Percy Grainger (photographer unknown)

THE NEW PERCY GRAINGER COMPANION

edited by
PENELOPE THWAITES

THE BOYDELL PRESS

© Editor and Contributors 2010
Appendices I–II © The Estate of Percy Grainger

All Rights Reserved. Except as permitted under current legislation
no part of this work may be photocopied, stored in a retrieval system,
published, performed in public, adapted, broadcast,
transmitted, recorded, or reproduced in any form or by any means,
without the prior permission of the copyright owner

First published 2010
The Boydell Press, Woodbridge
Paperback edition 2016

ISBN 978 1 84383 601 8 hardback
ISBN 978 1 78327 185 6 paperback

The Boydell Press is an imprint of Boydell & Brewer Ltd
PO Box 9, Woodbridge, Suffolk IP12 3DF, UK
and of Boydell & Brewer Inc.
668 Mount Hope Ave, Rochester, NY 14620, USA
website : www.boydellandbrewer.com

A CIP catalogue record for this book is available
from the British Library

The publisher has no responsibility for the continued existence or accuracy of URLs for
external or third-party internet websites referred to in this book, and does not guarantee
that any content on such websites is, or will remain, accurate or appropriate

Designed and typeset in Electra with Lydian display and Castellar initials by
The Stingray Office, Chorlton-cum-Hardy, Manchester

Foreword

In 1951, in a letter to Cyril Scott, Percy Grainger wrote: 'I don't think it any disgrace not to do some special thing well, as long as I can acquit myself reasonably as an all-round man.' He acquitted himself splendidly, and in *The New Percy Grainger Companion* this is made wondrously clear.

I was delighted when my dear friend Penelope Thwaites asked me to write about this book. She and I share a love of playing Grainger's piano music, although in my own case I do so with very much less skill. What I especially like about the *Companion* is that it gives rare insights into how to approach and play the music. It also tells of Grainger's own approach to it. For these reasons alone, the book is invaluable to me, just as it will be to all performers of his work.

The *Companion* contains an abundance of other such information that is quite new to me. It will be equally invaluable to composers and musicologists, and to all who care for Grainger's music. Furthermore, I would like to think that it will be of genuine interest to those who may not care for it. Grainger was far removed from Austro-German modernism, the prevailing musical idiom of the twentieth century. By placing him, and his wide interests, in this post-modern world, he emerges as a wholly contemporary composer.

I applaud the contributors to the *Companion*. Many are friends of mine, and all are distinguished Grainger scholars. I also applaud those whose belief and commitment helped the book come to fruition. *The New Percy Grainger Companion* is an exciting publication and a useful one. I have no doubt that it will bring about a wide dissemination of the music of this much-loved composer, this 'all-round man'.

Peter Sculthorpe.

For E.O.J.

Contents

Foreword by Peter Sculthorpe	v
Preface	ix
Acknowledgements	xi
List of Illustrations	xiii
List of Music Examples	xvi
List of Contributors	xvii
A Grainger Timeline	xix
Introduction Penelope Thwaites	1

The Music

1	Orchestral Music Penelope Thwaites, Geoffrey Simon, James Judd	7
2	Music for Wind Band Timothy Reynish	20
3	Grainger for Choirs Paul Jackson	30
4	Singing Grainger Solo Stephen Varcoe	46
5	At the Piano with Grainger Penelope Thwaites	58
6	Towards a Universal Language Paul Jackson, Barry Peter Ould	73
7	Programming Grainger Penelope Thwaites, James Koehne	87
8	Putting Grainger into Print Barry Peter Ould	107
9	Grainger's Pianism on Disc Murray McLachlan	114

Grainger in Context

10	Marvellous Melbourne, 1880–95 *David Walker*	123
11	The Family Background *Penelope Thwaites*	130
12	An Australian Composer? *Roger Covell*	140
13	The Grainger Museum: Then, Now, and In the Future *Brian Allison, Astrid Britt Krautschneider, Kay Dreyfus*	149
14	The Pursuit of Nordic Music *Bruce Clunies Ross*	157
15	At Home in New York *Stewart Manville*	166
16	Grainger and his Contemporaries *Lewis Foreman*	171
17	Reflection and Reminiscence *Desmond Scott, Ronald Stevenson, Peter Sculthorpe, and others*	181
18	The Spiritualising Influence of Music *Teresa Balough*	189

Appendices

I	Percy Grainger, *To Conductors*	199
II	Grainger's Statement on Free Music	207
III	The Family Trees and Family Groups	209
	Select Bibliography	221
	Select Discography	227
	Catalogue of Works	249
	Main Grainger Contacts	293
	Index	295

Preface

The reasonable man adapts himself to the world; the unreasonable one persists in trying to adapt the world to himself. Therefore all progress depends on the unreasonable man.

George Bernard Shaw, Man and Superman (1903),
'Maxims for Revolutionists'

It would be easy to dismiss this remark as typical Shavian paradox, but it seems to fit Percy Grainger like a glove. The extent to which his forward-thinking, pre-1920s ideas (exploration of non-western music, aleatoric methods, elastic instrumentation, adaptation of pre-Bach music, more sociable piano-playing, less formal concert presentation, the challenging of demarcation lines between amateurs and professionals, and between popular, folk and art musics) played an exclusive role in the progress of western music can be debated; but he is without doubt in the company of those who helped to bring about these developments.

In the thirty-five years since his centenary year (and the publication of Lewis Foreman's *The Percy Grainger Companion*) the world has certainly changed in its general awareness of Grainger. His music and life, with varying degrees of accuracy, are widely accessible through the internet. As I write, fifteen books about Grainger are before me, and he continues as a favourite subject for academic debate. He would surely have been pleased that his museum has been beautifully refurbished, and is finally assured of a secure place on the Melbourne University campus. Perhaps most important of all in his eyes, innumerable and continuing recordings of his music are bringing him the well-deserved notability he longed for in his lifetime. Not so encouraging to him would be the rarity of live performances of his works.

To address this latter point is the main aim of *The New Percy Grainger Companion*. There are many reasons why Grainger is so seldom performed, but those of us who love his music are unhappy to see the concert-going public deprived of it. The apparent problems can be overcome, and the practising musicians writing here share their experiences, their technical expertise and their programme suggestions for this gorgeous repertoire.

Grainger was clear that a composer's work is better understood by a knowledge of his or her life — or, to quote Kay Dreyfus, an understanding 'embedded in biography and social history'. He left much material relating to himself and other contemporaries available to the public in his museum. His writings cover a huge range of subjects.

Interpreting Grainger's words is a Sisyphean task. He uses the broadest of brushstrokes and is misleadingly prodigal in his use of the superlative. In his fury and resentment at things he does not like, he is wildly contradictory and at times offensive. He can tie himself in knots, trying to prove un-provable theories. Yet his use of language is unmistakeably individual and often wonderfully vivid, as the introductions to such works as *Green Bushes* and *The Warriors* illustrate. Perhaps this natural instinct for the music and rhythm of words was one of the attractions to him of Kipling's verse. His own titles are testament to it: for example, he cleverly exchanges the pun-worthy *Londonderry Air* for the much more evocative title *Irish Tune from County Derry*. Some of Grainger's verbal idiosyncrasies have led to the mistaken perception of him as some kind of musical court jester. On the contrary, he was a deeply serious thinker. In the final chapter of this book Teresa Balough highlights some of his most perceptive and stimulating thoughts on music and life.

He was a musician of genius, but he was much more than that. Explaining his baffling devotion to the Norse outlaw, Grettir the Strong, Grainger wrote, 'these chaps *really lived their lives out*'. So too did Percy Grainger: visionary, flawed, startlingly honest, ultimately (in his own estimation) a failure, he wrestled with the challenges that life threw at him, turning his experience into stirring and moving music. For all the millions of words he left behind him, his music is where the heart — the truth — of Grainger is to be found. To encourage that exploration is the purpose of this book.

Penelope Thwaites
London, 2016

Acknowledgements

MY DEBT TO RESEARCHERS AND BIOGRAPHERS from five decades and more is obvious, and the bibliography at the back of this volume gives some idea of the wealth of material already available to the Grainger investigator. I am especially grateful to my distinguished contributors, who have been generous enough to share their long experience, both as performers and scholars. Further thanks are due to the curatorial staff at the Grainger Museum in facilitating access to primary sources of material and for making me feel welcome on my research visits. Likewise, I was fortunate to have access to the unique collection held at Grainger's house in White Plains, New York, and for that privilege, for permission to take and use photographs, and for financial support, I thank Stewart Manville and the Grainger Estate. I am particularly grateful to both the Delius Trust and the Ralph Vaughan Williams Trust, as well as to Hector Walker, for their generous contributions towards the production of this book.

For permission to reproduce the illustrations, I am indebted to the following sources: The Grainger Museum for the front dust-jacket portrait of Percy Grainger by Rupert Bunny and for Plates 1, 2, 4, 5, 6, 9, 10, 13, 14, 16, 17, 18, 21, 22, 23, 24, 25, 31, 33, 34, 35, and 36; The Estate of Percy Grainger for the Frontispiece and for Plates 7, 12, 27, 29, and 37; West Point Military Academy for Plates 8 and 11, and for the signed portrait of Grainger on the back dust-jacket; The Brighton Historical Society (Melbourne, Australia) for Plate 19; The Delius Trust for Plate 28; Brian Allison for Plates 20 and 32; and Rita Boswell for Plates 15, 38, and 41. Plates 3, 26, 30, 39, and 40 are the editor's own. The programme examples, again, are from the editor's collection, permissions being granted for Figs. 7.1 and 7.2 by The Tait Memorial Trust, for Figs. 7.6 and 7.7 by Professor John Hopkins OBE, for Fig. 7.8 by The Monteverdi Choir and Orchestra, and for Fig. 7.12 by The Adelaide Symphony Orchestra. For permission to reproduce the musical examples, I wish to thank the following: Schott & Co. Ltd: Examples 1.1, 1.2, 2.1, 3.2, 3.3, 3.4, 4.1, 5.1, 5.6, and 5.7; Bardic Edition: Examples 4.2, 4.3, 5.2, 5.3, 5.4, 5.5, 6.1, 8.1, 8.2, and 8.3; Fischer/Schott: Example 2.2; Universal Edition: Example 3.1.

My work (like that, I suspect, of many other Grainger ventures) would have been infinitely more problematic without the invaluable support and generosity of Barry Peter Ould, who knows more about Grainger's music than anyone and is a walking library of essential information. My colleague John Lavender has also given helpful advice from long performing experience, and for that I am very grateful. In the largely unexplored area of Percy's Grainger forebears, as well as the Aldridge ancestors, I have been fortunate to have had the indispensable expertise of the archivist Rita Boswell, who has been most generous with her time and her suggestions. I am grateful also to Brian Allison for his sharing of information on that subject. I owe much to the advice of many Grainger colleagues, particularly Bruce Clunies Ross, Teresa Balough, Lionel Carley, Kay Dreyfus, Lewis Foreman, Stephen Lloyd, Stewart Manville, Alessandro Servadei, and Alan Woolgar. Over the years I have been regularly indebted to both Thomas Slattery's and John Bird's biographies. More recent published selections of Grainger's own writings, produced with exemplary scholarship by Teresa Balough, Kay Dreyfus, Malcolm Gillies, David Pear, Mark Carroll, and Bruce Clunies Ross, make reading these documents a pleasure rather than an obstacle course. Thomas Lewis's *A Source Guide to the Music of Percy Grainger* and Robert Simon's *Percy Grainger: The Pictorial Biography* have also been of special help.

For her painstaking work on the Index, I wish to thank Susan Foreman. Further valuable assistance, in a variety of ways, has been given by Hilary Belden, Colin Fox (ABC), Barrie Gavin, Professor John Hopkins, Astrid Krautschneider, John and Beryl Lindley, Rosalind McMillan, Megan and Miranda Passey, Ingrid Pearson, Bianca Rooman, Peter Thwaites, Professor David Tunley, Hector Walker, Sally and Virginia Wigan, and Joan Winterkorn. Earlier help with Grainger research, particularly from William L. Reed, and from John Amis, John Bird, Sir Frank Callaway and Rosemary Florrimell is gratefully acknowledged. The Aldridge family have provided invaluable contextual help, and my warm thanks go to Cara Aldridge Ham and Roderick Ham, Elspeth Aldridge, Sarah Frayne, John Morrish, Bill and Betty Morrish, Mary and Bob Hackett, James Aldridge, and Athalie Symons. My commissioning editor at Boydell & Brewer, Michael Middeke, has been most kind and patient in offering advice and guidance, and I am grateful also to his editorial and copy-editing team for all their help.

Heartfelt thanks go to my son and daughter, Matthew and Lucy. Their belief and encouragement have helped to make this book possible. To my late husband, Edward, I owe more than I can say. He was a huge admirer of Grainger's music and a discriminating and loyal supporter in so many projects over nearly thirty years. He did not live to see this book published but he knew that he would be its dedicatee.

List of Illustrations

Cover

Percy Grainger, oil on canvas, c.1902, by Rupert Bunny (1864–1947)

Frontispiece

Percy Grainger (photographer unknown)

Figures

2.1	West Point Military Academy concert programme, featuring Grainger, April 1948	29
7.1	1926 recital programme from Grainger's Australasian tour (dir. J. and N. Tait)	95
7.2	1934 recital programme from Grainger's Australasian tour (dir. J. and N. Tait)	96
7.3	1982 Centenary Day piano recital *Percy Grainger and his Circle* by Penelope Thwaites; 8 July, Purcell Room, Southbank Centre, London	97
7.4	1998 A *Grainger Song Gala*, Della Jones, mezzo, James Gilchrist, tenor, Stephen Varcoe, baritone, Penelope Thwaites, piano; 7 November, St John's, Smith Square, London	98
7.5	1998 A *Multi-Piano Extravaganza*, Wayne Marshall, Penelope Thwaites, John Lavender, Rhondda Gillespie, Antony Gray; 8 November, St John's, Smith Square, London	99
7.6	1982 Grainger Centenary Concert, Melbourne Symphony Orchestra, Royal Melbourne Philharmonic Society Choir, cond. John Hopkins OBE; 7 July, Melbourne Concert Hall	100
7.7	Grainger Centenary Programme, MSO, RMPSC, MUFMC, Hopkins, and soloists	101
7.8	1982 Grainger Centenary Concert, The Monteverdi Choir and Orchestra, cond. John Eliot Gardiner; 19 October, Queen Elizabeth Hall, London	102
7.9	1928 Hollywood Bowl Concert, cond. Percy Grainger; 9 August, Hollywood, USA, on the occasion of his marriage to Ella Viola Ström	103
7.10	1949 Houghton College Band, cond. H. Raynard Alger; pianist and conductor, Percy Grainger; 11 May, New York State, USA	104
7.11	1957 Aarhus Municipal Orchestra, cond. Per Dreier; piano soloist, Percy Grainger; 25 February, Aarhus Scala, Aarhus, Jutland, Denmark	105

7.12   2003 Adelaide Symphony Orchestra, Adelaide Chamber Singers, cond.   106
James Judd, piano soloists, Benjamin Martin, Penelope Thwaites;
9, 10, 11, 18 October, Adelaide Town Hall, Adelaide, South Australia

Plates

(between p. 74 and p. 75)

1. The 15th Band, Coast Artillery Corps of the US Army, Fort Hamilton, 1918
2. Grainger with Aeolian company recording producer W. Creary Woods, New York, August 1915
3. The Grainger house at 7 Cromwell Place, White Plains, New York, as it is today
4. Percy and Ella Grainger in wedding dress (photo taken at White Plains, 1928)
5. In towelling clothes, by the verandah at White Plains
6. In walking garb, Australia, 1934
7. Playing tuneful percussion, Salt Lake City, Utah, USA, 1946
8. West Point Military Academy band members, 1945, with Grainger's 'blind eye' conductor's prompt scores
9. Grainger with a group of students at the National Music Camp, Interlochen, Michigan, USA, c.1942
10. Grainger's Roller Desk with Grieg Piano Concerto cadenza prompts
11. Percy Grainger in rehearsal with the USMA band, March 1951
12. *The Warriors*; nineteen grand pianos rattle the rafters of the Chicago Civic Opera House, 18 June 1930. Rudolph Ganz conducts and Percy Grainger leads a team of pianists, including Australia's Vera Bradford[1]
13. *The Warriors* manuscript, page one, with Grainger's markings
14. Percy Grainger working at home

(between p. 138 and p. 139)

15. Aldridge's Horse Repository, St Martin's Lane, London, 1883
16. George Percy Grainger, aged three, with his mother
17. John Harry Grainger, Percy's father, around 1892
18. The young JHG sporting a monocle
19. Grainger's birthplace in the 1890s. The picket fence he remembered has been replaced by corrugated iron
20. John Grainger's Princes Bridge, as it looks today
21. The young prodigy, about the time he began to study with Louis Pabst, 1892
22. Page from an early composition, 1893
23. One of Grainger's early supporters, G. W. Marshall-Hall, painted by Tom Roberts, one of the 'Heidelberg School' of painters
24. Residents of the pension, Frankfurt-am-Main, 1895; Percy and Rose (seated) on the left
25. Fellow students: Percy Grainger with Cyril Scott, Frankfurt 1900
26. Percy with his uncle, James Henry Aldridge, Adelaide, probably 1909
27. The signed (later framed) photograph from Grieg, inscribed 'Mr Percy Grainger with my best thank[s] for your splendid folk-songs for mixed voices.'

---

[1] See Chapter 17, Vera Bradford's reminiscence

28. Grainger, 1923, with Frederick Delius and his artist wife, Jelka
29. The Lincolnshire folk singer George Gouldthorpe and fellow folk singer, c.1906
30. Exact replica (at White Plains) of the Edison Bell phonograph used by Grainger to collect folk tunes
31. The legendary Evald Tang Kristensen (seated) notates as Grainger encourages a Danish folk singer. The photo is inscribed *Lindebo-Herning 26.8.1922*

(between p. 170 and p. 171)

32. The Grainger Museum, 2010
33. Oscillator-playing tone-tool: Grainger's design for one of his Free Music machines
34. Liszt's box for letters, given to Grainger in 1910 by his patron, William Gair Rathbone
35. The Butterfly piano, tuned in sixth-tones for Grainger's Free Music experiments
36. The contents of Rose Grainger's handbag on the day she died, 30 April 1922
37. Building the Grainger Museum, 1938
38. The family headstone of Percy Grainger's great-grandfather, Jacob Grainger (1796–1880), Heighington, Co. Durham
39. Denton Chapel, Co. Durham, 2010, where Percy Grainger's grandfather, John, and his siblings were baptised
40. The family headstone of Grainger's great-uncle, Jacob Grainger jr (1830–1871), Heighington, Co. Durham
41. Heighington village, 2010

List of Music Examples

Chap. 1: Orchestral Music
1.1	*Eastern Intermezzo*, bars 98–105	8
1.2	*The Warriors*, bars 322–4 (with Geoffrey Simon's markings)	13

Chap. 2: Music for Wind Band
2.1	*Lincolnshire Posy*: 'Rufford Park Poachers', bars 52–8	23
2.2	*The Lads of Wamphray March*, showing Grainger's directions at rehearsal mark 10	25

Chap. 3: Grainger for Choirs
3.1	*Marching Song of Democracy* (vocal score), bars 117–22	33
3.2	*Brigg Fair*, bars 1–16	38
3.3	*Dollar and a Half a Day*, bars 49–57	41
3.4	*Danny Deever*, bars 2–9	43

Chap. 4: Singing Grainger Solo
4.1	*Bold William Taylor*, vocal line, bars 1–10	47
4.2	*Dedication* (first version), bars 1–6	51
4.3	*Creeping Jane*, vocal line, verses 1–5, bars 7–9	54

Chap. 5: At the Piano with Grainger
5.1	*Mock Morris* (concert version), bars 45–52	60
5.2	*Bridal Lullaby*, bars 1–5	60
5.3	*The Nightingale and The Two Sisters*, bars 1–5	61
5.4	*The Nightingale and The Two Sisters*, bar 16	61
5.5	*The Power of Love*, bars 1–6	62
5.6	*Colonial Song* (optional voice version), bars 64–70	66
5.7	*Lincolnshire Posy*: 'Lord Melbourne', bars 33–43	70

Chap. 6: Towards a Universal Language
6.1	*Mampahory Ny Masoandro Seranin-Javona*, bars 40–44	83

Chap. 8: Putting Grainger into Print
8.1	*The Song of Solomon*, Part 2, bars 21–6	109
8.2	*The Wraith of Odin*, bars 28–36	110
8.3	*Thanksgiving Song*, bars 181–92	111

List of Contributors

Brian Allison Currently Curator of Exhibitions and Public Programs at the Grainger Museum, University of Melbourne, with special interests in historical architecture, decorative arts and design.
Teresa Balough Adjunct Professor of Music at the University of Eastern Connecticut and author of many publications on Grainger, most recently editing the Grainger–Stevenson letters.
Rita Boswell Currently the Archivist at Harrow School and Consultant Archivist at Westminster School since 2007.
Vera Bradford Eminent Australian pianist, and pupil of Percy Grainger.
Colin Cameron Musician and former broadcaster for the Australian Broadcasting Corporation.
Bruce Clunies Ross Former Professor in the English Institute of the University of Copenhagen, who has researched and written extensively on Grainger's Nordic affiliations and language reformism.
Roger Covell Australian academic, critic and writer, whose *Australia's Music: Themes of a New Society* has become a classic survey of Australian composition up to the 1960s.
Kay Dreyfus In charge of the Grainger Museum in 1974–89, now a research officer in the School of Music, Conservatorium, and graduate student in the School of Historical Studies at Monash University.
Lewis Foreman Author or editor of many books on music, including the standard biography of Arnold Bax, and currently advises record companies on repertoire by British composers.
Gerald Gentry English conductor and teacher.
Cara Aldridge Ham Artist and jewellery designer and cousin of Percy Grainger.
John Hopkins Conductor and educator, Professorial Fellow in charge of Conducting at the University of Melbourne, who made pioneering recordings of Grainger's orchestral and choral music.
Paul Jackson Head of Music at Anglia Ruskin University, Cambridge, where he works as a teacher, pianist, conductor, composer, and writer, with a special research interest in Grainger.
James Judd Conducted orchestral concerts for the Adelaide Symphony Orchestra's two-week Grainger Festival 2003, including the Australian premiere of *Thanksgiving Song*.
James Koehne Music historian and writer; from 1998 to 2010 Manager of Artistic Planning for the Adelaide Symphony Orchestra, South Australia.
Astrid Britt Krautschneider Currently the Curator of Collections and Research at the Grainger Museum, University of Melbourne, holding a Masters degree in Art Curatorship.
Murray McLachlan Pianist with an international career that embraces performing, teaching, recording, writing, and administration.

Stewart Manville   Archivist and curator of the Estate of Percy Aldridge Grainger and the USA International Percy Grainger Society.

Barry Peter Ould   Secretary and archivist of the Percy Grainger Society (UK), publisher of Grainger's music for Bardic Edition, and President of the International Percy Grainger Society.

Timothy Reynish   Active in the world of wind band music as conductor, recording artist, and teacher, both in Europe and the USA.

Desmond Scott   Theatre director, actor, and sculptor; son of Cyril Scott, with the one regret that he never had the opportunity to meet his father's best friend, Percy Grainger.

Peter Sculthorpe   Composer deeply committed to Australia and to its music, not least to that of Percy Grainger.

Geoffrey Simon   London-based Australian conductor, who has appeared and recorded with major orchestras world-wide, including a much-admired *The Warriors* with the Melbourne Symphony Orchestra.

Ronald Stevenson   Scottish composer and pianist and correspondent with Percy Grainger.

Penelope Thwaites   British/Australian concert pianist, composer, broadcaster, writer, and recording artist, with an extensive Grainger discography.

Stephen Varcoe   Baritone, whose many recordings include Grainger songs, and whose publications include *Sing English Song* and a chapter on Art Song for *The Cambridge Companion to Singing*.

David Walker   Emeritus Professor at Deakin University, who has written extensively on Australian cultural history.

Alan Woolgar   Former Copyright Manager at Schott & Co., who for many years was associated wth Percy Grainger.

A Grainger Timeline

Interleaved with Grainger's own 'Compositional Life of Percy Aldridge Grainger: Dates and Details of Development as Composer' (*in italics*)[1]

1854	Birth of John Harry Grainger, London, England
1861	Birth of Rosa Annie Aldridge (later Rose), Adelaide, South Australia
1880	Marriage of John and Rose, Adelaide, South Australia. Move to Melbourne, where JHG sets up in business as an architect
1882	8 July: Birth of George Percy Grainger, Brighton (Melbourne), Victoria
	28 July: PG christened at St Andrew's C of E Church, Brighton
c. 1887	PG begins piano lessons with his mother
	Reading includes Hans Christian Andersen, Charles Dickens, Walter Scott
1888	Australian Centenary year; opening of Princes Bridge, Melbourne, designed by John Grainger
1890	John and Rose separate
1891	Studies acting and painting with Thomas Sisley and drawing with Frederick McCubbin
	Encounters the Icelandic saga 'Grettir the Strong'
About 1892:	*(aged 10) First contact with Bach's music*
	PG begins lessons with Louis Pabst, encounters the music of J. S. Bach, composes his first opus, *Birthday Gift*
About 1894:	*(aged 12) Conception of FREE MUSIC — music without beats, scales, set intervals or harmony*
	PG makes his official debut as a pianist 9 July at the Masonic Hall, Melbourne
	Stars in subsequent concert on 10 September, receiving critical acclaim for both
1895	Percy and Rose depart for Frankfurt and the Hoch Conservatorium
	Piano studies with James Kwast
	Friendships develop over the next five years with Cyril Scott, Balfour Gardiner, Roger Quilter, Norman O'Neill ('The Frankfurt Gang'), and the Danish cellist Herman Sandby
	In due course, abandons his official composition teacher, Ivan (or Iwan) Knorr, to study with Karl Klimsch
1897:	*Met CYRIL SCOTT in Frankfurt on Main, who encouraged me by his daring modernity and his belief in my gifts as a composer.*
1898:	*Closed a choral composition (AT TWILIGHT, mixed chorus) with the*

---

[1] Typewritten MS in Grainger Museum. It is included as a reflection of what Grainger himself felt was important in his musical progress.

	following discord (since much used by other composers and in Jazz): (intervals from bass upward) 1.5.3.6.1²
About 1898:	Influenced by arias, etc. in Bach Passions and Cantatas, started writing for LARGE ROOM-MUSIC — from 8 to 22 instruments, or for blends of single voices & large room-music combinations. These ideas and experiments led to³ Vaughan Williams' 'On Wenlock Edge', Schoenberg's 'Pierrot Lunaire' etc.
1898–1899:	First mature orchestral compositions (YOUTHFUL SUITE, etc) & chamber works (KIPLING SETTINGS for chorus & chamber music, etc)
1899–1901:	By studying the irregular rhythms of prose (The Song of Solomon) worked out my BEATLESS MUSIC (with continually changing time signatures) which was taken over by Cyril Scott in his Piano Sonata (1904) & thru him influenced Schoenberg, Stravinsky & the whole modern movement (atonalism, irregular barrings, etc.)
1900	Visits Paris Exposition (for which his father has designed the West Australian pavilion) and is captivated by the sounds of an Indonesian gamelan orchestra
1901	Thru Herman Sandby (Danish composer) came to know Grieg's settings of Norwegian Folksongs, Op 66 which helped to mould me as a folk-music setter (however I had made folk-music settings for several years before this.)
1901	May, finishes studies in Frankfurt and moves with his mother to London Career as solo pianist launched. Public debut at Steinway Hall on 29 October
1902	6 February, first appearance with orchestra (Bath, UK) playing Tchaikovsky Piano Concerto no. 1 Publication (La Scandinavie for cello and piano) by Schott & Co. (Mainz) Tour with Adelina Patti's concert party through English provinces
1902	First HILL SONG, for 6 oboes, 6 English horns, 6 bassoons, double bassoon, (published by Universal Edition, Vienna, in a revised scoring, about 1924).
1903	Meets Busoni and later studies with him in Berlin
1903–4	First tour of Australia with Ada Crossley
1904	First concert tour in Denmark. Meets Karen Holten, his girlfriend until 1912
1905–1908:	With the phonograph, collected about 500 English folksongs from country folk.
1905	Begins folk-song collecting in Lincolnshire (Brigg)
1906	Further folk-song collecting expedition, using Edison Bell phonograph
1906:	Met GRIEG in London (spent summer of 1907 with him in Norway). Works with Grieg on the Concerto, which he later performed in England
1907:	Second HILL SONG, for piccolo, 2 flutes, 3 oboes, English horn, 2 bassoons, double bassoon, E flat clar, 3 B flat clars, alto clar, bass clar, 4 saxophones, 2 trumpets, 2 horns, tuba, drums. Met Frederick Delius who became a great champion for my music
1908	First recordings with The Gramophone Company; meets Debussy
1908–9	Second Ada Crossley tour of Australia. Growing interest in Polynesian music and cultures
1909:	Collected Polynesian music of New Zealand & South Seas. At first Festival of British Music, organised by Frederick Delius and Edward

---

² The claim to have exclusive rights over the chord of the added sixth might be seen as debatable. (Ed.)

³ Without laying himself open to charges of overstating his claims, Grainger could accurately have said that his experiments preceded the publication of the works named. (Ed.)

	Elgar,[4] my choral compositions were performed in Liverpool and made a sensation.
1911	Adopts name of Percy Aldridge Grainger concurrently with first Schott (London) publications
1912:	*My ENGLISH DANCE (orchestra) performed by Thomas Beecham, London.* *This work (begun 1901, ended 1909) was the biggest example of my 'Big Form' music, in which there was little, if any, repetition of thematic ideas, but instead, a continual flow of new thoughts, welded together only by likeness of mood or of style.*
1912–13	Balfour Gardiner choral orchestral concerts feature Grainger for the first time as a composer. Grainger mentions *'my friend and fellow composer Balfour Gardiner'*
1912	May: All-Grainger concert, Aeolian Hall
1914	September: Leaves with his mother for the United States of America
1915	Hugely successful debut as pianist in USA, launching a hectic performing career, continuing at its height up to, during, and immediately after the Second World War
1916–17	Premieres of important orchestral works *In a Nutshell* (1916) and *The Warriors* (1917)[5]
1917	April: Death of John Grainger in Melbourne June: Percy Grainger enlists as bandsman in the US army
1917:	*First performance of my MARCHING SONG OF DEMOCRACY (my best work for chorus and orchestra) at Worcester (Mass.) festival under Dr Arthur Mees*
1918	Becomes American citizen
1919	Discharged from army; *Country Gardens* published Begins teaching at Chicago Musical College (summer school) which continued intermittently until 1931, supplanted by Interlochen summer schools starting in 1930
1921	Settles in White Plains, New York
1922	Rose Grainger commits suicide
1922–3	Visits Denmark (folk-collecting) and Frankfurt
1922–1927:	*Together with Evald Tang Kristensen (Danish 80-year-old folk-song collector) collected (phonograph) about 200 folksongs in Denmark.*
1924	Stages two large orchestral concerts in America including his own works and two Delius American premieres[6] Visits Australia
1926	Concert tour of Australia. Meets his future wife, Ella Viola Ström
1928	4 August: Civil marriage 9 August: Public marriage at Hollywood Bowl concert
1929	Harrogate Festival featuring music by the 'Frankfurt Group', organised by Grainger and the conductor, Basil Cameron
1931	Visit to the Haslemere Festival and the Dolmetsch family

---

[4] Organised by the short-lived Musical League, of which Elgar was president and Delius, vice-president.
[5] Strangely, neither work is mentioned in Grainger's 'Compositional Life'.
[6] *North Country Sketches* and *Song of the High Hills*

1932–3	Associate Professor and departmental Head at New York University. Meeting with Dom Anselm Hughes, leading to work with Hughes on English Gothic Music
1934–5	Tours Australasia and begins the establishment of the Grainger Museum in the grounds of Melbourne University
1935:	*First completed example of my FREE MUSIC performed under Percy Code at broadcast of Australian Broadcasting Commission*
1937:	*LINCOLNSHIRE POSY (my best work for wind band) played at Milwaukee*
	Begins regular teaching at Interlochen International Music Camp, Michigan, continuing until 1944
1938	Visits Australia. Museum officially opened
1940s	Concerts in America to support the war effort
1942:	*My completed KIPLING JUNGLE BOOK SETTINGS (about 14 choruses, some unaccompanied, some with chamber music accomp.) given by Adolph Nelson and the a cappella choir of Gustavus Adolphus College (St Peter, Minnesota) in 8 cities*
1945	Meets physicist Burnett Cross
1947	Delighted by outstanding performance of his *Hill-Song I* by the West Point Band
1948	Appears in his *Danish Folk-Music Suite* at the London Promenade Concerts
1950s	Works with Burnett Cross on machines to produce his 'Free Music'
1953	First operation (Aarhus, Denmark) for prostate cancer
1954	Awarded the St Olav Medal for services to Norwegian music
1955–6	Last visit, with Ella, to Australia for nine months. Works on his Museum collection
1957	Visit to Denmark; last recorded performance of Grieg piano concerto
1958	Visit to Europe. Meeting with Benjamin Britten. Projected Aldeburgh concerts
1959	Last visit to England
	Draws up final will, leaving the greater part of his estate to his Museum
1961	20 February: Dies of cancer at White Plains
	2 March: Buried at West Terrace Cemetery, Adelaide, South Australia

Introduction

Penelope Thwaites

THERE ARE MANY POSSIBLE APPROACHES to compiling a *Companion*. Uppermost in our mind has been the encouragement of readers to *experience* Grainger's music — whether as executants, professional or amateur, or as involved listeners. Academic analysis can take us so far, but to hear from performers who have lived in Grainger's musical world not only provides a fascinating look behind the scenes, but can awaken a desire for closer acquaintance with the music that inspired such enthusiasm. To that end, the tone of our professional performer-writers is more conversational than formal.

An emphasis on how to go about performing Grainger has rarely been attempted in the many publications, biographies, and collections of his writings that now exist, although Grainger himself went to considerable lengths to give suggestions within his scores and in the prefaces to several of them. Pianists, for example, are offered valuable insights on pedalling, phrasing, voicing of textures, and, in his own phrase, 'musicality before pianism'.[1] His own recordings, discussed in Chapter 9, are a remarkable demonstration of his pianistic canon.

Even for those of modest abilities, his songs, chamber pieces, and piano music include attractive and feasible works. Not only can they be purchased these days with relative ease, but they may also be heard — at least as examples — via the wonders of the internet. Schools, colleges, universities, wind bands, choirs, and orchestras have opportunities, as never before, of performing a whole range of works, not just the old favourites. Throughout the *Companion* we have tried to make helpful suggestions about programming this somewhat idiosyncratic repertoire, making a virtue rather than a problem out of the many short and often highly-charged pieces that Grainger offers. Indeed, for our sound-bite world, his comparatively short works fit rather well.

A note about Grainger's colourful titles: as our Catalogue shows,[2] he constantly recast his compositions for different genres. Hence, certain titles will appear in several chapters. The various versions are often quite distinct (e.g. the two-piano

---

[1] Grainger's *Guide to Virtuosity* is just one of a fascinating series of writings on music, gathered together in *Grainger on Music*, ed. Malcolm Gillies and Bruce Clunies Ross (Oxford and New York, 1999). See also the Select Bibliography, p. 222.

[2] Grainger was not consistent in the exact way he published a given title: e.g. *Hill Song* and *Hill-Song*. Our policy has been to include in the Catalogue the title as it appears most often on the printed score and to remain consistent with it throughout the book. On the other hand, within the Discography, including Grainger's own recordings, titles are given as printed on the recording.

versions of orchestral works, or versions that may be either sung or played). We have sought, as much as possible, to concentrate on the differences between these versions, although we have been aware that chapters may be read singly. Therefore, giving a little general background more than once has been unavoidable.

The discovery of Grainger's music is work in progress. A huge leap forward was taken with the rush of recordings in the late 1990s, and in particular, the decision of a major company to record a complete survey. This includes a significant body of new works and new versions of works, recorded for the first time.[3] The Edition's remit to cover all the original works and folk settings was a massive undertaking. The extensive area of Grainger's arrangements of other composers is an exploration also in hand, from a variety of recording companies, and our Discography gives current information. Our Catalogue of Works is as up to date as possible, although the odd unknown piece may yet surface, since the international dispersal of scores after Grainger's death has produced considerable problems in amassing a central archive. The Grainger Museum in Melbourne aims to hold copies of all scores for research purposes, and the major music publishers are responding to the growth in interest. In particular, Bardic Edition has been tireless in promoting the repertoire, and is now working in tandem with Grainger's original publisher, Schott & Co.

A convincing interpretation requires intelligent musical analysis, but a true understanding of Grainger rests, also, on a genuine attempt to try to understand his philosophy, his life, and some of the experiences that shaped him. Paradoxically, areas where Grainger himself was most vocal — at least in his writings — are some of the most misunderstood. The issue of racial difference has become one of the most sensitive issues of our age — not least, with the history of the twentieth century now behind us. Grainger grew up in a very different world. Our chapter on his pursuit of Nordic music reflects a deeper and much-needed look at this aspect of his life and its connection with his music. Similarly, his own close family background has been veiled in inaccuracies, concealment, and prejudice. And it is arguable that his exhaustive, not to say exhausting, quasi-confessional documentation of his private life, far from adding to a real understanding of the sheer stature of the man, has often, sadly, obscured it, for that is where many an over-excited commentator has become permanently marooned.

By contrast, certain facts in Grainger's family background, as they are beginning to emerge, explain with irresistible logic why he might have taken some of the directions he did. Their crafts and trades — whether as farming people or later in the town as dress-makers and tailors, as compositor, carpenter, and then, with his father, engineer and architect — this array of practical skills seemed to join with Grainger's artistic and intellectual gifts in an extraordinary way. One of the most striking discoveries is the parity between the lives of his great-grandfather Jacob Grainger's family in County Durham and those of the folk-singers in Lincolnshire with whom he had such innate understanding.[4]

---

[3] Chandos Records' *Grainger Edition* was launched at Australia House, London, on 9 October 1996.

[4] See Chap. 11, 'The Family Background'.

Apparently unaware of this heritage, Grainger's conscious encounter with British folk music went back to his student days in Frankfurt, when he began to make his own early settings. It really took flight when he followed Lucy Broadwood into the field of collecting, making fruitful visits between 1905 and 1908 to the festivals at Brigg in Lincolnshire, as well as undertaking collecting trips in Gloucestershire and elsewhere. The story is documented in detail, particularly in the Bird as well as the Slattery biographies, and vividly by Grainger himself through his letters in the Dreyfus collection, *The Farthest North of Humanness*. David Tall's article in *The Percy Grainger Companion* of 1981 gives a splendid overview of the topic, and readers are also referred to the web-site of the English Folk-Dance and Song Society for a list of publications on this much-documented subject. Grainger's visits to Denmark in 1922–7 were significant in his collection of about two hundred Danish tunes and subsequent use of some of them. David Walker's chapter on the cosmopolitan Melbourne of Grainger's childhood highlights the young boy's early awareness of non-western and native music traditions, a theme continued in Chapter 6. In our book, the significant relationship between Grainger and folk song is treated, not as a separate subject, but is interwoven with the various discussions of the repertoire, particularly in Chapters 3, 4, and 5.

Another subject covered extensively elsewhere and therefore not included as a chapter in this *Companion* is Grainger's concept of 'Free Music'.[5] In his childhood the sounds of nature, experienced on boating trips and expeditions into the Australian bush, had suggested to him the idea of a kind of music unconstrained by formal pitch or rhythm. In later life he worked to produce machines that would in turn produce such 'Free Music' (see Plate 33). The colleague and friend who would help him was the young American physicist Burnett Cross. Together they worked in the Grainger home at White Plains, New York (described and pictured in Stewart Manville's chapter), and these products of Grainger's imagination pre-dated some of the experiments later to be pursued in the electronic field. The concept was not unique to Grainger, and he produced very little music from it, but his vision indicates the unusual breadth of his musical mind — the refusal to cling to the old rules, but to go back to first principles and to think afresh. Typically, he overstated his case in denoting this as his 'only important contribution to music' — but in less dramatic ways, we can see throughout much of his composing oeuvre the impulse to stretch the boundaries, to discover freedom. Perhaps it could be said that the on-going tension between the necessary disciplines of an executant's and a composer's technique and the desire to break free from traditional constraints can be heard as an underlying characteristic of all his work. Indeed, it was an underlying characteristic of his life.

The editor acknowledges a strong Australian representation in our contents, an element, until now, rather less explored in the literature. Percy Grainger's forty-three years as an American citizen and resident of New York justify his listing in

---

[5] See Appendix 2, Grainger's statement on Free Music, Chap. 18 for Teresa Balough's thoughts on the subject, and articles by Ivor Dorum and Burnett Cross in *The Percy Grainger Companion*, ed. Lewis Foreman (1981).

some reference books as an American composer. He is a legend in the band world, and large areas of his American career deserve much more research attention. On the other hand, his parents' families, his residence in England from 1901 to 1914, and his significant work for its folk music link him to Britain. So Melbourne-born Percy Grainger represents — in his ancestry, experience, and loves — three continents. He played in a fourth (Africa) while reaching out to the music of a fifth (Asia). He is best seen as a world citizen. Ultimately, though, he decided that his life's collection should be housed in Australia, and he regularly and proudly described himself as an Australian composer. Not by inclination an inhabitant of the academic world, there is a certain irony in the fact that he chose the grounds of Melbourne University for his cherished museum. After the initial welcome and a preliminary opening in 1938, subsequent years saw various attempts to question, reassign, or entirely dislodge the building. Happily, a more enlightened view has now prevailed, acknowledging the museum collection's unique value, both in Australia's cultural heritage and to the world in general. As mentioned in the Preface, it is being superbly developed as an important international research centre.

Grainger was undoubtedly one of the most individual of people, but his friends and family were important to him, and some of his student friendships lasted a lifetime. He is placed among some of his contemporaries in Lewis Foreman's Chapter 16 and remembered by people who met or knew him in Chapter 17. One area we have not assessed is his long and successful marriage to Ella Viola Ström. But that would be the subject for another book.

THE MUSIC

1
Orchestral Music

Prelude: a bird's-eye view
Penelope Thwaites

THE INSIGHTS OF A CONDUCTOR who has actually performed Grainger are invaluable, but — to paraphrase Mrs Beeton — first catch your conductor. Conductors who have performed the repertoire, either on disc or in concert, are still a rare breed, and it is therefore particularly fortunate that two of them have been generous enough to share their experience of the particular works they have performed or recorded. Grainger's orchestral repertoire is still largely unknown in the concert hall. A preliminary overview of what is available, therefore, may help to place in context the more detailed comments below from Geoffrey Simon and James Judd, and perhaps may inspire more orchestras to venture into this exciting and colourful world. Listeners, of course, can now enjoy all this repertoire on disc, but a live performance is something special.

Since Grainger is widely regarded as a 'miniaturist', it is worth underlining that the three orchestral suites of between eighteen and twenty-five minutes (*Youthful Suite, Danish Folk-Music Suite*, and *In a Nutshell*) as well as the nineteen-minute *The Warriors* — can all contribute a substantial element to an orchestral programme. *Youthful Suite* (1899–1901) draws on some of the ideas preoccupying Grainger towards the end of his student years in Frankfurt, and it very much conveys that turn-of-the-century feeling (despite the fact that the whole work was revised and completed between 1940 and 1950). The movements touch variously on Grainger's interests in Norse culture, folk song, non-western traditions, and music hall. To the young composer, Wagner had been a powerful discovery, and the first movement *Northern March* starts with a fruity brass choir. Strings take over with a more jaunty air. *Rustic Dance* uses a drawing-room-cum-folk-like tune in swinging triple time (somewhat reminiscent of Edward German), encircling a broad optimistic melody. Rich brass writing returns in the sombre *Norse Dirge*, and the lavish percussion used throughout the suite foreshadows similar scoring in later works such as *The Warriors* and *To a Nordic Princess*. There are some effective solo opportunities for wind and string instruments and a rather sudden end to the *Dirge*. The fourth movement, *Eastern Intermezzo*, was one that Grainger used in other guises: for solo and duo pianos and also for percussion ensemble. It contains a succession of sixths that he felt was an important innovatory idea (see Example 1.1). In truth it is a very western eastern intermezzo, firmly of its period. The fifth movement, *English Waltz*, is a hilarious, somewhat galumphing portrait, exhibiting Grainger's outrageous, tongue-

Example 1.1 *Eastern Intermezzo*, bars 98–105

in-cheek, vulgar side — and on his terms, joyfully so! It is a shame that the *Youthful Suite* is rarely, if ever, programmed; in the right milieu it is hugely entertaining, and individual movements are also great fun in less formal orchestral programmes.

As James Judd confirms, the brilliant *In a Nutshell* (1916), with its huge colourful percussion section, once again evokes contrasting musical worlds. The suite was assembled from various pieces written at different times. Chronologically, *Pastoral*, its most complex movement, started earliest, from an idea the young composer had in 1906, at just the time when he had started collecting folk songs. The theme is artless enough, but by the time Grainger actually developed and scored it, ten years later, a luxuriant transformation had occurred. The plaintive tune is put through a series of strange experiences. Disparate snatches of themes 'undermine' it, chromatic harmonies grow from being lush to almost threatening. The colossal climax disperses in icy phrases. The imagination of this piece is truly spell-binding. *Arrival Platform Humlet* dates from 1908, at the height of Grainger's love affair with the Danish Karen Holten, and the excitement he describes of meeting at the railway station is clearly autobiographical. His favourite wild sounds of double reeds in unison carry the piece forward in feverish anticipation. *'The Gum-Suckers' March*, an easy-going, sometimes cacophonous swagger, dates from 1911. *Gay but Wistful* (1912), a gently sly popular song, draws on the style of the music hall.

Geoffrey Simon's accounts give background to both the *Danish Folk-Music Suite* and *The Warriors* — prodigal works, both of them. It is worth mentioning that although Grainger eschewed the concerto idea in his orchestral music, his method of building a suite from existing short works was echoed in the creation of a nine-minute *Grainger Suite* for solo piano and orchestra.[1] A subversive version of *Country Gardens* (in which Grainger vents his frustration on his musical albatross by means of some very rude discords) is effectively linked by a few orchestral bars leading into an arrangement by the composer John Pickard of Grainger's *Bridal Lullaby*.[2] The suite concludes with his 1952 version of *Handel in the Strand*. It makes an excellent component to any programme.

The scoring of *Thanksgiving Song* (1945), whose Australian premiere is described by James Judd and in a later chapter by James Koehne, raises the question of whether this work falls under the heading of purely orchestral works, or whether it belongs under the choral/orchestral heading. I would suggest that Grainger's use of wordless voices[3] (in this case off-stage) may be likened to Debussy's or Delius's use of voices *as orchestral sounds*. As to the logistical problems of Grainger's proposed transport of singers and instruments into the distance: a possible compromise might be to record this section of the work and gradually allow it to fade. Nevertheless, if space allows, Grainger's concept should of course be followed. It is a magical effect.

Three arresting orchestral works might best be described as tone poems: *English Dance*, *The Power of Rome and the Christian Heart*, and *To a Nordic Princess*. Each represents a different era in Grainger's life, and important strands therein. *English Dance*, upon which Grainger worked from 1899 to 1909, is an immensely energetic, exuberant piece — a young man's work, in which he sought to emulate the ongoing 'monochrome' textures of J. S. Bach. But to coin the phrase 'cheerfulness keeps breaking through', and Fauré's comment upon hearing it — 'It's as if the whole

---

[1] Premiered at a special Australia Day Concert at the Royal Opera House, London, in 1993.
[2] Used in 1992 as the theme for the Merchant Ivory film *Howards End*.
[3] Grainger also employs this effect in *Harvest Hymn*, *Afterword*, *County Derry Air* (1920 version, BFMS 29), and *The Immovable Do*.

population was dancing!' — sums up Grainger's mood of youthful optimism. *English Dance* is very much an Edwardian, pre-war piece. Dense in texture, it requires very clear dynamic shaping, but it can be tremendously effective.

By contrast, *The Power of Rome and the Christian Heart* (1918, 1943) is an anguished protest against the waste of war and the evils of oppression. It was inspired by Grainger's own involvement in the US army towards the end of World War I. The last section is in fact *Dreamery*, which is also listed as a separate work. In this context, it is as if the composer envisages a kinder, gentler post-war world. Grainger never hesitated to re-use good ideas and much of the material, particularly in *Dreamery*, can be heard in his two-piano sketch *The Warriors II*, as well as in his improvised piece, recorded as *Bridal Lullaby Ramble*,[4] and in his deeply pessimistic song setting *The Power of Love*. The third of these tone-poems, the opulent twelve-minute *To a Nordic Princess* (written in 1928 as a wedding gift for his Swedish wife, Ella) embodies an unapologetic full-on romance — no backward looks, no dark undercurrents, no jarring reservations. It can perhaps be compared with his *Colonial Song* as a love song, unusually free of lurking disaster.

Among several effective concert openers, the passacaglia on the folk tune *Green Bushes* is a nine-minute winner, its unceasing momentum rising to an ecstatic apotheosis. The American folk setting *Spoon River* is another piece which works well at the beginning of a programme. It has an almost cinematic suggestion of new-world America — the central fiddle tune to be played, says Grainger, with 'pioneer persistency'. His own modal extension of the tune lends nostalgia and breadth to the work.

The conductor's view (1)
Geoffrey Simon

Grainger's untrammelled musical imagination and unabashed hedonism produced orchestral works of boundless energy, flair — and complexity. They are delectable to listen to but sometimes daunting in their challenges. Yet for me, the rewards of performing and recording some of this amazing body of music have far outweighed the time and effort involved.

What appears to be the toughest problem turns out to be the easiest, and most fun, to deal with. Conductors have fretted about Grainger's 'elastic scoring' and the impossibly outré instruments he calls for. But these need not become reasons to avoid engaging with Grainger's scores. In his visionary essay of 2 December 1929, *To Conductors — and to those forming, or in charge of, amateur orchestras, high school, college and music school orchestras and chamber-music bodies* (and, I would add, professional orchestras as well),[5] the pivotal paragraph states:

What we need in our composers and in our leaders of musical thought is an

---

[4] Recorded by Penelope Thwaites, piano, Chandos CHAN 10205.
[5] See Appendix 1.

attitude like Bach's: he seems to have been willing enough to experiment with all the instruments known to him and to arrange and rearrange all kinds of works for all sorts of combinations of those instruments. It's easy to guess what liberal uses he would have made of the marvellous instruments of to-day.

The article gives us interpreters further comfort: 'My music tells its story mainly by means of intervals and the liveliness of the part-writing, rather than by means of tone-colour.' So, in short, if you don't have a sarrusophone, a dulcitone, a heckelphone or a bass glockenspiel, don't worry, just use what you do have. '(My music) is . . . well fitted to be played by almost any . . . combination of instruments, provided a proper *balance of tone* is kept.' Grainger's scores usually suggest alternative instruments for consideration, and many also make it clear that the music can be played by anything 'from four single instruments up to massed orchestra'.

I confess that when *recording* Grainger's music, the orchestras and I did go to great lengths to unearth exactly the instruments he specifies. Recordings, after all, are reference documents. On the other hand, in my live performances I have found it wonderfully liberating to take Grainger at his word and improvise. This has even extended to introducing synthesised sounds, now that the generators are so sophisticated and today's musicians so at ease with them. But crucially, and always, the character of the music — the essential gritty core of it — had to come across.

That said, Grainger's orchestral masterpiece *The Warriors* (c.18 mins.; first performed in 1917) is the exception to the rule, and it does pose a conundrum to conductors and concert presenters. Nothing can really replace the spectacle of three massive grand pianos pounding against the large orchestra. But the difficulties of squeezing them onto the stage — not to mention affording them and the virtuoso pianists who will play them — have scuppered many an intended performance. Yes, you are permitted to perform the piece with only six of the ideal dozen percussionists and their instruments, and the bass oboe can be omitted. But without all six horns and the full complement of other brass to match, not only do the massive tutti textures become unacceptably thin but the off-stage brass sextet will hardly work.

What a show-stopper of a work this is, however, once its logistical problems have been resolved! Grainger's warriors are not at war but at play. His exuberant programme note is as unmissable as the music itself:

> Often the scenes of a ballet have flitted before the eyes of my imagination, in which the ghosts of male and female warrior types of all times and places are spirited together for an orgy of war-like dances, processions and merry-makings broken, or accompanied, by amorous interludes; their frolics tinged with just that faint suspicion of wistfulness all holiday gladness wears.
>
> I see the action of the ballet shot through, again and again, with the surging onslaughts of good-humouredly mischievous revellers who carry all before them in the pursuit of voluptuous pleasures. At times the lovemakers close at hand hear from afar the proud passage of harnessed fighting-men, and for the final picture I like to think of them all lining up together in brotherly fellowship and wholesale animal glee; all bitter and vengeful memories

vanished, all hardships forgot; a sort of Valhalla gathering of childishly overbearing and arrogant savage men and women of all ages; — the old Greek heroes with fluttering horse-haired helms; shining black Zulus, their perfect limbs lit with fire-red blossoms; flaxenhaired Vikings clad in scarlet and sky-blue; lithe bright Amazons in windswept garments side by side with squat Greenland women in ornately patterned furs; Red Indians resplendent in bead-heavy dresses and negrito Fijians terrible with sharks' teeth ornaments, their woolly hair dyed pale ochre with lime; graceful cannibal Polynesians of both sexes, their golden skins wreathed with flowers and winding tendrils; — these and all the rest, arm in arm in a united show of gay and innocent pride and animal spirits, fierce and exultant.

Despite Grainger's famous call for no fewer than three conductors, the fact is that one conductor can handle the piece perfectly well, and Grainger not only indicates this in his introductory note, but explains the detail on the appropriate pages.[6] First, there's the section from bar 292 where a group of four players is told to carry on with the patterns they have been playing, ignoring the conductor who has to take the orchestra into different tempos and melodies. Players enjoy that. Then at bar 298 there is a long fermata, during which the one and only maestro has time to give a slow pulse to the second harp, who in turn is watched and followed by the others in her small group for the remainder of that section. And finally, the fantastical off-stage brass passage can more than ably be led by the fifth horn, once set underway during the fermata in bar 322 (see Example 1.2). If you read the (very) small print in Alessandro Servadei's admirable performing edition, Grainger points out how all this can be done. Sadly, this little joke may have been one more factor in needlessly dissuading dozens of orchestras from tackling a truly magnificent and iconic piece.

Whilst the *Danish Folk-Music Suite* (c.19 mins.; completed 1928, revised 1941) is more flexible in scoring than *The Warriors*, and far less heavy on orchestral resources, it does present some challenges before its deep and passionate beauty can be offered confidently to audiences. Chief amongst these is the need for a harmonium and an organ, or, as Grainger directs, either of them. With versatile electronic keyboards so readily available and high-quality amplification so much less expensive than it used to be, this need not be an issue. Electronic solutions may now be seen as perfectly valid, rather than as artificial and eviscerating compromises. Support is provided by Grainger himself. In one place on the score (please note the date: 1923) he calls for 'Pipe (or electric) Organ'. He also describes what stops should be used, when an organ substitutes for the harmonium. Put these two together and we see he is telling us that the approximation of a harmonium sound by an electric organ is perfectly acceptable. He does say that a big organ sonority is needed in full orchestral versions — but electronics can deal with this, too — particularly since

---

[6] In Example 1.2, Grainger's detailed suggestions appear at the top left-hand corner of the page (here too small to read). They explain how the offices of a second conductor may be dispensed with, as well as giving logistical instructions on how to achieve the desired balance of sound between the off-stage group and the main orchestra. The conductor's hand-written markings on the score are Geoffrey Simon's.

1. ORCHESTRAL MUSIC

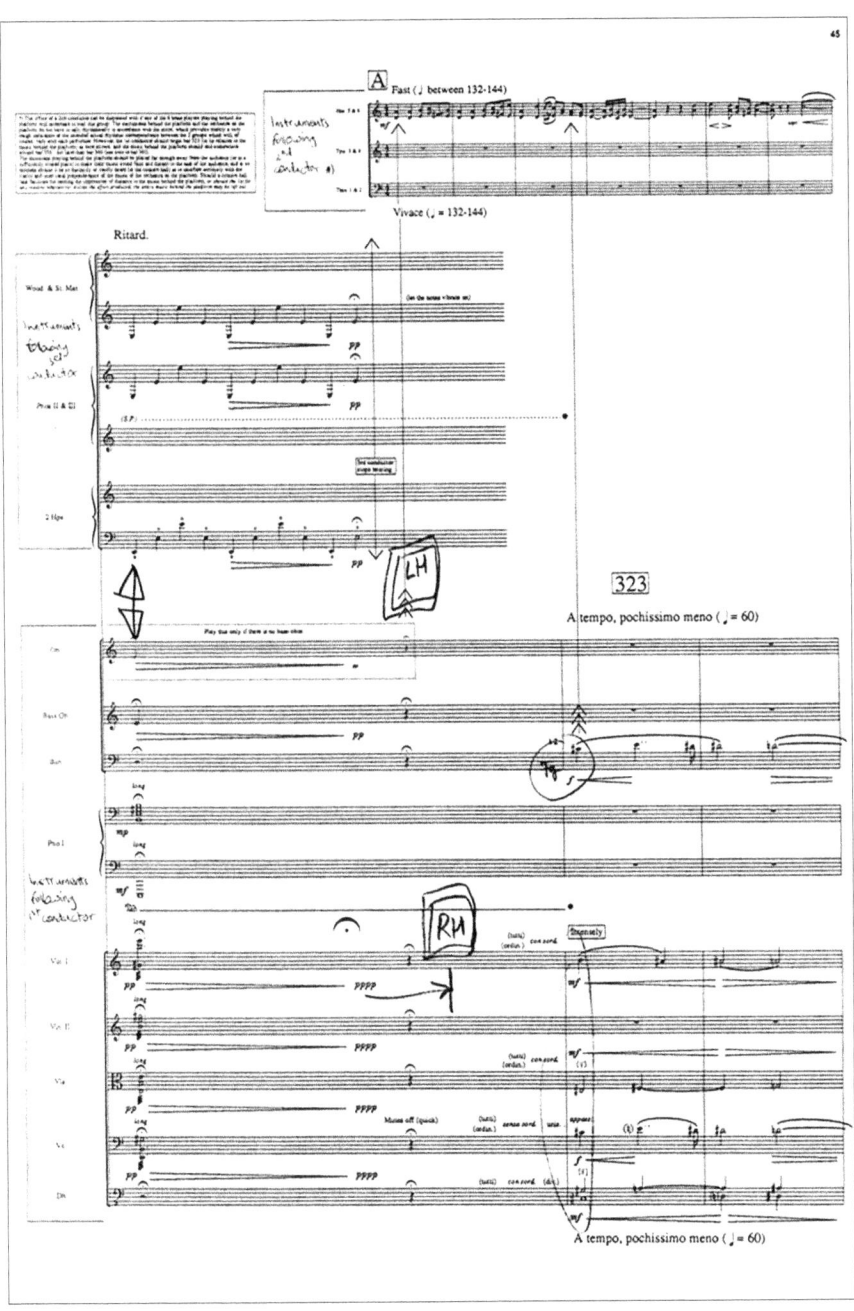

Example 1.2 *The Warriors*, bars 322–4

the organ/harmonium parts only ever provide colour. There are no solo melodies for these instruments, during which their traditional timbre would be closely scrutinised. The task is merely to come up with an attractive and appropriate synthesised 'supportive' sound. That done, the piece will work.

In general, Grainger's printed scores can be off-putting. In the cause of 'elastic scoring' he gives many notes and options, and it is something of an act of faith on the conductor's part to accept that the composer has been consistent, and above all, practical — not only in the score but in the printed parts as well. But since he clearly indicates where one instrument is cued in the part of another, the conductor only needs to decide whether the particular instruments at his disposal will all have a part to play, and whether all the musical lines will indeed be covered. With a standard orchestra, they are. Smaller combinations will need a bit more analysis. (The *Danish Folk-Music Suite*, for example, can abandon its luxuriant instrumentation and be performed with as few as four instruments, two of which are keyboards — piano and organ/harmonium.) All of this suggests that Grainger wanted each performance to take on its own unique character, according to the number and kind of instruments used. Nothing would be routine, or predictable. What an opportunity this is — if we can but embrace the freedom of choice Grainger has afforded us!

The *Danish Folk-Music Suite* is built on folk songs collected by Grainger in the Jutland region of Denmark in 1922, 1925, and 1927. He travelled with a phonograph, recording folk singers with the help of three Danish experts in the field: Evald Tang Kristensen, H. P. Hansen, and Poul Lorenzen. The first two movements—*The Power of Love* and *Lord Peter's Stable-Boy*—are 'lovingly honor-tokened' to the memory of his mother, Rose Grainger.[7] The third movement, dedicated to Grainger's friend, the Danish cellist Herman Sandby, uses two folk songs, *The Nightingale* and *The Two Sisters*. The finale, *Jutish Medley*, is dedicated to Kristensen 'as a token of boundless admiration' and incorporates four tunes: *Choosing the Bride*, *The Dragoon's Farewell*, *The Shoemaker from Jerusalem* (collected from the singing of Tang Kristensen's wife), and *Husband and Wife* (a quarrelling duet). The slow melodies are all of surpassing beauty, and Grainger helps us to maximise their impact by offering suggestions for rubato. The fast tunes are typically bustling and ebullient. The *Suite* makes for a marvellously effective, varied, and entertaining addition to a concert, and a richly rewarding experience for the participating musicians.

The two *Hill-Songs* are striking evocations of the wild spirit of the unpeopled highlands of Scotland's West Argyllshire. *Hill-Song I* (c.13 mins.; 1901/2, rescored 1923) was Grainger's direct response not only to 'the soul-shaking hillscapes' of the region but also to some of the musical timbres which he had encountered on his Continental travels: the 'hard-toned rustic oboe' in Italy, 'some extremely nasal Egyptian double-reeds at the Paris Exhibition', and 'bagpipes in the Scottish Highlands'. *Hill-Song II* (c.5 mins.; 1907) emerged as 'the result of a wish to present the fast, energetic elements of *Hill-Song I* as a single-type whole, without contrasting types of a slower, more dreamy nature'.[8] Unlike the ravishing, voluptuous textures

---

[7] Rose Grainger had committed suicide in April 1922.
[8] See Chap. 2, 'Music for Wind Band'

of *The Warriors* and the *Danish Folk-Music Suite*, the music of the *Hill-Songs* is for the most part hard-edged and glittering. The original 1901 scoring of *Hill-Song I* was for 2 piccolos, 6 oboes, 6 cors anglais, 6 bassoons, and 1 contra-bassoon — just imagine! The tempo marking for *Hill-Song II* says it well: 'Fierce and keen, at fast walking speed.'

When rescored twenty-one years after its composition, *Hill-Song I* became *Room-music for 22-some (23-some at will)*. The score makes it clear that Grainger wants only one player per part, although he helpfully gives a number of options for several less-than-readily-available wind instruments. As a result, the piece is suitable as a moment of stark contrast in a symphonic concert — not least visually — as it calls for just seven solo string players instead of a string section. It will of course also work in a band programme, if a string septet is importable. *Hill-Song II* is much shorter and more straightforward, and accordingly is offered more flexibly: '(*a*) Solo Wind Ensemble (23 or 24 wind instruments and cymbal); or (*b*) Band; or (*c*) Symphony Orchestra (omitting trombones, tuba and violins).' Again, Grainger gives possible doublings in addition to alternative instruments.

Once all this has been deciphered, the true, if entirely conventional, challenge of these works emerges: they are seriously difficult to play and to conduct. The scores abound with written-in rubato indications, cross-rhythms, multi-meters, and tempo changes. *Hill-Song II* is somewhat easier than *Hill-Song I* but it is no push-over. Both works, however, more than repay the effort they demand, just as Grainger expressed it towards the end of his life: 'I consider *Hill-Song I* by far the best of all my compositions.'

Not surprisingly, the orchestral music most frequently performed is drawn from the substantial body of delightful and evocative short pieces which he either composed or arranged for large ensembles. I have selected a handful of them, which I have found to be particularly effective and rewarding.

Of the numerous arrangements Grainger made of *Irish Tune from County Derry*, the one I prefer by far is his *British Folk-Music Setting no. 29* (*c*.6 mins.; 1920), entitled in this version *County Derry Air*. It is 'large room-music, elastically scored' and employs a highly chromatic and disturbingly effective harmonisation, totally at odds with the sometimes sentimentalised treatment of this tune. I've had the privilege of performing it orchestrally, both with and without chorus. It is utterly breathtaking for audiences and performers alike as they experience the immortal melody soaring over the heart-wrenching harmonies at its dénouement.

In his ingenious orchestration of *La Vallée des cloches* (*Valley of the Bells*, the fifth and final piece of Ravel's piano set *Miroirs*; *c*.6 mins.; 1944) for 'tuneful percussion', harp, piano, and strings, Grainger takes a literal view of the valley, populating it with bell-like sounds on glockenspiel, staff bells, vibraphone, marimba, celesta, dulcitone, and the strings of a piano struck by mallets. Whereas there are three distinct bell sonorities in Ravel's piano manuscript, we can count at least six in Grainger's version. For orchestras with large percussion resources this piece makes a highly atmospheric interlude.

Grainger's arrangement of *Pagodes* (the first of the three *Estampes* for piano by Debussy; *c*.6 mins.; 1928) is, if anything, even more extraordinary. Scored for twelve percussionists, four grand pianos, celesta, dulcitone and harmonium, it succeeds in evoking with western instruments the haunting sounds of the gamelan which had so captivated Debussy many years earlier. With such scoring this piece belongs only to special occasions; but it is mentioned here for its luminous, enthralling beauty.[9]

Finally, I would recommend three pieces readily manageable by small, conventional orchestras. Grainger made eight settings of *Early One Morning*, and the last of these (*c*.4 mins.; 1950) is for chamber orchestra (double winds) enlarged only by a bass clarinet, trombone, and euphonium. It is particularly expressive and effective in concert, and neither difficult nor complicated to prepare. *Colleen Dhas* (or *The Valley Lay Smiling*; *c*.3 mins.; 1907) is for flute, cor anglais, guitar, and string orchestra (or string quintet). 'Colleen Dhas' is Gaelic for 'pretty maid', and Grainger found the folk-song within Thomas Moore's ten volumes of Irish Melodies. Its delicate lyricism provides a nice vehicle for an expressive flute player. Grainger took the popular Chinese folk song *Beautiful Fresh Flower* (*c*.3 mins.; 1935) and set it for piano solo, harmonising it by using only the tune's pentatonic notes. Peter Sculthorpe has made a delightful orchestration for strings, vibraphone, and tam-tam as well as a version for string quartet.

The conductor's view (2)
James Judd

After years of programming and conducting concerts and ignorantly neglecting to include Grainger's music, an opportunity to revel in his works came with the Adelaide Grainger Festival organised by Jim Koehne in 2003. Amongst the works I conducted was the suite *In a Nutshell* for orchestra, piano, and Deagan percussion instruments. Opening the score for the first time, one is struck by the helpful and quite precise requirements. John Calhorn Deagan was a clarinettist fascinated by the science of acoustics and by the theory and practice of tuning, and the company he founded in Chicago produced a huge variety of instruments. Clearly, Grainger sought instruments capable of producing very specific colours. Equally specifically, he would convey his thoughts to conductors with helpful notes containing interpretative and practical suggestions, something we are used to encountering in the works of Mahler.

The score of *In a Nutshell* commences with five pages of such advice! For example, aware that not every performance could muster eight percussionists, alternative scenarios are offered on how to proceed with four, five, six, or seven players if necessary. Then to the first page of music: *Arrival Platform Humlet* 'started at Liverpool St. and Waterloo Stations in London, awaiting the arrival of a belated train bringing one's sweetheart from foreign parts' does not so much sound of trains but rather the excited beating of the composer's heart. We are advised to set off 'Fast; about minim = 126' and 'with healthy and somewhat fierce "go"'. The woodwinds are required to be 'nasal, reedy and snarling', producing a steady stream of tunes and rhythms

---

[9] See Chap. 6, 'Towards a Universal Language'.

— accumulating and shattering page after page of text-book rules — crazy octaves of tunes, searching for harmony until, at the command 'louden lots', we reach an excited arrival.

Gay but Wistful at first tenderly, and later exuberantly evokes the London music hall. With most delicate use of percussion, harp, celesta, and piano, Grainger surrounds the memories with a depth and space that hints to me that we are at an uninhibited rehearsal in an empty theatre. Lovingly placed directions — 'more clingingly', 'very feelingly' — help the performers achieve the right sentiments through to the abrupt bringing down of the curtain. *Pastoral* invites us to be 'restful and dreamy, but wayward in time'. Before long, though, we find Grainger hurling a palette of his unique and exotic orchestral colours around the simple haunting melodies. Again, as with Mahler, Grainger keeps a practical eye on the conductor, advising when to change from conducting crotchets to quavers. *'The Gum-Suckers' March* ('Gum-suckers' is a nickname for people from his home state of Victoria) sets off 'at a quick walking speed' on a carefree journey. Throngs of harmonies march head on through each other while diverse characters (it seems) join Grainger's celebration of life. Unusually, in this movement we find *tenuto, expressivo, crescendo* replacing *clingingly, feelingly, louden lots*.

At the Adelaide Grainger Festival I had the thrill, for the first time, of conducting many of his orchestral works, but I suppose the most intriguing was the Australian premiere of *Thanksgiving Song* (1945), which had just been newly edited and prepared by Barry Peter Ould. Whilst this was not the only work I conducted involving off-stage music (we also performed *Tribute to Foster*), it was the most daunting, since it entailed moving instruments and musicians from the stage in the middle of the performance.[10] Grainger 'honor-tokened' the work to all his 'life's sweethearts' . . . and so the music starts with romantic memories conjured up by luscious string harmonies, gradually becoming excitable, with a solo trumpet hinting at a thanksgiving hymn, perhaps. As percussion are added, the movement builds to a furious frenzy and then . . . silence. At this point in the score, various players with their instruments discreetly leave the platform for backstage. There is a sense of great tension and anticipation as the stunned quiet is accompanied by the soft departures. This silence is vibrant music in itself. The spell is broken, or rather enhanced, by a distant, magical choir and orchestra, which repeat glorious yearning harmonies as they are towed further and further away. We are never sure at what point we really stop hearing the sound, and at what point the vibrant silence is in fact the music. We simply want it to last forever, as for me, the memory of it does.

---

[10] Described by James Koehne in Chap. 7, 'Programming Grainger: Au tombeau de Percy'.

Postlude

The following selections of works, including those discussed above, are offered as a starting point. Full details of timings and orchestration are given in the Catalogue of Works.

WORKS FOR FULL ORCHESTRA (25 MINUTES DOWN TO 9 MINUTES)

Youthful Suite
In a Nutshell
Danish Folk-Music Suite
The Warriors
Hill-Song I
Thanksgiving Song
The Power of Rome and the Christian Heart
English Dance
To a Nordic Princess
Green Bushes

SHORTER WORKS FOR FULL ORCHESTRA (7 MINUTES DOWNWARDS)

Original works

Blithe Bells
Colonial Song
Dreamery
Handel in the Strand (with solo piano)
Harvest Hymn
Hill-Song II
Mock Morris
The Immovable Do
Walking Tune (for symphonic winds)
Youthful Rapture (with solo violoncello)

Folk settings

Colleen Dhas
Country Gardens
Early One Morning
Irish Tune from County Derry
Molly on the Shore
Shepherd's Hey
The Merry King (with solo piano)

WORKS FOR STRING ORCHESTRA

Died for Love
Early One Morning
The Immovable Do
Irish Tune from County Derry
Mock Morris

1. ORCHESTRAL MUSIC

Molly on the Shore
Handel in the Strand (with solo piano)
Ye Banks and Braes

WORKS FOR ORCHESTRAL WIND/BRASS

Children's March: 'Over the Hills and Far Away'
Duke of Marlborough Fanfare
Walking Tune
Ye Banks and Braes o' Bonnie Doon

The following are of interest particularly from the point of view of Grainger's developing ideas.

YOUTHFUL TONE-WORKS

Fisher's Boarding House
Kleine Variationen-Form
Scherzo
The Crew of the Long Serpent
There were Three Friends
We were Dreamers

ARRANGEMENTS

Beautiful Fresh Flower (Chinese trad., arr. Grainger/Sculthorpe)
La Vallée des cloches (Ravel, arr. Grainger)
Pagodes (Debussy, arr. Grainger)

The elasticity Grainger allows in so many of his works makes them ideal for inclusion and adaptation, and an energetic conductor in an educational establishment, well supplied with both instruments and players, has quite a collection at his disposal. For professional orchestras, today's emphasis on including the young in 'outreach' programmes links in well with both Grainger's philosophy and the music he provides. His absence from concert programmes was perhaps understandable in the old days of the standard layout of overture, concerto and symphony — in none of which forms he wrote. But with today's more adventurous approach, and with the necessary and creative emphasis on introducing the young of all ages to the joys of seventy instruments playing as one, Grainger's kaleidoscopic repertoire is a gift.

2
Music for Wind Band
Timothy Reynish

Percy Grainger is undoubtedly the greatest composer in the past century to be involved in the wind band and its development. He is the only composer of stature to consider military bands the equal, if not the superior, in expressive potential to symphony orchestras (or as he described them 'bow-down-to-blend bands'). His earliest works predate those by Holst and Vaughan Williams. For half a century he was constantly contributing major and minor works to the genre as well as writing persuasively about it. From his programme note to *Lincolnshire Posy* (1939):

> Why this cold-shouldering of the wind band by most composers? Is the wind band — with its varied assortment of reeds (so much richer than the reeds of the symphony orchestra), its complete saxophone family that is found nowhere else . . . its army of brass (both wide-bore and narrow-bore) — not the equal of any medium ever conceived? As a vehicle of deeply emotional expression it seems to me unrivalled.

The absence of conventional large-scale works in his oeuvre militates against the ready acceptance of Percy Grainger in the canon of 'great' composers. Yet in the world of the wind band it is precisely the wealth of miniatures that makes him so very popular. Even the work acknowledged as one of his greatest achievements, *Lincolnshire Posy*, is a suite of six movements, each of three or four minutes or less. Most of his works for wind take less than six minutes. It is a tragedy that, fifty years after his death, four major works for wind are still rarely played or recorded: the two *Hill-Songs*, *Marching Song of Democracy*, and *The Power of Rome and the Christian Heart*, arguably with *Posy* his greatest contributions to the repertoire. Although, strictly speaking, arrangements *of* Grainger do not fall within the remit of this essay, I would like to add a passing mention of the arrangement by Frank Pappajohn (US Air Force Band) of Grainger's orchestral work *The Warriors* as a further example of his most adventurous writing expressed in wind-band terms.

'I'd much rather hear you make a mess of typical modern music than hear you tootling forever at a lot of baby's stuff.' So wrote Percy Grainger in 1943 in one of his famous 'Round letters'.[1] There is no longer any excuse for tootling these days, as critical editions of his more challenging works are freely available. A listing of

---

[1] 3 Sept. 1943 (Springfield, Missouri).

his original wind-band works may be divided, perhaps arbitrarily, into four groups. The chronology is sometimes hard to divine, as Grainger frequently revisited scores, and many of these works are reworkings of earlier versions for chorus, piano/s or orchestra.

Masterpieces

Hill-Song I (1901–21)
Hill-Song II (1907–29)
Lincolnshire Posy (1937)
The Power of Rome and the Christian Heart (1918–43)

Marching Song of Democracy (1901–48)
Colonial Song (1911–14)
Duke of Marlborough Fanfare (1939)

Hill-Song I is a remarkable work,[2] not only for its bizarre scoring for six each of oboes, cors anglais, and bassoons, with two piccolos and contra-bassoon, or its extraordinary compositional process of 'democratic' continuous melodic polyphony, but also for the early date of the first sketches, 1901. In 1955 Grainger said that his music 'should be fiercely & wildly performed, rather than in a staid & modest manner',[3] and he adds in a programme note: 'I consider *Hill-Song I* by far the best of all my compositions . . . At the time of composing it [1901–2, aged 19–20] wildness and fierceness were the qualities in life and nature that I prized the most and wished to express in my music.' Realising its impracticalities, he rescored it between 1921 and 1923 for twenty-two or twenty-three instruments, including strings. He also made a version for two pianos, four hands.[4]

Hill-Song II was written in 1907, is derived from the fast, wild music of *Hill-Song I*, and is scored for twenty-three or twenty-four solo players: piccolo and two flutes, three oboes and cor anglais, two bassoons and contra, E-flat, B-flat (three), alto, and bass clarinets, saxophone quartet, two cornets, and two horns. In 1921, he completely rebarred and rescored *Hill-Song I* for an ensemble of piccolo, flute, six double reeds, two saxophones, three brass, harmonium, percussion, piano, and six string parts. In the later versions, the original bars of 10/4, 11/4, 12/4, or 13/4 are broken into shorter metrical concepts, which are far more practical, but still vividly indicate his rhythmic freedom. Grainger refers to his tonal experiments of the 1890s: 'wide-tone scales', 'irregular rhythms', 'democratic polyphony', semi-discordant triads', and 'non-repetition of themes' among them. There is little development, and his melodic and harmonic approaches predate the future innovations of Schoenberg and Debussy. Either of the *Hill-Songs* in any version would be worthy regular additions to the orchestral or wind band repertoire.

---

[2] The two *Hill-Songs* are also discussed in Chap. 1, pp. 14–15, but in different (orchestral) versions.
[3] Gillies and Clunies Ross (eds.), *Grainger on Music*, 375, from a response to a Questionnaire.
[4] A wind-band score is now published by Southern Music in an arrangement prepared meticulously by Mark Rogers. It is scored for piccolo and two flutes, two oboes and cor anglais with bass oboe, two bassoons and contra, clarinets in E-flat, B-flat (two), A, alto and bass, saxophone quartet (including Grainger's beloved soprano), two cornets, two horns, euphonium, string-bass, percussion, and piano. It is well worth exploring for a dedicated wind ensemble.

Grainger's *Lincolnshire Posy* — 'Lisbon', 'Horkstow Grange', 'Rufford Park Poachers', 'The Brisk Young Sailor', 'Lord Melbourne', 'The Lost Lady Found' — demonstrates almost every facet of his compositional vocabulary. For many years it was only available as a condensed score plus the original parts, riddled with mistakes. Now there is a fine edition edited by the late Frederick Fennell and published by Ludwig. Any conductor beginning to work on *Posy* should set aside several weeks to study, first, Grainger's own programme note in the printed score, then Fennell's perceptive notes on interpretation in *The Instrumentalist*.[5] Finally, there is a wonderful resource from Robert Garafalo in Volume 4 of his series of books *Folk Songs & Dances in Wind Band Classics*, published by Whirlwind Music Publications. It is packed with useful background information and includes recordings sung by Grainger's original folk singers, together with updated recordings of each song by contemporary folk singers, and a bonus of both Grainger and Fennel singing *Lord Melbourne*. The less expert ensemble might consider tackling the opening movement *Lisbon* (sometimes titled *Dublin Bay*), the second movement *Horkstow Grange*, possibly *The Brisk Young Sailor*, and the finale *The Lost Lady Found*. *Rufford Park Poachers* and *Lord Melbourne* present a challenge to the most expert ensemble, but when surmounted, offer atmospheric sounds unique in the repertory (see Example 2.1).

Throughout his life, Grainger repeatedly revised and rescored earlier works, and when in 1947 he was invited to write a band work in honour of the seventieth birthday of Edwin Franko Goldman, he turned to *The Power of Rome and the Christian Heart*, first sketched in 1918, scored in 1943 for organ and orchestra with an enlarged wind section, and eventually rescored and premiered in 1948. Its initial inspiration was drawn from his military service (see Plate 1), and his anger at seeing young soldiers in training before being sent to their deaths in the battlefields of France. More universally, the work reflects his bitterness at the influence on the civilised world of the 'Roman Empire's conception of life (a privileged few catered to by a host of slaves)'. Elsewhere there is a note on the score which describes the piece as 'the unfoldment of musical feelings started by thoughts of the agony of Individual Souls in conflict with The-Powers-That-Be — as when the Early Christians found themselves at strife with the Power of Ancient Rome'. The passionate intensity of these feelings draws some of his most heartfelt music, but unfortunately the complexity of the scoring and the demands of the orchestration militate against frequent performances (for example, he asks for six harps, although it is possible to perform it with only one). However this is a magnificent work, predating the Second Viennese School in many of its harmonic procedures, but ending with a lyrical pastoral which would not be out of place in a work by George Butterworth or Vaughan Williams.

Marching Song of Democracy can be performed by band, with or without a wordless chorus.[6] Grainger's first sketches were in 1901. He worked on the chorus and orchestral version over the next fifteen years, and finally arranged it for band in 1948. *Marching Song of Democracy* is far more diatonic than *Power of Rome*, but there is

---

[5] Frederick Fennel, 'An Interpretative Analysis', *The Instrumentalist* (May, September, October 1980); repr. in *Conductor's Anthology*, published by *The Instrumentalist* in 1980.

[6] See Chap. 3, p. 31 below.

2. MUSIC FOR WIND BAND

Example 2.1   *Lincolnshire Posy*: 'Rufford Park Poachers', bars 52–8

a fluidity of harmonic movement, a constant ebb and flow, taking the work from a tonal centre of C to a final coda in F sharp. The work has the romantic sweep of a tone-poem by Strauss or Elgar, and in the new edition by Keith Brion, published by G. Schirmer, all the problems of the old edition have disappeared. The composer, conductor, and Grainger scholar Joseph Kreines writes, 'This mighty, epic conclusion provides a stunning peroration to a remarkable work which, for all its stylistic disparities, remains one of Grainger's greatest achievements, and certainly deserves to be ranked with the finest compositions for wind band.'

The band version of *Colonial Song* remains one of the great examples of subtle scoring. Grainger gives a vivid clue to the style of performance needed in his preface: 'I have . . . noticed curious, almost Italian-like, musical tendencies in brass band performances and ways of singing in Australia (such as a preference for richness and intensity of tone and soulful breadth of phrasing over more subtly and sensitively varied delicacies of expression) which are also reflected here.' His own piano recording is quite wayward, with considerable slowing-offs and careful placing of cadences — the pauses not too exaggerated, and with a sense of urgency in the middle section building to a huge climax. It is worth noting, too, the almost exaggerated placing of the small notes after that climax, the emphatic articulation of the little turns and the carefully controlled, gradual slowing-off towards the final few bars. Of course the piano cannot replicate the magical overlapping diminuendo in the flutes and horns.

Grainger's music is so full of joyful energy and picaresque inspiration that it lends itself to imaginative presentation. A concert in Sweden recently began with the *Duke of Marlborough Fanfare* (scored for brass ensemble), but with the ensemble offstage and the solo horn wandering through the audience. At the end, the audience was suddenly aware that the players on stage had surreptitiously started *The Immovable Do*, the brass sneaked back in, and eventually the conductor started to conduct: a magical opening to a concert.

The concert marches

The Lads of Wamphray March (1905–37/8)   '*The Gum-Suckers' March* (1905–42)
Children's March (1917–19)

Percy Grainger's preface to *The Lads of Wamphray March* gives a clue to his own ideas on performance. Based on themes from his ballad for men's chorus and orchestra, it was 'tone-wrought for band' between 1904 and 1905, pre-dating Holst's First Suite in E flat by four years. Upon hearing a read-through by the Band of the Coldstream Guards, however, Grainger was very self-critical. His subsequent experiences during the Great War in the 15th Band, Coast Artillery, under Rocco Resta gave him a useful opportunity to experiment with scoring for band, and he continued throughout his life to make revisions and improvements to his works. In 1937 he was invited to contribute to the convention of the American Bandmasters Association in Milwaukee, and he undertook a revision of the *March*.

Example 2.2 *The Lads of Wamphray March*,
showing Grainger's directions at rehearsal mark 10

In his preface 'To Bandmasters' he gives some interesting suggestions for performance and interpretation. The soprano saxophone can be replaced by a muted trumpet sitting with the saxophones; *ad libitum* tin whistles or fifes can be played by any number of instruments (the more the merrier); the E-flat clarinet and third flute part are interchangeable. He demands a metrical, unyielding beat throughout — 'the kind of stoical steadiness to be found in Bach's energetic movements, rather than the volatility of Chopin or Liszt'. Grainger is perhaps most interesting in matters of balance, deploring the over-weight of B-flat clarinets (a throw-back to the scoring tradition where the violins are replaced by the clarinet section), and he demands good tonal balance with an increase, if possible, in alto and bass clarinets. In bar 10 he puts in a note, 'N.B. The bars beginning at [rehearsal mark] 10 should sound like a mobilized (de-droned) bagpipe — as nasal, reedy and raucous in each reed part as possible' (see Example 2.2). He is meticulous about dynamics, accents and tenutos, commenting that 'it is very important that their full duration-values be given to notes (that they be not clipped short) over which a stress or a stress and accent are placed'. Throughout the work, we are aware of the detail which is so essential to give his music vitality and virtuosity, the wild swings of emotion and extreme dynamic contrasts which veer from *pp* to *fff* — 'louden hugely'.

Children's March: Over the Hills and Far Away was written between 1916 and 1918 and has three special characteristics: the introduction of a piano[7] (at one stage he instructs the pianist to strike the strings with a mallet), the inclusion of two short passages where the players sing a wordless chorus, and the concentration at the start and finish on low wind including the bass oboe and low brass. There were no problems with the orchestration, and the work was published in 1919. This is the most practical of the marches for less-experienced bands. There is a misleading if very exciting recording of the piano-duo version by Grainger and Lotta Mills Hough,[8] played at a breakneck speed which, if attempted by a band, would be disastrously unclear.

His third concert march, 'The Gum-Suckers' March, became the fourth movement of his orchestral suite *In a Nutshell*. It was scored for band in 1942. It is worth listening to an orchestral version of *In a Nutshell* to catch a speed determined by string phrasing. While encompassing the jaunty energy of the piece, it is important to give time for all the detail to emerge. For example, incorporating a tune from *Colonial Song*, he submits it to some humorously complex chromatic treatment. As in the *Children's March*, there is a major part for piano, along with a huge percussion section.

'Easier' music: the challenges

Irish Tune from County Derry (1918)
Ye Banks and Braes (1901–32)
The Merry King (1936–9)

Let's Dance Gay in Green Meadow (1943)
The Immovable Do (1933–9)

Irish Tune from County Derry was first set in 1902 for unaccompanied wordless chorus. For the piano solo version of 1911 he writes, 'slow-ish, but not dragged, and wayward in time' — perhaps a useful indication for the band version, which appeared in 1916. It remains a fine example of band scoring, and a considerable test of a conductor's control and a band's flexibility. It demands the highest professional playing to achieve a great performance, since the dynamic range is from triple *pianissimo* to quadruple *fortissimo*, and back. It is worth noting that there is little of his democratic independence of part-writing here, and special care must be taken with the *tutti* dynamics. For instance, when the brass choir join the woodwind in bar 49, they must almost creep in, with an accompanying *forte* (perhaps more of a rich *mp*) well under the woodwind colour. They can then open out into the glorious *ff*, *fff*, and *ffff* at bar 58, swamping the woodwind and then quickly getting out of the way. In 1920 Grainger made a further version, this time for voices with organ and wind band. The accompaniment is treated very chromatically, giving an intense air of pathos and nostalgia. Without voice, this version is a little easier to bring off, and is effective in a completely different way. *Irish Tune* is well worth tackling by the inexperienced

---

[7] See Plate 11.
[8] *Grainger Plays Grainger (Grand Piano Project)*, Nimbus NI 8809; see Discography.

band. It is a wonderful training in balance, dynamic control and intonation. Incidentally, the very difficult entry on a high G for first clarinet in bar 40 might be more effectively slipped onto the E-flat clarinet if (s)he is a competent player.

While all of Grainger presents challenges, there are four pieces well within most bands' capabilities, the easiest being *Ye Banks and Braes*. It was originally written in 1901 for voices and whistlers, and when he returned to it in the early thirties it was to devise several versions. It is a simple two-verse setting of the song, with a countermelody for whistlers (perhaps an opportunity for audience participation), and in its 'elastic' scoring it is available for any combination of wind or brass instruments. Not quite as simple in its technical demands but still very possible for school bands is the less well-known *The Merry King*, a band version with piano 'dished-up' between 1936 and 1939. A simple theme is stated on the woodwind and followed by four variations. The full title of *The Faeroe Island Dance* is *Let's Dance Gay in Green Meadow* and, as so often, the work began life for chorus (1905). It was later arranged for harmonium, for piano, and finally for band in 1954. The structure is unusual as it has a seven-bar theme which never cadences, rather like *The Dargason*, and so is a set of continuous variants on the theme, ending very abruptly.

Like so many composers in the early part of the last century, Grainger was devoted to amateur music-making, and many of his scores are planned for the widest possible use. In the preface to the choral version of *The Immovable Do*, he writes, 'This choral version may be used together with any or all of the other editions of this piece: Organ or Harmonium, 9 strings or String Orchestra, Small or Full Orchestra, Clarinet Choir, Saxophone Choir, Wood-Wind Choir, Band. The composition is naturally fitted to be used on occasions (such as high school & competition festivals) when many different organizations are massed together.'

Two rambles

Blithe Bells (free ramble on Bach's 'Sheep may safely graze' from Cantata 208) (1930–32)

Bell Piece (after Dowland) (1953)

Grainger was an enthusiastic arranger of other composers, especially from the pre-Bach era, and many of these *Chosen Gems for Winds* are discussed elsewhere.[9] *Blithe Bells*, a 'free ramble' on J. S. Bach's 'Sheep may safely graze', is a fine introduction for the high school band, as long as there are many tuned percussion available. His other ramble for band is *Bell Piece*, based on the John Dowland song 'Now, O now, I needs must part'. First set for solo piano and later arranged for band, it constitutes a simple setting of the first verse and a more elaborate setting of the second. This verse is described by John Pickard[10] as transporting Dowland's melody 'into the world of Duke Ellington by way of the chromaticism of Delius'. Both works

---

[9] See Chap. 6, 'Towards a Universal Language'.
[10] Notes to *Percy Grainger — Dished up for Piano: The Complete Piano Music*, Vol. 2: 'Arrangements', Martin Jones, Nimbus CD NI 5232.

provide a wonderful change of pace for wind band programmes and are relatively easy to tackle.

Three lollipops[11]

Molly on the Shore (1907–20) Country Gardens (1918–53)
Shepherd's Hey (1913–18)

The virtuoso 'lollipops', on which Grainger's fame was largely based, are not so easy. The late Lt Colonel Rodney Bashford, Director of Music at Kneller Hall, discussed the interpretation of these in an article in Winds Magazine:

> Percy Grainger, with his wife, visited Kneller Hall in 1957, its centenary year, to conduct four of his lollipops at a summer concert. During his stay he watched me, then staff bandmaster of the school, rehearse the four pieces (Shepherd's Hey, Molly on the Shore, Irish Tune from County Derry, Country Gardens) and greeted me as I left the rostrum with 'Everyone plays my music too slowly.' My deflation was only slightly tempered by his rider, 'it was good to hear it up to speed for once'. I didn't believe him for a moment, especially when next day he took them all at a furious pace, far outstripping mine.[12]

Grainger was scathing about the feeble effects usually achieved in Molly on the Shore, particularly at the 'banshee cry'. In Shepherd's Hey there was never enough 'hey'. The Tune from County Derry was not a setting of Danny Boy. Country Gardens were too often full of exotic arum lilies instead of dog roses.

Now that many more modern works have arrived, with their rhythmic complexities and outrageous demands on technique, perhaps these wonderful evocations of a rural life that Grainger knew and loved will be treated with less awe (and dare one say, respect) and a little more joy. 'Dullsome' is a word Grainger did not coin, though he might well consider it, were he alive today. Here then is the dilemma of performance of Grainger's wind music: capturing the fastidious elegance of the composer without losing that elemental lust-for-life, the fierceness, the energy, the brilliance of scoring and of harmonic progressions, the fun and good humour, alongside the depth of sadness. Thomas Slattery quotes the composer as claiming 'I have never written a part that I did not sing myself',[13] and indeed it is the singable quality of his part-writing which makes his contribution to wind music so unique.

We should not be afraid of tackling his music. It is now over sixty years since he so famously wrote, 'As I said to them at the last rehearsal of Lincolnshire Posy about the changing barrings: "Don't mind if you play a few wrong notes; don't mind if you get the rhythms wrong. Please don't think I will suffer if you do. My job is to show

---

[11] Not necessarily easy.
[12] Rodney Bashford, 'A Plea for the Posy', Winds Magazine (Winter 1989).
[13] The Percy Grainger Companion (1981), 104.

2. MUSIC FOR WIND BAND

PROGRAM

I. Overture—Cockaigne (In London Town) .... Edward Elgar

II. *Concerto for Piano, in A Minor .... Edward Grieg
    (a) Allegro molto moderato, animato, piu lento, animato, piu lento, poco piu allegro
    (b) Adagio
    (c) Allegro moderato molto e marcato
PERCY GRAINGER

III. Hill-song No. 2, for 24 single wind instruments .. Percy Grainger

IV. Two Movements from "Celtic Set" .... Henry Cowell
    (a) Caoine (Irish Lament for the Dead)
    (b) Hornpipe

INTERMISSION (Ten Minutes)

The second half of this program is devoted entirely to compositions
by Percy Grainger

V. (a) **The Duke of Marlborough** (Fanfare for Brass Choir)
   (b) **Dublin Bay,** English Folk-song (set for five single instruments)
   (c) **The Merry King,** English Folk-song (set for ten single instruments and piano)
   (d) **Children's March,** "Over the Hills and Far Away," for piano and band

VI. (a) **The Immovable Do**
    (b) **Irish Tune** from County Derry
    (c) **Shepherd's Hey**
Conducted by the Composer

VII. **"The Gum-suckers" March,** from the suite **"In a Nutshell"** for piano and band

Henry Cowell's and all of Percy Grainger's compositions
appearing on this program were written for band by the composers.

*Arranged for band for this concert by Lieut. Resta

Figure 2.1 West Point Military Academy concert programme, featuring Grainger, April 1948

you what modern music is like. These irregular barrings were started over forty years ago, so it's about time you began to get used to them."[14]

Now that critical editions of most of the band music are available, the question remains about how to programme such a heterogeneous group of works. *Irish Tune from County Derry* and *Molly On The Shore* were published together, and the pairing works well. A concert given in April 1948 by Percy Grainger at the United States Military Academy, West Point, gives some nice ideas on organising the smaller pieces (see Figure 2.1).

---

[14] Round Letter to Kin & Friends, 3 Sept. 1943 (Springfield, Missouri).

3
Grainger for Choirs
Paul Jackson

IN HIS 1942 ARTICLE, 'The Culturizing Possibilities of the Instrumentally Supplemented *A Cappella* Choir',[1] Grainger recalls the words of the English Elizabethan composer William Byrd: 'There is not any Musicke of Instruments whatsoever, comparable to that which is made of the voyces of Men, where the voyces are good, and the same well sorted and ordered.' These words are as apposite to Grainger as they are to his musical forebear; for him, singing, and more specifically, communal singing, was perhaps the most direct and expressive form of musical utterance. Grainger wrote music for voices throughout his life, and his choral oeuvre presents us not only with some startlingly original works, but also with a summary of his musical, literary, and philosophical preoccupations. His vocal writing generally tends to favour male voices (see the Sea Chanty settings, for example), a preference perhaps in part arising from the popularity of men's choruses in turn-of-the-century Germany, where the young Australian spent his student years. In a literal sense, male singers also provide voice for the sentiments of two of his favourite writers, Rudyard Kipling and Walt Whitman.

Upon his arrival in Frankfurt-am-Main in 1895, Grainger studied composition first with Iwan (or Ivan) Knorr, and later with Karl Klimsch. Fuelled by a sense of experimentation and a growing love for and awareness of the writings of Kipling, Whitman, Swinburne, and others, he began producing large-scale works for singers and orchestra that sought to convey the immediacy of the speech-rhythms of the text in music through the use of irregular and constantly changing bar lengths. The concept of musical phrase structures mirroring the inherently irregular metres of prose (albeit in poetic form) also found resonance with Grainger's developing conceptions of 'musical democracy' and Free Music.[2]

His early compositions, writings, and experiments, whilst varied in the particularities of the methods of their realisation, share the sense of a composer in search of new methods of articulating musical form. As Grainger was studying at the end of the nineteenth century in Germany, the putative seat of western musical development, he was undoubtedly exposed to the increasingly saturated harmonic language and sometimes bloated orchestration employed by many composers of the time.

---

[1] *The Musical Quarterly*, 28/2 (April 1942), repr. in Teresa Balough (ed.), *A Musical Genius from Australia: Selected Writings by and about Percy Grainger* (Nedlands, W.A., 1982).

[2] See Introduction and Appendix II.

Unsurprisingly, therefore, several of the early works for orchestra and voices employ huge forces and use a dense and wandering chromatic language, a language that Grainger would later adapt and refine once his encounter with British folk music began in 1905.

Works for orchestra and chorus

Among his earlier settings, *Love Verses from the 'Song of Solomon'* and *King Solomon's Espousals*, of 1899 and 1900 respectively, were Grainger's only completed sections of what was planned to be a fourteen-part setting of the Old Testament *Song of Solomon*, using the authorised Douay translation. In their first incarnations, *Love Verses from the 'Song of Solomon'* (Part II of the cycle) employs a mezzo-soprano and tenor soloist with mixed chorus and orchestra, whilst Part V of the cycle, *King Solomon's Espousals*, is for chorus and orchestra alone. Grainger's gargantuan orchestra calls for up to thirty-two woodwind parts, eleven brass parts, and strings, making performances of these works unfeasible for many choirs and orchestras. Aware of the difficulty, Grainger revised *Love Verses from the 'Song of Solomon'* in 1931 for altogether more reasonable forces — soprano and tenor soloist, mixed chorus, and single wind and brass with strings[3] — and the sumptuous writing realises the intimacy of the songs beautifully and sensitively through a sustained melodic unfolding of the text.

Experiments in rhythmic irregularity abounded in Grainger's music at this time. For choral forces, one of the most striking examples is the Whitmanesque *Marching Song of Democracy*, which was to occupy him from 1901 to 1917.[4] Grainger's original plan was

> to write my *Marching Song of Democracy* for voices and whistlers only (no instruments), and have it performed by a chorus of men, women, and children singing and whistling to the rhythmic accompaniment of their tramping feet as they marched along in the open air; but a later realization of the need for instrumental color inherent in the character of the music from the first ultimately led me to score it for the concert-hall. An athletic out-of-door spirit must, however, be understood to be behind the piece from start to finish.[5]

Grainger sets no text but employs wordless syllables (see Example 3.1), and his explanation for this decision helps to clarify his views on vocalisation (and particularly massed vocalisation) and assists in the realisation of a possible approach to performance practice in his choral music:

> The vocal parts are sung to 'nonsense syllables' such as children use in their thoughtless singing; firstly, because I thought that a more varied and

---

[3] Grainger also allows this version for accompaniment by pipe organ and two Solovoxes, the latter featuring prominently in his later Free Music experiments.
[4] See also Chap. 2, 'Music for Wind Band'.
[5] From Grainger's programme notes to *Marching Song of Democracy*.

instinctive vocalism could be obtained without the use of words in music of a polyphonic nature (a freely-moving many-voicedness is the natural musical counterpart of individualistic democratic tendencies), and secondly, because I did not want to pin the music down, at each moment, to the precise expression of such definite and concrete thoughts as words inevitably convey, but aimed at devoting it, rather, to a less 'mental' immersion in a general central emotional mood.[6]

The instrumental forces accompanying the double chorus are again large, notably employing the orchestral 'gamelan' — glockenspiels, bells, and metal marimba — that was to become characteristic of many of his later works. *Marching Song of Democracy* is a fine example of Grainger's attempt to allow 'each phrase to grow naturally out of what foreran it & to keep the music continually at a white heat of melodic & harmonic inventiveness — never slowed up by cerebral afterthoughts or formulas.'[7] A reworked version emerged in 1930, renamed *Australian Marching Song*, scored for mixed chorus and a chamber-music ensemble of brass, strings, two pianos, organ (or harmonium), and optional expanded percussion.

Grainger returned to setting texts for chorus in 1903 with *The Wraith of Odin*,[8] the only completed movement of what was planned to be a larger cycle of settings of Henry Wadsworth Longfellow's *The Saga of King Olaf* (itself part of a larger work, *The Musician's Tale*). *The Wraith of Odin*, for double five-part chorus, again accompanied by a large orchestra, is a stirring piece that captures the mysterious, rough urgency of Longfellow's story with vivid vocal and orchestral writing. Grainger makes extensive use of vocal glissandi, a technique that does not perhaps come easily, either technically or philosophically, to many a choir, but one which serves to root his writing in the kind of 'instinctive vocalism' he sought in *Marching Song of Democracy*. The vocal writing is challenging, particularly for the sopranos and tenors. Divided tenor parts reach up to F *in alt*, a range well beyond most choral singers of today, and more the province of the operatic *tenore contraltino*.[9]

Male voices take centre stage in *The Lads of Wamphray*, Grainger's 1904 setting of one of the ballads from Sir Walter Scott's *Minstrelsy of the Scottish Border*. This rumbustious piece, in Scots dialect, originally scored for tenor and baritone soloists, four-part male chorus, and (very) large orchestra may also be performed in Grainger's version for voices and two (or more) pianos. Grainger similarly drew on traditional ballads when he used William Chappell's 1838–40 collection *Old English Popular Music* for his setting of *The Hunter in his Career*, for men's chorus and orchestra. From John Stafford Smith's 1812 collection, *Musica Antiqua*, he set *Sir Eglamore* (begun in 1904 and revised between 1912 and 1913) for double mixed chorus, brass,

---

[6] From Grainger's programme notes to *Marching Song of Democracy*.
[7] From Grainger's programme notes to *Hill-Song I*.
[8] See Chap. 8, Example 8.2.
[9] See, for example, Grainger's 1901 version of *The Peora Hunt*, scored for 5-part male chorus and contraltino (in the last bar only!).

Example 3.1 *Marching Song of Democracy* (vocal score), bars 117–22

percussion, and string orchestra.[10] The English poet Algernon Charles Swinburne, whom Grainger admired for his 'superb riming, anti-morality & deep philosophy',[11] provided the text for *The Bride's Tragedy*, one of the composer's most complex and anguished works for chorus and orchestra. Written in a pseudo-Scots dialect, it recounts the tragic story of two lovers who, fleeing from the bride's loveless marriage ceremony with another man, drown in a river which 'smote them hand and head'.

Two works, concluding this section, are drawn from folk poems from the Faeroe Islands, *The Merry Wedding (Bridal Dance)* and *Fadir og Dóttir (Father and Daughter)*. The *Merry Wedding*, written between 1912 and 1915, was inspired by a refrain from the folk poem *Brúnsveins Vísa (The Song of Brownswain)*, drawn from the folklorist V. U. Hammershaimb's *Færøsk Antologi*. This delightful piece, scored for nine solo voices, chorus, and small orchestra, finds a character all of its own, quite distinct from both his earlier works for chorus and from the English folk-song settings. He remarks in his introduction that 'the lines seemed to me to breathe a spirit closely akin to the gentle glowing joyousness of Denmark, which I was longing to thankfully give voice at that time'. The composer enjoyed enormous success with his setting of *Father and Daughter* (1908–9), prompting the critic of *The Daily Telegraph* to write that the piece was 'in very truth the most stupendous crescendo from strength to strength that has come within our ken: its effect was literally terrific and the piece had to be repeated'.[12] It skilfully combines traditional folk material, collected by the Danish musicologist Hjalmar Thuren[13] and by V. U. Hammershaimb, with melodies of his own invention. A prime example of the technique of gradual reinforcement through repetition, and one of his most exhilarating settings, *Father and Daughter* captures the spirit of the native Faeroese dance-fuelled epic ballad-song. Scored for five men's voices, double mixed chorus, strings, brass, and optional mandolin and guitar band,[14] it makes a rousing addition to any choir's repertoire, although it requires exceptional discipline in its breathless, unrelenting articulation.

The extraordinary *Tribute to Foster*, first sketched in 1913 but not completed until 1931, sets and transforms Stephen Foster's *Camptown Races*, recalling, in the process, memories of Grainger's mother singing him to sleep with 'this entrancing ditty'. Foster's tune is treated both as dance-song and lullaby, giving 'musical expression . . . to my love and reverence for this exquisite American genius — one of the

---

[10] Unusually, in the 1904 version Grainger calls for antiphonal brass with different instruments in the gallery, behind the platform, in front of the platform, and to the right and left of the platform.

[11] 'Why "My Wretched Tone-Life"?', repr. in Gillies, Pear and Carroll (eds.), *Self-Portrait of Percy Grainger* (Oxford, 2006).

[12] Cited in Kay Dreyfus (ed.), *The Farthest North of Humanness: Letters of Percy Grainger, 1901–1914* (Melbourne and London, 1985), 451.

[13] Hjalmar Lauritz Thuren (1873–1911), a member of the Folk-Song Society, recorded traditional folk music of the Faeroe Islands with the aid of a phonograph between 1901 and 1902, publishing his findings in *Folkesangen paa Færøerne* [Folksong in the Faeroe Islands].

[14] Whilst Grainger directs that 'the mandolins and guitars can be left out at will', the effectiveness of the piece is considerably enhanced by their inclusion. The parts are not difficult and are ideally suited to the kind of massed forces that the resourceful conductor could muster through wider community involvement. Grainger calls for as many instruments as possible.

most tender, touching and subtle melodists and poets of all time; a mystic dreamer no less than a whimsical humorist'.[15] Humour and dreamery are certainly evoked in the piece, which combines expert scoring for five single voices, mixed chorus, musical glasses, solo piano, and orchestra with some of Grainger's experimental and quasi-aleatoric techniques that were also to feature in such works as *Pastoral* and *The Warriors*. In these pieces bell-like ostinato figures veritably explode from points of climax, only to subside in intensity, subsequently providing the background for new material. In the central lullaby section of *Tribute to Foster*, a sustained piece of ensemble vocal writing, recalling Puccini or Verdi, emerges from such a moment. The effect is further enhanced by a sustained 'black-note' cluster of bowed metal marimba notes and rubbed wine-glasses[16] — played by members of the (now silent) chorus in an act of musical communality — which contains the vocal ensemble within a numinous aura of resonance.

The final bars of *Tribute to Foster* provide a notable example of what might be termed 'textural democracy', the music splitting into three layers — chorus and orchestra, offstage men's voices and piano, and offstage ensemble — each of which, in turn, is constituted from harmonically ambiguous and temporally independent musical elements. The effect is akin to a group of street musicians or marching bands (albeit, in this case, symphonic ones) literally going their separate ways at the conclusion of their musical celebrations. For the ever-anguished Grainger this conclusion is, however, strangely indefinite, a reference to an earlier work, *The Lonely Desert Man Sees the Tents of the Happy Tribes* (1911–49), providing a note of disquiet. This little piece, which was to become a kind of *idée fixe* for Grainger, following its first incarnation in 1911, exists in various versions for solo or mixed voices and instrumental accompaniment. The wordless and impassioned incantation recalls Grainger's encounters with Rarotongan music in 1909 (albeit at a more sedate tempo than the South Sea Island music), and was to feature at key moments in various other works, most notably as the central section *The Warriors* (1913).

John Hopkins, a pioneer in conducting and recording Grainger, points out the similarity with Charles Ives in Grainger's aleatoric effects. He mentions how, in introducing the bowed metal marimba (or vibraphone or metallophone) members of the string section are given special instructions on how their bows should be drawn at right angles across the metal bar. The music for the latter group is printed in the orchestral string parts, and an instrument, now held in the Grainger Museum, University of Melbourne, retains marks clearly showing how it was prepared for use in this work. On this instrument the individual bars, with resonators attached, can easily be removed and distributed among the nominated string players.

---

[15] From the programme notes to *Tribute to Foster*.
[16] Grainger calls for a wide range of tuning for the glasses, necessitating the procurement of some vessels of unusually large size.

British folk-music settings

For Grainger, the folk music of rural Britain provided a well-spring of melodic material that was to form the inspiration for a significant proportion of his compositional activity. His love of 'primitive' music, which he judged to be both superior to, and more complex than, western art music, was matched by his admiration for the personal qualities and unselfconscious expression of the peasant performers he encountered.[17] However, Grainger's genius lay not simply in his ability to recognise the value of this fast-disappearing native music of Britain and Scandinavia, but also in the way in which his settings both capture and reinvigorate the essence of the original music, transforming the music into something new, vital, and wholly original. His attention to details of rhythmic phrasing, vocal 'orchestration', texture, language, and dialect, make the folk-music settings particularly rich and rewarding ground for performers and listeners alike.

One of Grainger's earliest settings is *The Three Ravens* (1902–50), a version of an old English song, scored for baritone solo, mixed chorus, and woodwind (or harmonium) accompaniment. In this brief but intense setting of 'a knight slain under his shield', Grainger captures the bittersweet sentiment of the original in a work of restrained, but complex, inventiveness. The detailed score, a typical example of Grainger's idiosyncratic but marvellously clear notational practices, contains bar-by-bar instructions for dynamic phrasing, methods of vocal production (this is another piece which features prominent use of vocal glissandi), and the balance and distribution of voice parts. In the same year, Grainger began work on what was to become one of his most popular and ubiquitous pieces, *Irish Tune from County Derry* (also known as *Old Irish Tune*, *Londonderry Air*, and *County Derry Air*). Existing in a proliferation of versions, Grainger set the tune for wordless chorus several times. At first glance, a straightforward homophonic harmonisation of the melody, Grainger's 1902 version (revised and published in 1912) for five-part mixed chorus, provides a masterful example of his ability to realise the polyphonic potential of melodic material.[18] His use of semi-discordant harmonies, together with the use of carefully-balanced weighting of the inner voices, have arguably made this version the definitive setting.[19]

Grainger collected folk music throughout the British Isles, but his most fruitful location was Lincolnshire, which he visited between 1905 and 1909. His 1905

---

[17] See Grainger's article 'The Impress of Personality in Unwritten Music' (1915) for a full account of his views of folk music and its singers. Repr. in Gillies and Clunies Ross (eds.), *Grainger on Music*.

[18] 'All my textal settings are rhythmically homophonic, the same word being sung simultaneously in all parts. This is to ensure easy intelligibility. Melodically, however, the part-writing is free & polyphonic.' Ibid., 19.

[19] In the 1919–20 version, titled *County Derry Air* (BFMS no. 29), Grainger sets the tune for women's chorus, optional unison men's voices, harmonium (pipe-organ), and three single instruments up to full orchestra, military band or two pianos. See Geoffrey Simon's comments in Chap. 1, 'Orchestral Music: The conductor's view (1)'.

visit to Brigg, in the north of the county, provided him for the first time with direct experience of the music of indigenous folk singers, an event that left an indelible impression on the young composer.[20] One of his first responses was the 1906 setting of *Brigg Fair*, a traditional tune noted down from the singing of Joseph Taylor, a farm bailiff from nearby Saxby-All-Saints.[21] Taylor had earlier won the folk-song class of the Musical Competition Festival, organised by Lady Winefride Elwes, wife of the English tenor Gervase Elwes, with his rendition of *Creeping Jane*. *Brigg Fair*, for tenor solo and unaccompanied mixed chorus, is a finely wrought but nevertheless passionate setting of the melody. Modern-day visitors to Brigg will still encounter the melody, sung in the streets of Brigg at festival time, including — perhaps unknowingly on the part of the performers — the additional verses Grainger borrowed from other songs to expand the two verses Joseph Taylor could remember (see Example 3.2).[22]

The question of dialect and accent becomes a consideration in the performance of these settings, and Grainger gives some guidance in the score for the realisation of the original pronunciation. In *I'm Seventeen Come Sunday*, an energetic setting for mixed chorus and brass band (or piano) drawn from Grainger's noting of the singing of Mr Fred Atkinson in 1905, he directs the piece to be sung with a Lincolnshire (Lindsey) accent if possible.[23] Atkinson also provided the source material, together with Lucy Broadwood's transcription of the singing of her Lincolnshire nurse, for *The Lost Lady Found*, set in 1910. A wonderful example of Grainger's ever-pragmatic 'elastic scoring' approach, the piece can be performed by mixed chorus and small orchestra, smaller mixed chorus and large room-music ensemble, or a single voice or unison voices with either the small orchestra, large room-music, or piano accompaniment. Grainger's 'Hints to Performers', reproduced in the score, not only provide guidance on pronunciation and performance practice but also contain an entreaty for the solo singer or conductor to mirror the dance-actions of the original performers in various sections of the piece. Such an approach, if confidently embracing the spirit of the piece, will help towards a performance that should, in Grainger's words, 'begin primly and neatly and bit by bit rouse up to a great and rowdy to-do'.[24] *The Lost Lady Found* is unusual in Grainger's choral work, as the female voices take prominence, and we must look to the setting of *There was a pig went out to dig* for one of his few examples of music for women's voices alone. This

---

[20] Whilst Grainger's contribution to the collection, recording and notation of British folk music was invaluable, he also used field material collected by others, including Cecil Sharp and Lucy Broadwood, as well as earlier published collections of traditional tunes. See Chap. 4, 'Singing Grainger Solo', for additional background.

[21] Modern transfers of Grainger's original recordings are available and should certainly be consulted where possible. See, for example, Folktrax Archive (http://folktrax-archive.org/).

[22] Grainger had earlier (1905) set the tune *Once I Courted a Damsel*, sung by Joseph Taylor, as *Marching Tune* for mixed chorus, brass band, and percussion. As with *Brigg Fair*, Taylor could only remember partial verses, forcing Grainger to add additional words from ballad-sheets held in the British Museum.

[23] Recordings of Lincolnshire dialect are available, and conductors are directed to the county's libraries in the first instance.

[24] From the 'Hints to Performers' in *The Lost Lady Found*.

Example 3.2 *Brigg Fair*, bars 1–16

a cappella setting provides a virtuoso test for the singers in Grainger's ever-changing passacaglia-like treatment of the simple refrain.

Standing alone, and sharing some kinship with the Sea Chanty settings (although very different in sentiment) is *Scotch Strathspey and Reel* (1901–1911) for four-part men's voices and small orchestra comprising four woodwinds, baritone concertina (or harmonium), xylophone, two guitars (or piano), and eight strings. Grainger had noticed several elements of commonality in Celtic dance tunes and, in his introduction to *Scotch Strathspey and Reel*, imagined that

If a room full of Scotch and Irish fiddlers and pipers and any nationality of English-speaking chanty-singing deep-sea sailors could be spirited together and suddenly miraculously endowed with the gift for polyphonic improvisation enjoyed, for instance, by South Sea Island Polynesians what a strange merry friendly Babel of tune, harmony and rhythm might result!

The rendition of the sea chanty *What shall we do with a drunken sailor?* requires lusty singing on the part of the men, and is interwoven with the other material with relentless energy and invention. The melody and words of the chanty were taken from the collection of Charles Rosher, a painter, author, collector, and singer of sea chanties with whom Grainger worked between 1906 and 1908. It was Rosher, together with the deep-sea sailor and chantyman John Perring of Dartmouth, who provided Grainger with the source material for some of his most sensitive and moving realisations, the Sea Chanty settings.

Sea Chanty settings

If Grainger's response to the folk music of Britain found an even more poignant manifestation, it is arguably in his Sea Chanty settings, composed between 1907 and 1910.[25] He was clearly influenced by the singing of Perring, whom he encountered through his work with the Folk-Song Society in the preparation for his seminal 1908 *Journal of the Folk-Song Society* article 'Collecting with the Phonograph'.[26] Grainger notes of Perring that he had 'a strong rich voice, capable of extreme modulation. He sings with a nasal drawl, sliding up to his high notes, and down to his low notes with searching intensity. He invests chanties (and these, to my mind, have as great an emotional charm as country folk-songs), with a strange blend of sea-born weirdness and human tenderness . . . He seems to me one of the most creatively gifted, fiery spirited traditional singers I have yet heard.'[27]

Grainger drew on the singing of Rosher and Perring[28] for his settings of *Shenandoah* and *Stormy* (1907), *Dollar and a Half a Day* (1908–9), and *Shallow Brown* (1910). He notes that 'Chantymen, are, I think, more inclined [than folk singers] to sing whole phrases with the full strength of the voice; doubtless because they have been accustomed to make themselves heard above wind and weather',[29] and

---

[25] Grainger's Sea Chanty setting no. 1 is the piano solo piece, *One More Day, My John*, composed in 1915 and reset in an easy version in 1932. As with most of Grainger's collections, the numbering reflects the date of publication rather than composition.

[26] Partially repr. in Balough (ed.), *A Musical Genius from Australia*.

[27] *Journal of the Folk-Song Society*, 3/12 (May 1908), 231.

[28] Writing in the 1916 *Journal of the Folk-Song Society*, Grainger's fellow collector Harry Piggott gives a vivid portrait of the singing of Perring and his fellow coal-lumpers: 'Mr. Perring or one of the others would stand in the middle and sing the solo parts while the chorus were grouped around. They always sang unaccompanied ("We do not sing to music" as they once explained to me), and in unison except for the occasional addition of an under part, generally in thirds, for a few notes.'

[29] 'Collecting with the Phonograph' (1908).

it is doubtless this contrast in vocal styles that sets Grainger's realisations apart from his British Folk-Music Settings, and which lends them an intensity of expression not found elsewhere. *Shenandoah* and *Stormy*, for solo male voice, refrain chorus, and accompanying single voices, recapture the practice of Perring's singers in arrangements that require the full vocal range of the male voice. *Dollar and a Half a Day*, scored for five single voices, refrain chorus, and accompanying chorus, similarly combines different versions of the original chanties on which it is based within a more sustained and detailed setting. Grainger's control of the vocal forces is masterful, his quasi-orchestral treatment of the vocal ensemble making this short piece one of his most sophisticated and heart-felt settings (see Example 3.3).

Sea Chanty setting no. 3, *Shallow Brown* (1910), for solo male voice and unison male chorus or mixed unison chorus, is an equally intense setting, this time employing additional instrumental forces. Perring recounts that the tune 'was supposed to be sung by a woman standing on the quay to Shallow Brown as his ship was weighing anchor',[30] yet the piece is equally effective sung by a male or female soloist. The vocal lines are presented almost exactly as Grainger originally noted them from Perring's singing, with harmonic and textural variation supplied by the orchestra of winds, harmonium, piano, strings, and optional ukuleles, mandolins, mandolas, and guitars. Whilst the piece may alternatively be performed with piano accompaniment, it is worth while realising Grainger's more ambitious scoring intentions. The guitar band not only allows for the participation of a wider range of instrumentalists than is usual, but also contributes considerably to the unique wave-like textures of *Shallow Brown*. Grainger directs that each player's instrument is to be restrung with its own identically-tuned strings, and to be played in the 'Australian' manner (that is, with the hand over the top of the neck)[31] in a constant cross-string tremolo fashion, producing an effect that is both extraordinary and unique.

The Kipling settings

Grainger first encountered Kipling's writings around 1897 and he began his first settings a year later. His Kipling settings were to occupy him throughout his compositional life: the earliest, *Northern Ballad*, *The Sea Wife*, *Verses from the Jungle Book*, and *Soldier, Soldier* dating from 1898, and the last, *The Only Son*, from 1947.[32] His explanation of this lifetime interest was simple: 'I set Kipling's rime-pieces to tone-art, because I deemed Kipling the seer of the English-speaking folk.'[33]

Grainger completed thirty-three Kipling settings,[34] twenty-two of which were

---

[30] From the programme notes to *Shallow Brown*. See also Chap. 4, 'Singing Grainger Solo'.
[31] Grainger supplies full instructions for playing guitar in the 'Australian' manner in the preface to the printed guitar parts for *Scotch Strathspey and Reel*.
[32] The final revision of *Mowgli's Song Against People* was finished in 1956 when Grainger was seventy-four years old, some fifty-three years after its initial composition.
[33] Unpublished Round Letter, 15–17 February 1942.
[34] Grainger began over fifty works inspired by Kipling, including instrumental pieces such as *Eastern Intermezzo*, *We Were Dreamers*, and *Zanzibar Boat Song*.

Example 3.3 *Dollar and a Half a Day*, bars 49–57

published in a numbered sequence between 1912 and 1958. Scored for a variety of ensembles, ranging from solo voice and piano to mixed chorus with orchestra, the collection centres around the Kipling *Jungle Book* cycle, which was to occupy him for fifty-nine years. The *Jungle Book* settings were not published as a cycle until 1947, and the variety of vocal and instrumental forces Grainger calls for tends to favour the performance of selected numbers in concert. Writing to the pianist Harold Bauer in 1947, Grainger explained that the Kipling Settings were 'an outcome of the influence emanating from the vocal-solo numbers-with-accompaniment-of-solo-instruments in Bach's *Matthew Passion*, as I heard it when a boy of 12, 13, 14, in Frankfurt'.[35] Bach's influence, never far beneath the surface of Grainger's music, is also revealed in the eleven movements that make up the *Jungle Book* cycle through the regular use of expressive solo lines set against refrain textures of often homophonic harmonisations of the melody. The eleven brief movements of the *Jungle Book*, which Grainger regarded as among his finest work, form a compendium of Grainger's compositional techniques, and reveal text setting of great ingenuity and sensitivity. The cycle comprises the following:

'The Fall of the Stone'	mixed chorus with instruments
'Morning Song in the Jungle'	a cappella mixed chorus
'Night Song in the Jungle'	a cappella male voices
'The Inuit'	a cappella mixed chorus
'The Beaches of Lukannon'	a cappella male voices, mixed chorus with instruments
'Red Dog'	a cappella male voices
'The Peora Hunt'	mixed chorus with instruments
'The Hunting Song of the Seeonee Pack'	male voices and strings
'Tiger! Tiger!'	a cappella male voices
'The Only Son'	soloists, mixed chorus with instruments
'Mowgli's Song Against People'	mixed chorus with instruments

The technique of solo and choral refrain, much favoured by Grainger, is also employed in a Kipling setting of quite different temperament, *Danny Deever*. The words come from the poet's *Barrack Room Ballads*, which were published in two series, in 1892 and 1896. Grainger clearly identified with Kipling's blend of heroic stoicism and patriotic imperialism, the poet's ability to speak through the voice of the common man finding particular resonance with the composer. Grainger had set two other Barrack Room Ballads, *Soldier, Soldier* (1898–9) and *The Young British Soldier* (1899),[36] before sketching out *Danny Deever* in the summer of 1903. The piece was reworked in 1922 and published by Schott in 1924. Recounting the tale of the execution, by hanging, of a young soldier accused of murder, Kipling's poem employs a question, answer, and commentary structure that combines grim humour with the chilling horror of the act of execution as witnessed by Danny Deever's fellow soldiers. Scored for double men's chorus and orchestra or baritone solo, men's

---

[35] Letter from Grainger to Harold Bauer, reproduced in Thomas C. Slattery, *Percy Grainger: The Inveterate Innovator* (Evanston, Ill., 1974), 115.

[36] The third setting, *The Widow's Party*, followed in 1906.

Example 3.4 *Danny Deever*, bars 2–9

chorus, and piano, *Danny Deever* provides a telling example of Grainger's ability to respond to the theatricality of a text in both sentiment and means of realisation (see Example 3.4).[37]

Postlude

The following selective list is given as a guide to choirs to begin exploring Grainger's wide-ranging choral legacy. The categories are not exclusive, and it should be remembered that Grainger frequently wrote different versions of his musical works, of sometimes quite contrasting levels of difficulty and vocal and instrumental resources. With this in mind, the full catalogue of works contained in this volume should be consulted, in conjunction with the range of recordings currently (and historically) available. Let the last word remain with Cyril Scott, writing in 1916, who simply remarked that 'Grainger is a choral writer of exceptional power . . . for he manages to draw effects from a chorus which have remained latent heretofore, and the choral writers that will come after his day will owe him a debt in the field of technique.'[38]

COMPETENT CHOIRS — SCHOOL OR COLLEGE

Angelus ad Virginem
Australian Up-Country Song
I'm Seventeen Come Sunday
Morning Song in the Jungle
Random Round[39]
Recessional
The Lost Lady Found
The Widow's Party

CHORAL SOCIETIES

A Song of Värmeland
March of the Men of Harlech
Marching-Tune
Selections from Jungle Book Cycle
Shallow Brown
Six Dukes went a-Fishin'
The Hunter in his Career
The Lads of Wamphray
The Lonely Desert-Man Sees the Tents of the Happy Tribes
The Love Song of Har Dyal

---

[37] Grainger recalls Kipling's response to hearing an early draft of *Danny Deever* in 1905, the poet noting that 'Till now I've had to rely on black and white, but you do the thing for me in color.' Cited in Dreyfus (ed.), *The Farthest North of Humanness*, 50.

[38] Cyril Scott, 'Percy Grainger: The Music and the Man', *The Musical Quarterly*, 2 (July 1916).

[39] See Chap. 6, p. 81, and Chap. 7, p. 90 below.

The Three Ravens
Tribute to Foster
Willow, Willow

PROFESSIONAL CHOIRS[40]

Danny Deever
Father and Daughter
Love Verses from the 'Song of Solomon'
Marching Song of Democracy
Scotch Strathspey and Reel
The Bride's Tragedy
The Merry Wedding

A CAPPELLA GROUPS

Brigg Fair
Dollar and a Half a Day
Irish Tune from County Derry
Mo Nighean Dubh
Morning Song in the Jungle
Shenandoah
Soldier, Soldier
Stormy
The Gypsy's Wedding Day
There was a pig went out to dig

---

[40] A late-night BBC Proms concert in 2000 with the Joyful Company of Singers conducted by the late Richard Hickox presented a programme which included *The Widow's Party, The Power of Love, Dollar and a Half a Day, The Keel Row, The Lonely Desert Man Sees the Tents of the Happy Tribes, Scotch Strathspey and Reel, Ye Banks and Braes o' Bonnie Doon, Danny Deever, Shenandoah, Stormy, Colonial Song, Shallow Brown,* and *Random Round*.

4
Singing Grainger Solo

Stephen Varcoe

GRAINGER'S SONGS offer marvellous opportunities to singers who are not afraid to be daring and imaginative. The strange sounds which are so effective in *The Twa Corbies*, the broad cockney of *The Young British Soldier*, the extreme vocal demands of *Dedication* or *The Beaches of Lukannon*, or the robust story-telling of *Hard-hearted Barb'ra (H)Ellen* — these are just a few of the exciting challenges he sets us. But there is a deep sincerity of feeling at the heart of this music, and the odd eccentricities which we find scattered about are themselves a by-product of that sincerity. *The Lost Lady Found*, for example, was sung to Lucy Broadwood, the pioneering folk-song collector, by her Lincolnshire nurse, Mrs Hill, who danced as she sang; in his setting of 1910, Grainger actually gives dance steps for performers to use as they sing. If this strikes today's conservatoire-trained recitalist as fun but odd, it must have appeared positively offensive to the serious musicians of a century ago. Yet his purpose was not simply to be capricious but to attempt to recapture something of the true quality of the original dance-song.

For singers who may not be confident enough to have a go at some of the more demanding numbers, there are many folk settings which require a more conventional approach (with or without some dialect sounds), and there are original songs which are nearer in style to the songs of his contemporaries. *Willow Willow, My faithful fond one*, or *A Song of Autumn* are examples of both these types, and it would be a pity if singers were discouraged from programming such beautiful songs because of a misconception that all of Grainger is somehow 'difficult'. Here I ought perhaps to qualify my use of the word 'conventional' in the context of this highly unconventional man: even when he is composing 'serious' concert songs, his distinctive voice is always heard. And as we should expect from a pianist of such renown, the same fascination and fantasy abound in his piano writing.

British folk-music settings

Percy Grainger showed an interest in folk music at the very beginning of his composing life, and his first setting of a traditional tune was *Willow Willow* in 1898, when he was only sixteen; this was from Chappell's collection *Old English Popular Music*. His two other early sources of traditional songs were Augener's *Minstrelsy of England* and Cramer's *Songs of the North*. It was not until 1905 that he started collecting

Example 4.1 *Bold William Taylor*, vocal line, bars 1–10

folk songs himself. He joined the English Folk-Song Society, a distinguished band of enthusiasts led by Lucy Broadwood, Cecil Sharp, and Ralph Vaughan Williams, and it is in this work that he made his most important contribution to the music of Great Britain. In 1906 he was among the first song collectors to use the wax-cylinder recorder, and some of his original recordings have been transferred to digital format. We can hear again the singers he wrote about with such respect and affection: the likes of Joseph Taylor, Joseph Leaning, and George Gouldthorpe.

The settings he made from these collected songs show a fastidious attention to detail. Typically they were published in various different formats — in his words, 'elastic scoring' — either with piano, orchestra, or small instrumental ensemble. The ensemble for *Bold William Taylor*, for example, has clarinets, strings, and either harmonium, reed-organ, concertina, or accordion. In his introduction to the song he writes that these instruments 'conjure up some suggestions of countryfied sounds'.[1] His philosophy was to recreate as much as possible of the original performances as he had heard and recorded them, preserving as faithfully as he could the diction, the dynamic ebb and flow, and the melodic variations between each verse. The resulting scores can be difficult for a musician to interpret, certainly one trained in standard European art-singing. Almost every note has its own set of instructions for dynamic and attack, and every syllable has its strange dialect sound.[2] Grainger himself bemoaned the inadequacies of conventional notation to convey the flexible nature of the rhythm as originally recorded, and described the outcome (see Example 4.1) as making a 'regrettably disturbing picture to the eye'.[3]

---

[1] Percy Grainger, Introduction to 'Bold William Taylor', BFMS no. 43 (1952).

[2] In 1906, after a concert in the Aeolian Hall, London, where Grainger had accompanied the famous tenor Gervase Elwes in several of his folk-song arrangements, the *Guardian* said, 'He [Elwes] was an ideal interpreter, and that in two of them he used his native Lincolnshire dialect with irresistibly humorous effect.' Winefride Elwes and Richard Elwes, *Gervase Elwes: The Story of His Life* (London, 1935), 166. Performers without that knowledge of the dialect sounds are at a disadvantage.

[3] Preface to a selection of songs published in the *Journal of the Folk-Song Society*, 3/3 no. 12 (May 1908), cited in John Bird, *Percy Grainger* (London, 1976), 112.

The score of *Bold William Taylor* also has some of Grainger's idiosyncratic indications of mood: verses 3 and 4 have 'frolicsomely' followed by 'boldly' in line 3; halfway through verse 6 there is 'clingingly' and 'plaintively', and 'still more plaintively'; verses 7 and 8 both start with 'feelinglessly', and verse 8 later has 'brightly, crisply'. These are his interpretations of what he heard, revealing the subtle variations made by old Joseph Taylor. He wrote that 'the interest taken by folksingers in the stories related in their songs shows how alive their minds are to the narrative element'.[4]

Listening to the modern vinyl copy of some of the original cylinder recordings of these old singers made by Grainger himself in 1906, and the disc recordings he made two years later, I think he was exaggerating the dynamic contrasts actually present.[5] The performances on these recordings possess much more of his description of George Gouldthorpe's singing: 'He gave out his tunes in all possible gauntness and plainness, for the most part in broad even notes.'[6] A. L. Lloyd, the eminent folklorist and an admirer of Grainger's style of folk-song arrangement, suggests that expression was conveyed by the traditional singers not by grand, sweeping gesture, but by tiny nuances of tone, rhythmic alteration, and ornament.[7] I would emphasise the word 'tiny'.

That being said, conservatoire-trained singers would do well to approach these songs in the spirit of Grainger's philosophy, and use their imaginations to enter the special musical world of these old folk singers. Treating these folk songs as if they are arrangements by Quilter or Vaughan Williams (much as I admire those composers) will not do justice to what Grainger was trying to create. The most telling of his comments is this: 'The greatest crime against folksong is to "middle-class" it — to sing it with a "white collar" voice production and other townified suggestions.'[8]

It will be seen from the example above that many of the vowels have strange symbols above them. Grainger was not only at great pains to try to indicate as much as possible of the nuance of time and dynamic which he heard, but also the sounds of the local dialect. Without these dialect sounds, the song 'loses its charm as surely as would Kathleen Mavourin, *Coming Through the Rye* or an American-Negro spiritual if sung in "Standard Southern English"'. This comment should be born in mind when considering not only the folk songs but many of the Kipling settings as well, since it is part and parcel of his philosophy of music.

Songs of the North and Minstrelsy of the Scottish Border

Grainger's first visit to Scotland in 1900 made a very strong impression upon him, and his Scottish songs show how powerfully his imagination was stimulated by the landscape, the people and their history. Already at the age of sixteen he had writ-

---

[4] Grainger, introduction to 'Bold William Taylor'.
[5] *Unto Brigg Fair*, Leader LEA 4050 (1972).
[6] Percy Grainger, Introduction to 'Six Dukes went a-fishin", BFMS no. 11 (1913). The direction at the start of the song is: 'Very simply and with a childlike unconscious pathos.'
[7] A. L. Lloyd, *Folk Song in England* (London and New York, 1967), 83.
[8] Grainger, introduction to 'Bold William Taylor'.

ten some original songs to poems of Robert Burns, with melodies that are distinctly Graingerish, but his fourteen *Songs of the North* are settings of traditional words and tunes, and they exhibit much more characteristic harmonies. They also cover a wide variety of moods, from the vigorous *The Women are a' gane wud* and *Willie's gane to Melville Castle* to the slow and quiet *O'er the moor* or the lyrical *My faithful fond one*.

For the most part the texts are in Scots dialect:

> The women are a' gane wud,
> Oh, that he had biden awa'!
> He's turn'd their heads, the lad,
> And ruin will bring on us a'.
> George was a peaceable man,
> My wife she did doucely behave;
> But now dae a' that I can,
> She's just as wild as the lave . . .[9]

It seems clear to me that with all these dialect words the singer must make the effort to mimic a Scots accent. Here is the distinctive language of the people, and we can easily imagine Percy's horror at the performer who would give it the middle-class Standard Southern treatment.

One of these songs, *Drowned*, is a translation from the Gaelic into standard English, and there is nothing in the text to suggest Scottishness:

> No wonder my heart it is sore,
> No wonder the tears that I weep;
> My true love I'll see him no more,
> He lies fathoms down in the deep . . .[10]

Because the language here carries no hint of the poem's Scottish roots, I believe it should be performed with our normal sung English pronunciation, just as one would expect to hear Vaughan Williams's *Songs of Travel* sung, even though those poems were by Robert Louis Stevenson, also a Scotsman. However much it may have been a creation of 'the folk', the original Gaelic poem of *Drowned* has become, in the translation by the Rev. A. Stewart, a middle-class thing more akin to the texts of Victorian parlour songs.

---

[9] Charles Rogers (ed.), *The Modern Scottish Minstrel, or The Songs of Scotland of the Past Half Century*, 6 vols. (Edinburgh, 1855–7), I. 227.
[10] Dugald Mitchell (ed.), *The Book of Highland Verse: An (English) Anthology Consisting of (a) Translations from Gaelic, (b) English Verse Relating to the Highlands* (Paisley and London, 1912), 180–81. Anon., trans. Alex Stewart.

Rudyard Kipling settings

Another important influence on Grainger was Kipling's poetry, several volumes of which his father gave him, and from these come some of his earliest songs. *Northern Ballad* is the first, written when he was not yet sixteen, and it was followed by thirteen more settings. As with the Scottish songs we find a great range of moods and styles. There is the energetic *Ride with an Idle Whip*, lasting a mere twenty seconds, and the even more energetic *The Young British Soldier*, which lasts seven minutes. The strange, haunting *The Beaches of Lukannon* offers us a song Greenpeace might use as an anthem for promoting its ecological message, while *The Widow's Party* is a bitter denunciation of war and its consequences for the common soldier. Some of these songs are astonishing in their boldness, not least the first (1901) setting of *Dedication* (Example 4.2). It requires considerable technical expertise.

The question of suitable accent again arises, and it seems clear to me that a song like *Dedication* should be sung with normal sung English, since there is nothing in the text to suggest otherwise. *The Beaches of Lukannon, Merciful Town*, and *The Men of the Sea* should be treated similarly. But the settings of *Barrack-Room Ballads* and others like *Ganges Pilot* should certainly have a full-on cockney intonation. Here's the first stanza of *The Young British Soldier*:

> When the 'arf-made recruity goes out to the East
> 'E acts like a babe an' 'e drinks like a beast,
> An' 'e wonders because 'e is frequent deceased.
> Ere 'e's fit for to serve as a soldier.
>   Serve, serve, serve as a soldier,
>   Serve, serve, serve as a soldier,
>   Serve, serve, serve as a soldier,
>   So-oldier OF the Queen! [11]

It's hard to imagine anyone attempting that with middle-class tones.

Sea Chanty settings and other songs of the sea

Grainger's most remarkable and powerful song, in my opinion, is *Shallow Brown*, the third of his *Sea Chanty settings*. They all involve chorus, but there is a version of *Shallow Brown* just for solo voice and piano. The chanty was collected from the singing of John Perring, a sailor from Dartmouth. In its full orchestration, which includes mandolins, mandolas, ukeleles, guitars, and saxophones, it evokes surging sea, moaning wind, and the cries of the people on the shore. The opportunities for performing this version are for obvious reasons rather few and far between, but his arrangement for piano, as one might expect, is wonderfully impressive. The voice

---

[11] Rudyard Kipling, *Barrack-Room Ballads and Other Verses* (1st edn, London, 1892; many repr.).

Example 4.2 *Dedication* (first version), bars 1–6

part has a dynamic range from *pp* to *fff*, with great swelling surges and retreats as it rides the rolling sea of the accompanying piano. The last verse starts softly and gets softer, finally fading away to nothing on the high last phrase — not easy when you've been contending with all the huge sounds that have gone before.

Several of the Kipling songs (*Anchor Song* and *The First Chanty* among them) are about the sea, as are two fine early settings of Longfellow and Conan Doyle — *The Secret of the Sea*, which uses the whole-tone scale, and *Sailor's Chanty*, which tells a gripping tale of pirates, murder, and sexual awakening.

Danish folk-music settings and other songs

Grainger's song collecting took him to Denmark in the 1920s, and he made several settings for multiple voices of what he found there. *Husband and Wife* has two characters, but it can be sung by just one voice with piano. *Proud Vesselil* is a fairytale with many stanzas, and as with all story-songs it needs really crisp diction. For sheer passionate music-making there cannot be many songs to rival *The Power of Love*. Though there is only one stanza, it is repeated after the most spine-tingling extended piano writing. The music builds in emotional strength until it seems that the singer has no choice but to join in and repeat the words with heart-breaking intensity. That Grainger found such depths of feeling for this song can be explained by the recent suicide of his beloved mother, who had in effect been the lode-star of his life for forty years.

Amongst 'other songs' we have *Dafydd y Gareg Wen* (David of the White Rock) in a luscious arrangement which starts off quite conventionally, but as we would expect, begins to develop some strange corners, especially in the piano interlude between the two stanzas. The splendid *A Reiver's Neck-Verse* has plenty of rich harmonisation and a full-toned vocal line, with (to my ears) a hint of *Handel in the Strand* in the accompaniment.

Five songs by Percy's wife Ella were harmonised and, in four cases, scored by her husband: *Crying for the Moon, Farewell to an Atoll, Honey-Pot Bee, Love at First Sight, To Echo.*

Songs with several voices

Some of the very best of Grainger's songs are for more than one voice, and one of these, *Brigg Fair*, in his arrangement for tenor and chorus, must be the most famous of all his vocal works. It seems such a pity to deprive audiences of opportunities to hear this that I have performed a homemade version with tenor, baritone (for various hummings, as well as the words of the fourth verse) and piano. I wonder if he would have approved? One of the Danish folk-music settings, *Under en Bro* (Under a Bridge), is for mezzo and baritone accompanied by an interesting instrumental ensemble and piano, or by piano alone. The long unaccompanied opening presents a challenge for the singers' intonation, but the piece is fun to perform, and it is completed by two pages of terrific dance music for the pianist. From the Kipling songs comes *The Only Son*, a duet for soprano and tenor with optional chorus. It is elastically scored for room-music ensemble, though it is very effective with piano accompaniment. The tenor takes the part of Mowgli, telling a strange and gripping story from *The Jungle Book*.

Then there is one of his more eccentric creations, *The Lonely Desert-Man Sees the Tents of the Happy Tribes* from *Room-Music Tit Bits*, for soprano, tenor, and baritone. This has wordless syllables throughout, though he offers the performers the choice of making up their own if they wish. At the beginning the desert-man (tenor) sings what sounds like a lament, and he is followed by one of the happy tribes (distant baritone) singing a jaunty 'Yum, pum, pum, puppa, puppa, pum': he is soon joined by a friend (soprano), and they carry on together to a quiet but happy conclusion.

Gender of singer and song

To the folk singers from whom Grainger collected his songs it seems that matching the gender of the singer with that of the song was not an important issue. John Perring sang *Shallow Brown*, a song for a woman desperately bewailing the loss of her man as his ship leaves harbour. A baritone normally sings this song, with or without male chorus interjections, and this would be entirely appropriate for a sea chanty. Joseph Taylor sang *The Sprig of Thyme*, a song of innocence, virginity, and love, and a more 'female' piece could hardly be imagined: this is no male-only sea chanty but a beautiful evocation of disappointment and loss. Yet it seems that the folk tradition wore this vocal cross-dressing without demur.

It must be admitted that the singers Grainger recorded were nearly all men, and it looks as though they held the field in terms of singing in public. Perhaps in the public arena this was the case, but as we have already seen, *The Lost Lady Found* was collected from a woman's singing, and Grainger himself collected *The Brisk Young Sailor* from a Mrs Thompson. We also know that in another context, Thomas Hardy learnt many of the old songs from his grandmother, and doubtless a good number of these would have been narrated by male characters. Whatever the history of these and other songs, we are now quite prepared to hear the 'wrong' sex holding forth. After all, it is the singer's job to take on any number of different roles, even in the course of a single concert, and impersonating the opposite sex should not be viewed with any more alarm than pretending to be a lovesick pirate one moment and a dying mother the next.

Some important issues in singing Grainger's songs

As indicated above, the use of dialect and regional accent was a subject close to Grainger's heart. He was excited by the idea of music as something organic, grown in the soil of a collective imagination, and he abhorred anything which would stifle the connection with the original artistic impulse. Hence his search for 'authenticity' in performance — not sterile mimicry but inventive re-creation. Hence, too, his continual reworking of earlier material for new forces and flexible instrumental groupings. His preface to *Lincolnshire Posy* (1937), saluting the folk singers he had heard, should be required reading for anyone attempting to perform his songs, and, I suggest, anyone else's songs:

> No concert singer I have ever heard approached these rural warblers in variety of tone-quality, range of dynamics, rhythmic resourcefulness and individuality of style. For while our concert singers (dull dogs that they are with their monotonous mooing and bellowing between *mf* and *ff* and with never a *pp* to their name) can show nothing better than (and often nothing as good as) slavish obedience to the tyrannical behests of composers, our folksingers were lords of their own domain — were at once performers and creators.

Grainger's words suggest two major elements: *variety* in all aspects of performance; and *obedience* to the composer's demands. Even after all this time, singers tend not to see the need for that variety of tone, dialect, and dynamic which he called for. Training to be Mimi, Rodolfo, Don Giovanni, or Adalgisa requires, first, a gorgeous, big voice with a seamless legato. But if Grainger were miraculously to be among us again today, I would sit him down with some of the Chandos song recordings — say, Martyn Hill singing *The Twa Corbies* or *Ganges Pilot*, or Della Jones singing *Weaving Song*, or perhaps me singing *Willie's gane to Melville Castle*, and I hope he would feel that, to an extent at least, much progress had been made.[12]

In his article 'Collecting with the Phonograph' Grainger emphasises the chief types of detail needing attention. He includes 'length of notes, staccatos, legatos etc.'

---

[12] Chandos CHAN 9610, tracks 18 and 4; CHAN 9730, track 8; CHAN 9503, track 11.

Example 4.3 *Creeping Jane*, vocal line, verses 1–5, bars 7–9

and 'component notes of ornaments that are hard to catch at the original speed of a performance'.[13] Example 4.3 from *Creeping Jane* shows the results of this kind of research, in the minute adjustments he makes to the precise rhythm and attack for each verse.

Obedience to the 'tyrannical behests of composers' was clearly seen by Grainger as the last refuge of the vocal scoundrel who was too weak-willed to do anything more interesting. But presumably he did not mean that we should ignore the detailed markings he gives in his own scores. If he asks for a crescendo and diminuendo on a held note, and I feel like doing the opposite, that surely was not what he had in mind: that smacks of mutiny!

Near the end of *Hard-hearted Barb'ra (H)Ellen*[14] we hear how this cruel girl, who mocked her lover as he lay dying, finally admits that she really loved him after all. She tells her mother to make her a bed that she might die and join him. The next verse has pianist and singer following independent speeds: the voice at MM 104, singing expressively, the piano at MM 120, marked 'lightly, gaily':

> Her mother dear she made her a bed,
> Both soft and fit for dyin'.
> 'For O I reeoo, for O I reeoo,
> I reeoo that I denied him.'

The voice then speeds up to coincide with the piano on MM 120, but in spite of the words, the singer has the marking 'warmly, heartily' for half the verse:

---

[13] Percy Grainger, 'Collecting with the Phonograph', *Journal of the Folk-Song Society*, 3/3 no. 12 (May 1908), 22.

[14] Noted down in 1906 from the singing of Mr James Hornby of Crosby, Scunthorpe, NE Lincolnshire. The strange spellings in these extracts are Grainger's transcriptions of what he heard, some of them obvious, some less so: 'reoo' = rue; 'shaller' = shallow; 'Addend' = And; 'kwier' = quire; 'greeoo' = grew; 'treeoo' = true; 'Fower' = For; 'wurruld' = world; 'admiyer' = admire.

> Her mother dear, she made her a bed,
> She made it both soft and shaller.

Then both voice and piano accelerate again to MM 132, with the singer marked 'exultantly':

> She turned her pale white face to the wall
> Addend death came creepin' on her.

The singer who decided to rebel here and go against Grainger's 'tyrannical behests' would be making a bad error, in spite of the strangeness of his instructions. To turn her face to the wall and sing 'exultantly' is surely beyond all reason. Yet it is precisely by such means that Grainger underlines the emotional dislocation of the girl throughout the song, including her heartless, inappropriate reaction to the dying man. And he is also looking ahead to the triumphant dénouement of the story. The music now becomes more and more impassioned as it approaches the end, with fistfuls of notes from the pianist, and *ff* and even *fff* from the singer.

> The won was buried in the 'igh church-yard,
> And the other in the kwier;
> The won sprung up a red rose-bud,
> And the other a green brier.

> Then they greeoo and they greeoo to the high church top
> And could not get any higher.
> And they met and they tied of a treeoo lovers knot
> Fower all the wurruld to admiyer.

Grainger's extraordinary imagination is completely vindicated. Mutiny? Elsewhere maybe, but not here. He described his old singers as 'lords of their own domain . . . at once performers and creators'. We do not have quite the degree of freedom they had when we take the music off the page, but we can take the lead he has given us and stretch our imaginations as performers. And we can take his meticulous and idiosyncratic notation as a basis on which to create anew.

Grading songs for difficulty

I shall list a cross-section of the songs according to their degree of difficulty, starting with the most straightforward. But first a word of warning: the simpler a song may appear to be, the more scrupulous we have to be about it. Broad sounds in a big song can cover up a multitude of faults, whereas we can be cruelly exposed in a 'little' song. Reasons for upgrading the difficulty quotient may include vocal or dynamic range, length of song, rhythmic drive, melodic factors, or odd twiddles.

ELEMENTARY

British Folk-Music Settings

Willow Willow (two versions)
Near Woodstock Town (two versions)
Died for Love

Songs of the North

Turn ye to me
Skye Boat Song
Fair young Mary
Drowned
Leezie Lindsay
My faithful fond one

Various

Evan Banks
A Song of Autumn
The Land o' the Leal

INTERMEDIATE

British Folk-Music Settings

Creeping Jane
Six Dukes went a-fishin'
The Sprig of Thyme
British Waterside
The Pretty Maid Milking her Cow
The Lost Lady Found
Lord Maxwell's Goodnight

Songs of the North

Willie's gane to Melville Castle
This is no my Plaid
Weaving Song
The Women are a' gane wud
Bonnie George Campbell
O'er the moor

Danish Folk-Music Settings

Proud Vesselil

Kipling Settings

Merciful Town
Ride with an Idle Whip
Northern Ballad
Soldier, Soldier (two versions)
Anchor Song
The Sea Wife
The Men of the Sea

Various

5 Ella Grainger songs
Afton Water
David of the White Rock (Dafydd y Gareg Wen)

MODERATELY DIFFICULT

British Folk-Music Settings

Bold William Taylor

Danish Folk-Music Settings

Husband and Wife

Kipling Settings

Ganges Pilot
The First Chanty
The Young British Soldier
The Widow's Party
The Love Song of Har Dyal

Various

The Secret of the Sea
Sailor's Chanty
Yon wild mossy mountains
A Reiver's Neck-Verse
The Twa Corbies

VERY DIFFICULT

British Folk-Music Settings

Hard-hearted Barb'ra (H)Ellen
Early one morning

Danish Folk-Music Settings

The Power of Love

Kipling Settings

Dedication
The Beaches of Lukannon

Various

Shallow Brown

5
At the Piano with Grainger

Penelope Thwaites

GRAINGER ONCE REMARKED: 'One reason why things of mine like *Shepherd's Hey* and *Molly on the Shore* are good is because there is so little gaiety and fun in them. Where others would have been jolly in setting them, I have been sad and furious.'[1] His emotions were always intense, his life celebration laced with manic joy or bitterness — sometimes a mixture of the two. Wherever you start, it is vital to grasp the character of Grainger's music. Vitality, in fact, is the key. Intensity underlies much of his music — the slow and quiet as well as the lively.

Organising the piano works

The vast majority of Grainger's compositions include the piano. Around twenty-five works, both solo and multi-hand, began or exist only as piano pieces,[2] but most began in vocal or instrumental form. This gives the pianist a wonderful range of colouristic references with which to enrich an interpretation. Current catalogues will reveal useful comparative versions.[3]

The piano works are bewildering to categorise since they tend to avoid conventional forms. Overall, the original works and folk settings for solo, four hands, and six to eleven hands cover nearly one hundred titles. Thirty more are arrangements or reworkings of other composers. There are a number of chamber works, some important orchestral piano parts and, not least, the song accompaniments, in many of which the piano is a true partner to the singer. Chapter 4 indicates several examples.

Organisational problems became endemic from the moment when Grainger hit on the ideal of what he termed 'elastic scoring'. His aim was to adapt a work to

---

[1] His introduction to *Lincolnshire Posy*, deploring the harsh treatment of the folk singers, illuminates this statement.

[2] *A Bridal Lullaby*; *Bridal Lullaby Ramble*; *Andante con moto*; *Beautiful Fresh Flower*; *Gigue*; *In Dahomey*; four *Klavierstücke*; *Knight and Shepherd's Daughter*; *One More Day, My John*; *Paraphrase on Tchaikovsky's Flower-Waltz*; *Peace*; *Preludes in G and C*; *Prittling, Prattling, Pretty Poll Parrot*; *Ramble on the last love-duet from 'Der Rosenkavalier'*; *Saxon Twi-Play*; *The Warriors II*; 'The Widow's Party' March; *Two Musical Relics of My Mother*; *When the World was Young*; *Zanzibar Boat Song*. The Tchaikovsky *Paraphrase* and the Strauss *Ramble* are included because each contains original material and is not simply a transcription.

[3] See the complete Catalogue at the end of this book and associated references.

a variety of forces, ranging from perhaps one or two players right up to full orchestra. In presenting such a wide array of choices, Grainger in effect invites us to be part of the creative process. The composer's own making of more than one version under the same title (or even more confusingly, under a different title[4]) can be misleading. A work may acquire a whole new section (as in the two-piano version of *Spoon River*), or, at the other extreme, a rollicking wind-band-and-piano work like *Children's March* may be pared down to a solo piano piece using the main refrain only.

Grainger had his reasons for these approaches. For example, there are around twenty pianistic 'fragments' which simply give the main theme of a work. Some of these were made for pedagogical reasons — simplified for pupils and beginners, and actually full of rhythmic and textural instruction. Some fragments are archival — themes from uncompleted works (his *Sea Song* and *Train Music*, for example) where he may have wished to leave a record of his more experimental ideas. Other, longer multi-hand versions were made for his students at the Chicago and Interlochen summer schools, at which he taught intermittently between 1919 and 1944.

His piano writing can be flamboyantly virtuosic and ingeniously colouristic. It can supply orchestral texture, or, as in the multi-hand works, it can spell out themes which may be less obvious in orchestral versions. In the song accompaniments it can be wickedly subversive in musical asides,[5] or heart-rendingly supportive of a mood or story.

Some general technical considerations

An element that often discourages would-be performers of Grainger's piano music is the prevalence of large stretches, often changing at speed. He wrote for his own unusually large span. A large hand will always tend to be an advantage, but there are at least four ways of overcoming the difficulty.

1. Grainger, being aware of the problem, often provided *ossias* for passages with large chords (say, a tenth with two or three notes in between; see Example 5.1). These *ossias* can be incorporated happily, especially if, in quick music, they enable a more dance-like flow.

2. He also suggests 'harping' wide-spread chords, if necessary. Certainly essential at times, this tactic should be used with a sensitive ear. The actual spreading of accompanying chords should be extremely quick and light in fast passages. In a work like *Colonial Song*, where the right-hand harped chords in the recapitulation amount to more of a musical rather than technical device, good musical sense will keep these harped chords light and silvery, rather than glutinous. As in his *Bridal Lullaby* (Example 5.2), *One More Day, My John*, and many other pieces, the top notes of the spread chords must ring out as a *line* of melody — whatever the dynamic.

---

[4] For example, *Always Merry and Bright* is the four-hand version of *Mock Morris*.
[5] An excellent example is the accompaniment to *Bold William Taylor*.

Example 5.1 *Mock Morris* (concert version), bars 45–52

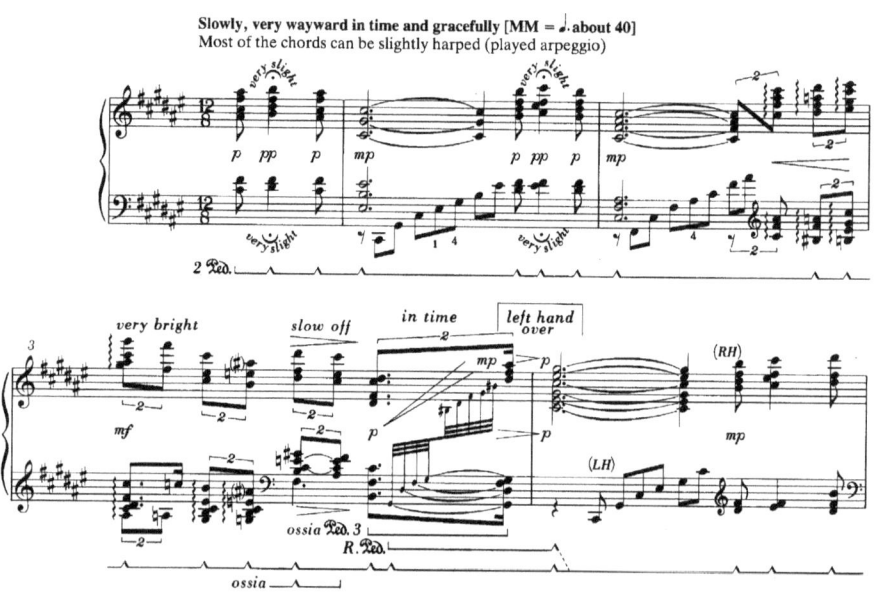

Example 5.2 *Bridal Lullaby*, bars 1–5

Example 5.3   *The Nightingale and The Two Sisters*, bars 1–5

Example 5.4   *The Nightingale and The Two Sisters*, bar 16

3. The occasional stretch sometimes occurs in a more static atmospheric piece such as *The Nightingale and The Two Sisters*. The last thing one wants is to spoil its floating quality. Rather than spreading the chord, the first (bass) note may be played gently as a tied acciaccatura (Example 5.3). Or there may be enough time to prepare a large stretch, and to depress both notes simultaneously on the extreme edge of the keys (Example 5.4). Similarly, the notes at the top of the right-hand chord and the bottom of the left-hand chord may be played (with pedal) on the beat, and the inner notes quickly and subtly added.

4. Chords may be redistributed between left and right hands.

The question of arpeggiating or 'harping' chords arises constantly in Grainger's piano music. Unafraid of being deemed 'vulgar' (indeed proud of its democratic meaning), Grainger uses the device, at times with strong effect, to 'wrench the heartstrings'. The introductory bars of *The Power of Love* (Example 5.5) illustrate this exactly. At other times he uses it to produce his favourite 'far-away, wafted' atmosphere,[6] or to enrich the texture.[7] Ask yourself *why*, in any given passage, he

---

[6] See *One More Day, My John*.
[7] See *Ramble on the last love-duet from 'Der Rosenkavalier'*.

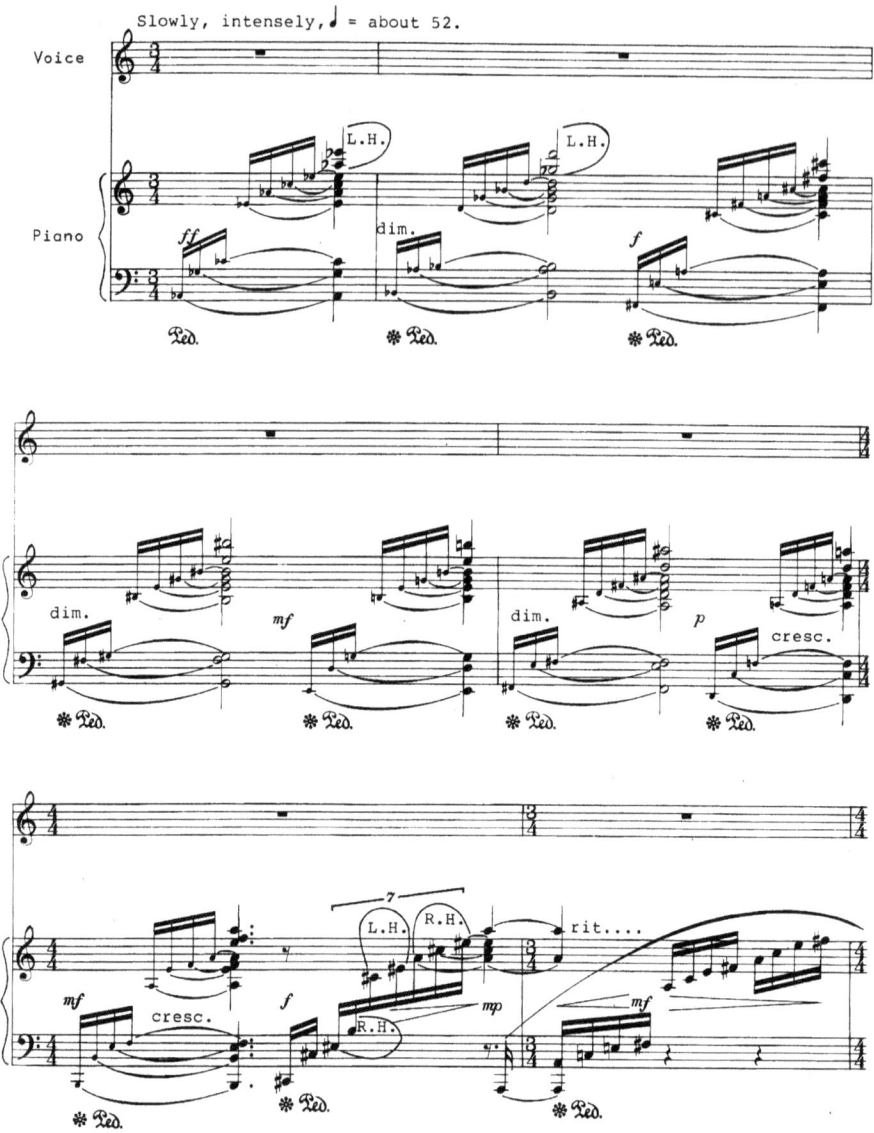

Example 5.5 *The Power of Love*, bars 1–6

spreads *this* chord. There are many answers. And where chords must be spread, of necessity, a musically resourceful pianist can make a virtue of it.

Grainger's scores feature detailed notation of pedalling, including imaginative use of the middle (sustaining) pedal. Pianists should therefore acquaint themselves with its possibilities. He also went into some detail about the importance of voicing chords and even had them printed so that the important note was larger than the others.[8] Pianists may also be required to use marimba mallets (gently) on the piano strings, and this, too, takes practice. A Grainger pianist must know how to be a team player. The works for four, six, eight, ten, eleven hands, or multiples thereof, are more than a stunt. Pianists learn that the more fingers there are at work, the more sensitive must be the listening ear. Although (or perhaps because) he earned his living as a famous concerto player, Grainger avoided writing such soloistic works and explored more communal piano writing. This included the extravagant suggestion in certain works (*Handel in the Strand*, for instance) of massed pianos for what he felt would be a more mellow effect. Sadly, these innovative ideas tend to go unexplored for obvious reasons of economy, although there is a photograph (reproduced here as Plate 12) of one American performance of *The Warriors* with nineteen grand pianos and their players in serried ranks.

Solo piano works

Grainger's own pre-eminence as a performer is reflected in a collection of virtuoso works admirably suited to concert programmes and requiring a concert technique. The works under 'Advanced students' represent a range of particular keyboard skills suitable for gifted tertiary-level students. A third list gives works which may be useful for teaching at a reasonable level of technical ability — or simply a place to start for an able pianist. The pieces under 'Ways in' make up the small collection of works or versions suitable for small hands. Children of ability may also enjoy the Schott collection *The Young Pianist's Grainger*, which includes six of Grainger's simplified versions and a further nine arrangements by Ronald Stevenson, together with useful background notes.

The selections listed in each category below are simply a guide and obviously intersect at many points, depending on particular pianistic abilities and programming requirements. Our comments on particular works are necessarily brief, and in the context of one chapter, not every work listed can be annotated.

VIRTUOSO WORKS

In a Nutshell (Suite)[9]
 ('Arrival Platform Humlet', 'Gay but Wistful', 'Pastoral', '"The Gum-Suckers" March')
Danish Folk-Music Suite
 ('The Power of Love', 'The Nightingale and The Two Sisters', 'Jutish Medley')

English Waltz	*Mock Morris* (concert version)
Scotch Strathspey and Reel	*Paraphrase on Tchaikovsky's Flower Waltz*
In Dahomey	*Ramble on the last love-duet from 'Der Rosenkavalier* (Strauss)
Lullaby from 'Tribute to Foster'	*Four Irish Dances* (Stanford)

---

[8] See for example *Irish Tune from County Derry*.
[9] See also Chap. 1, 'Orchestral Music', and Chap. 7, 'Programming Grainger'.

Each of the two suites was assembled from earlier-written individual works. They are both very effective, either in their entirety as twenty-minute segments of a programme or as separate pieces, possibly in other groupings. *Arrival Platform Humlet* makes a splendid opening to a concert or section of a concert — and it should be fierce and exhilarating. Do not play *Gay but Wistful* if you detest music-hall — it needs that happy/sad lilt and a little heart-twist. Note the characteristic descending chromatics in the left hand — a true Grainger signature. *Pastoral* is one of Grainger's most interesting works — a perfect example of a simple lilting tune developed into something a great deal more complex — even threatening — sumptuous in its harmonies. It is essential to hear its orchestral version if attempting the piano one. In contrast to this highly sophisticated piece, *'The Gum-Suckers'*[10] *March* presents the 'artless' Grainger — upbeat, athletic (horribly athletic), amusing, iconoclastic. It is a furiously difficult piece that needs to sound carefree and fun.

Solo pianists can now present the whole of the *Danish Folk-Music Suite*, since *The Power of Love* has been transcribed for solo piano.[11] *The Nightingale and The Two Sisters* makes a most lovely interlude before the huge technical demands of *Jutish Medley* (not *Melody*). Here, Grainger uses the folk tunes he collected in 1922 and 1927 in the Danish province of Jutland. Deceptively relaxed at the opening, it soon introduces some favourite devices: successions of wide accompanying chords (harp them very quickly), hectic asides between phrases, relentless right hand double-note chords at speed, and so on. Yet what varied character in the different numbers: humour, pathos, and then the final *Lord Peter's Stable Boy*, ending triumphantly at *ffff*.

Many of the same factors will be found in his hilarious *English Waltz* and the knockabout *In Dahomey*. The idioms (not the usual content of a classical training) should be understood; for example, the cakewalk was a humorous (Black American) imitation of the white employers, and was taken at a steady tempo. Played in this way, its character is fully realised and the temptation merely to use it as a vehicle for keyboard velocity is avoided. Character is also important in his gorgeous *Scotch Strathspey* — a real piece of impressionism, featuring at one point a drunken sailor and the suggestion of an increasingly drunken chorus. It requires fingers of steel and a sensitive ear. F-sharp major was the key of dreams for Grainger, and his *Lullaby from 'Tribute to Foster'* mimics the effect of the musical glasses used in the orchestral piece. It is indeed a 'sound study', as Grainger explains. To my ears, his own recording rather hammers the repeated notes, but this *can* be the most beautiful impressionistic piece. *Mock Morris* in its concert version represents the problem mentioned above — perpetual, extended, fast-moving chords, proudly designed for an exceptionally wide reach (tenths with one or two notes in between). The two show-pieces based on Tchaikovsky and Richard Strauss are splendid, and the Strauss in particular is revealingly annotated. Less known are the delicious Stanford arrangements. The fourth, *A Reel*, inspired Grainger's first 'hit', *Molly on the Shore*, which was also based on County Cork reel tunes.

---

[10] A nickname for Australians from the state of Victoria.
[11] Transcribed by Penelope Thwaites and available from Bardic Edition.

5. AT THE PIANO WITH GRAINGER

FOR ADVANCED STUDENTS

Blithe Bells
A Bridal Lullaby
Colonial Song
Country Gardens
Died for Love
Eastern Intermezzo
Handel in the Strand
Klavierstück in A minor
Klavierstück in E
Molly on the Shore
My Robin is to the Greenwood Gone

Shepherd's Hey
Spoon River
The Hunter in his Career
The Merry King
To a Nordic Princess
Bridal Lullaby Ramble[12]
Après un rêve ⎫
Nell ⎬ (after Fauré)
Love Walked In ⎫
The Man I Love ⎬ (after Gershwin)
Now, O now, I needs must part (after Dowland)

Much may be learned and enjoyed from Grainger's piano works. I would suggest his *Colonial Song* as a good starting point. It demands a huge dynamic range, a full-blooded cantabile, whether *mp* or *ff*, and the pianist must weave the melody and counter-melodies back and forth convincingly within the texture. It is noble rather than self-indulgent. The recapitulation should be magically quiet. My preference is for the original piano version of the orchestral score (with optional singers) rather than the 'solo version' later produced. It has a fascinating ending of a slow glissando and tremolando in which the work dissolves (Example 5.6). His haunting *Bridal Lullaby*, written for a former girlfriend on her marriage, demands super-sensitive ears for pedalling and chord balance.[13] His improvised extension of the piece (now transcribed as *Bridal Lullaby Ramble*) reveals lush romanticism to rival Rachmaninov and some really beautiful tunes.[14] And talking of tunes — many of Grainger's works are simply songs for the piano itself to sing. Try his *Died for Love* — tricky but effective figuration that must leave the melody distinct. It is a sound picture of a deserted pregnant girl, the steady ache of the musical motive so evocative. Grainger fell in love with the 'many-strandedness' of Bach's music, and his studies with Busoni turned him into a masterly Bach player. His own part-playing was astonishingly clear and is a model for interpreting his compositions.[15]

For full-on virtuosity, try *The Hunter in his Career* and the 'hits': *Country Gardens* needs an almost double-dotted rhythm and an easy swinging left hand; *Molly on the Shore* and *Shepherd's Hey* require considerable finger strength and endurance in order to realise their contrapuntal element. *The Merry King* exemplifies the folk singers' ability to give each verse a different character. Again, the piano must be the singer as well as the accompanist. Grainger's arrangements of the two Fauré songs, *Après un rêve* and *Nell*, like the Gershwin arrangements *The Man I Love* and *Love Walked In* make wonderful encores — as he himself used them. His approach to

---

[12] Realised from Grainger's improvised recording.
[13] In the wake of *Bridal Lullaby* being used as the theme for the film *Howards End*, a simplified arrangement was issued by Bardic Edition.
[14] Some of these are recycled in his duo-piano *The Warriors II*, recorded on Pearl SHE 9623.
[15] See Chap. 9, 'Grainger's Pianism on Disc', and Grainger's own recordings, listed in the Discography.

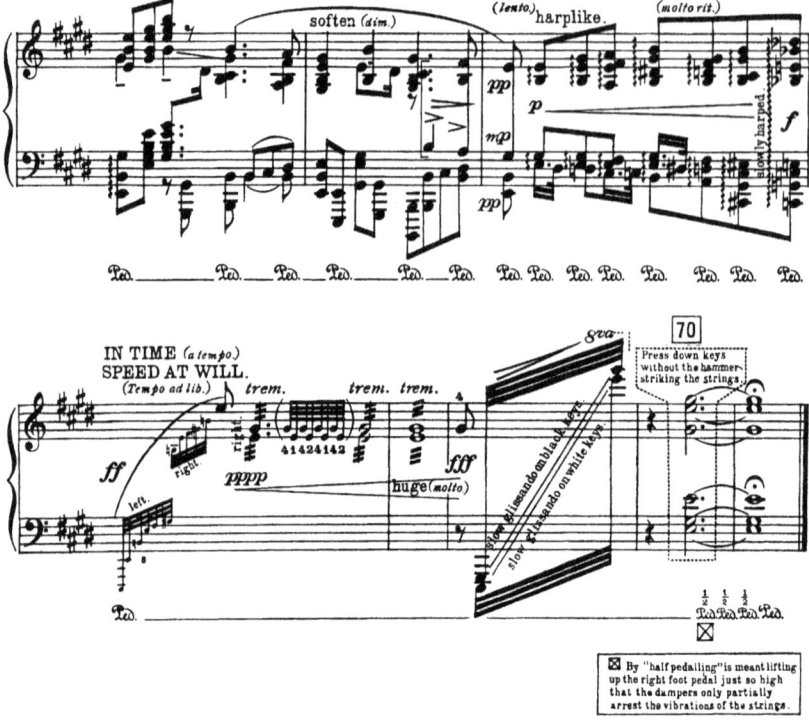

Example 5.6 *Colonial Song* (optional voice version), bars 64–70

Dowland's *Now, O now, I needs must part* — totally *un*authentic — is strangely moving.

FOR ABLE PIANISTS

Andante con moto
Beautiful Fresh Flower
A Bridal Lullaby (easy version)
Children's March
Harvest Hymn
Irish Tune from County Derry
Klavierstück in D
Knight and Shepherd's Daughter
Mock Morris (popular version)
Near Woodstock Town

One More Day, My John
Peace and *Saxon Twi-Play*
Prelude in C
Prelude in G
Sailor's Song (1954 version)
The Immovable Do
The Sussex Mummers' Christmas Carol
The Widow's Party
Three Scotch Folksongs
Walking Tune

Many of the general points mentioned above will apply to this list. The early preludes, written at the age of ten, are delightful. The *Andante con moto* is a good piece for trying the various approaches to large chords, mentioned above. Songs and dances abound here: dances — *Prelude in C, Children's March, Mock Mor-*

ris, *Saxon Twi-Play*, *The Widow's Party*, *Sailor's Song* (in a simplified but still quite tricky version).[16] As for songs: the youthful *Klavierstück in D* (dedicated to his father) has a Mendelssohnian warmth, *One More Day, My John* is a rewarding exercise in balancing chords. In *The Sussex Mummers' Christmas Carol* and *Irish Tune from County Derry* Grainger has found his true voice and individual style. *Beautiful Fresh Flower* touches a non-European world.

WAYS IN (SIMPLER SHORT PIECES)

At Twilight
Gigue in C[17]
In Bristol Town
Lisbon

The Brisk Young Sailor
The Rival Brothers
Walking Tune (easy version)
The Young Pianist's Grainger (a collection of fifteen pieces)[18]

Apart from the *Gigue*, all these short pieces are themes taken from longer works. They contain dancing rhythms, harmonic charm and an excellent introduction to Grainger's world. *The Young Pianist's Grainger* collection should not be despised by older beginners. Even the simpler versions of *Now, O now, I needs must part* and *Blithe Bells* provide challenges of tonal balance — the latter introducing the middle (sustaining) pedal. *Shepherd's Hey* minus the huge accompanying chords is still fun to play, and Grainger provides for his 'especially easy' *Country Gardens* a cheeky 'tailpiece' which, if taken at speed, is most effective.

Piano works for four hands

Grainger's four-hand works range from domestic versions to full-scale quasi-orchestral concert works. A list of duet pieces would include:

DUETS

Early One Morning (for harmonium)
Embraceable You (after Gershwin)
Harvest Hymn
Let's Dance Gay in Green Meadow
The Lonely Desert-Man Sees the Tents of the Happy Tribes

The Widow's Party
Tiger, Tiger (for harmonium)
Walking Tune (1957)
Walking Tune (easiest version)
Ye Banks and Braes

MORE DEMANDING

Country Gardens
English Waltz (arr. Palmer)

Rondo (1897)
The Crew of the Long Serpent (1898)

---

[16] The full version (published by Peters) bears all the marks of a short score and needs more editing to become truly pianistic.
[17] See Plate 22 for the 1893 MS.
[18] Published by Schott & Co. Edited and annotated by Ronald Stevenson (1966).

With the exception of the first, these include adult-sized chords. However, it is often the case in Grainger's multi-hand works that *one* of the parts will be perfectly possible for a small hand, which makes them ideal for teachers to use with their pupils. A busy teacher himself, Grainger made constant use of his compositions, or adapted versions thereof. It is fairly clear that he would have preferred his music to be played with a few adaptations than for it to be left on the shelf. For example, in order to realise his appealing *Rondo* and the other teenage duet *The Crew of the Long Serpent*, it is actually more effective to use two pianos and to re-distribute some of the phrases. The more mature duet *Let's Dance Gay in Green Meadow* is strongly recommended. As so often, within a few minutes Grainger conjures up a whole world, far from our own. His illuminating background notes are included with the score. The duet *Country Gardens* presents some enjoyable challenges. The Palmer arrangement of *English Waltz* requires a fully-fledged technique. Grainger's duet arrangement of Gershwin's *Embraceable You* is an embraceable delight.

TWO PIANOS FOUR HANDS

Blithe Bells
Children's March: Over the Hills and Far Away
Hill-Song I
Lincolnshire Posy
  ('Lisbon (Dublin Bay)', 'Horkstow Grange', 'Rufford Park Poachers', 'The Brisk Young Sailor', 'Lord Melbourne', 'The Lost Lady Found')

Hill-Song II
In A Nutshell
Konzertstück 1896

Always Merry and Bright (Mock Morris)
Country Gardens
Duke of Marlborough Fanfare
Eastern Intermezzo
Handel in the Strand
Molly on the Shore

Pritteling, Prattling, Pretty Poll Parrot
Shepherd's Hey
Spoon River
The Rival Brothers
Two Musical Relics of My Mother
When the World was Young

Mowgli's Song Against People
The Wraith of Odin

The Warriors II

ARRANGEMENTS

A Dance Rhapsody No. 1 (Delius)
Song of the High Hills (Delius)
Fantasy on George Gershwin's 'Porgy and Bess'
Festival (Richard Addinsell)
Warsaw Concerto (Richard Addinsell)

Knut Lurasen's Halling II (Grieg)
La Bel' Aronde (two versions; Claude le Jeune)
Three Symphonic Dances (Cyril Scott)
English Dance (Balfour Gardiner)
Six Part Fantasy & Air (William Lawes)

The lists above are not exhaustive but may serve as reference for various purposes. The first group comprises major Grainger works, suitable for a substantial slot in a concert programme. Then follows a list of shorter works which all go well in performance. In a group of their own are two interesting versions he made of orchestral/choral works which suit study purposes. Placed with these is the lovely, slightly mysterious *The Warriors II* — a work completed according to his instructions,[19] and

---

[19] Recorded by Penelope Thwaites and John Lavender on Pearl SHE 9623.

revealing a 'romantic' Grainger found elsewhere in his improvised *Bridal Lullaby Ramble*. Finally, there is a selection of arrangements of other composers' music, which provides a gold mine for both study and performance purposes.

Lincolnshire Posy — six settings of Lincolnshire folk tunes — is a Grainger classic, equally distinguished in its wind-band or two-piano versions.[20] Of particular interest are the *Rufford Park Poachers* and *Lord Melbourne* movements, both of which match the free rhythms of the folk singers and include some startling effects — see for example bar 35, where one tremolando emerges from behind another (Example 5.7). *In A Nutshell* is ideal for two pianos, altogether richer than the solo version, and better than the orchestral one in making clear the musical strands. The same might be said of the work Grainger rated as his best — *Hill-Song I*. It is a fascinating piece to analyse, and students can take the use of leitmotifs, sprinkled throughout, as a clue to its structural cohesion. The shorter *Hill-Song II* is perhaps a better choice for a concert and audiences may appreciate an introductory comment. *Children's March*, written after the wind-band-and-piano version, has grit as well as fun. The temptation to pound should be avoided if the wit is to come through.

Amateur pianists may enjoy many of the shorter pieces. The two *Relics* were written for Grainger's mother to play with him — a simpler part being matched with the more demanding. A similar pattern follows in *When the World was Young* and *Always Merry and Bright* — both dedicated to Rose. *Spoon River* is a most effective work, with a lovely extra melody at its heart. The two-piano *Handel in the Strand* is, in my opinion, the most delightful of all versions. Concert pianists have long enjoyed the magnificent *Porgy and Bess* fantasy. For another substantial work, the Cyril Scott *Three Symphonic Dances* are both demanding and rewarding. Delius's haunting *Dance Rhapsody* is surprisingly effective in this medium.

Piano works for six or more hands

MAJOR WORKS

English Dance (6 hands, 2/3 pianos)
Green Bushes (6 hands, 2/3 pianos)
Jutish Medley (6 hands, 2/3 pianos)
Thanksgiving Song (6 hands, 2 pianos)

Random Round (11 hands, 2/3 pianos)
The Warriors (6 hands, 2/3 pianos)
The Widow's Party March (6 hands, 3 pianos)

SHORTER WORKS

Country Gardens (8 hands, 2 pianos)
Harvest Hymn (8 hands, 2 pianos)
The Keel Row (10 hands, 2 pianos)

In Bristol Town (6 hands, 1 piano)
Ye Banks and Braes (6 hands, 1 piano)
Zanzibar Boat Song (6 hands, 1 piano)

The Warriors needs three very strong pianists to explore this most exciting orchestral work of Grainger. Optional brass may be added, but the slow sections inevitably

---

[20] The Schott publication now includes Leslie Howard's essential essay, correcting the many mistakes which for some years languished unacknowledged in the original.

Example 5.7 *Lincolnshire Posy*: 'Lord Melbourne', bars 33–43

suffer in comparison with the orchestral piece. However, in the absence of an orchestra, this is stirring stuff. More grateful in performance are *Jutish Medley* and particularly *Green Bushes*, whose steadily building passacaglia is positively orgiastic. Paradoxically, the effectiveness of this work depends on the performers being able to listen and, at times, to play quietly, rather than to compete. The many countermelodies can then emerge tellingly from the texture. The impact will come as much from rhythmic unanimity as from sheer force. *Random Round* — notated in one version very *un*randomly — may also be performed as Grainger envisaged — mixing and matching the various components at will.

The number of instruments used in these works will vary: for the most part two pianos will suffice, as the six-hand works were conceived for Pianist 1 at one piano, Pianists 2 and 3 at the second piano. A different kind of balancing must be achieved if three instruments are used. Educational institutions lend themselves most readily to pianistic extravaganzas, and they can be enjoyable for all.[21] The exquisite *Zan-*

---

[21] In Chap. 6, Barry Peter Ould's essay on Grainger's early-music settings includes a list of the multi-hand Bach arrangements Grainger made for his students. Further solo piano arrangements

zibar Boat Song makes a lovely encore — it needs a magical lightness to create its atmosphere. Whistling parts for the audience add fun to Ye Banks and Braes.

Orchestral piano parts

The Warriors, Grainger's 'Music to an Imaginary Ballet', stipulates three pianos with pianists of 'exceptional strength'. It is indeed exciting to participate in this wild jubilant work. The three pianists need to rehearse as a unit, which in turn is closely integrated with the large percussion section. (The pianists all perform, at times, directly on the piano strings.) A similar co-working with the percussion arises for the one solo pianist in the choral/orchestral Tribute to Foster.

In many orchestral works Grainger simply wants the piano sound to emerge occasionally, as it does in the suite In a Nutshell and the Danish Folk-Music Suite. It is also intermittently audible in the luscious To a Nordic Princess and Green Bushes. The orchestral/choral Thanksgiving Song — rarely performed — makes use of three pianists, one of them playing from outside the hall! Grainger wanted to emphasise the piano's colouristic qualities in a communal setting — the communal idea was ever present with him. In these orchestral parts the pianist is an energetic team player, contributing particularly through the instrument's percussive qualities, but wary of spoiling the string or wind lines by over-intrusiveness or by ill-judged entries. The café-orchestra sound is not what is required. Grainger himself appeared as pianist in orchestral performances of his Danish Folk-Music Suite, and, with his exceptional power, he certainly made himself heard.[22] But the truth is that these are, on the whole, *concertante* parts; there to enrich the texture (and perhaps, in Grainger's case, to have more performance input, in terms of tempi).

Despite, or perhaps because of, his career as a powerful and exciting concerto soloist, the notion of writing a concerto was rejected. (His early — incomplete — essay under this name emerges as a quasi-Beethovenian student exercise.) There is only one work where a solo pianist is truly central: Handel in the Strand, for piano and strings. The writing is classic Grainger with dense chords in both hands, constantly changing at speed, with no let-up and interspersed with (what should be) sparkling finger-work. All this makes for a demanding four minutes. In his introduction, the composer suggests the idea of 'massed pianos' for an ideal balance — a fascinating idea requiring a quixotic promoter. In 1952 he recast the work in full orchestral garb, and this version (preceded by Country Gardens and Bridal Lullaby) has been most effectively used as the final movement of a nine-minute composite Grainger Suite.[23]

---

of early music are also included in this chapter, as well as appearing in the main Catalogue of Works.

[22] For example, his 1957 recording with Per Dreier and the Aarhus Municipal Orchestra, available on Vanguard Classics USA CD: OVC 8205 (see also the Discography).

[23] See Chap. 1, 'Orchestral Music', for further details.

Room-music

The chamber works with piano contain some gems[24] — particularly those for cello and piano, many of which were written for Grainger's lifelong friend, the Danish cellist Hermann Sandby. The enchanting suites of Scandinavian tunes (under the title *La Scandinavie*) make some unusual technical demands on both players, such as the glissandi in thirds for the cello and some fast-moving complex chordal leaps for the pianist. *La Scandinavie* makes an excellent programme companion to the Grieg cello sonata in A Minor, Op. 36, and indeed Grainger and Sandby did combine them on at least one occasion. *The Sussex Mummers' Christmas Carol* attains a new and passionate life with its cello obbligato. *Youthful Rapture* (1901) forsakes the world of folk song for the Edwardian drawing-room. It emerges as a rhapsodic piece, which (although he originally entitled it 'A Lot of Rot') Grainger must have liked, since he later arranged it for solo cello and orchestra, in which version it was recorded by the cellist Beatrice Harrison. Piano trio arrangements of *My Robin is to the Greenwood Gone*, *Harvest Hymn* and *Colonial Song* are beautiful additions to the repertory, as are *Mock Morris* and *Molly on the Shore* for violin and piano: two showpieces requiring agility and panache from both players.

Grainger's 'elastic scoring' of certain works allowed for performances by a nucleus of instruments, and into this category come several scaled-down movements from the *Danish Folk-Music Suite* arranged for strings with piano and/or harmonium: *The Power of Love, The Nightingale, The Two Sisters, Lord Peter's Stable Boy* and *The Shoemaker from Jerusalem*. *Handel in the Strand* works well for piano and string quartet, and there is also a version for piano trio.

When planning concert repertoire, performers (particularly chamber groups) may naturally gravitate towards longer works, but these short gems by Grainger — usually between two and six minutes in length — have the same validity as many of the solo song masterpieces, and they demand and deserve a similar commitment. Intelligently grouped in threes or fours, they can provide a welcome variety of pace and a refreshing change of tone and mood. The chapter on programming gives some successful examples.

---

[24] See also Chap. 7, 'Programming Grainger'.

6
Towards a Universal Language
Grainger and Early Music; Grainger and World Music

Paul Jackson and Barry Peter Ould

DURING THE 1930S Grainger entered a sustained period of activity that saw his musicological and educational work come to the fore as his compositional output declined. Driven by a passionate belief that the general public was both indifferent to — even intolerant of — music that lay outside the 1700–1900 western canon, he worked tirelessly to bring to the public's attention little-known music from the pre-Classical period, as well as examples of music from India, Indonesia, Polynesia, Africa, and elsewhere. In 1932 he was invited to take up the post of Head of Music at New York University, and his class lectures *A General Study of the Manifold Nature of Music* provide a summary of his musical preoccupations at the time.

Beginning with a series of twenty *Statements*, the lectures attempt to 'show the threads of unity, running through all kinds of music', by freely juxtaposing examples from the English polyphonic tradition with 'primitive music, folk-music, jazz, Oriental and Western art-music'. From 1931 to 1934 Grainger produced a constant stream of lectures, broadcasts, and articles exploring his developing world music view, including *Democracy in Music* in 1931, *Arnold Dolmetsch: Musical Confucius* and *Can Music Become a Universal Language?* in 1933, and the Australian Broadcasting Commission series *Music: A Commonsense View of All Types* in 1934.

Grainger's contribution to what he termed a 'universalist attitude toward music'[1] took many forms, but it is his often pioneering work in the transcription, arranging, and performing of early and non-European music that most directly addresses the task of bringing unfamiliar works — unfamiliar, at least, to western ears — into circulation. The establishment of the Grainger Museum in Melbourne in 1938 provided a further focus for his proselytising work, and among the many aims of the museum, Grainger included the creation of centres 'for the preservation and study of the early music of Europe' and 'for the preservation and study of native music in, or adjacent to Australia, such as aboriginal Australian music, the art-musics of Java, Siam, Bali and the Hybrid music of the South Sea'.[2] It is within this context that we now explore Grainger's legacy.

---

[1] Lecture 1 from John Blacking, '*A Commonsense View of All Music': Reflections on Percy Grainger's Contribution to Ethnomusicology and Music Education* (Cambridge, 1987).

[2] Letter to James Barrett, Chancellor of Melbourne University, 24 August 1938.

Grainger and early music

By the time Grainger commenced his duties at New York University in September 1932, he was on the brink of entering a new stage of consuming interest in early (pre-Bach) music that would last for three decades. The music of J. S. Bach himself had held a special place in Grainger's affections since childhood, and he regularly programmed and recorded his works. Now his ongoing curiosity to learn more about early music had led him, in the previous year, to write to Arnold Dolmetsch expressing his intention to attend the Dolmetsch Festival in Haslemere, Surrey, England. After years of admiration for Dolmetsch's work, Grainger was able at last to hear music for viol consort hitherto unknown to him. The performances he attended left a tremendous impression and at the final concert he attended, one of the pieces, William Lawes' *Fantasy and Air* was encored at Grainger's request. Dolmetsch had discovered this piece and many others from manuscript sources in the British Museum and had been in the process of editing them for performance. Grainger's praise was effusive and not long afterwards his thoughts on Dolmetsch and his work appeared in print.[3]

The Dolmetsch Consorts

A grand project was initiated to publish some of these discoveries under the collective — and lengthy — title *The Dolmetsch Collection of English Consorts, Eleven Fantasies, Airs, Pavans, Galliards, Almains etc. by 16th and 17th Century Composers*.[4] Grainger's collaboration with Arnold Dolmetsch lasted until the latter's death in 1940, and his continuing correspondence with Mabel Dolmetsch expressed his faith in the educational value of these consorts. The Dolmetsch family had hoped to publish a collection of twenty-five such works, and an initial batch of eleven were sent to Grainger in 1941, but their publication was a protracted affair. Grainger was entrusted to sort out the terms with Schirmer and generously offered, in addition, a lump sum towards costs. Schirmer's Carl Engel[5] stipulated that each fantasy should be published in two versions: Dolmetsch's original for viols and Grainger's edition for modern string instruments.

Unfortunately, only three of the projected series eventually appeared in print (in 1944).[6] Further editions were discussed, but Grainger seems to have done very little other than to make some initial preparations towards publication. Despite expressing his intentions to continue the project in a letter to Dolmetsch's daughter

---

[3] Percy Grainger, 'Arnold Dolmetsch: Musical Confucius', *The Musical Quarterly*, 19/2 (1933). Reprinted in Gillies and Clunies Ross (eds.), *Grainger on Music*, 232–45.

[4] Generic title for the projected series edited by Arnold Dolmetsch and Percy Grainger.

[5] Carl Engel, Paris-born composer and musicologist, headed G. Schirmer from 1929 until his death in 1944. Founder of the Library of Congress Archive of American Folk Song, Engel also founded Schirmer's extensive catalogue of folk-music materials, to which he brought such collectors and composers as John Jacob Niles.

[6] Consorts by Ferrabosco, Jenkins, and Lawes (New York, 1944).

Plate 1. The 15th Band, Coast Artillery Corps of the US Army, Fort Hamilton, 1918 (Grainger seated, fifth from right)

Plate 2. Grainger with Aeolian company recording producer W. Creary Woods, New York, August 1915

Plate 3. The Grainger house at 7 Cromwell Place, White Plains, New York, as it is today

Plate 4. Percy and Ella Grainger in wedding dress (photo taken at White Plains, 1928)

Plate 6. In walking garb, Australia, 1934

Plate 5. In towelling clothes, by the verandah at White Plains

Plate 7. Playing tuneful percussion, Salt Lake City, Utah, USA, 1946

Plate 8. West Point Military Academy band members, 1945, with Grainger's 'blind eye' conductor's prompt scores

Plate 9. Grainger with a group of students at the National Music Camp, Interlochen, Michigan, USA, c.1942

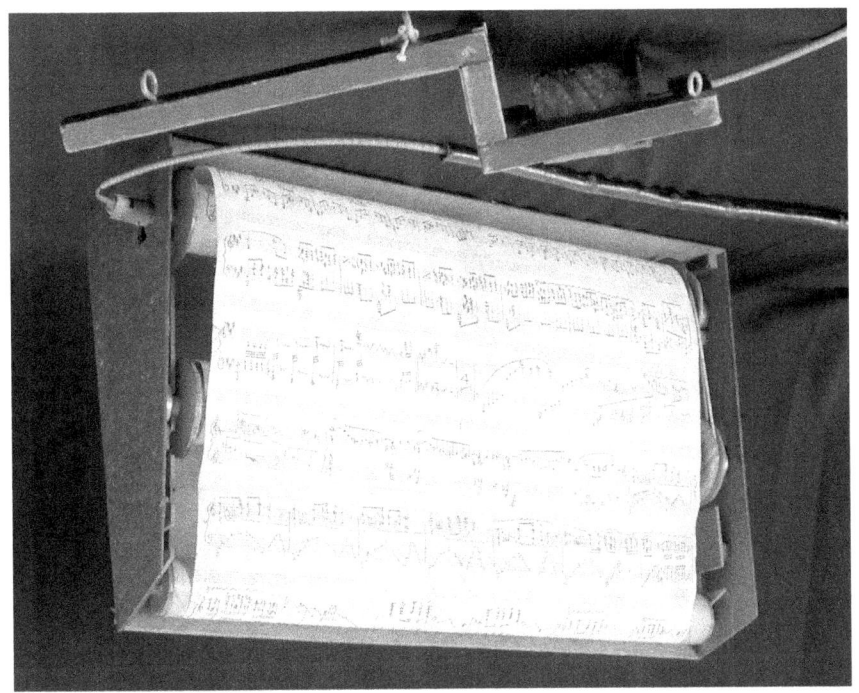

Plate 10. Grainger's Roller Desk with Grieg Piano Concerto cadenza prompts

Plate 11. Percy Grainger in rehearsal with the USMA band, March 1951

Plate 12. *The Warriors*; nineteen grand pianos rattle the rafters of the Chicago Civic Opera House, 18 June 1930. Rudolph Ganz conducts and Percy Grainger leads a team of pianists, including Australia's Vera Bradford

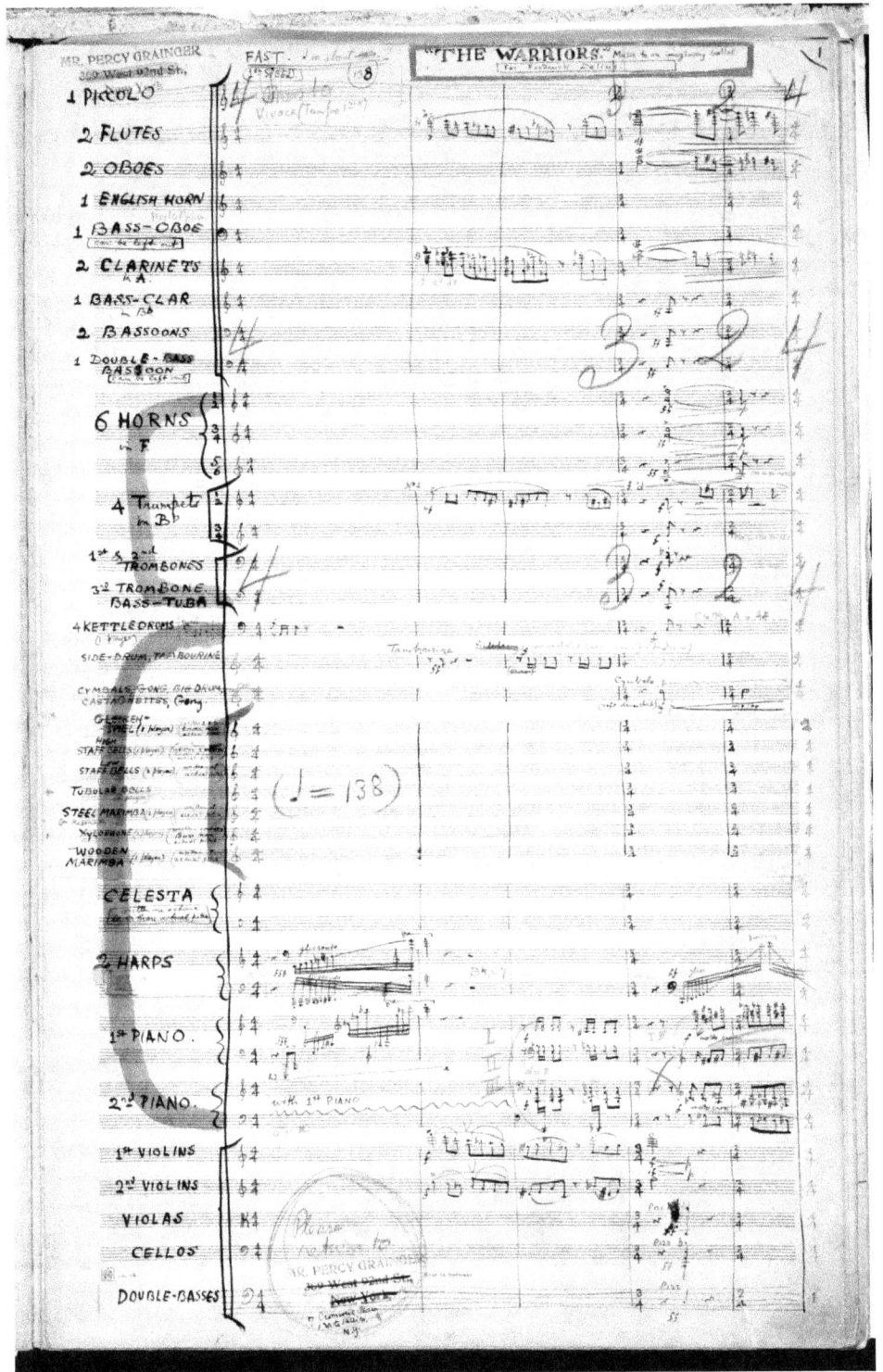

Plate 13. *The Warriors* manuscript, page one, with Grainger's markings

Plate 14. Percy Grainger working at home

Nathalie in 1949, no further editions in the series appeared. Copies of the remaining eight Dolmetsch manuscripts reside in the Grainger Museum, Melbourne,[7] and it is unclear whether any of these found publication elsewhere.[8] The preface to the published editions, however, makes Grainger's enthusiasm plain: 'They are as polyphonically melodious, in their own instrumental way, as are the vocal perfections of Palestrina — but they are more varied, in mood and style, than Palestrina. They do not suffer, as does much string writing of later periods, from being orchestrally or pianistically conceived or influenced.'[9] All three published editions are well worth exploration.[10] They can be played either by single strings (violin family) or by string orchestra.

English Gothic Music

On taking up his duties at New York University, Grainger became reacquainted with Gustave Reese.[11] Reese had worked for Grainger's American publisher, G. Schirmer, and had first met him in 1924. Working as a part-time instructor at NYU, Reese gave classes in medieval and Renaissance music, which Grainger would occasionally attend. He began to introduce into his own lectures — along with the Dolmetsch pieces — other early music, probably encountered in the recently published anthology by Arnold Schering, *History of Music in Examples*.[12]

Through Reese, Grainger was made aware of the work of Dom Anselm Hughes (Humphrey Vaughan; 1889–1974), a Benedictine monk who had deciphered from old vellums, and later published, over one hundred pieces of music that had been sung in Worcester Cathedral in the thirteenth and fourteenth centuries.[13] A recording of one of these pieces, *Alleluia Psallat*, so impressed Grainger that he wrote to Hughes, requesting life membership of The Plainsong and Medieval Music Society, of which at the time Hughes was secretary. It is unclear whether the two met first in New York when Hughes was undertaking a lecture tour in 1932, or on Grainger's visit to England in 1933. Whenever it happened, it prompted Grainger once again to propose a collaboration: this time, with Hughes, for a series under the title of

---

[7] John Jenkins, *Fantasy no. 8* for 3 viols; Thomas Tomkins, *Pavan no. 1 in F* for 5 viols; Martin Pierson, *Fantasy and 2 Almaines no. 6* for 6 viols; Richard Deering, *Fantasy* for 6 viols; Alfonso Ferrabosco II, *Dove House Pavan* for 5 viols; Michael Easte, '*Triumphavi*' *Fantasy* for 5 viols; Coperario (i.e., John Cooper), '*Chi pue miraryi*' *Fantasy* for 5 viols; Thomas Weelkes, *Fantasy* for 6 viols.

[8] In a letter to Grainger dated 2 May 1949, Nathalie Dolmetsch informs Grainger that some of the consort pieces were under consideration for publication by the newly founded Viola da Gamba Society.

[9] Percy Aldridge Grainger, Foreword to *The Dolmetsch Collection of English Consorts* (New York, 1944).

[10] Available from Bardic Edition UK; G. Schirmer USA.

[11] Gustave Reese (1899–1974), American musicologist and teacher, mainly known for his work on medieval and Renaissance music: *Music in the Middle Ages* (New York, 1940); *Music in the Renaissance* (New York, 1954).

[12] Arnold Schering, *Geschichte der Music in Beispielen* (Leipzig, 1931).

[13] Dom Anselm Hughes, *Worcester Mediæval Harmony of the Thirteenth & Fourteenth Centuries*, The Plainsong and Medieval Music Society, 11 (Burnham, Bucks., 1928).

English Gothic Music. The object was to produce editions of medieval English music for the non-specialist as well as amateur performers.

The association with Dom Anselm Hughes over a period of nearly three decades was to produce a rich collection of choral works dating from the tenth to fifteenth centuries. Hughes supplied Grainger with the texts and music copied from the original manuscripts so that he could make editorial decisions regarding presentation, scoring, and dynamics. Eighteen works were selected for the series, but only seven separate editions were ever published during Grainger's and Hughes's lifetime. Hughes was dismayed at the slow progress, but Grainger was cautious about publication. He insisted that 'all these things should be tried out, if they are to be worthwhile'. The collection never appeared in book form, but Dom Anselm did write an Introduction in which he spoke of the three stages in the rediscovery of early music:

1. the presentation of the music in both original and modern editions to interest the practical musician as well as the antiquarian;
2. to have the music sounded, in order that it might not only be performed but tested and its quality judged;
3. the publication of *English Gothic Music*:

    offered to all musicians, amateur and professional, singers and instrumentalists, who love to make music. Special qualifications they need possess, none; if such are found to be necessary, this book will have failed of its first object. We are offering this music to the public in order that they may not merely hear it as part of a specialised programme performed by a specialised choir, but may take it to themselves as a part of their own musical repertoire, to sing in choral societies, church choirs, school, and even (as our own Elizabethan forefathers did) as family music round the table.[14]

Chosen Gems

The educational value of both the Dolmetsch and the Hughes collections was also foremost in Grainger's mind. He felt that modern performances could awaken interest in discovering the originals: 'When we have become familiar with the great works of all times and all countries through the medium of arrangements and transcriptions we will find ourselves the more ready for the reception of those works in their original scoring.'[15] He set about adapting a selection of early music compositions for modern use so that different instrumental and vocal groups would be able to perform them. A projected series, given the title of *Chosen Gems*, involved two groups — strings and winds. For some of the works within the wind group, Grainger employed his concept of 'elastic scoring', in which each voice or part of the original is assigned a letter: A for the highest line, B, C, D, E, etc. down to the bass line.

---

[14] Dom Anselm Hughes, Introduction to *English Gothic Music*, unpublished.
[15] Percy Grainger, 'The Gregarious Art of Music', *Australian Musical News*, 16/9 (1927); repr. in Gillies and Clunies Ross (eds.), *Grainger on Music*, 179–83 at 180.

Grainger termed these parts 'Tone Strands', and he would assign to each strand instruments suitable to their range, dynamics, and properties of tone colour. Many of the *Chosen Gems* were tried and tested by students attending the Interlochen International Music Camp in Michigan, where Grainger taught between 1937 and 1944. Of them Grainger wrote:

> Many of these early pieces of music (alive as the day they were written, and performable by small solo groups of wind instruments or by larger band groups such as the saxophone family, the clarinet family, the complete reed band, the brass band) are ideal for giving soloistic chamber-music opportunities to the more skilful band members, and for bringing tonal variety into band programmes . . .[16]

Whilst the wind versions of the *Gems* have had much exposure in recent years, the string versions remain virtually unknown. Overall, these editions remain a remarkable testament to Grainger's unique scoring capabilities and are well worth further investigation. For him, the music of the past was an essential part of his vision for the music of the future.

Collaborations with Arnold Dolmetsch

The Dolmetsch Collection of English Consorts — Eleven Fantasies, Airs, Pavans, Galliards, Almains, etc. by 16th and 17th Century Composers. Scored from the Original Version for Viols by Arnold Dolmetsch, Version for Modern String Instruments by Percy Aldridge Grainger with Bowing and Fingering by Ottokar Čadek.[17]

> Alfonso Ferrabosco II (d. 1628): *The Four Note Pavan*
> John Jenkins (1592–1678): *Five Part Fantasy No. 1*
> William Lawes (d. 1645): *Six part Fantasy and Air No. 1*

Collaborations with Dom Anselm Hughes

ENGLISH GOTHIC MUSIC
(original choral versions)

Ad cantum laetitiae (anon.)
Alleluia Psallat (anon.)
Angelus ad Virginem (anon.)
Beata viscera (anon.)
Credo (anon.)
Edi beo thu (anon.)
Foweles in the frith (anon.)
Fulget coelestis curia (anon.)
Hac in anni janua (anon.)

Jubilemus omnes una (anon.)
Marionette douce (anon.)
O rosa bella (John Dunstable)
Princesse of youth (anon.)
Puellare gremium (anon.)
Sanctus (Lionel Power)
Veni Sancte Spiritus (Dunstable)
Worcester Sanctus (anon.)

---

[16] Grainger, Foreword to *The Band's Music* by Richard Franko Goldman (London, 1938).
[17] See also 'Chosen Gems for Strings', p. 78 below.

Chosen Gems for Strings

A l'heure que je vous (Josquin des Prez)
Allemande (William Brade)
Alleluia Psallat [EGM] (anon.)
Angelus ad Virginem [EGM] (anon.)
Anima mea liquefacta est [EGM] (Power)
Ballade no. 17 'Sans cuer m'en vois' (Guillaume de Machaut)
Credo [EGM] (anon.)
Edi beo thu [EGM] (anon.)
Five Part Fantasy (Jenkins)
The Four Note Pavan (Ferrabosco)
Fulget coelestis curia [EGM] (anon.)
Hac in anni janua [EGM] (anon.)
Harraytre Amours (Johannes Stokem)
La bel' aronde (Claude Le Jeune)
La Bernardina (Josquin)
Le jour s'endort (Guillaume Dufay)
Marionette douce [EGM] (anon.)
Nenciozza mia (Johannes Jappart)
O begl'anni dell'oro (Francesco Corteccia)
O praeclara patriae [EGM] (anon.)
O rosa bella [EGM] (Dunstable)
O salutaris hostia (Adrian Willaert)
O schönes Weib (Heinrich Finck)
Paesabase, The Moorish King (Diego de Pisador)
Prelude and Fugue V (WTK Book II) (Bach)
Prelude in the Dorian Mode (Antonio de Cabezón)
Princesse of youth [EGM] (anon.)
Pro Beata Pauli — O praeclara patriae [EGM] (anon.)
Puellare gremium [EGM] (anon.)
The Quiet Brook (Alessandro Scarlatti)
Quis tibi Christe meritas (anon.)
Rondeau no. 14 'Ma fin est mon commencement' (Machaut)
Six Part Fantasy and Air (Lawes)
Veni Sancte Spiritus [EGM] (Dunstable)
Worcester Sanctus [EGM] (anon.)

Chosen Gems for Winds

Alleluia Psallat [EGM] (anon.)
Angelus ad Virginem [EGM] (anon.)
Ballade no. 17 (Machaut)
Beata Viscera [EGM] (anon.)
Edi beo thu [EGM] (anon.)
Five Part Fantasy (Jenkins)
Five Part Fugue (WTK Book I/4) (Bach)
The Four Note Pavan (Ferrabosco)
La bel' aronde (Le Jeune)
La Bernardina (Josquin)
March (Notebook for Anna Magdalena Bach) (Bach)
O Mensch, bewein' dein' Sünde gross (Bach)
O salutaris hostia (Adrian Willaert)
Prelude in the Dorian Mode (Cabezón)
Prelude and Fugue V (WTK Book II) (Bach)
The Quiet Brook (Domenico Scarlatti)
Royal Fanfare (Josquin)
Seht, was die Liebe tut (Bach)
Six Part Fantasy and Air (Lawes)
Veni Sancte Spiritus (Dunstable)

Additional selected transcriptions and arrangements

ORCHESTRA

Alleluia Psallat [EGM] (anon.)
Angelus ad Virginem [EGM] (anon.)
Blithe Bells (after Bach's Sheep may safely graze)[18] (also for military band)
Paseabase, The Moorish King (Pisador)
Puellare Gremium [EGM] (anon.)
Veni Sancte Spiritus [EGM] (Dunstable)

---

[18] One of several Grainger works inhabiting the borderline between original work and arrangement.

STRINGS WITH PIANO

Brandenburg Concerto no. 3 (Bach)
Four Part Fantasy no. 8 (Purcell)

VOICE(S) AND INSTRUMENTS

O salutaris hostia (Willaert) — 2-part voices and strings
Bell Piece (after Dowland) — tenor and wind band
O begl'anni dell'oro (Corteccia) — voice and piano (harmonium)
Variations on Handel's 'The Harmonious Blacksmith' — voice (or cello) and piano

A CAPPELLA

Ballade no. 2 'Helas! tant ay dolour' (Machaut) — 2-part voices
La bel' aronde (Le Jeune) — sattbb
O Mistress Mine (Morley) — sattbb
O praise the Lord, all ye heathen (Bach) — satb
Salve porta paradisi [EGM] (Damett) — sattbb

PIANO(S)

Angelus ad Virginem [EGM] (anon.) — piano solo
Blithe Bells (after Bach) — piano solo, two pianos four hands
Fantasy and Air no. 1 (Lawes) — two pianos four hands
Five Part Fantasy (Jenkins) — piano solo
Fugue in A minor (Bach) — piano solo, two pianos eight hands
Fugue in C (Bach) — two pianos (or harmoniums) four hands
Fugue in D-sharp minor (Bach) — piano solo, two pianos four hands
Fugue in E (Bach) — piano solo, two pianos four hands
Hornpipe (Handel) — piano solo
La bel' aronde (Le Jeune) — piano solo, piano four hands, two pianos (or harmoniums) four hands
Mori quasi il mio core (Palestrina) — two pianos (or harmoniums) four hands
Now, O now, I needs must part (Dowland) — piano solo
The Carman's Whistle (William Byrd) — piano solo
Toccata and Fugue in D minor (Bach) — piano solo
Toccata in F (Bach) — massed pianos

Grainger and world music

Whilst his natural enthusiasm for simultaneously engaging in a range of projects often meant that many of his new ideas remained only partially realised, Grainger's attempts at what might be termed the concertisation of non-western music has left us with a small number of beautifully-crafted realisations of melodies from Indonesia, India, and Africa, among tantalising sketches of music from Polynesia, Australia, and elsewhere. In addition to providing a means of preserving music that might otherwise be lost to contemporary audiences, Grainger's 'world music' arrangements reveal both an acutely sensitive and detailed transcriptive ear and a mastery of orchestration that enables the idiomatic sound world of the original to be effectively realised with conventional western instrumental and vocal forces.

His work on non-western music had begun in earnest in 1909 during a concert tour of Australia, but it was in the 1930s that Grainger was able to take advantage of the wealth of commercially-available field recordings that arose from the pioneering work of the Berliner Phonogramm-Archiv.[19] In 1931, under the auspices of that archive, the comparative musicologist Erich Moritz von Hornbostel oversaw the issuing of the seminal twenty-four-gramophone-record set *Musik des Orients*.[20] The collection featured examples of traditional music from 'Japan, China, Java, Bali, Siam, India, Persia, Egypt, and Tunisia'. Grainger repeatedly drew on these recordings, both as a means of illustration for his lectures, and as a source for his transcriptions.

Broadly speaking, Grainger's transcriptions and arrangements divide into four types:

1. partially-completed transcriptions, not intended for performance — here we include the various Rarotongan part songs and the Maori folksongs, both made from field recordings collected in 1909, as well as the unfinished sketches for music from Australia, Somalia, Yemen, and Africa, made from a variety of second-hand sources;

2. harmonisations and arrangements of material collected by others — this includes the two Mexican pieces, *'Matachina' Dance* and *Lenten Chant*, the *Negro Lullaby*, and the African *Songs of Love*, all originally collected, notated and arranged by Natalie Curtis;

3. fully orchestrated original transcriptions, made from commercially-released gramophone records in the 1930s, that provide an aural equivalence of the originals; into this category fall *Bahariyale V. Palaniyandi* (India), *Gamelan Anklung: Berong Pengètjèt* (Bali), *Sekar Gadung* (Java) and *Mampahory Ny Masoandro Seranin-Javona* (Madagascar);

4. arrangements of 'mock' Asiatic music, which nevertheless capture the sound world of authentic instruments — Debussy's *Pagodes*, orchestrated in 1928, and Ravel's *La Vallée des cloches*, orchestrated in 1944. The piano miniature, *Beautiful Fresh Flower*, based on a traditional Chinese tune, completes this section.

Early transcriptions

In his activity as a collector of folk songs in the early years of the twentieth century, Grainger quickly recognised the benefit of utilising the emergent recording technology of the day, purchasing his own Edison phonograph in 1908 for the purpose

---

[19] Now held within the Ethnological Museum, part of the National Museum of Berlin.

[20] Erich Moritz von Hornbostel, *Musik des Orients: Eine Schallplattenfolge* (Berlin: Lindstrom A.-G., 1931). English ed., *Music of the Orient* (London: Parlophone Co., 1934).

of capturing performances in the field. The phonograph aided considerably the arduous process of notational transcription with its ability to replay music back at slower speeds.

Aside from his English and Danish music collecting, Grainger's most significant work at this time arose from his experiences with the music of Australasia and Polynesia — specifically with Maori music of New Zealand and Rarotongan part songs from the Cook Islands. Rarotongan music, in particular, was something of a revelation to Grainger, who maintained its importance and superiority to western art music throughout this life. The legacy of this experience is to be heard most notably in the various versions of his experimental piece *Random Round*. In 1909 Grainger had made a number of detailed transcriptions of performances, recorded by A. J. Knocks of Otaki, of a troupe of South Sea islanders who visited the 1906–7 International Exhibition in Christchurch, New Zealand. The most complete transcriptions are those identified as *Rarotonga I* and *Fierce Rarotonga I*. They reveal a music characterised by an energetic vocalisation around melodic motifs based on extended pentatonic scales. The transcriptions are sufficiently detailed to allow for modern-day performances (although *Fierce Rarotonga I* is the only transcription with words), and would provide a fascinating addition to the vocal repertoire of small choirs.

The Americas

Grainger found a kindred spirit in the person of Natalie Curtis (1875–1921), whose pioneering work in the study and recording of Native American, African-American, and African music moved Grainger to publish the article 'The Unique Value of Natalie Curtis' Notations of American Folksongs' in the *New York Times Book Review* in 1918.[21] Curtis's seminal publications, *The Indians Book* (1907), *Negro Folk Songs* (1918–19), and *Songs and Tales from the Dark Continent* (1920), bear certain similarities with Grainger's early writings on English folk music, and Curtis's ability to 'enter into the soul life of an alien race' matches Grainger's own. Grainger was particularly impressed with Curtis's transcriptions and arrangements of Negro folk music, a music he felt occupied 'the first place in my mind, as regards its sheer acoustical beauty, its emotional depth, and by reason of its musico-historical import'. Grainger's most sustained adaptations of Curtis's work appear in '*Matachina' Dance* and *Sangre de Cristo* (Lenten Chant) of 1925 — orchestrations of Curtis's own *Memories of New Mexico* (1921), which was based on Spanish-Indian melodies from Santa Fe, New Mexico.

Indonesia, India, and Madagascar

The 1926 essay 'The Completion of the Percussion Family in the Orchestra' outlined Grainger's advocacy of tuned percussion, although he first encountered Javanese instruments in 1913 whilst visiting the Ethnomusicological Museum in Leyden, Holland. It is this sound world that Grainger employs most effectively in

---

[21] Repr. in Gillies and Clunies Ross (ed.), *Grainger on Music*.

his realisations of the 5-tone Javanese Gamelan Slendro in *Sekar Gadung* and the 4-tone Balinese Gamelan Anklung in *Berong Pengètjèt*. The orchestration of *Berong Pengètjèt* is particularly skilful, employing an ensemble comprising flute or piccolo, doubled with harmonium, in place of the traditional Indonesian flute known as the *suling*; two players each on the metal marimba and chime bells replacing the various *pemade, kantilan, rejong,* and *jegogan* melody instruments of the Balinese gamelan (with optional tam-tams, played with the fingers, emulating drums (*kendang*) and *ceng-ceng*); and finally, piano strings struck with soft mallets, doubled with pizzicato double bass, for the punctuating gongs. The use of multiple players on the melodic instruments allows for massed involvement, whilst the simplification of the complex interlocking patterns so characteristic of the original makes this an ideal piece for non-specialist performers and a good 'hands-on' introduction to the clangorous euphonicity of traditional gamelan music.

Bahariyale V. Palaniyandi, Grainger's only known foray into Indian music, takes the ancient *jaltarang* ('water waves') as its textural inspiration. The piece, scored for Indian cup bells, harmonium, three hand drums, and bass drum (substituting for *tabla* and other Indian drums), was transcribed from a Columbia recording in 1935. As with the Indonesian pieces — *jaltarang* were initially made from metal and shared a timbral similarity with gamelan gongs — Grainger captures, by the most economical and subtle means, the sound world of the original in a piece that also lends itself to performance by non-specialists. Modern *jaltarang* comprise a set of china bowls of various sizes (in this case, eight), finely tuned by filling each bowl with the appropriate amount of water. The bowls are arranged in a semicircle around the player and are struck with a wooden stick. Whilst it would be possible to substitute an appropriately pitched metallophone in performance, a homemade version may be constructed with a little care and ingenuity, using thin-walled china, porcelain, or other resonant bowls.[22]

Grainger's seminal transcriptions of English folk music, first published in the 1908 article 'Collecting with the Phonograph', revealed an approach to notating aurally-transmitted music that attempted to remain faithful to the details of performance, especially in terms of complex rhythms, expression, articulation, and 'uncertainties' of tuning. He adopted a similar approach in the transcription of *Two Madigascar [sic] Records* in 1933, which contain examples of traditional *chant malgaches* sung in the island's native tongue, Malagasy. Originally performed by women and men's voices accompanied by the *valiha* (the traditional Madagascan bamboo tube zither), Grainger transcribed the first of the two songs,[23] *Mampahory Ny Masoandro Seranin-Javona*, for voices and plucked strings. He produced at least two good copies

---

[22] Grainger's friend and assistant, the American composer Henry Cowell, composed original music for *jaltarang* in his *Pianissimo Ostinato* of 1934. Cowell embraced non-western music even more vigorously than Grainger and, in 1931, went to Berlin to study Javanese and Indian music, and also comparative musicology with E. M. von Hornbostel.

[23] Grainger references the second of the two songs, *Oay Lahy E*, in various articles and broadcasts of the 1930s, but the whereabouts of his transcription, if it exists, remains unknown. A recording of the piece, presumably the one Grainger used, is available via Smithsonian Global Sound (www.smithsonianglobalsound.org).

6. TOWARDS A UNIVERSAL LANGUAGE

Example 6.1 *Mampahory Ny Masoandro Seranin-Javona*, bars 40–44

of this transcription, with sufficient detail to make modern performances of this delightful piece worthy of investigation (see Example 6.1 for an example of Grainger's typically detailed notation).

Debussy, Ravel, and the Orient

It is in the evocations of the Indonesian gamelan, through the reimagining of piano works by Debussy (*Pagodes*) and Ravel (*La Vallée des cloches*), that Grainger's most developed exercises in percussion orchestration are to be heard. Whilst neither piece is based on original Indonesian music, Grainger's versions successfully realise both the implied orchestral sonorities of the piano originals and the sound world of the gamelan, taking them, in his words, 'back to the sound-type from which [they] originally emerged'.[24] Scored for large tuneful percussion ensembles, these pieces attend to Grainger's notions of democratic — and non-specialist — music-making. 'A good amateur band, if . . . conducted by a real genius of a conductor, is just alive with joy and with a love of music.'[25] Such ensembles also rectify what Grainger saw as an inherent problem of tonal balance within modern orchestras — namely the tendency to give undue importance to the higher-register melody instruments and to use unbalanced choirs of instruments by selecting only certain commonly-used types. 'To use, orchestrally, a glockenspiel without a metal marimba, a xylophone without a wooden marimba, is just as absurd and incomplete as it would be to use piccolo without flute, violins without lower strings, the two top octaves of the piano without the lower octaves.'[26] In *Pagodes* and *La Vallée des cloches*, Grainger employs balanced families of tuned wooden idiophones (xylophone and wooden marimba) and tuned metal idiophones (glockenspiel, staff bells, tubular bells, metal marimba, dulcitone, and celesta), with pianos (played both by the keyboard and internally, with marimba mallets), gongs, harmonium, and double bass providing additional resonance and melodic definition.

This enthusiasm for such gamelan-like ensembles — also to be found in larger orchestral works (Suite *In a Nutshell*, *The Warriors*, *Marching Song of Democracy*) — does however provide some challenging performance problems. In particular,

---

[24] Percy Grainger, 'A Commonsense View of All Music' (broadcasts, Australian Broadcasting Corporation, 1934), quoted in Blacking, '*A Commonsense View of All Music*', 178.
[25] Quoted in James Michael Floyd, 'An Interview with Percy Grainger', *Tempo* 61 (2007), 18–26.
[26] Percy Grainger, Preface to *Jutish Medley*.

Grainger's much beloved but now defunct metal marimba and staff bells[27] must usually be substituted by instruments such as the vibraphone (generally, harder mallets are required to emulate the sound of its larger parent), hand bells (which can be mounted and struck with beaters), or other types of metallophones. Grainger's scoring is usually sufficiently flexible to allow for the omission of some instruments, and in the spirit of 'elastic scoring' the inventive conductor needs mainly to ensure tonal balance is maintained when making substitutions. The predecessor to the celesta, the dulcitone,[28] may still be found in auction houses. The delicate sound of the dulcitone, quite distinct from the celesta, is produced by a keyboard mechanism striking U-shaped tuning forks. Grainger sometimes indicates that this instrument may be replaced by a piano, although carefully programmed synthesisers or samplers may also provide a workable alternative.[29]

Finally, in this section we might also include Grainger's 'pianisation' of the traditional Chinese melody *Mo-li-hua*,[30] published as *Beautiful Fresh Flower* for solo piano (black keys only) in 1935. Grainger based his realisation on a example by the musicologist Joseph Yasser, who used the melody in his 1932 book *A Theory of Evolving Tonality* to illustrate his notion of 'unigenous' harmonisation. This was a technique that sought to preserve 'the psychological unity between Harmony and Melody' by allowing 'Chinese, Celtic and other "pentatonic" tunes to be harmonised within the tonal possibilities of their underlying infra-diatonic [i.e. pentatonic] scale'.

Grainger's work as music educator, his enthusiasm for the artistic expression of cultures that lay outside the prevailing western experience, and his love of tuneful music — whether from the voices of 'primitive' musicians or from the medieval abbeys of England — manifest themselves as elements of his two abiding preoccupations: the notions of democracy in music, and Free Music. His belief that 'music is always perfect amongst all races, at all times and in all places', itself a remarkable acceptance of the plurality of artistic expression, was nevertheless framed within a conviction that an observable line of progress ran through all musics, from 'highly artificial and rule-clad forms… towards ever greater freedom and irregularity.'[31] An understanding of this complex, if at times, idiosyncratic view of the inter-relatedness of all music provides us not just with an insight into Grainger's thought processes as an educator and composer, but also with a model of musical panhumanity that remains intriguing and persuasive.

---

[27] Arising from his close interest in the developments of the American mallet-instrument manufacturer J. C. Deagan (1853–1934)
[28] Manufactured by Thomas Machell of Glasgow (1841–1915).
[29] A 'virtual' dulcitone is available through www.soundsonline.com.
[30] Puccini used the same melody throughout the score of his 1924 opera, *Turandot*.
[31] Quoted in Blacking, 'A *Commonsense View of All Music*', 158.

World music settings

AFRICA

Zulu Love Songs: 'Igáma lo Tándo' I & II (Zulu), 'Lúmbo lgo Lúdo' (Chindaú)
Source: Natalie Curtis, from *Songs and Tales from the Dark Continent* (New York, 1920). Grainger reproduces Curtis' original notations, appending his own performance notes.

AMERICAS

Negro Lullaby
Orchestration: 1934: mixed voices; 1939: string orchestra.
Source: Natalie Curtis, published in *Negro Folk-Songs (Hampton Series)* (New York, 1918).

'Matachina' Dance
Orchestration: 1925: Group 1 (on platform): oboe, clarinet, bassoon, horn, harmonium, harp, piano I, 2 violins, viola I, cello I; Group 2 (behind platform): flute, piano II, viola II, cello II, bass.
Lenten Chant (Crucifixion Hymn): *Sangre de Cristo* [Blood of Christ]
Orchestration: 1925: flute (also piccolo), oboe, clarinet, bassoon, 2 horns, timpani, bells [tubular, staff, metal marimba], harmonium, piano (4 hands) + ad lib., harp, strings.
Source: Spanish-Indian melodies from Santa Fe, New Mexico, collected and arranged by Natalie Curtis as *Memories of New Mexico* (1921).

BALI

Berong Pengètjèt
Orchestration: Flute or Piccolo (or both), harmonium, metal marimba (2 players) (or vibraphone or vibraharp), chime bells (hand bells) (2 players), two tam-tams, piano (2–4 players with mallets), double bass.
Source: *Musik des Orients*, no. 12, Odeon O4492b (Berlin, 1931). Reissued as *Music of the Orient: Dr E. M. von Hornbostel* (1979), Ethnic Folkways Records FWO 4157, available at Smithsonian Folkways (http://www.folkways.si.edu/albumdetails.aspx?itemid=686; accessed 21 July 2010).
Original forces: 4-tone *Gamelan Anklung*.
Transcribed 1935: with James Scott-Power (Hobart, Tasmania).

CHINA

Beautiful Fresh Flower
Pianisation: 1935: based on a harmonisation of the traditional Chinese song known as *Mo-li-hua* by Joseph Yasser, from Addendum I in *A Theory of Evolving Tonality*, American Library of Musicology: Contemporary Series, 1 (New York, 1932).

INDIA

Bahariyale V. Palaniyandi
Orchestration: 1935: Indian cup-bells; harmonium; three hand drums; bass drum.
Source: Columbia Records 19588 (80335), Oriental, instrumental (*jalatarangan*).
Original forces: *jalatarang*, harmonium, drums.

JAVA

Sekar Gadung
Orchestration: Voices, piccolo or harmonium, xylophone, wooden marimba, metal marimba, staff bells.
Source: *Musik des Orients*, no. 9, Odeon O1936a (Berlin, 1930). See *Berong Pengètjèt*, above, for reissue details.
Original forces: 5-tone *Gamelan Slendro*, from the court gamelan of Prince Pakoe Alam of Jogjakarta.
Transcribed 1932–3: with Norman Voelcker.

MADAGASCAR

Two Madagascar Records, no. 1. *Mampahory Ny Masoandro Seranin-Javona* [La soleil caché par le nuage nous rend tristes]
Orchestration: 1933: plucked strings, women's and men's voices.
Source: Disque Gramophone, K-4502, 50-1597-8 (Nogent S/M).
Available on *The Music Of Madagascar: Classic Traditional Recordings From The 1930s*, Yazoo YAZCD 7003 (USA, 1995).
Original forces: *Valiha*; women's and men's voices (Hiran'ny Tanoran'ny Ntao Lo, Mpilalao Ao Fenoarivo).

'ORIENTAL'

Pagodes (Estampes) — Debussy (1903)
Orchestration: 1928: harmonium, glockenspiel, metal marimba, celesta, dulcitone (or harp), staff bells, tubular chimes, gong, xylophone, wooden marimba, three or four pianos.

Eastern Intermezzo
Orchestration: 1933–7 and 1943: xylophone, metal marimba, wooden marimba, tubular bells, glockenspiel/chimes, staff bells, dulcitone, two pianos, harmonium, double bass.
Original forces: 1898: small orchestra; 1922: piano; 2 pianos 4 hands.

La Vallée des cloches — Ravel (1904–5)
Orchestration: 1944: harp, staff bells, tubular bells, gong, metal marimba, wooden marimba, Dulcitone/piano 2, piano, celesta, violins, viols, violoncello, double bass.

RAROTONGA

Rarotonga I, Rarotonga II, Fierce Rarotonga I
Source: Field recordings made by A. J. Knocks, Otaki, New Zealand, 1907, not commercially available.
Original forces: men's voices.
Transcribed 1909, 1947: Grainger Museum catalogue nos. SL1 MG13/6-3:1-2; /6-4:1-5; /6-5:1-4.

Other sketches and incomplete transcriptions for music from New Zealand, Australia, Africa, Somalia, and Yemen are to be found in the Grainger Museum archives. None of the transcriptions is complete enough for performance. Grainger also made his own field recordings of a number of Maori tunes in 1909.

7

Programming Grainger

Penelope Thwaites

THE SPECIALIST MUSIC CHAPTERS give some indications of choices for public performance. Grainger repertoire exists for all the following types of programmes:

Orchestral programmes
Orchestral/choral concerts
Choral programmes
Wind band concerts
Chamber recitals (violin and piano, cello and piano, piano trio, string quartet (sometimes with other instruments), wind quintet, cello quintet, small non-western ensembles, guitar and voices)
Song recitals (solo, duo, trio)
Duo-piano/multi-piano recitals
Solo piano recitals

There is no doubt that putting together a Grainger programme can be demanding. The brevity and unconventional scoring of many of his works makes it so, and it is just as well to expect this at the outset. Yet despite the challenges, more often than not, promoters have found that a Grainger programme turns out to be something special — a rewarding and memorable event. The 'longer' works — of anything between twelve and twenty-five minutes — will be particularly favourable where large forces are involved, not least from the stage-management point of view. But in general, if the programmer thinks like a singer designing a song recital, he or she has the chance of creating groups of short works, perhaps with the occasional longer work to give ballast.[1]

The repertoire in all genres lends itself to a variety of themes which can hold sections of a programme together. To name a few of them: the sea; settings of Rudyard Kipling; war; Scandinavia (particularly Denmark); death and destruction — both personal and general; Scotland; love (often betrayed or doomed). The more general themes of folk song have been much explored, and continue to offer rich possibilities. Grainger's arrangements of non-western music are well worth investigating, as are his highly idiosyncratic early-music arrangements.[2]

---

[1] See Fig. 7.7, MSO Centenary programme, p. 101 below.
[2] See Chap. 6, 'Towards a Universal Language'.

The comprehensive Catalogue of Works at the back of this volume gives detailed information on forces required. Both amateurs and professionals should be aware that — notwithstanding the misleading informality of some of his titles — Grainger is technically demanding. Singers must reach uncomfortable registers and articulate vital rhythms. Pianists are stretched. Orchestral balance and co-ordination will require razor-sharp concentration. (A performance of a 'lollipop' like *Molly on the Shore* may have been approached with light-hearted nonchalance, only to emerge as heavy, unco-ordinated, and lacking the sparkling incisiveness necessary for a truly Graingeresque performance.) There is usually a lot going on in Grainger's scores — contrapuntal lines at speed, vigorous interpolations. Pianists find this out soon enough. Listening to the best recordings can be inspirational: once you hear the Grainger magic at work, nothing seems too much trouble in order to participate in it. For me, as for many others, Benjamin Britten's 1969 recording *Salute to Percy Grainger* was the seminal encounter.[3] Since then I have found myself designing, with others, programmes of all kinds, from solo piano and duo-piano — sometimes in an informal lecture-recital format — through song and choral programmes to purely instrumental concerts, using small to large ensembles.

There is ample scope, too, for placing Grainger in the company of other composers. His own solo piano programmes are an interesting study in this respect (see Figures 7.1 and 7.2, at the end of this chapter). Edwardian times rather favoured his preferred option of groups of shorter pieces. Certainly he would never have programmed two or three sonatas in a single recital. Grieg, Delius, and other kindred spirits, such as his composer friends from student days, Cyril Scott, Roger Quilter (for a song programme), and Balfour Gardiner, go well with Grainger (see Figure 7.3). As has been mentioned elsewhere, composers such as Debussy, with an accent on colour and painting in sound, often fit with Grainger's works. His own writings and concert programmes make clear the composers of keyboard repertoire he chiefly admired — J. S. Bach being probably at the top of the list, but Grieg, Debussy, Cyril Scott, Chopin, Schumann, and Brahms feature often, as well. Pianists have many possibilities for logical combinations.

The largest field of choice might appear to be Grainger's folk-music settings, and here he is in extensive company. For example, Grieg's *Norwegian Peasant Dances*, Op. 66 and Op. 72, were a special inspiration to him, and Grieg goes well with Grainger, but Bartók's folk settings, amongst others, could also be considered. The Scandinavian link was strong, and it was easy enough for me to put together a piano recital for a Danish tour entitled 'Percy Grainger and Denmark: A Love Story'. Mixed programmes of solo piano and solo song give many more options. Singers have a wonderful choice, either in an all-Grainger programme (see Fig. 7.4), or in a mixed recital including other folk settings. And Grainger's themes, as mentioned above, can lead in all sorts of directions.

His Australian background, albeit a very anglicised one, makes him an interesting comparison with other Australian composers, both from the early part of the twentieth century and from more recent times. A centenary tribute to Australia's Margaret

---

[3] Decca UK SXL 6410; later issued, with added tracks, as a CD: Decca 425 159-2.

Sutherland (1897–1984)[4], a composer of very different style but a friend of Grainger, included some of his piano music with groups of songs by the skilful Arthur Benjamin (1893–1960), Fritz Hart (1874–1949), and the much younger Alison Bauld (b. 1944) — the songs all presented with characteristic flair by the indefatigable Jane Manning. In his own concerts, Grainger was interested in bridging the gap between performer and audience, and he often said a few words about the work he was going to play. Imaginative presentation makes all the difference, particularly if remarks are pithy and clearly projected, and perhaps contain a touch of humour.

In designing an orchestral programme, absolute essentials in the scoring will need consideration.[5] For example, Grainger was much enamoured of the harmonium and introduces it at key moments in such works as *The Power of Rome and the Christian Heart*, *The Immovable Do*, *To a Nordic Princess*, and many more. The search for a harmonium can be difficult and expensive. (Being aware of this, Grainger used to keep an instrument at his house in White Plains, specifically to lend out to prospective performers.) His fascination with unusual instruments — vibraphone, sarrusophone, dulcitone, bass oboe, to name but a few — makes a daunting prospect for all but the dedicated and adventurous. However, there are mitigating factors. In particular, he provides for what he termed 'elastic scoring'. A scaled-down version — or versions — can be made from most of his larger works. They may, therefore, be given with more manageable forces. On the other hand, in music schools, colleges and university faculties, well endowed with instruments, here is a chance for an exciting extravaganza. There is a wonderful photograph (Plate 12) of a 1930 performance of *The Warriors* in the Chicago Civic Opera House with eighteen pianos and twenty-seven pianists, arranged in serried ranks behind the orchestra, with Grainger solo and central at a nineteenth piano.

The implications of Grainger's elastic scoring are endless. For example, he indicates parts for brass sextet in the latter section of his six-hand piano arrangement of *The Warriors*. No-one would deny the preference for hearing this fabulous work in full orchestral garb, yet there was a most effective occasion when three pianists at three pianos were playing this work in its six-hand version as the finale to a concert (see Figure 7.5). Six (unannounced) brass players[6] were concealed behind a curtain at the back of the platform. Their blazing entry as the curtains swung back produced a gasp of delight in the audience, and the work was carried — like a surfer on a particularly powerful wave — to its exultant conclusion.

In Grainger's centenary year (1982) a 'room-music' (small chamber-music) programme was given at the Dulwich Picture Gallery,[7] including the smallest possible elastic scoring of his darkly dramatic Danish folk-song setting *The Power of Love*. Lacking a harmonium, a small (Casio) electronic keyboard was brought into play. The arranger, whilst leaving a pianist to undertake the keyboard part, experienced

---

[4] Wigmore Hall, 20 Nov. 1997.
[5] See Chap. 1, 'Orchestral Music: The conductor's view (1)', by Geoffrey Simon.
[6] Kingston Brass.
[7] Stephen Bryant, violin, Garth Knox, viola, Helen Verney, cello, John Lavender, piano, Penelope Thwaites, piano.

the thrill of sitting at the volume controls and slowly creating a massive crescendo. In such a programme, five competent players — in this case, violinist, cellist, violist, and two pianists — can, between them, produce a most enjoyable concert. Other works on that occasion included, for violin and piano, *Mock Morris*, *Molly on the Shore* (a real fire-cracker), and *Harvest Hymn*. Cellist and pianist presented *The Sussex Mummers' Christmas Carol*, the suite *La Scandinavie* (Grainger rarely used French; one suspects the marketing manager's hand), and *Youthful Rapture* (once entitled by the composer *A Lot of Rot*). The violist had his solo innings with *Arrival Platform Humlet*, and the pianists duetted in *Let's Dance Gay in Green Meadow*, *Country Gardens*, and several other arrangements. The lovely *My Robin is to the Greenwood Gone* and *Colonial Song* were given as piano trios, *The Power of Love* (as above) and *Handel in the Strand* in piano-quartet versions.

Grainger's improvisatory work *Random Round* can be presented just with guitar(s) and voices, or with more instruments, as required. It depends, as in jazz, on a certain relaxed competence in the performers, and a 'produced' style of singing does not really suit Grainger's inspiration for this piece, which was the vocal music of the South Pacific. His mix-and-match elements of musical material provide endlessly varied possibilities, and in terms of involving an audience, it has enjoyable potential. A string quartet can present his *Free Music* no. 1, lasting all of one minute (perhaps meriting a return performance later in the programme). It is but a tiny sample of a grand concept which Grainger was never able to bring to fruition, although the ideas behind it put him in the company of many a twentieth-century musical adventurer.[8] Programmers in search of unconventional chamber items can also turn to his two settings of Asian music — *Bahariyale V. Palaniyandi* for Indian cup bells, harmonium, and three or four hand drums, and the Javanese *Sekar Gadung*, for voices, flute, and percussion.[9]

Grainger's solo songs include several which conjure a real scena, lending drama to a programme (see Figure 7.4). The most taxing is probably *Hard-hearted Barb'ra (H)Ellen* — a tour de force for both singer and pianist. The unfolding story of an unbalanced heroine, besotted lover (and seemingly unbalanced parents), ending in the lovers' final unity in death (as two intertwining vines), is deranged enough to satisfy the most melodramatic taste. In a wry setting of Kipling's acidly-mooded Barrack Room Ballad *The Young British Soldier*, the tenor may characterise to his heart's delight the worldly-wise sergeant advising the young recruit. Robust humour marks the Danish setting, *Husband and Wife* — a duet of marital conflict — and its companion piece *Under a Bridge*, where the betrothed couple good-naturedly taunt each other, only to end in a wild, bitonally-accompanied dance. *The Old Woman at the Christening* is another uninhibited Danish song, describing the god Thor, disguised as an old crone, arriving at a christening and devouring horrifying amounts of food. In complete contrast, and this time for three voices, there is a magical setting of Kipling's poem *The Only Son*. The young son (Mowgli) dreams of childhood days when he lived amongst the wolves. He recollects fleeting scenes and sounds, and as

---

[8] See Appendix II.
[9] See Chap. 6, pp. 81, 82 above.

the tension builds, his mother opens the door of their house and sees the she-wolf come out of the shadows and fawn affectionately on her son. The musical setting is truly exquisite.

Once you get into the chorus and orchestra repertoire, the powerful scenes are such that one wishes that Grainger had written an opera (see Figures 7.6, 7.7, and 7.8). *Father and Daughter*, for example, requires top vocal accomplishment. Taken at speed, the breathless question-and-answer story, which ends in two murders, is driven to a wildly exciting conclusion. A dark and gruesome tale of a different kind is told in the execution of the erring soldier *Danny Deever* — a kind of miniature Berlioz *March to the Scaffold*. One of the most widely-known and loved settings is *Shallow Brown*,[10] a sea chanty collected from John Perring. Grainger uses the highly effective (and expensive) idea of including in his orchestra two each of ukeleles, mandolins, and mandolas, as well as four guitars, piano, harmonium, and a variety of winds and strings. Few settings can match the surging, keening sounds Grainger produces as the forsaken heroine stands on the quay, knowing her 'shallow Brown' will not come back. Both baritone and soprano soloists have recorded the song, accompanied by male chorus. In contrast, the *Scotch Strathspey and Reel* lends itself to a wild rambunctiousness, combining Scottish and Irish reels with a very English *What Shall We Do with a Drunken Sailor?*

A sideways move may be made at this point to the solo pianist and programming Grainger. Sadly, his music is still a rarity in concert recitals, and yet groups of his works can fit beautifully into a programme. A selection of folk settings can provide an excellent conclusion to a more serious programme. As indicated above, some of his 'impressionistic'[11] works go very well alongside a composer like Debussy. Grieg is another natural companion. I have grouped pieces by Grainger into little suites (for example his *Lullaby from 'Tribute to Foster'*, *Bridal Lullaby Ramble*, and *Scotch Strathspey and Reel*). As always, one considers key sequences, contrasts, or connections of mood and theme, and builds a 'segment'. This is precisely what Debussy does in his much-loved *Estampes* — three unrelated pieces, though all pictorial. For pianists of strong technique, Grainger's longer suites, *In a Nutshell* and his *Danish Folk-Music Suite* (incorporating the brilliant 'Jutish Medley'), make at least a quarter of a programme.

The duo piano repertoire is rich indeed, and there is plenty enough of contrast to make an all-Grainger programme with ample choice for mixing and matching works. The duo *Lincolnshire Posy* is a sixteen-minute gem, and the duo *In a Nutshell* works particularly well (the first pianist will need a marimba mallet to play on the piano strings the final ghostly notes of *Pastoral*). The *Fantasy on Themes from 'Porgy and Bess'* has been much played and recorded — Gershwin's tunes, after all, are sure-fire winners — and it is beautifully written for the two instruments.

A final comment on Grainger's own uninhibited approach to programming: where he was given a free hand, such as in the series he conducted at the Hollywood Bowl in August 1928, his tastes ranged from Purcell and Bach to his friends

---

[10] See also Chap. 3, 'Grainger for Choirs' and Chap. 4, 'Singing Grainger Solo'.
[11] *Lullaby from 'Tribute to Foster'* and *Pastoral*, to name two.

Delius and Grieg, Sandby and Hanson, Dillon and Goldmark, and of course his own music — culminating on his wedding day, Thursday 9 August, with *The Warriors* and then his tribute to his wife-to-be, *To a Nordic Princess* (see Figure 7.9). In his later years, his concerts often took place in schools or colleges and with local bands and orchestras. He would usually agree to appear in one of the popular war-horse concertos — particularly the Grieg or Tchaikovsky — on condition that his own compositions and arrangements would also be included in the programme. A band programme from 1949 (Figure 7.10), bearing Grainger's own red pencilled markings, illustrates the scope of the repertoire. A particularly poignant appearance took place in February 1957 at Aarhus, Jutland, Denmark (see Figure 7.11). A pairing of Grieg and Grainger in the music made clear their affinity — including the *Peer Gynt Suite* as inspiration for Grainger's *Danish Folk-Music Suite* — on that occasion played in the very region from which he and Evald Tang Kristensen had gathered the tunes thirty years before.[12]

To organise a Grainger concert is work enough — to organise a two-week festival, reflecting most aspects of his work, is an enormous undertaking. In October 2003 the Adelaide Symphony Orchestra did just that. The personal account of its then Director of Artistic Planning follows.

Au tombeau de Percy
James Koehne

The city of Adelaide in South Australia had a special place in the life — and the death — of Percy Grainger. The hometown of his beloved mother, Rose, it is also his own final resting place, at the Aldridge family plot in the West Terrace Cemetery. The modest memorial has become a place of pilgrimage for visiting musicians. This fact alone makes a convenient excuse for claiming that Adelaide should celebrate the work of the composer, but the real motivation for mounting a Grainger Festival here in 2003 was actually musical. In realising my idea, I was indeed fortunate to have the support of the ASO's then Managing Director, Robert Clarke, who was easily convinced of the musical, historical, and cultural relevance of the project.

Grainger's image is often frustratingly constrained to half-baked ideas of the sado-masochistic weirdo or the English folklorist. In setting up our Grainger Festival, I hoped for an event that would reveal the many dimensions of Percy Grainger the tone artist; to allow Grainger's spirit and music to radiate upon Adelaide audiences and, through broadcasts on ABC Classic FM radio, upon a national audience as well. To achieve this grand aim, I was fortunate to be able to enlist the support of a small team of dedicated souls who made huge personal efforts to bring the Festival to life.

---

[12] See 'A Grainger Timeline'.

Two concert programmes[13] with the Adelaide Symphony Orchestra formed the core of the Festival, conducted by our Principal Guest, James Judd. One programme of our main subscription concert series (a concert given three times) was devoted to music of Grainger or music associated with him: Grieg's Piano Concerto was an obvious choice, together with a selection of pieces that I considered would be familiar to audiences, and importantly, that did not give rise to excessive extra costs of orchestral augmentation. A one-night-only concert 'special' was programmed as the Festival's Grand Finale, in which the scope for unusual and additional elements was expanded. It included a fine local choir, the Adelaide Chamber Singers, directed by Carl Crossin, and the enlarged percussion section required for such pieces as *In a Nutshell* and *Tribute to Foster* (with its direct references to Adelaide). An early work by Bernard Herrmann, dating from the time of his influential encounter with Grainger at New York University, was also included.

The quantities of tuned percussion that Grainger so loved often cause concern for programmers in professional orchestras, but it is important to examine the scores in more detail before dismissing them as impractical. Grainger himself usually provides the solutions.

In particular, Grainger's suggestion that students and amateur musicians should be drawn into the performances of his music as players of tuned percussion is an idea that I wish I had explored in the Festival, though in the event I took the easier, more practical path of using the minimum of tuned percussion. Though it requires special negotiation in any professional orchestral organisation, the prospect of a massed tuned percussion section chiming in to add another dimension of orchestral colour in many of Grainger's pieces would be awe-inspiring.

Grainger's musical vision is broad and embracing, seeking a spirit of participation and individual creativity that can seem to be at odds with the structures of musical production in the busy professional orchestra. Many of his pieces include opportunities for both player and audience participation. Grainger makes extraordinary demands — not necessarily matters of serious cost so much as of time and creative energy. Having the right leaders in place, who are willing and able to marshal the musical resources, solve the problems and idiosyncrasies, and realise the opportunities of Percy's musical challenges, is one of the keys to presenting his music.

Surrounding the Festival's orchestral concerts, we placed a range of events which gave a taste of the further dimensions of Grainger. ABC Classic FM Radio, through Station Manager John Crawford, helped put together and resource additional concerts of Grainger rarities and ensemble music. Melbourne-based experimental composer Warren Burt devised and presented an investigation of Grainger's sonic experimentations, building his own versions of Grainger's proto-electronic inventions. A humble overhead projector was adapted into a reconstruction, based on Grainger's original drawings, of the 'Electric Eye Music Machine'. Burt's low-tech inventiveness celebrated and perfectly captured the home-made sensibility of Grainger's own experiments. Penelope Thwaites led an ensemble of pianists presenting a selection

---

[13] See Fig. 7.12. In the event, the Grainger special concert placed 'Thanksgiving Song' just before the interval, its impact creating a pin-drop silence at the end. See also Chap. 1, p. 17 above.

of Grainger's multi-piano compositions featuring eleven pianistic hands at three pianos, and joined with a small array of contemporary music specialist performers to present an illuminating selection of Grainger byways — including his Balinese transcriptions and the original improvised version of *Random Round* — under the appropriate heading 'Radical Thinking'. The local Kensington & Norwood Brass Band contributed a Sunday afternoon concert of Grainger's music mixed with popular band favourites from his time. Special late-night live radio broadcasts from Grainger's grave and a walking tour of Grainger sites in Adelaide added promotional value to draw public attention to Grainger and the Festival. I was also indebted to Barry Ould, Grainger custodian and music publisher, who made the pilgrimage to Adelaide and participated as a speaker and interview subject, as well as providing eminently practical advice about Grainger scores and musical issues.

One personal moment from the Grainger Festival deserves to be recounted as an epiphanic illustration of Grainger's musical power, and an example of the need for determination in seeking to achieve Grainger's often half-realised musical visions. Barry Ould persuaded me to include a Grainger premiere in one of the Festival's orchestral concerts, a reconstruction of the *Thanksgiving Song* for choir and orchestra, hitherto unperformed in Australia. At one point, the score instructs that the orchestra and choir should begin to disappear, sonically, from the concert hall — physically moving into the distance while continuing to play and sing. I imagined we would indicate this obviously impractical suggestion in some straightforward way, but conductor James Judd rightly insisted that we should attempt to realise fully the composer's instructions. After discussions with players, choristers, and the orchestra's operational personnel, a system for moving the players and singers on a series of trolleys was devised. At the final rehearsal, I was assigned to stay in the hall, while the mechanics of mobilising the orchestra and choir was put into action, to judge the effectiveness of our solution to Grainger's logistical challenge.

Alone in the hall, while James Judd conducted before a closed-circuit camera, and the trolleys bearing players and choristers were set in motion to move gradually away from the auditorium and eventually into the street outside, I was transfixed by the simple beauty of the repetitive chorale which gradually faded into the sonic distance, evoking a majestic sense of homage to all the women Grainger had loved. In this moment of radiant beauty, brought about through the co-operation and unified effort of a large group of people, the power and spiritual depth of Grainger's musical vision was unleashed upon me. All thoughts of Grainger's 'scandalous' image were banished as I experienced the musical benediction of his beautiful artistic imagination.

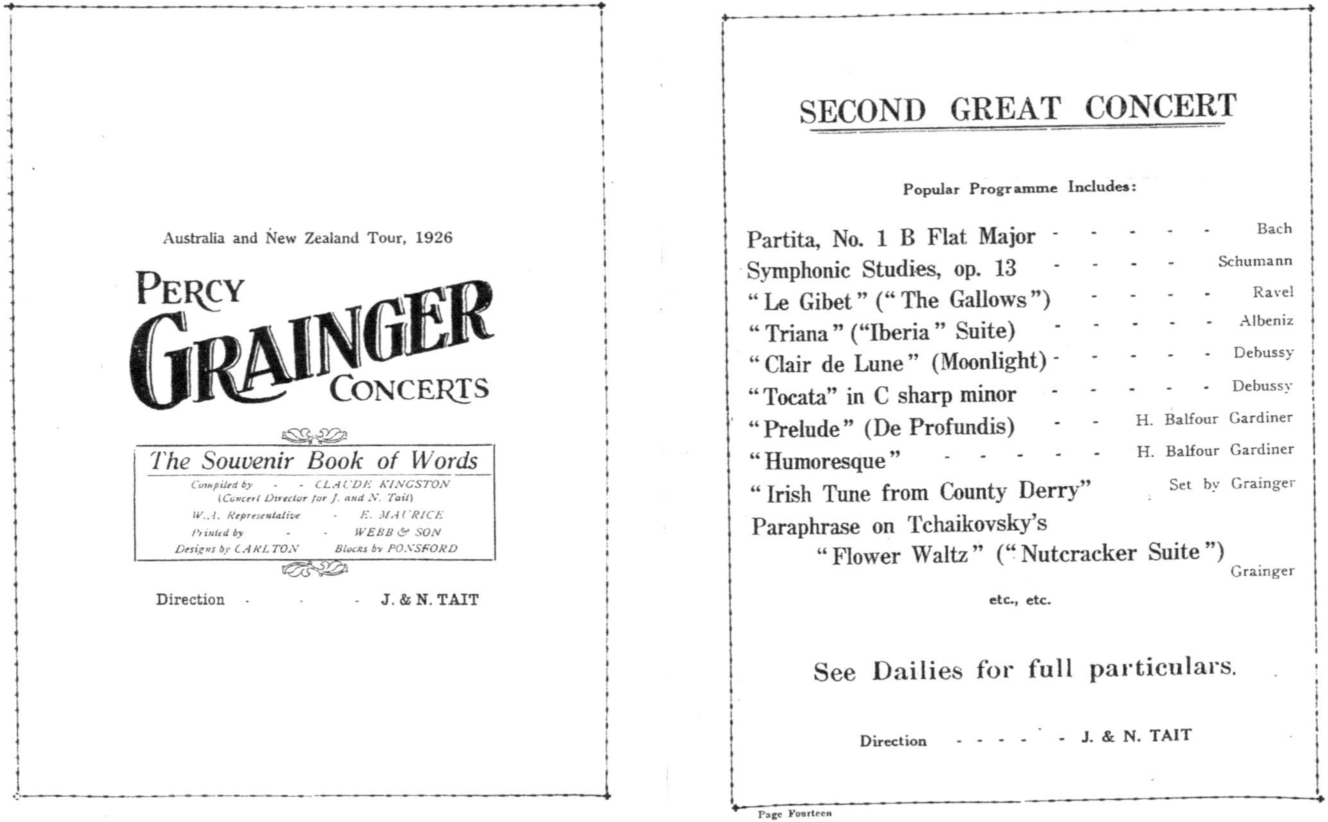

7. PROGRAMMING GRAINGER

SECOND GREAT CONCERT

Popular Programme Includes:

Partita, No. 1 B Flat Major	Bach
Symphonic Studies, op. 13	Schumann
"Le Gibet" ("The Gallows")	Ravel
"Triana" ("Iberia" Suite)	Albeniz
"Clair de Lune" (Moonlight)	Debussy
"Tocata" in C sharp minor	Debussy
"Prelude" (De Profundis)	H. Balfour Gardiner
"Humoresque"	H. Balfour Gardiner
"Irish Tune from County Derry"	Set by Grainger
Paraphrase on Tchaikovsky's "Flower Waltz" ("Nutcracker Suite")	Grainger

etc., etc.

See Dailies for full particulars.

Direction - - - - J. & N. TAIT

Page Fourteen

Australia and New Zealand Tour, 1926

PERCY GRAINGER CONCERTS

The Souvenir Book of Words

Compiled by - - CLAUDE KINGSTON
(Concert Director for J. and N. Tait)
W.J. Representative - - E. MAURICE
Printed by - - WEBB & SON
Designs by CARLTON — Blocks by PONSFORD

Direction - - - J. & N. TAIT

Figure 7.1 1926 recital programme from Grainger's Australasian tour (dir. J. and N. Tait)

96 · THE MUSIC

Figure 7.2 1934 recital programme from Grainger's Australasian tour (dir. J. and N. Tait)

Figure 7.3 1982 Centenary Day piano recital *Percy Grainger and his Circle* by Penelope Thwaites; 8 July, Purcell Room, Southbank Centre, London

7.30 pm: GALA CONCERT I

"UNTO BRIGG FAIR...... and beyond"

An exploration of Grainger's songs interspersed with readings from his letters

Della Jones, mezzo-soprano, *Stephen Varcoe*, baritone,
James Gilchrist, tenor, *Penelope Thwaites*, piano

BRIGG FAIR

BOLD WILLIAM TAYLOR
SPRIG OF THYME

DIED FOR LOVE

ANCHOR SONG†
GANGES PILOT†
THE BRITISH WATERSIDE

SHALLOW BROWN

MY FAITHFUL FOND ONE
WILLY'S GANG TO MELVILLE CASTLE
TURN YE TO ME
SKYE BOAT SONG

HARD HEARTED BARBRA' (H)ELLEN
LORD MAXWELL'S GOODNIGHT

Interval (20 minutes)

DAVID OF THE WHITE ROCK

THE LONELY DESERT-MAN SEES THE TENTS
    OF THE HAPPY TRIBES

A SONG OF AUTUMN

DEDICATION
THE LOVE SONG OF HAR DYAL

THE WIDOW'S PARTY
with *John Lavender*, piano
MERCIFUL TOWN†
RIDE WITH AN IDLE WHIP†
THE ONLY SON

THE POWER OF LOVE

LOVE AT FIRST SIGHT (*Ella Grainger*)†

UNDER A BRIDGE

HUBBY AND WIFEY

NOW, O NOW, I NEEDS MUST PART
  (*Dowland arr. Grainger*)

† *first London performance*

Figure 7.4 1998 *A Grainger Song Gala*; 7 November, St John's, Smith Square, London

7.30 pm: GALA CONCERT II

A MULTI-PIANO EXTRAVAGANZA for 2, 4, 6, 8, 10 and 11 hands

PENELOPE THWAITES, JOHN LAVENDER, WAYNE MARSHALL
with *RHONDDA GILLESPIE* and *ANTONY GRAY*

GREEN BUSHES

ZANZIBAR BOAT-SONG

YE BANKS AND BRAES O BONNIE DOON

"THE WIDOW'S PARTY" MARCH†

PASTORAL

JUTISH MEDLEY

INTERVAL (20 minutes)

COUNTRY GARDENS

HARVEST HYMN

RANDOM ROUND

THE KEEL ROW *(realised Ould)*†

THE WARRIORS

† *first public performance*

Figure 7.5 1998 A *Multi-Piano Extravaganza*;
8 November, St John's, Smith Square, London

The University of Melbourne
in association with the
Australian Broadcasting Commission

In the distinguished presence of the Governor General of Australia
His Excellency, The Right Honourable Sir Zelman Cowen
A.K., G.C.M.G., G.C.V.O., K.St.J., Q.C.
and Lady Cowen

presents

PERCY GRAINGER CENTENARY CONCERT

Melbourne Symphony Orchestra

Royal Melbourne Philharmonic Society Choir

Conductor:

John Hopkins OBE

Piano Soloists:

Michael Brimer
May Clifford, Ronald Farren-Price, Mack Jost,
Margaret Schofield, Donald Thornton, Kenneth Weir

MELBOURNE CONCERT HALL
Victorian Arts Centre

WEDNESDAY, 7th JULY AT 8.00 P.M.

*This concert is arranged by the
Australian Broadcasting Commission in conjunction with the
Government of Victoria.*

PROGRAM: ONE DOLLAR

Figure 7.6 1982 Grainger Centenary Concert, Melbourne Symphony Orchestra, Royal Melbourne Philharmonic Society Choir, cond. John Hopkins OBE; 7 July, Melbourne Concert Hall

PROGRAM

CHILDREN'S MARCH—OVER THE HILLS AND FAR AWAY

THE MERRY WEDDING
> Royal Melbourne Philharmonic Society Choir

TO A NORDIC PRINCESS

TRIBUTE TO STEPHEN FOSTER
> Royal Melbourne Philharmonic Society Choir
> Off-Stage Choir:
>> The University of Melbourne Faculty of Music Choir
>
> Soloist: Michael Brimer, piano

Interval

MOCK MORRIS

BLITHE BELLS

MOLLY ON THE SHORE

THE WARRIORS
> Piano Soloists:
> May Clifford, Ronald Farren-Price, Mack Jost, Margaret Schofield, Donald Thornton, Kenneth Weir

Figure 7.7 Grainger Centenary Programme, MSO, RMPSC, MUFMC, Hopkins, and soloists

Monteverdi Choir and Orchestra Ltd

Greater London Council
Queen Elizabeth Hall
General Administrator: Michael Kaye

Tuesday 19 October 1982

The Monteverdi Choir
The Monteverdi Orchestra
Nona Liddell *leader*

John Eliot Gardiner *conductor*

William Kendall *tenor*

PERCY GRAINGER CENTENARY CONCERT

Rustic Dance
Lost Lady Found
Australian Up-Country Song
Spoon River
Brigg Fair
I'm Seventeen Come Sunday
Kipling's "Jungle Book" Cycle

Interval

Father and Daughter
Hermundur Illi
Hill Song No. 1
Stormy
Scotch Strathspey and Reel
Shallow Brown
Molly on the Shore
Irish Tune

Sponsored by the Hongkong Bank Group

Programme 50p

Figure 7.8 1982 Grainger Centenary Concert, The Monteverdi Choir and Orchestra, cond. John Eliot Gardiner; 19 October, Queen Elizabeth Hall, London

HOLLYWOOD BOWL :: SEASON 1928

EIGHTEENTH PROGRAM
Thursday, August 9, 1928, 8:30 P. M.
Conductor: PERCY GRAINGER

1. Fantasia in Four Voices for Strings, G-Major - - - Purcell
   (First Performance in Los Angeles)
2. a. Brandenburg Concerto, No. 3, G-major, First Movement, Bach
   b. Air, D-major, from Overture No. 3 (for Strings and Organ) - - - - - - - - - - - - Bach
   c. Brandenburg Concerto, No. 3, Second Movement - - Bach

Assisting Artists: Ralph Dobbs, George H. Greenwood, Alexander Kosloff, Willard MacGregor, Harold P. Smyth, Marshall Sumner, Pianists.
(First Performance in Los Angeles Preserving the Tonal Balance Present in the Original Score.)

3. Suite: "In a Mission Garden," Opus 52 - Fannie Charles Dillon
   a. Flower of Gethsemane (Passiflora).   b. A Story of the Bells.   c. Humming-Birds.
   (First Performance of Version for Full Orchestra)

INTERMISSION—(Fifteen Minutes)

4. "The Warriors": Music to an Imaginary Ballet - - Grainger

Assisting Artists: Ralph Dobbs, George H. Greenwood, Alexander Kosloff, Willard MacGregor, Harold P. Smyth, Marshall Sumner, Pianists.
(First Performance on the Pacific Coast)

5. "To a Nordic Princess" - - - - - - - - Grainger
   (Bridal Song, dedicated to the composer's bride-to-be, Ella Viola Strom.)
   (First Performance Anywhere)

(Steinway Pianos and Estey Reed and Pipe Organs Used, Courtesy Birkel Co.)

At the conclusion of the above program, Ella Viola Strom and Percy Grainger will be united in marriage in a brief ceremony conducted by the Reverend J. Herman Olsson (Swedish Lutheran Church) on the Bowl platform. As part of this ceremony two unaccompanied part-songs will be sung by the Smallman a Cappella Choir (Conductor: John Smallman):
   a. "A Song of Vermeland" (Swedish Folksong, set by Grainger)
   b. Australian Up-Country Song (Grainger)

Figure 7.9 1928 Hollywood Bowl Concert, cond. Percy Grainger;
9 August, Hollywood, USA,
on the occasion of his marriage to Ella Viola Ström

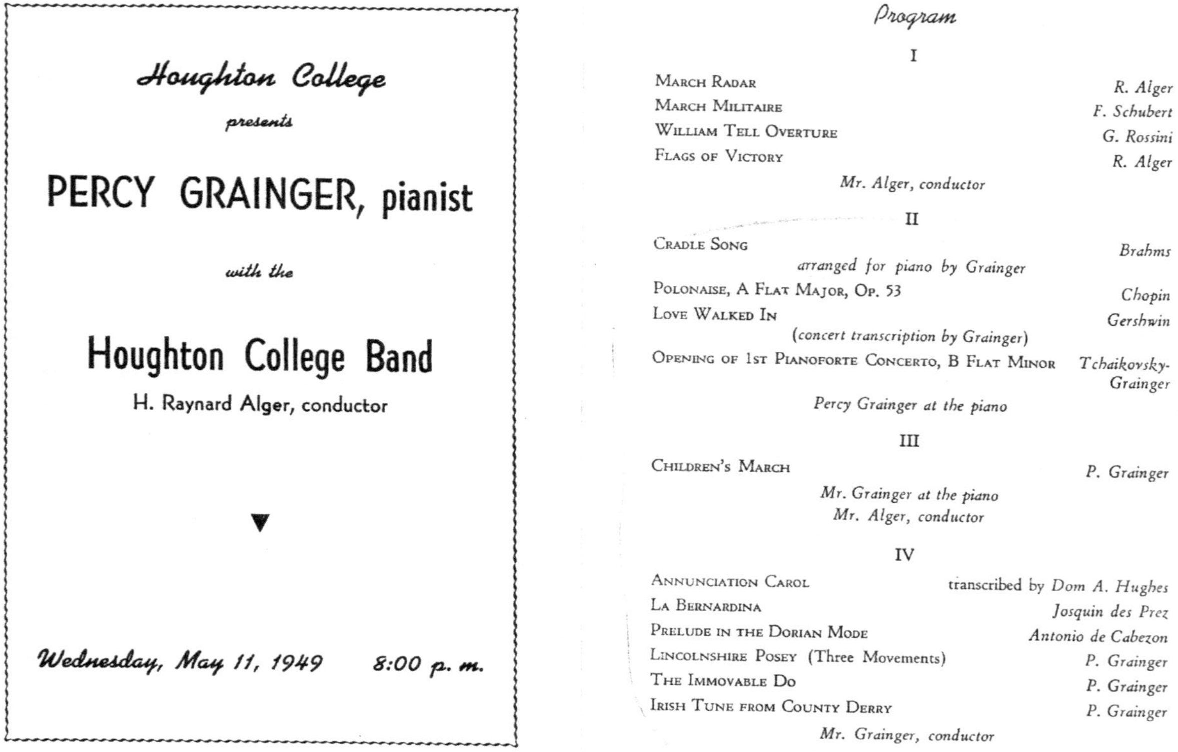

Houghton College
presents

PERCY GRAINGER, pianist

with the

Houghton College Band

H. Raynard Alger, conductor

▶

Wednesday, May 11, 1949   8:00 p.m.

Program

I

MARCH RADAR	R. Alger
MARCH MILITAIRE	F. Schubert
WILLIAM TELL OVERTURE	G. Rossini
FLAGS OF VICTORY	R. Alger

Mr. Alger, conductor

II

CRADLE SONG *arranged for piano by Grainger*	Brahms
POLONAISE, A FLAT MAJOR, OP. 53	Chopin
LOVE WALKED IN	Gershwin
(concert transcription by Grainger)	
OPENING OF 1ST PIANOFORTE CONCERTO, B FLAT MINOR	Tchaikovsky-Grainger

Percy Grainger at the piano

III

CHILDREN'S MARCH — P. Grainger

Mr. Grainger at the piano
Mr. Alger, conductor

IV

ANNUNCIATION CAROL *transcribed by Dom A. Hughes*	
LA BERNARDINA	Josquin des Prez
PRELUDE IN THE DORIAN MODE	Antonio de Cabezon
LINCOLNSHIRE POSEY (Three Movements)	P. Grainger
THE IMMOVABLE DO	P. Grainger
IRISH TUNE FROM COUNTY DERRY	P. Grainger

Mr. Grainger, conductor

Figure 7.10 1949 Houghton College Band, cond. H. Raynard Alger; pianist and conductor, Percy Grainger; 11 May, Houghton College, New York State, USA

7. PROGRAMMING GRAINGER

AARHUS BY-ORKESTER
JYDSK SYMFONISK ORKESTER

SÆSONEN 1956-57

PRIS: 25 ØRE

MANDAG DEN 25. FEBRUAR 1957

6. ORKESTER- og SOLISTKONCERT

Mandag den 25. februar kl. 20

Dirigent: *Per Dreier*

Solist: Den australske pianist og komponist *Percy Grainger*
Medv.: Jydsk Akademisk Kor, dirigent: *Walter Børner*

Edvard Grieg: Hyldningsmarch af dramaet
"Sigurd Jorsalfar". Op. 56 nr. 3

Edvard Grieg: Klaverkoncert i a-moll. Op. 16
  Allegro molto moderato
  Adagio
  Allegro moderato molto e marcato —
  Quasi presto — Andante maestoso
  Percy Grainger

PAUSE

Percy Grainger: 3 sange for kor og orkester
  Dirigent: *Walter Børner*
  1. Love verses from "The song of Solomon"
  2. Mowgli's song against people
  3. The sea-wife
  Mezzo-sopran: *Inger Kyrne Frandsen*
  Tenor: *Torben Viskum Sørensen*

Percy Grainger: Dansk folkemusik-suite
  "Kærligheds styrke" — "Herr Peders stalddreng"
  "Nattergalen" og "De to søstre"
  "Jydsk fantasi"

Edvard Grieg: Peer Gynt suite nr. 1. Op. 46
  Morgenstemning — Åses død
  Anitras dans — I Dovregubbens hal

Flygel: *Hornung & Møller*

7. orkester- og solistkoncert: mandag den 7. marts kl. 20

Figure 7.11 1957 Aarhus Municipal Orchestra, cond. Per Dreier, piano soloist, Percy Grainger; 25 February, Aarhus Scala, Aarhus, Jutland, Denmark

program: a grainger harvest

Master Series 10

Adelaide Town Hall
Thursday 09 October, 2003 – 6.30pm
Friday 10 October, 2003 – 8.00pm
Saturday 11 October, 2003 – 6.30pm

Delius	*In a Summer Garden*
Grieg	Piano Concerto
	INTERVAL
Grainger	*The Immovable 'Do' (The Cyphering C)*
	Colonial Song
	Suite for Piano and Orchestra
	Country Gardens
	A Bridal Lullaby
	Handel in the Strand
	The Merry King
	To A Nordic Princess
	Green Bushes

Conductor	James Judd
Piano	Benjamin Martin (Grieg)
Piano	Penelope Thwaites (Grainger)

program: grainger special concert

Adelaide Town Hall
Saturday 18 October 2003 – 8.00pm

Grainger	*Thanksgiving Song*
	In a Nutshell
	INTERVAL
Hermann	*Silent Noon*
Grainger	*The Lost Lady Found*
	Marching Tune
	Scotch Strathspey and Reel
	Irish Tune from County Derry
	Tribute to Foster

Conductor	James Judd
Piano	Penelope Thwaites
Choir	Adelaide Chamber Singers

Figure 7.12 2003 Adelaide Symphony Orchestra, Adelaide Chamber Singers, cond. James Judd, piano soloists, Benjamin Martin, Penelope Thwaites; 9, 10, 11, 18 October, Adelaide Town Hall, Adelaide, South Australia

8

Putting Grainger into Print

Barry Peter Ould

Hearing Grainger's *Brigg Fair* in 1971 was a revelation. The Benjamin Britten recording *Salute to Percy Grainger* fuelled my enthusiasm still further, and upon consulting Teresa Balough's catalogue of Grainger's works,[1] it was obvious how much more there was to discover. I wrote to the American Grainger archivist Stewart Manville (then married to Grainger's widow, Ella) with the idea of forming a Grainger appreciation society. Stewart put me in touch with another British enthusiast, David Tall, and together we formed the Percy Grainger Society as a focus for the enjoyment and dissemination of Grainger's music.[2] The formation of the Society was followed in 1978 by a significant donation of unpublished Grainger scores, generously given by Ella Grainger from the archive of her home in White Plains, New York. Thus my first venture in putting Grainger into print, with full encouragement from the Grainger Estate, was providing short works for inclusion in our bi-annual Journal. At first these were done by hand, but in due course they were set by music typewriter. In the course of music studies both at school and at WEA evening classes, and later, working for publishers such as J. & W. Chester and Novello, I had become intrigued with the graphic processes of printing music. (At the time, this was mostly done by hand. The standard methods were either engraving musical symbols on copper plates, or hand-copying with pen and ink or stencils.) Pursuing a career as a music copyist had greatly expanded my practical knowledge of instruments, their ranges and respective transpositions, as well as the complexities of putting together a choral or orchestral score.

During a visit to White Plains in 1979 I found myself cataloguing the contents of the filing cabinets in the large fireproof room in the basement of the house. At that time, all the material contained therein consisted of original manuscripts, either on paper or transparencies. After Ella Grainger's death, and according to the instructions in Grainger's will, all these originals were transferred to the Grainger Museum. The lists I had made earlier became a very useful reference tool, until the items were issued by the Grainger Museum in a supplementary catalogue.[3] At

---

[1] Teresa Balough, *A Complete Catalogue of the Works of Percy Grainger*, Music Monograph 2 (Nedlands, W.A., 1975).

[2] As distinct from the American Percy Grainger Library Society, now the International Percy Grainger Society.

[3] Kay Dreyfus, *Supplementary List and Index: Music by Percy Aldridge Grainger*, Percy Grainger Music Collection, 3; Grainger Museum, University of Melbourne, Catalogue 4 (Parkville, Vic., 1995).

around the same time, the composer and pianist Ronald Stevenson had been asked by Peters Edition, New York, to edit the *Three Scottish Folksongs* for piano. My services were called upon to typeset master copies from the edited manuscript. For this work I was honoured to receive the Paul Revere Award for music origination, issued by the Music Publishers Association of America. Much later, also for Peters Edition, I originated for publication both Grainger's *Two Sea Chanties* and *In Dahomey*.

Over the next seven years, the Percy Grainger Society Music Archive was to grow considerably, becoming the largest Grainger music resource in the world outside the Grainger Museum collection in Melbourne and the International Percy Grainger Society's collection in White Plains. However, it seemed that neither of those institutions was in a position to publish the music. During that period I was working for Roberton Publications, where some of my time was spent in proof-reading and preparing manuscripts for typesetting. Shortly after this, the first computer music-engraving program became available for use with the Macintosh computer, and, being curious, I purchased the software, even before acquiring a computer. In August 1987 I launched my own publishing company, Bardic Edition, in order to put into print the works of several composers whose music was of interest to me. Amongst these was, of course, Grainger, and with the blessing of the Grainger Estate, I began to publish some of his hitherto unknown works. One of the first pieces issued under the Bardic imprint was *A Bridal Lullaby* — a copy of which I had been able to bring back earlier from the Grainger house. It was later used as the theme for the Merchant Ivory film of E. M. Forster's *Howards End*. As demand for Grainger's music grew, more pieces were published, and by 1995 Bardic had a sizeable catalogue, with Grainger as the dominant composer.

Grainger performances and recordings were proliferating. In 1991, Penelope Thwaites had suggested to me the idea of a complete Grainger recording series. We had several meetings with interested parties, discussing the considerable implications of bringing such an idea to fruition. Eventually, in 1995, Chandos Records took up the challenge, and with subsequent correspondence resulting in a meeting with conductor Richard Hickox,[4] I was asked to prepare repertoire lists which would encompass all Grainger's original and folk-based compositions, a project amounting to twenty-five CD albums.[5]

To provide reliable scores for solo artists, chamber groups, choirs, bands, and orchestras was a daunting task. In some instances, especially in the manuscript scores, a great deal of editing was involved. Details in the full scores naturally had to match every detail in the instrumental parts. Given Grainger's not uncommon habit of dispensing with a complete score and simply writing out the instrumental or choral parts, the editor had to construct the full score from scratch. The early works proved to be the most challenging. Where complete scores existed they tended to be condensed (the woodwind, brass, and strings intricately notated on two or three staves).

---

[4] Richard Hickox completed many of the choral and orchestral recordings before his untimely death in November 2008.

[5] See Discography.

8. PUTTING GRAINGER INTO PRINT · 109

Example 8.1 *The Song of Solomon*, Part 2, bars 21–6

An example of this problematic situation is his ambitious choral/orchestral setting dating from 1899 of the *Song of Solomon* (Example 8.1).

Grainger's habit of indicating the flow of instrumental lines with dashes sometimes called for the use of a magnifying glass. In some cases, he wrote for instruments not commonly in use by today's orchestras,[6] which would involve transposing or adapting to suit the modern orchestra. In other cases, he suddenly changes the layout of the instrumental lines from one page to the next of his manuscript, and following his scoring becomes rather like a puzzle. Sometimes an instrument will be added which has never appeared in the score until that point. At other times, he may suddenly divide the cellos into eight individual solo parts (see Example 8.2).

When full scores are eventually assembled, checking them for wrong notes can be an exhausting business. A particular instance was Grainger's exciting and moving choral and orchestral work *Thanksgiving Song* (Example 8.3), which had languished since its one and only performance in Florida in 1945. In the process of producing a new score and parts for its Australian premiere at the Adelaide Grainger Festival in October 2003, a great many mistakes were found in the manuscript parts. Thankfully, with some careful editing, the new full score and parts enabled smooth rehearsals, and the performance was a triumph.

Editing Grainger's music has also involved working in close co-operation with performers who have been able to provide useful practical insights, particularly where the manuscript was ambivalent. In a couple of cases, works have had to be transcribed from Grainger's private recordings as these were the only available source. John Lavender and Penelope Thwaites worked with me on several four-hand pieces, including one quite substantial work which Grainger never completed. This consisted of sketches for another version of *The Warriors* which he sub-titled

---

[6] See his inclusion of horns and trumpets in A in *Kleine Variationen-Form* (full score, Dec. 1898: Grainger Museum, MG3/102-7-6).

Example 8.2   *The Wraith of Odin*, bars 28–36

'slow music movement'. Putting together and trying out this work from Grainger's sketches and a (somewhat cryptic) skeletal plan became a lesson of immense value and an insight into Grainger's creative process. In order to distinguish this from the orchestral version of *The Warriors*, we renamed it *The Warriors II*.[7] A related work was found on a piano roll that Grainger had made in 1918. The music contained similar material to the 'slow music' *Warriors* but also included an extended version of the *Bridal Lullaby*. This piece is now published and recorded as *Bridal Lullaby Ramble*.[8] Both Martin Jones and Penelope Thwaites made helpful suggestions in the course of recording the early *Klavierstücke*, and Penelope chose and edited the most convincing of Grainger's childhood works.

In a very few cases, it has been necessary to realise the music from whatever sketches Grainger left. In all instances where this has happened, Grainger's instructions have been followed to the letter. In the case of my realisation of *The Keel Row*, I based the orchestra I used on a similar scoring Grainger was using at the time he sketched this work (*c*.1902). The addition of a four-part chorus, starting with 'whistlers', was also in keeping with Grainger's scoring practices employed at that time.

In his frequent dissatisfaction with a given work, he would experiment with several different versions. Such key works as *Colonial Song, English Dance*, and *Green Bushes* followed this process. From the publisher's standpoint, and with the development of computer technology, it now becomes possible to input the original scoring of a work so that it can be saved as a template; it may then be adapted to accommodate the different instrumental lines of any particular version. The work is ongoing,

---

[7] Percy Grainger, *The Warriors II* (Aylesbury, 1991). Recorded on Pearl SHE 9623.
[8] Recorded by Penelope Thwaites on Chandos CHAN 10205.

Example 8.3 *Thanksgiving Song*, bars 181–92

for there are still many areas (such as his arrangements of other composers) waiting to be explored and brought into print. One particular hope of mine would be to see the commencement of a complete Grainger Edition in print (akin to the complete Delius Edition edited by Robert Threlfall[9]). With digital technology coming 'to the

---

[9] Frederick Delius, *Complete Works*, ed. Thomas Beecham and Robert Threlfall (London, 1951–93).

fore', as Grainger would say, it will be possible for this edition to be made available on-line so that anyone wanting to obtain particular works will be able to do so.

Being so closely involved with Grainger's music, I see all of his works as having importance. Since Grainger never destroyed anything, it is possible to trace the way in which he developed — something far more interesting to the scholar than having only a composer's last thoughts. In a very few cases, there are some tantalising gaps in Grainger's output: works which may be alluded to in his autobiographical writings or letters to colleagues but which appear to be lost. Moreover, Grainger's expressed intention to complete a work did not always materialise. Indeed, in some instances, works were advertised as being published, but were never fully completed.[10] Among the 'alluded to' scores are the first two movements of the *Thanksgiving Song*. The second movement I believe we already have, which is the slow music for *The Warriors* mentioned above. However, the first movement remains a mystery, despite the fact that Grainger states that it is based on the faster elements of the orchestral *Warriors* music. Does it perhaps relate to the 'actual ballet music' he briefly mentions in one of his notebooks? Again and again we can sense the urgency in Grainger's creative powers in deciding to write about a work, even before — if ever — it reached fruition.

Amongst the works that I have been issuing under the Bardic imprint there are certain ones that are of particular importance in the Grainger oeuvre. Some works, although recorded years before I came across the actual manuscripts in the archive at White Plains, had never been put into print. For instance, *The Lonely Desert-Man Sees the Tents of the Happy Tribes*, recorded by John Hopkins and the Sydney Symphony Orchestra,[11] is a natural for others to play and enjoy, and I was delighted to be able to publish it. The list continues with such works as *Afterword*, *Dreamery*, *Random Round*, and the three Danish folk-music settings, *Husband and Wife*, *The Old Woman at the Christening*, and *Under a Bridge*. The discoveries along the way have been intriguing and exciting, and unravelling all the details is like detective work. Grainger never ceases to surprise — for example, with a recent discovery of his arrangement for five cellos of the chorus 'Wach' auf' from Act III of Wagner's *Die Meistersinger*.

Amongst other works, I am especially proud to have published *Lord Maxwell's Goodnight* in all of its various versions. Grainger's ability to identify with the opening four bars of someone else's melody, and then to continue in similar vein has, to my mind, a touch of genius — and what heightened emotion is conveyed by this composite creation![12] *My Love's in Germanie* is another exquisitely heartfelt setting for solo voices and mixed chorus in which the sense of loss is dramatically felt in the closing page. *Colleen Dhas*, a simple tune set for flute, cor anglais, guitar, and strings was Grainger's first attempt at setting a folk melody and is related to

---

[10] A notable example of this is his intended choral setting of *Lord Peter's Stable-Boy*, which appears in an advertisement for his music by G. Schirmer Inc.

[11] *Country Gardens: The Orchestral Works of Percy Grainger*, John Hopkins conducting the Sydney Symphony Orchestra, EMI 5514 (LP: 12″, 33⅓ rpm).

[12] A procedure he also adopts with telling effect in *My Robin is to the Greenwood Gone*. (Ed.)

the folk song *The Pretty Maid Milking her Cow*. It already shows signs of his 'heart-wrenching' harmonies, especially in the string writing.

Since the formation of the Grainger Society I naturally became closely associated with Grainger's original publisher, Schott, and have worked with them in promoting Grainger's music through the publication of lists and catalogues. From 1994 I have worked as their official consultant on all matters relating to Grainger, including all of the works published by Schott. Several new albums of piano and organ music have been the result. This association has now progressed to a formalised co-operation between Bardic Edition and Schott in regard to distribution and sub-publishing of all Bardic Grainger titles.

To be involved in helping to establish further Grainger's name in musical history has been a privilege and one that I hope will long continue. I look forward to the day when all of Grainger's music will be available both in print and in recorded format so that we can do justice to the man. He once wrote: 'I do not mind being "found wanting", as long as I am "weighed in the balance" first. I (in common with most composers) do not like to be condemned unheard.'[13]

---

[13] *Percy Aldridge Grainger's published compositions, 1st editions*. Display legend, Grainger Museum, Melbourne.

9
Grainger's Pianism on Disc
Murray McLachlan

THE RANGE OF RECORDED MATERIAL Grainger has left to posterity is both prolific and fascinating.[1] The repertoire ranges from Bach, or arranged by Bach, to Grainger's own arrangements and compositions. Along the way are substantial offerings from Brahms, Chopin, Grieg, Liszt, Schumann, and Tchaikovsky as well as music by Debussy, Gershwin, Scharwenka, Sinding, and others. There have been numerous remasterings of Grainger's recordings on various labels over the years, but inevitably many of these admirable issues and reissues have long since been deleted. At the time of writing (2009) many important recordings by Percy Grainger are sadly missing from the catalogue. However a significant collection of discs remains currently available, made up either completely or substantially from Grainger's own playing.

Grainger's first known acoustic recordings were made on 16 May 1908 for HMV (originally called 'The Gramophone Company'). They comprised the cadenza from Grieg's concerto, a shortened version of the *Hungarian Rhapsody* no. 12 of Liszt, and the Stanford-Grainger *Irish Dance* no. 1 (*March Jig*, known as *McGuire's Kick*). The last can be heard on a remastered recording,[2] full of his trademark virtuosity and demonic intensity. The playing also demonstrates his contrapuntal understanding and tonal variety, with none of the wilful eccentricity of which Grainger is often (unfairly) accused. There is a subtle rhythmic skill at work in the playing here, something totally removed from mere metronomic correctness, and the clarity and definition of articulation is also special. The final pages are dispatched at breakneck speed (and this recording was made long before the days of editing), yet there is never any loss of focus, accuracy, or definition.

Also notable from Grainger's earliest recordings is his performance of the *Toccata* from Debussy's suite *Pour le piano* (recorded 14 July 1914).[3] The thirty-two-year-old Grainger gives a performance full of wonderfully volatile dynamic inflexions as well as daring surges of tempo. Unexpected inner melodies are highlighted and there is a consistent celebration of off-beat rhythmic inflexions, challenging any narrow-minded notions of 'good taste'. The recording contains other Graingeresque

---

[1] Currently available recordings of Grainger's pianism are listed in the first section of the Discography.
[2] Pearl GEMM 9013.
[3] Pearl GEMM 9957.

hallmarks: articulation that is always strong and clear, as well as the tendency suddenly to drop the dynamic level. Note too the wonderfully expansive *rallentando* on the final page, as well as the characteristic addition of an acciaccatura to repeat the final triumphant C-sharp major chord. Such showmanship ensured even greater applause!

There are many piano rolls made by Grainger for the Duo-Art Company, for whom he worked exclusively from 1915 and for whom he became a best-selling artist (see Plate 2).[4] Many of the piano rolls are duplicated in later recordings of the same repertoire for the Columbia label. One of Grainger's most striking performances for Duo-Art is his remarkable rendering of Grieg's *Lyric Piece*, Op. 43 no. 5, *Poème érotique*, recorded in 1923,[5] and the most emotionally charged recording this writer has yet heard. To describe in detail what Grainger actually does here in terms of rubato, spread chords, fermatas, and unusual voicings would probably take an entire essay in itself — and this is only a 36-bar miniature. All the more remarkable, then, that this performance never breaks Grieg's musical line, never sounds over-laden with ideas, and never sounds complicated. Of course Grainger had a special affinity with Grieg and his music, and the Norwegian master was effusive in his praise of his younger colleague's pianism: 'Possibly I am partial to him because he has actually realised my ideals of piano playing.'[6]

It is fascinating to remember that Grainger actually edited his own piano rolls, and that he was probably unique in being able to do so amongst pianists of his time — or indeed of any time. There are particularly interesting versions of the Grieg[7] and first Tchaikovsky concertos (1921 and 1925 respectively). Only the solo part of the Tchaikovsky was recorded, but it is possible to perform it today with a live orchestral accompaniment if a concert instrument equipped with the Duo-Art mechanism is used. For the Grieg, Grainger edited and arranged the orchestral part so that both solo part and accompaniment fuse together with remarkable lucidity. The spectacular results can be heard in a modern, remastered recording of the original Duo-Art roll.[8] It illustrates how Grainger's many, sometimes controversial, ideas — outlined in his own edition of the concerto — actually work out in practice.

In the Duo-Art recording Grainger's approach to the concerto's famous opening flourish is characteristically monumental. The bass acciaccatura fifths at the opening of the first subject theme (bar 17) are held in the middle pedal, as suggested in the Schirmer edition. Indeed, much use is made of the sostenuto pedal throughout this performance, making for stronger contrapuntal clarity, as well as creating unusually sonorous power in the various crescendi. As well as proving the potency of the middle pedal, Grainger's playing also shows just how practical and effective the recommended fingerings and arrangements of pianistic flourishes in this edition

---

[4] David Dubal, sleeve notes to *Percy Grainger plays Grainger*, Nimbus NI 8809.
[5] Dal Segno DSPRCD020; also Klavier KCD-11075.
[6] Dubal, sleeve notes to *Percy Grainger plays Grainger*, Nimbus NI 8809.
[7] The Grieg roll has been used with live orchestral accompaniment in Australia (1978) and in England at the Henry Wood Promenade Concerts (1988). See also the Discography for recorded versions.
[8] Klavier KCD-11075.

actually are. The accentuation at the top of the arpeggios in the first movement's development could only be achieved by the use of the thumb on the top notes (rather than the fifth finger), whilst in the finale the eighth bar is spread out over four rather than two beats (performers usually either squeeze it into two beats as written, or else extend the bar by an extra crotchet beat).

Detailed examination of the Schirmer edition in conjunction with repeated listening to this recording will elicit many more revelations. But even without a score, the listener will be immediately struck by the degree of rhythmic freedom Grainger displays within an overall sense of discipline and structural command. His contrapuntal clarity and voicing makes the 'two-piano' experience in the piano roll's modern remastered format multifaceted. In Grainger's hands the many tremolandos in the orchestral part are always emotionally charged, often with changes of dynamics and tempo. Such a moment, for example, comes at the end of the first movement exposition, where the impact created is reminiscent of the emotional power generated by the instrumentation in Grainger's masterful choral folk song *Shallow Brown*.[9] Clearly, tremolandos were a Grainger speciality.

His recording of the Chopin B minor sonata for Columbia was made on 10 and 11 June 1925. He was the first artist to record the work (on six discs) using the electrical process,[10] and this performance remains one of the most celebrated recordings of all time. Admired greatly by Benjamin Britten, and described by John Bird as 'the recording to which connoisseurs always turn when Grainger's greatness as a pianist is being discussed',[11] it contains an enormous range of contrasting colours, dynamics, and touches. It is big-boned, monumental, and quite unlike any other performance of the work in the catalogue. It also embraces many of the essential qualities of Grainger's pianism, so deserves special examination.

His creativity with subsidiary 'voices' is especially notable throughout the whole of the sonata's first movement, so that inner melodic fragments (such as the projection of the alto voice from bars 86–90) are often made to glow in revelatory ways. Also striking are the original means by which the overall structure (sometimes felt to be 'problematic') is controlled. Within the expansive aesthetic adopted, Grainger utilises an unusual range of tempo and rubato. This can be heard in the transition towards the second subject, which includes sweeping triplets from bar 17, soaring semiquavers (bars 20–21, 23–9, and 31–8), and enormous *ritenutos* (bars 22 and 39–41). Indeed the final gear shift for the second subject entry at bar 41 takes the music to a tempo almost one-third slower than that adopted at the opening bar! This, of course, goes against the advice of many a respected pedagogue in many a distinguished conservatoire. Indeed it is hard to imagine any modern-day pianist who would wish to emulate Grainger's flexibility, or indeed be capable of imitating it with conviction. Though it certainly takes time to get used to his often volatile

---

[9] Recording by the Monteverdi Choir and John Eliot Gardiner on Philips Classics CD 446 657-2, reissued as Philips Classics CD 475 213-2.
[10] See Dubal, sleeve notes to *Percy Grainger plays Grainger*, Nimbus NI 8809.
[11] Bird, *Percy Grainger* (1976).

accelerandos, strettos, ritenutos, and rallentandos, they are utilised in the same way as his shifts of colour, pedal, and touch.

Such an approach may seem bewildering, but if viewed in terms of sheer primal feeling (think of sorrowful melancholy in the *molto ritenutos* of bars 68 and 71–2, and passionate excitement in the *accelerandos* of bars 66–7 and 70), then they make perfect sense. It is so much more pleasurable to enter Grainger's pianistic treasure house — his recorded legacy — if one lays aside preconceptions and conventions beforehand. His often extreme musical approaches in this recording, as elsewhere, reflect the intensity of his musical instincts — instincts even more extreme when measured against the musical sentiments displayed on disc by many of today's recording artists. Grainger's recordings are often the antithesis of refinement, bringing a quasi-animalistic savagery to the instrument that makes his playing shocking to the unwary. With an almost tiger-like attack, he literally tears into the exciting double-note run at the beginning of the recapitulation in the first movement (bars 140–41). At this particularly awkward corner, one that most pianists recognise as being rather dangerous, Grainger is fearless in his resolve. Passages like this are tackled head on, the result always confident and assured. Grainger's own description of his piano teacher Ferruccio Busoni's playing, 'He did not seem to "feel" his way about the keyboard by touching adjacent notes — as most of us do — he smacked the keys right in the middle',[12] comes to mind, as does his apparent motivation to cultivate sound 'as hard as nails'.[13] This is not Chopin for the faint-hearted.

Grainger's realisation of the outer sections in the scherzo second movement of the sonata may not be perfect in terms of synchronisation between the hands, but the approach is certainly exciting, especially in bars 53–6, when the inner hemiola accentuations are emphasised as the notes pour forth in earnest, giving the impression of an expert gymnast tumbling towards a flourishing conclusion. In the trio section of the movement, Grainger tenderly arpeggiates selected chords to beautiful effect within an expansive tempo, whilst still allowing the tenor voice to sing sonorously.

Within the first two lines of the third, slow movement Grainger uses at least three different tempi, but he soon settles into a wonderful outpouring of lyricism that is consistently subtle and creative. Notes are held, pinpointed, hurried from, delayed, and revoiced. It is as though Grainger is raising his eyebrows, bowing and saluting in turn to a series of key figures in a regal procession, but the overview is consistently natural and unaffected. His approach to the central section of the movement — substantially cut — is particularly free, almost sounding at times like an improvisation. So slow do the triplets eventually become (bars 65–8) that the music almost seems to change into the opening motif of 'Morning' from Grieg's *Peer Gynt*. The *accelerando* that follows (bars 89–98) then comes as a quickening of the pulse, or a sudden rush of blood to the head, rather than as an intellectual miscalculation.

In the finale we have perhaps the greatest example on disc of Grainger's courage as a pianist. His control of rhythm is ruthless and intense, displaying almost demonic force as it continues inexorably through extremely challenging and varied

---

[12] Ibid.
[13] See sleeve notes by Allan Evans to Pearl GEMM 9013.

figurations. Within this remarkable force of intensity and white heat there is a great deal of colouristic subtlety, not only in terms of changing dynamics, but also in terms of variety in pedalling and touch. This leads towards the blazing B-major coda, a veritable Promethean display of glory, charisma and transcendental power.

We cannot ignore Grainger's changes to the text in this recording. They fall into various categories, and in this sense reflect on Grainger's extensive discography as a whole. On the one hand there are the notes and dynamics that modern editions now recognise as being incorrect (e.g. the upbeat to bar 99, as well as various ties, many of which Grainger plays), and on the other there are minor 'fluffs', tiny mistakes that remain tiny even for today's hardened listeners by virtue of the fact that Grainger's artistic priorities are elsewhere (one could cite various left-hand octaves in the development in this connection).

But on a more creative level, there are re-readings which can be extremely beautiful. Accented *forte* triplets are vaporised into *leggiero* piano gestures at bar 30, whilst at the first *forte* passage of the development (from bar 98) Grainger stays *sotto voce*, his piano execution making the music all the more frightening and ominous. Elsewhere there are tenderly realised arpeggiations of block chords (bars 183 and 189) and in the finale, added double octaves and a final rapidly executed double attack (an acciaccatura) on the final chord. These latter additions breathe the world of show business and 'playing to the gallery'. As already noted, Grainger had quite a penchant for flourishes at the ends of pieces, and on disc he can be heard repeating final chords in the finales of the Brahms F-minor sonata, the Grieg concerto, and elsewhere (and why not?).

Turning to a much smaller-scale work, the 1926 recording of Brahms' celebrated Waltz in A flat, Op. 39 no. 15, provides ninety-eight seconds' worth of charming subtlety. Grainger is not afraid to bring the lower voice of the right hand to the fore on the theme's repetition, whilst the time taken on the crests of phrases is as striking as the *accelerandos* that follow. Grainger's dancers impulsively linger, then push forward. The rubato taken is considerable, but always tender and loving.

In contrast, the melodic contour of Schumann's *Romanze* in F sharp (from 1928) is much less subtle, if equally striking, in a rendering evidently devoid of all sentimentality. There is an organ-like depth to the sound in the middle section here, whilst the concluding stretto is red-blooded and passionate, before finally yielding to delicacy and fantasy with a melting arpeggio and a drop in sonority at its conclusion.

A similar lack of sentiment can be heard at the opening of the slow movement in the Brahms F-minor sonata, but then again it could be argued that too many performances miss the 'walking pace' implication normally associated with *andante espressivo*. Grainger's approach reminds one of the outdoors, making the continuation at bar 12 all the more telling. The clarity and strength from bar 26 hints at the use of the middle pedal, and the trills in this section are executed without ambiguity. Modern listeners may find the *accelerandos* that follow in this movement a little too much to take, but few will fail to be impressed by the sheer vibrancy projected in the repeated left-hand octaves of the closing page as the climax is reached. The final chords appear as a descent into the abyss, with extremely penetrating and powerful arpeggios.

Space forbids more than brief mention of Grainger's recording of Schumann's *Études symphoniques*,[14] but it is important to note how magical his realisation of this composer's endless dotted rhythms becomes in the finale (variation 12). By shortening the semiquavers and almost overlapping the dotted quavers, there is a wonderful dovetailing of the latter, which takes away the unyielding aspect that can be all too present in many a modern-day performance. Grainger executes the dots almost to the point of double-dotting them, nearly obscuring the semiquavers in the process. Elsewhere Grainger shows his characteristic strength of articulation and clarity. Perhaps more delicacy would be welcome in places (for example the third variation), but the eleventh étude, realised with very little pedal and even less rubato, convinces through its sheer directness and simplicity.

Grainger's performances of Bach transcriptions show steely finger-work, extensive use of the middle pedal, heroic conceptions, and vast tonal climaxes. His D-minor Toccata (a combination of the Tausig and Busoni arrangements, along with some Grainger) may not be the most accurate, but it certainly brings the gypsy into the world of the neo-Baroque.[15] His performance of the Bach/Liszt G minor Fantasie is equally heroic in terms of expansiveness and improvisatory freedom.[16] The Fugue demonstrates contrapuntal playing of exceptional clarity and technical control.

In lighter vein, Grainger shows considerable charm as well as rhythmic skill in his handling of miniatures, particularly in the collection of piano rolls. Amidst an embarrassment of riches one example will have to suffice: his duet arrangement of Tchaikovsky's *Nutcracker Suite*, with Grainger taking both parts. Both the 'March' and 'Russian Dance' movements show tremendous rhythmic buoyancy as well as impressive pianistic precision and clarity. With the 'Arab Dance', synchronisation between *secondo* and *primo* parts is far from exact — literally waxing and waning in the opening section. Most notable of all in the Suite is the exquisite colouring and voicing in the 'Dance of the Sugar Plum Fairy', particularly in its middle and final sections.

As an interpreter of his own music, Grainger was invariably persuasive, as one might expect. *Percy Grainger plays Grainger* on Nimbus provides us with an outstanding testament to Grainger's brilliance and authority as an interpreter of his own works.[17] Anyone who thinks it is impractical to follow Grainger's extensive and explicit performance directions — and they are often extremely detailed and specific — should listen with score in hand to his own rendering of *Jutish Medley*. Everything requested on the printed page is faithfully realised — a remarkable feat by any standards. At the same time this recording shows just how limited printed directions will always be, for Grainger's interpretation of his own articulation markings is vibrantly creative, leading to a plethora of inflexions. This is perhaps most notable in the section 'The Dragoon's Farewell', where the accompanying figurations under Grainger's hands become aquiline, wave-like, and fluid, confirming that

---

[14] Pearl GEMM 9013.
[15] Pearl GEMM 9957.
[16] Nimbus NI 8808.
[17] Ibid.

the slurs and pianistic groupings on the page are merely a superficial indication of the sonorities that their author had in mind when he wrote them down. In short, Grainger transcends his own text as a performer in terms of voicing, rubato, and variety of touch, showing triumphantly the extent to which his particular re-creative genius can soar. Grainger's pianism was a constant voyage of discovery in which there would never be a definitive 'final word'. Perhaps this is most strongly felt in the recordings in which he plays his own piano music.

The recording legacy ended with some sadness and controversy. His final disc, a 1957 live performance of the Grieg concerto with the Aarhus Municipal Orchestra for Vanguard) was initially withdrawn after only a few hundred pressings, on the presumption that listeners would find it too insecure to accept.[18] By 1957 the ailing Grainger was certainly far from 'accurate' in the sense that modern listeners may understand the word, yet unquestionably his interpretive insights were still exceptional. His association with the work and its composer makes any performance from him worthy of the greatest attention. Moreover, musicians of the standing of Benjamin Britten have praised this version of the Grieg as 'the noblest ever committed to record'.[19] It seems unfair that Grainger's performance had to wait so long in order to enjoy wide circulation. Fortunately today there are listeners who can see beyond wrong notes and who deeply appreciate and admire the unique intensity, authority, and connection that Grainger always brought to his piano playing. Through the refinement and remastering of his recordings, the particular genius of Grainger's pianism will continue to live and be admired by present and indeed future generations of listeners.

---

[18] Transferred to CD on Vanguard Classics USA OVC 8205 (see Discography). Cadenza only: Simax PSC 1809 (1).

[19] Quoted in Bird, *Percy Grainger* (1976).

GRAINGER IN CONTEXT

10

Marvellous Melbourne, 1880-95

David Walker

John and Rose Grainger arrived in Melbourne from Adelaide in October 1880. Two years later, Percy was born in the comfortable seaside suburb of Brighton. By 1895 he and Rose had departed the colony for Germany. Melbourne in these years was a tale of two cities. The 1880s was a decade of extravagant growth. Fortunes were made and speculation was rife. The English journalist George Augustus Sala was astonished by the hustle and bustle of it all. He had not anticipated so much energy, drive, and brassy confidence. Melbourne, he wrote in London's *Daily Telegraph*, 'teems with wealth even as it does with humanity'.[1] Sala coined the term 'Marvellous Melbourne', and it stuck. The Sydney *Bulletin* was unimpressed and referred, with some justification, to 'Marvellous Smellbourne'. Victoria was the leading manufacturing colony. Melbourne had open sewers, grimy factories, and infamously pungent tanneries and breweries. While there was already a great rivalry between Australia's two foremost cities, in the 1880s it was agreed that 'go-ahead' Melbourne was altogether more advanced than 'sleepy' Sydney. The novelist Anthony Trollope considered Melbourne Australia's 'undoubted capital'.[2] R. E. N. Twopeny, the English author of *Town Life in Australia* (1883), went a step further, calling Melbourne 'the metropolis of the Southern Hemisphere.'

When, forty years ago, the distinguished British urban historian Asa Briggs wrote his fine study of the nineteenth-century city, *Victorian Cities*, Melbourne stood out as the wonder city of the newly settled Australian continent. Melbourne's phenomenal rise from the 1850s to the 1880s marked it as one of the great cities of the British Empire. Briggs placed it alongside Manchester, Leeds, Birmingham, and Middlesbrough. Where contemporaries rushed to hyperbole, Briggs offered more sober measures of urban growth: by 1891 the 'rateable value of Melbourne was surpassed in the Empire only by London and, by a small margin, Glasgow'.[3] So phenomenal was Melbourne's economic growth in the fifty years since 1830, when the first small settlement was established, that a plot of land bought for £38 in 1837 would have been worth £250,000 in 1881.[4]

---

[1] Tim Flannery (ed.), *The Birth of Melbourne* (Melbourne, 2002), 327.
[2] Ibid., 281.
[3] Asa Briggs, *Victorian Cities*, new edn (Harmondsworth, 1968), 278.
[4] Ibid., 279.

Melbourne was renowned as a city that 'likes to "go ahead"',[5] and it was regularly compared by overseas visitors to London, Paris, New York, and San Francisco. Trollope compared Melbourne's suburbs to London's Southwark, its Yarra River to the Seine, and the visibility of its poverty to that of London, Paris, and New York. Rudyard Kipling, visiting in 1891, was especially struck by how American Melbourne seemed, 'with its square blocks and straight streets . . . and the trams of Frisco'.[6] According to the poet Francis Adams, the city had a *metropolitan tone* and a *metropolitan look*.[7] Melbourne, he thought, had a 'general sense of movement, of progress, of conscious power', unlike its 'quieter, more civilised' rival Sydney.[8] But Melbourne prided itself on having more books, more men of education and intellect, better-quality shops, more theatres, more music, more racing, cricket, and football, all of which serviced a large 'leisured class'.[9]

Visitors to Melbourne were invariably impressed by the size of its buildings. Twopeny declared, 'There is certainly no city in England which can boast of nearly as many fine buildings, or as large ones, proportionately to its size, as Melbourne.'[10] The 1880s were a boom time for engineers, builders, and architects, John Grainger among them. William Pitt was the best known for his extravagant designs, which, apart from his 'greatest triumph', the Princess Theatre, included the Melbourne Stock Exchange, the city's first coffee palace, and various suburban town halls.[11] Melbourne, Trollope observed, was given the 'appearance of magnificence' by the width of its streets and 'the devotion of very large spaces within the city to public gardens'.[12]

If the city centre was impressive, it was in the suburbs that one really gained a sense of Melbourne's wealth. Twopeny noted that there were 'thousands of large roomy houses and well-kept gardens which betoken incomes of over two thousand a year, and the tens of thousands of villas whose occupants must be spending from a thousand to fifteen hundred a year'.[13] Brighton, where the Graingers lived until 1890, was such a suburb, prosperous, leafy, and expensive. After her separation, Rose took Percy to live in elegant Hawthorn, linked to the city by the railway and electric trams. In the boom years of the 1880s, land speculators were busy creating new suburbs at such a rate that 'by 1888 more allotments had been subdivided in Melbourne than were needed to house the population of London'.[14] Members of the colonial government approved railway lines extending to imaginary suburbs in order to boost the price of land. Melburnians' land-investment mania was fuelled by the fact that virtually anyone could set up a bank; the free market was left to run

---

[5] Flannery (ed.), *The Birth of Melbourne*, 331.
[6] Ibid., 358.
[7] Ibid., 331.
[8] Briggs, *Victorian Cities*, 288.
[9] R. E. N. Twopeny, *Town Life in Australia* (London, 1883; facs. repr. Sydney, 1973), 3–12.
[10] Ibid., 11.
[11] Michael Cannon, *The Land Boomers*, new illus. edn (Melbourne, 1976), 13.
[12] Quoted in Flannery (ed.), *The Birth of Melbourne*, 282.
[13] Twopeny, *Town Life in Australia*, 16.
[14] Cannon, *The Land Boomers*, 40.

a disastrous course. The inevitable crash came in 1891. Two years later, the Sydney *Bulletin* pronounced, with undisguised pleasure, that 'the policy of the continent at large should be to declare Victoria an infected province until its moral character has been renovated and its reputation restored'.[15] The 1890s collapse halted Melbourne's growth and brought wholesale demoralisation and painful soul-searching. Sydney began to overtake Melbourne as Australia's pre-eminent city.

When John and Rose Grainger had arrived in Melbourne in 1880, all the talk was of growth and opportunity. John Grainger had been commissioned to design the Princes Bridge across the Yarra River. There was no more important bridge, for it marked the point at which Melbourne's most gracious boulevard, St Kilda Road, became Swanston Street, the main thoroughfare through the city centre. This was a momentous time in the colony of Victoria. On 30 October 1880, Australia's most infamous bushranger, Ned Kelly, was sentenced to death. On sentencing Kelly, Judge Redmond Barry pronounced the customary words: 'May the Lord have mercy on your soul.' Kelly replied, 'I will go a little further than that and say I will see you there where I go.'[16] On 11 November 1880, Ned Kelly was hanged. Redmond Barry died suddenly just twelve days later.

Barry had been appointed to the Supreme Court of Victoria while still in his late thirties. His contribution in laying the foundations for what would become 'Marvellous Melbourne' was immense: he founded the University of Melbourne and was the driving force behind the creation of the State Library and the Art Gallery. By the 1880s, both institutions were among the finest of their kind in the British Empire. He played a part in founding the Philosophical Institute, the Philharmonic Society, the Horticultural Society, the Melbourne Hospital, and the Melbourne Club, the best appointed club in the colonies[17] and the seat of Melbourne 'power brokers' well into the next century. Barry's achievements exemplify the Melbourne establishment's efforts to dignify the colony's gold-rush prosperity by creating in Melbourne great public monuments to culture and learning.

While it is no doubt easy to overstate the colonial thirst for culture, it was none the less a phenomenon that attracted the attention of visitors. Owning a piano was a mark of good taste, and amateur concerts were frequent. In the 1880s, a visiting Frenchman, Oscar Comettant, noted that some 700,000 pianos had been imported into Australia. This moved him to compose a triumphant march for piano, *Salut à Melbourne*, to mark his visit.[18] The popularity of piano playing and singing, however, was not necessarily matched by ability. 'Most young people think they can sing', Twopeny observed rather tartly, but 'sometimes when you are bored in a drawing-room by bad music and poor singing, you are inclined to think that the colonial love of music is an intolerable nuisance'.[19] While Twopeny was critical, he did not appear to doubt 'the colonial love of music'. 'If you are out for a walk on

---

[15] Briggs, *Victorian Cities*, 291.
[16] Flannery (ed.), *The Birth of Melbourne*, 313.
[17] Twopeny, *Town Life in Australia*, 14.
[18] Jill Eastwood, *Melbourne: The Growth of a Metropolis* (Melbourne, 1983), 82.
[19] Twopeny, *Town Life in Australia*, 218.

a summer's evening, and look into the windows of working-men's cottages', Twopeny added, 'you will see the old folk after their day's labour gathered round the piano in the sitting-room to hear their daughters play.'[20]

Popular culture provided a considerable range of amusements. Bourke Street was the most popular entertainment strip, particularly after the Eastern Market was established in the 'Excitable Eighties' at the cost of £33,000. Bourke Street had been the first city street to feature gas lamps in the 1850s, and in the 1880s Eastern Market was the first building to be lit up with electric lights. Downstairs, a large, rambling indoor market featured peep shows, tattoo shops, hoop-la games, shooting galleries, snake charmers, and fire-eaters. Upstairs, a German brass band provided entertainment for patrons browsing among florists, shops selling 'fancy goods', and crockery. In the 'Naughty Nineties', new technologies brought novel amusements, such as Edison's first recordings of the human voice. 'Customers paid 3d each, put a "doctor's stethoscope" in their ears and heard a human voice reproduced',[21] much to their astonishment.

The more genteel classes enjoyed the European opera companies that frequently toured the colonies. Victorians were never too far behind in their musical tastes: *Carmen* premiered in Melbourne in May 1879, only four years after its world premiere. A review in Melbourne's *Argus* credited its leading lady Rose Hersée with a performance of 'infinite grace and spirit'.[22] Hersée was a well-known opera singer in Melbourne at the time and much loved by Melburnians. Twopeny, however, was not impressed: 'The class of opera company that usually comes out here may be imagined when I tell you that Rose Hersée was a favourite *prima donna!*'[23]

It was generally believed that Melbourne still required the assistance of Europeans to mount a musical performance of quality. This was very much the case with the 1888 Melbourne Centennial International Exhibition. Music was to be a central feature of the Exhibition, but its Executive Commissioners were conscious of steering Melburnian tastes in the right direction. They wanted concerts that were 'both a source of attraction and an educational factor' at the Exhibition. The public would be presented with 'not only the standard classics of the great masters, but also the best works of modern composers, interspersed with pieces of a light and agreeable character, yet possessing artistic value'.[24]

Frederic H. Cowen of London was engaged as Musical Director from May 1888 to March 1889 at the handsome sum of £5,000. He brought 'about 15 good instrumental musicians' to 'strengthen the orchestra',[25] which comprised 73 musicians, accompanied by a massive choir of 709. Cowen was one of Victorian England's most successful composer-conductors. Like Percy Grainger, he had demonstrated a precocious musical talent, composing his first piece of published music, *The Minna-*

---

[20] Twopeny, *Town Life in Australia*, 218.
[21] Ron Testro, 'Lively days in the Eastern Market', *The Argus* (25 March 1939).
[22] Katherine Brisbane (ed.), *Entertaining Australia: An Illustrated History* (Sydney, 1991), 92.
[23] Twopeny, *Town Life in Australia*, 216.
[24] *Official Record of the Melbourne Centennial International Exhibition, 1888-89* (Melbourne, 1890), 259.
[25] Ibid., 260.

Waltz, at the age of six. Indeed, the six-year-old Grainger went to the Exhibition with his mother and governess, who recalled that he was 'very excited over the music . . . He was presented to Frederick Cowen [who] patted Percy on the head & asked what he was going to be when he grew up. Percy answered, "A musician like you."'[26]

Rose Grainger recalled hearing Wagner at the Exhibition for the first time.[27] Melbourne's love affair with Wagner began in the 1870s, when *Lohengrin* was performed at the Prince of Wales Opera House in 1877, only two years after its London premiere. Alberto Zelman, who 'had probably never heard any Wagner performed',[28] conducted, and the German soprano Antonietta Link sang the part of Elsa, having performed this role in Leipzig and Vienna and gained the approval of Wagner himself. 'The *Argus* thought the introduction of Wagner into Melbourne marked "another period of the musical history of the city".'[29]

In selecting the programme of music for the Exhibition of 1888, there was concern that the public would tire of 'more lengthy and elaborate works'.[30] In an extraordinarily democratic move, a plebiscite vote was taken on three occasions to gauge the musical tastes of Melburnians. The top five were: Beethoven's symphony in F ('Pastoral'), Wagner's overture to *Tannhaüser*, Handel's *Largo* for organ, harp, and strings, Liszt's *Hungarian Rhapsody* (no. 1 in F), and Wagner's overture to *Rienzi*. The Executive Committee for the Exhibition noted with pride that the two favourites 'are among the most widely popular in their class in the principal musical centres of the old world. This is an interesting coincidence, and a valuable indication of the correctness of the musical taste which is so rapidly developing in Australia.'[31]

Melbourne's musical culture was fostered by European musicians such as Cowen, who had been performing on tours to the colonies since the gold rush era. The French violinist Camilla Urso toured in 1879, performing with local musicians in Melbourne. She performed the Mendelssohn violin concerto at the Melbourne Town Hall and introduced several new European works to colonial audiences. Many other famous musicians of the era toured, including the Hungarian violinist Eduard Reményi, a friend of Johannes Brahms, who brought gypsy music to Melbourne, Sydney, and Tasmania.[32] Another famous visitor to Melbourne was the French actress Sarah Bernhardt, who toured in 1890. She performed to rapturous audiences in the colonies for two and a half years, always in French, with audiences leafing through the programme to keep up with the dialogue in English.

Along with sudden wealth, Victoria's gold discoveries had brought a diverse population to the colony, including many Chinese gold seekers. The Chinese miners performed Cantonese operas for each other on the goldfields in the 1850s and 1860s,

---

[26] Gillies and Pear (eds.), *Portrait of Percy Grainger*, Eastman Studies in Music, 18 (Rochester, N.Y., 2002), 8.
[27] Ibid., 5.
[28] Brisbane (ed.), *Entertaining Australia*, 88–9.
[29] Ibid.
[30] *Official Record of the Melbourne Centennial International Exhibition*, 264.
[31] Ibid.
[32] Brisbane (ed.), *Entertaining Australia*, 103.

and Chinese opera companies toured Melbourne and the goldfields.[33] By the 1870s and 1880s the number of Chinese in Victoria had significantly decreased, and Chinese musicians similarly decreased: 'The table of "Occupations of Chinese males 1861–1891" shows there were 48 Chinese people recorded as musicians and actors in 1871', and this had fallen to just two Chinese recorded as musicians and actors in 1881.[34] However, several Chinese merchants had risen to positions of respectability in the colony. Included among the members of the Commission appointed to the Centennial International Exhibition on 6 January 1886 was L. Kong Meng Esq., an influential Chinese businessman and trader.[35]

The Melbourne Exhibition was divided into 'courts', or exhibition spaces, which were dominated in size by the colonies of Australia, followed by Britain, America, Germany, France, Austro-Hungary, and then Belgium, Holland, Italy, and so on, all of which were positioned in the main hall. Spaces in annexes were allotted to Asian and Pacific exhibitors, the largest of which was China, followed by Japan and India. It was noted at the end of the section on Chinese exhibits that 'The principal Chinese residents in Melbourne formed a committee for the purpose of representing their country, and exhibited a very interesting collection of articles of Chinese manufacture.'[36] China, it was recorded after the Exhibition 'showed teas, carved cabinets, fancy articles, general goods, and toys, the three last named being remarkable for their gorgeous colouring.'[37]

The Japanese and Indian exhibits were also extensive and popular, and these may well have been seen by a precocious six-year-old Percy Grainger. The Japanese court occupied over 3,200 feet, and though the exhibits were few in number, most of them were very interesting. 'A fine display was made of vases in porcelain and cloisonné ware, other porcelain articles, bronzes, embroidery, and carved work in wood and ivory . . . India was represented by silks, muslins, shawls, and carpets, from Cashmere; bronze and copperware, Benares brassware, fancy articles made from sandalwood, ebony, tortoise-shell, and ivory; gold and silver lace filigree-work, jewellery, precious stones, tobacco, cigars, condiments, and tea.'[38]

The 1888 Centenary Exhibition epitomised the prosperity and confidence of the decade. Yet two years later, when Rose Grainger was a single mother, moving from house to house around the suburbs of Hawthorn and South Yarra, 'the bottom had completely dropped out of the market'.[39] Banks collapsed, and scores of people lost everything. By 1892 there was mass unemployment in Melbourne, malnutrition was

---

[33] Brisbane (ed.), *Entertaining Australia*, 62.
[34] Kathryn Cronin, *Colonial Casualties: Chinese in Early Victoria* (Carlton, Vic., and Beaverton, Ore., 1982), 144, quoted in Wang Zheng-Ting, *Chinese Music in Australia: Victoria, 1850s to mid-1990s* (Melbourne, 1997), 31.
[35] *Official Record of the Melbourne Centennial International Exhibition*, 3.
[36] Ibid., 379.
[37] Ibid., 250.
[38] Ibid., 250–51.
[39] Cannon, *The Land Boomers*, 32.

rife, and the city suffered influenza, typhoid, and measles epidemics.[40] There was a mass exodus from the colony, some 50,000 leaving to find work in South Australia and New South Wales; many returned to England, and many died of disease or committed suicide.[41]

The 1890s brought a significant shift in colonial sentiment. The labour movement, the franchise for women, legislative reforms to banking and business, and moves towards federalism became priorities in a much more sober Melbourne. With it came growing Australian nationalist sentiments that valorised the bush as the symbol of Australianness. This was evident in the Australian art and literature of the 1890s. A group of markedly Australian landscape painters, known as 'the Heidelberg School', was formed in 1891; they were the first to use a distinctively Australian pallette, in paintings that celebrated bush settings and the rural workforce as the embodiment of a national spirit. When Banjo Paterson and Henry Lawson published books of verse, *The Man from Snowy River* in 1895 and *While the Billy Boils* in 1896, it was the bush rather than the city they celebrated. The 'Marvellous Melbourne' of Percy Grainger's childhood had been tainted by greed and excess and the devastating financial collapse that had followed.

---

[40] Fear of infection was one strong reason why Grainger was not sent to school but educated at home.
[41] Cannon, *The Land Boomers*, 48.

11

The Family Background

Penelope Thwaites

GRAINGER'S DECISION to include much personal information in his music Museum was fired by his belief that everything about a composer was relevant to a true understanding of him:

> Destroy nothing, forget nothing. Remember all, say all. Trust life, trust mankind. As long as the picture of truth is placed in the right form (art, science, history) it will offend none![1]

Such an ideal makes it all the more surprising that in the fundamental area of his own parentage there are major omissions. His father, John Harry Grainger, pursued the typical path of many who emigrated to the colonies — he reinvented himself. In many respects the real story of the gifted, upwardly-mobile young architect is more impressive than the romanticised and inaccurate picture he created, and which has been widely accepted. As for Percy's mother, Rose: although the facts of her background are clearer, developments in attitudes to women over the last hundred years suggest that the time is long overdue for a complete re-evaluation of her life.

Scholars will find disappointingly little about the Grainger family in the Grainger Museum. There are, however, three charming letters (1932–3) to Percy from a distant cousin, signing himself only T. Grainger, which suggest how differently things might have turned out. The cousin writes from Stockton-on-Tees, Durham, inviting his relative to visit, and offering a small oil painting of Percy's father, aged three. Although Percy replied with interest, the painting, it seems, was never collected — again, surprising, in the light of his obsessive collecting methods.

Three short biographical accounts of John Grainger — one by his younger friend Amy Chalk, née Black, and two by Winifred Falconer, his companion in later life — concentrate, perhaps inevitably, on John Grainger's professional achievements and his engaging personality, although even the admiring Amy Black admits 'my hero had some grave defects and gave his wife much anxiety'.[2] They all contain factual inaccuracies. In the display legend he prepared for the Museum, Percy expresses admiration for his father as an artist and acknowledges the visual awareness he inherited from him, but elsewhere his tone is restrained. The fact that he has not even

---

[1] Letter from Grainger, 13 Nov. 1936, to Richard Hindle Fowler: with his wife, Dorothy, the first curator of the Grainger Museum.

[2] Amy Chalk (née Black), *John Grainger*, MS A34, Grainger Museum.

consulted (or perhaps did not possess) his father's birth certificate in order to give the correct date, and that he depends largely on vague and inaccurate information, suggests a certain lack of real interest.

To reach the truth about John Grainger's early history is no easy task. One after another of the facts recorded by his early biographers and then repeated by others (including his son) turns out to be either untrue or else impossible to substantiate. John Grainger's assertion that he came from a 'Northumbrian family of builders, architects and engineers' certainly fitted in with his own aspirations as an architect. Richard Grainger (1797–1861), the Newcastle property developer whose partnership with the architect John Dobson, amongst others, transformed Newcastle, rose from humble beginnings, worked hard, married well, and went on to make a notable career. Richard was a contemporary of Percy's great-grandfather, Jacob (1796–1880), but, despite strenuous attempts for the purposes of this essay to find some link between the two, there appears to be none.

The Public Record Office in Durham shows that Grainger's father's family are recorded from the late eighteenth century in the southern area of County Durham as working people — carpenters, joiners, and farm-workers. Visitors to the church of St Michael, Heighington, will be able to see five of the Grainger family graves. Surrounded by rolling countryside, the nearby hamlet of Denton[3] is where Percy's great-grandfather, Jacob Grainger, married Jane Willis in 1818 and with her brought up their family of six (a seventh dying in infancy). Born in Auckland Bolam, Jacob is described on his son John's marriage certificate as a 'carpenter and joiner' and later as 'farmer' with a holding of thirty-six acres. Appropriately, the name Grainger (or Granger) came from the Old French *grangier*, meaning a farm-bailiff, or one in charge of a grange.[4] This was exactly the occupation of the Lincolnshire folk singer Joseph Taylor, whom Grainger so admired.[5]

Jacob Grainger lived to an impressive age, and the home he occupied latterly at Walworth Gate was a focus for the family, including Percy's father, John Harry, as a child, as well as John's two older sisters, both recorded in 1861 as staying with their grandfather. Jane kept house for him, and Annie worked as a dairymaid. Whether any family members were musical is not known, but they would surely have sung and heard the folk songs of the area, and Percy's father is recalled as performing some of them.[6] The Grainger family came from precisely the background celebrated by Percy again and again, both in his music and in his almost romantic love

---

[3] See photograph of Denton Chapel, Plate 39.
[4] Since Grainger's Anglo-Saxon convictions led him to write of his sense of 'humiliation' at the Battle of Hastings, and the wish that his music should 'make good' for it, there is some irony in the fact that, according to several sources, both the names 'Percy' (meaning 'to pierce or breach') and 'Grainger' entered England in the wake of the Norman Conquest. 'Aldridge', on the other hand, stemmed from Old English: Ælfric (elf-ruler) or Æthelric (noble ruler). In 1911, Grainger changed his name from George Percy Grainger to Percy Aldridge Grainger. Grainger's knowledge of his mother's English forebears is based on the Australian branch's recollections. Did he ever visit the site of 'Aldridge's Horse Repository' in St Martin's Lane, London (see Plate 15) — a considerable family business?
[5] Described by Grainger in the preface to *Lincolnshire Posy*.
[6] Amy Chalk, *John Grainger*.

for the yeoman traditions of Old England. It seems extraordinary that he had (apparently) no knowledge of these forebears.

The Graingers were affected, like so many rural families, by the great nineteenth-century migrations to major industrial centres. While the rest of the family carried on their traditional trades locally, Jacob's second son, John (1821–1897), left for London and an apprenticeship which would eventually make him a Master Tailor. He married a shirt-maker, Mary Ann Parsons, the daughter of a compositor, in 1843 in the borough of Westminster.[7] Their children,[8] born between 1844 and 1865, were Jane and Annie (mentioned above), Herodias (Rhode), Mary Ann, Elizabeth, John Harry (Percy's father), Henry, Frederick, Henrietta, and Arthur. The latter appears, many years later, as the recipient of a letter from his brother John in Australia, indicating at least one remaining link at that time.[9] Despite having such a large family in London, there is no evidence that in the years he lived there (between 1901 and 1914) Percy ever made contact with any of them. Certainly his father's two oldest sisters, Jane and Annie, were alive at the time, Jane listed in the 1901 census as the proprietor of a coffee shop in Barons Court, Fulham. The clue may lie in the personal history of his father, John Harry Grainger.

John's birth certificate shows that he was born at 1 New Street, Westminster (now Maunsell Street, London SW1). Even the dates of his birth have caused confusion, as his birth certificate gives the date as 30 November 1854. But since the birth was only registered in 1855, the latter year has been wrongly given by biographers as his birth year. He may well have lived with his Durham relatives in his early years, as stated — the three-year-old portrait suggests it, as does the evidence of other siblings staying with their grandfather Jacob.

There is in fact no sign that John Harry Grainger lived with his parents. Given their large family, it would have been quite possible, as was often the custom at the time, for the boy to be 'farmed out' to a relative. One could speculate on the effect this might have had. John Grainger certainly showed signs at times of living in a fantasy world. Winifred Falconer writes that he attended a 'monastery school at Yvetot in France' when he was around fourteen years old. Possibly by this time he had moved back from Durham to London and was staying with the unidentified 'uncle' whom Falconer also mentions.[10] The gentleman in question, it appears, was a friend of John Henry (later Cardinal) Newman, and may even have suggested the monastery school. The Roman Catholic influence remained with JHG for life.

The time in France would fit with John Grainger's affection for French revivalist architecture, although, as George Tibbits points out,[11] his style was eclectic.[12] Less

---

[7] Copy of marriage certificate in the Grainger Museum.

[8] Census records 1851, 1861, 1871.

[9] Grainger Museum collection, letter from John Harry Grainger to his brother Arthur.

[10] Falconer's second (typed) account mentions that 'he went to live with an uncle (in) Westminster'.

[11] George Tibbits, 'John Grainger in Australia', in Brian Allison (ed.), *John Harry Grainger: Architect and Civil Engineer* (Melbourne, 2007).

[12] JHG was destined to return triumphantly to France in 1900, when, as Chief Government Architect for Western Australia, his designs for the West Australian Court at the Great Exposition

11. THE FAMILY BACKGROUND

plausible is JHG's claim to have been in Paris during the 1870/71 siege. The claim would appear to conflict with his assertion in a later (unsuccessful) application to join the Royal Victorian Institute of Architects[13] that he was 'apprenticed to a civil engineer at the age of fifteen'.[14] That would have been in 1869/70. He is listed in the 1871 census as a 'clerk' living with his brother Henry (listed as 'tailor's apprentice') at 5 Prince Street, Westminster.[15] It is physically possible that he could, Scarlet Pimpernel-like, have nipped across the Channel, but it seems highly unlikely for one just beginning his apprenticeship. This census gives a number of illuminating facts about John Grainger senior's large family. While John junior and his brother Henry were lodging together in Prince Street, his second eldest sister, Annie, and her husband, the licensed victualler George Cave, were running a popular public house known as The Blue Posts at 59 Haymarket, just off Trafalgar Square. Three of her sisters, Jane (soon to marry a caterer, Phineas Romanel), Mary Ann, and Elizabeth were lodging there. Presumably their seventeen-year-old brother was a regular visitor.

John's apprenticeship was to a well-known engineer who had worked with the Metropolitan and District Railway, William Wilson, MICE, originally from Newcastle. Wilson's offices were at 4 Victoria Street, St Margaret's, Westminster, and later, almost next door at 13 Dean's Yard. Contrary to the story related by all his major biographers, there is no sign in the archives of John Harry Grainger as a pupil of Westminster School. But the ancient school does occupy buildings precisely in Dean's Yard. If JHG spent the next seven or eight years as an apprentice in civil engineering with Wilson, he might have considered it irresistible to throw in that useful adjustment of the facts. According to the Australian architect David Beauchamp,[16] he also studied architecture under I. J. Eden and W. K. Green of Westminster. One way and another, John Harry was moving up in the world. According to his account, the uncle who had taken him on introduced him to the world of classical music. The concerts they attended 'at the Queen's Hall'[17] were probably the 'Monday Pops' concerts, a title JHG later used for the concerts he organised in Adelaide. He developed an impressive knowledge of music, including opera, later remarked upon in the memoir of a musical colleague in Adelaide, Herman Schrader.[18] Percy

---

in Paris won him silver and gold medals, as well as membership of the Société Centrale des Architects Françaises.

[13] i.e. in the state of Victoria, Australia.

[14] Grainger's application for RVIA Fellowship, dated 17 Sept. 1906, RVIA Papers, Australian Manuscript Collection, State Library of Victoria, Australia.

[15] Probably Princes Street, London W1.

[16] George Tibbits and David Beauchamp, 'John Harry Grainger, Engineer and Architect', unpublished paper for the 3rd Australasian Engineering Heritage Conference, 2009.

[17] Queen's Hall was not built until 1893. This would have been St James's Hall, Piccadilly, London W1, which opened on 25 March 1858 with frontages on Regent Street and Piccadilly. It was London's principal concert hall until it was demolished in 1905. Famous for its Monday and Saturday Popular Classical Concerts, the St James's concerts brought access to musical entertainment within the reach of the middle and working classes.

[18] Hermann Schrader, *Reminiscences of J. H. Grainger and the Adelaide String Quartet*, MS in the Grainger Museum.

regarded his father's musical tastes as conservative, and he never remembered any paternal praise for his own compositions — merely remarks of dissatisfaction and some patronage. But he admired the trenchant way John Grainger would express his views about the great masterpieces. And his father was to have 'a decisive effect on my compositional life' when in 1897 he provided him with several books of Kipling's works. Setting Kipling to music became a life-long theme.

In the RVIA application John Grainger also states that during 'the mid-1870s' he travelled through France, Spain, and Italy. With the reservation that JHG was unreliable with facts, this might well have been true; if he was emerging as a talented young architect, his boss may have considered that he would make good use of the education, and, therefore, perhaps have financed it. But also, presumably, he would have expected a longer association with his young beneficiary. Another possibility is that JHG's uncle financed him — in which case, again, his departure for Australia in 1877 would not have been well regarded. Falconer's account mentions a 'quarrel with his uncle'.

John's departure for Australia, aged twenty-three, seems to have been expedient. It is claimed that having got a young woman pregnant, he decided to emigrate to the colonies. (The woman in question was later to write to Rose Grainger wishing her all the unhappiness she herself had endured.)[19] As it happened, the South Australian government was calling for draughtsmen, and John was accepted. He did not become, as Falconer states, 'Assistant Architect and Engineer' — he was employed as a draughtsman by the man who actually filled that position.[20] Nevertheless, John — cultured, enterprising, and enthusiastic — did well. He soon set up his own practice and before long was winning prizes for his architectural designs. One of the most notable was a design for the Princes Bridge which leads into the city of Melbourne. It is strongly based on London's Victoria Bridge — a construction with which John Grainger would have been completely familiar. His later failure to be accepted by the Royal Victorian Institute of Architects suggests that he may have been unable to produce formal qualifications, but the proof of his brilliance can be seen in a whole range of buildings — including Melbourne's Masonic Hall, the Perth Town Hall, and the Auckland Public Library — well documented in a detailed publication from the University of Melbourne.[21] Music remained a passion for John. He instigated Adelaide's first string quartet, running regular chamber concerts at his rooms, and thereby gained the interest of some leading lights in the burgeoning city. His extraordinary house for Sir Thomas Elder[22] can still be seen in the Adelaide hills — a touch of baronial Scotland in the bush. His design for the equally wealthy Barr Smith family's mansion was on the grandest scale.

---

[19] Gillies, Pear, and Carroll (eds.), *Self-Portrait of Percy Grainger*, 25: 'My Father in my Childhood' (1954).

[20] Extracts from S.A. Library Division Archives, 'J. H. Grainger — Adelaide Appointment 1876–78', quoted in Peter Kinsella, *John Harry Grainger* (Grainger Museum).

[21] Allison (ed.), *John Harry Grainger: Architect and Civil Engineer*.

[22] A wealthy entrepreneur who founded the Elder Conservatorium of Music. His partnership with Robert Barr Smith became the firm Elder Smith.

11. THE FAMILY BACKGROUND

John Grainger's rooms were situated near a large family hotel owned by George Aldridge. According to Cara Aldridge, a cousin of Percy Grainger, the Aldridges had been associated with a coaching business in London.[23] In Australia their name is still synonymous with horse-breeding and horse-racing. Grandfather George (b. London, 1818) left his first wife to emigrate to Australia, arriving in Adelaide in 1847 with his new love, Sarah Jane Brown, their baby son George, and Sarah Jane's mother. After working hard at several interim jobs, George senior eventually became successful as an hotelier in Adelaide. He and Sarah raised their nine children there, formalising their marriage on 4 September 1856[24]. In common with many early pioneering families, they evinced a certain spirit of enterprise, toughness, and very hard work, supported necessarily by the family structure itself. Family was the only element that could be relied upon in an often hostile and insecure environment. The Aldridge pride in their fair-haired and blue-eyed characteristics has been disapprovingly emphasised. It certainly did not prevent them from welcoming into their midst the dark-haired, dark-eyed John Grainger. He became popular with the family, sharing a drink with George Aldridge and no doubt feeling thoroughly at home in such surroundings. The Aldridge sons approved of his sporting pursuits; the daughters enjoyed his reading aloud to them from the classics. George Aldridge's death in 1879 hastened the need for his daughters to be settled. Rose, the youngest and prettiest, had already attracted John's attention, and they were married on 1 October 1880. (As it happened, the eldest daughter, Emma, died in 1881. Clara remained unmarried and was the ongoing 'rock' for the family, looking after, first, her mentally retarded younger brother, Frank, and then her widowed mother, outliving all eight of her siblings by many years. Until her death in 1944 she remained Percy Grainger's fondest link with his family, and her house, Claremont, housed his first museum collection.)

Rosa Annie — later Rose — (b. 1861) inherited the strength and combative spirit of her father. But she was far more art-worshipping than any of her relatives, playing the piano well and appreciating with passion the music at the concerts organised by John Grainger. There is little doubt that the economic and social pressures of the day were a factor in the marriage between the two, but there also seems to have been genuine affection at the outset.[25] Percy later described the attraction between the culture-mad young woman and a man of similar enthusiasms: 'I can quite see how my mother must have felt herself tempted to take the leap off the yeoman Aldridge furrow into the airier, less earthbound Grainger brain-life.' Moving to Melbourne after their marriage, the gifted young couple led a comfortable life in a well-

---

[23] 'The Aldridge Family: Penelope Thwaites meets Cara Ham', *Grainger Society Journal*, 6/2 (1984). The 1852 London Post Office Directory mentions Aldridge's Horse Repository in St Martin's Lane. The 1846 Commercial Directory also mentions Aldridge's Repository, 6 Upper Street, St Martin's Lane. The rate books record as occupants (amonst others) James Aldridge 1776–82, Thomas Aldridge 1783–6 and Joseph Aldridge 1787–1826.

[24] A private ceremony by John Gardner, Minister of the Free Presbyterian Church. 'Aunty Clara's Aldridge History' includes the marriage certificate.

[25] 'Aunty Clara's Aldridge History', p. 7, relates her role in assisting their courtship.

appointed house in Brighton, Melbourne. They had a circle of congenial friends. John's architectural work flourished.

The birth of a son, named George Percy Grainger,[26] on 8 July 1882 brought both parents pride and delight, but it was soon to be blighted. Percy's own account of this turning point appears in a letter to Karen Kellerman in 1926, four years after his mother's death:[27]

> Soon after I was born . . . my father got syphilis and infected my mother with it in a quite unnecessary way. That is to say, my mother was staying in the country, while father caught the disease in the town, travelled to her, infected her and told her the whole thing afterwards . . . My mother wasn't bitter towards him although she thought that to lose one's health was the worst thing that could happen to anyone. After that she never lived with him as man and wife because she did not want to give birth to sick children. I have seen her drive him out of the room with a riding-whip when he was drunk and unwilling to follow her wishes in this matter.

Percy's nurse, Mabel Todhunter, was with the Graingers from 1886 until 1894. In an otherwise idyllic written recollection of her charge, including happy children's parties, outings and so on, she enclosed her own account of 'things one cannot talk about':

> We all had some very nice times together and then your father got worse and worse. Came home so very drunk and fell down in the hall as he opened the front door, and your mother and myself used to pull him up. I got him to his room and when he was like that we used to go to bed and put the chest of drawers in front of our bedroom door. Your mother was very frightened of him when he was very bad. She was so frightened he might hurt you.[28]

Grainger's own account continues:

> She kept house for him until I was about 8–9 years old, as she hoped to be able to get the better of his drunkenness. But when she realised that it was no good, then they separated — in all friendship.[29] Shortly after that the disease manifested itself in terrible neuralgic pains, and she was never really well again thereafter. If she wrote or read she got pains in her eyes or arms, when she walked, in her back . . . her face drawn with pain was dreadful to see. I will never forget it.

---

[26] Perhaps John Grainger had in mind naming his son after the aristocratic Percy family of Northumberland.

[27] The whole of this long letter to his former lover (then Karen Holten), puts a number of misrepresented facts in context. It is reproduced in Gillies and Pear (eds.), *The All-Round Man: Selected Letters of Percy Grainger, 1914–1961* (Oxford, 1994), 76–82.

[28] From an unpublished recollection, attached to a letter to Percy Grainger, 30 March 1938, held in the Grainger Museum, and reproduced in Gillies and Pear (eds.), *Portrait of Percy Grainger*.

[29] Around this time, an attempt by John in 1890 to effect a reconciliation with his English relatives during a visit to London appears to have failed.

11. THE FAMILY BACKGROUND

Any medical dictionary spells out the shocking effects of syphilis — which before penicillin were often untreatable. John Grainger was to end his days, cared for by Winifred Falconer, as a semi-paralysed wreck. From the age of twenty-two, and for her remaining thirty-nine years, Rose experienced the disease's escalating attack on both body and brain. Much for which she has been routinely criticised can surely be related to her pitiful condition. What it must have been like *for her* to have to deal with the recurrent nightmare of a violent syphilitic drunkard — with the accompanying fear and loneliness — is an aspect barely acknowledged in most accounts. Instead she has usually been made the villain of the piece for standing up to him. Nor is it acknowledged how fortunate was John that, owing to his wife's discretion, her family had no idea of the truth and offered him their warm hospitality when the marriage finally ended. While she was still trying to hold the family together, Rose dragged herself around to piano pupils to be sure there was enough to live on. At times she had to borrow money, but she managed to keep private the humiliations of their life. After all, seen in good times, John was a fond father, lending financial support and proud of his wife, and they had a warm circle of friends. But Rose must have needed all the stoicism of the Norse heroes she so much admired in order to cope.

After they separated, Rose and John continued to write regularly to each other. Rose did not alienate Percy from his father, as one can see from his accounts of their meetings, and John remained fully apprised of his son's progress. In 1893, in a religious mood, he prepared a beautifully-written book for his son, with a Bible quotation for each day of the year. Percy had been baptised, although not as a Catholic, and they very occasionally went to church. Rose was less enthusiastically religious. It is hardly surprising that, isolated as she was in a predicament that could not be mentioned, Rose should concentrate all her energies and devotion on her unusually gifted son. Here, at least, was one way in which she could make sense of her — and their — life. She turned out to be a dedicated if selective educator, teaching him at the piano for two hours a day, as well as reading with him Hans Christian Andersen, Walter Scott, Dickens, and others of the classics, and overseeing his lessons in drawing, writing, history, and natural science. Outdoor pursuits included gardening and various sports (his father encouraged football and cricket). Childhood friends joined in. As Percy grew older, his mother found the best music and art teachers in Melbourne and worked effectively to find supporters and sponsors. By the age of eleven, Percy was composing quite ambitiously, as his touchingly aspiring *Birthday Gift* (1893) attests. The critical success of his several public appearances as 'The Young Prodigy, Master Percy Grainger', sealed his fate. With the help of £50 raised by friends, Percy and his mother set sail for Europe in 1895, so that he could commence his studies at the Hoch Conservatorium in Frankfurt.

Rose trained her son in habits of discipline and hard work that followed him throughout his life. Her belief in the common contemporary maxim 'spare the rod and spoil the child' would have been seen simply as her duty.[30] His mother's love was never in doubt, but what does become clear from reading her letters is that, for

---

[30] To claim this as the sole reason for Grainger's later predilections would appear to circumvent historical context: corporal punishment was taken for granted in Victorian families, including

Rose, everything depended on her son's love for her, sometimes driving her to unattractive 'tests' of his feelings and putting him under the wrong kind of pressure. Her earliest surviving letter to the ten-year-old is worrying in its tugging intensity — and so her letters continued through the years — always anxious, always desperate to direct and protect.[31] However, it should be acknowledged, in all fairness, that the letters reflect Rose as she was when away from her son, and therefore do not reflect the fun and companionship they enjoyed when they were together, something to which Grainger himself often refers. Rose's underlying anxiety, exacerbated by the advance of syphilis, probably brought about the two major nervous breakdowns (1899 and 1900) during Percy's years of study in Frankfurt. The truth of those breakdowns is discussed in a little-known interview recorded in 1981 by Grainger's doctor in later life, the Norwegian K. K. Nygaard. Dismayed by the many accusations against Rose which had begun to emerge in print, and speaking with Grainger's close associate, Burnett Cross, Dr Nygaard elucidates the relationship between Percy and his mother, as he came to see it. Describing it as an 'heroic tragedy', Nygaard draws on his own conversations with Grainger about those Frankfurt years.

By 1898 Percy was in the midst of an adolescence of intense compositional creativity. He was boiling with ideas; he was discovering what it was to fall in love. Yet his life was hemmed around with the pressure to succeed as a pianist (not least for economic reasons) and to maintain strict disciplines of work. The sexual turmoil must have an outlet, and he found it, with huge relief, in real and imagined acts of self-harm, and in flagellation — mostly self-affecting, but ultimately as part of his love affairs. Nygaard suggests convincingly that this discovery played its part in his mother's initial breakdown. She feared that this addiction risked the very social disgrace she had been so desperately trying to avoid. It could end his career. At the same time, Percy heard from her, for the first time, the full truth of his parents' separation and the nature of her illness. An agreement was reached. Rose would 'manage' his professional and social affairs, allowing him to develop musically and support them both, avoiding the risk of scandal. Nygaard expresses his conclusion that Grainger 'was not a weak mind but a willing co-worker in the family problem . . . Percy would not have developed his gift without the protection of a great mother'.[32]

In her introduction to the collection of Grainger letters, *The Farthest North of Humanness*, Kay Dreyfus spells out, particularly in reference to their years in London (1901–14), the unremitting work that was Rose Grainger's contribution to her son's career. The spectres of poverty and failure were ever present in that highly competitive environment. All her life, whether in Frankfurt, London, or New York (where they settled in 1914) she was there to support him; writing endless professional letters, entertaining his friends, organising his teaching schedules, advising

---

affectionate ones, and the Aldridges and Graingers were no exception. The emotive word 'whipping' was Victorian for 'smacking' or more extremely 'beating'.

[31] Interestingly, his replies, written later in the thick of a successfully expanding career, are more often than not, breezy, amusing, and upbeat: see Dreyfus (ed.), *The Farthest North of Humanness*.

[32] The transcript and the tape, dated 9 January 1983, are available for research purposes from the Percy Grainger Society UK and from the Grainger Museum.

Plate 15. Aldridge's Horse Repository, St Martin's Lane, London, 1883

Plate 16. George Percy Grainger, aged three, with his mother

Plate 17. John Harry Grainger, Percy's father, around 1892

Plate 18. The young JHG sporting a monocle

Plate 19. Grainger's birthplace in the 1890s. The picket fence he remembered has been replaced by corrugated iron

Plate 20. John Grainger's Princes Bridge, as it looks today

Plate 21. The young prodigy, about the time he began to study with Louis Pabst, 1892

Plate 22. Page from an early composition, 1893

Plate 23. One of Grainger's early supporters, G. W. Marshall-Hall, painted by Tom Roberts, one of the 'Heidelberg School' of painters

Plate 24. Residents of the pension, Frankfurt-am-Main, 1895; Percy and Rose (seated) on the left

Plate 25. Fellow students: Grainger with Cyril Scott, Frankfurt, 1900

Plate 26. Percy with his uncle, James Henry Aldridge, Adelaide, probably 1909

Plate 27. The signed (later framed) photograph from Grieg inscribed 'Mr Percy Grainger with my best thank[s] for your splendid folk-songs for mixed voices.' This was kept in Grainger's music room in White Plains, where it remains today

Plate 28. Grainger, 1923, with Frederick Delius and his artist wife, Jelka

Plate 29. The Lincolnshire folk singer George Gouldthorpe and fellow folk singer, c.1906

Plate 30. Exact replica (at White Plains) of the Edison Bell phonograph used by Grainger to collect folk tunes

Plate 31. The legendary Evald Tang Kristensen (seated) notates as Grainger encourages a Danish folk singer. The photo is inscribed 'Lindebo-Herning 26.8.1922'

him on professional diplomacy, somehow earning or finding the money to create the background of his life: something any extremely busy artist needs. She did all this as an intermittent invalid. Her eventual suicide on 30 April 1922 came at a point of particular mental disturbance and vulnerability during Percy's prolonged absence on a concert tour. Whether her decision to remove herself as the decisive element in his life was rational or irrational, it matches the 'drastic' Nordic spirit he so admired, the stoic self-sacrifice of the hero.

Rose Grainger's tragedy has been two-fold. The physical and mental injury done to her at the age of twenty-two led, as we have seen, to lifelong physical and mental decline. But that has been followed in almost all biographical accounts by an empathy-free assessment — an unthinking, overwhelmingly negative picture. It is high time for a more balanced view. Without the heroic efforts of Rose, we would have had no Percy Grainger.

Four years after the trauma of his mother's death, Percy was to meet the Swedish artist Ella Viola Ström, who became his ideal helpmate and wife of thirty-three years. Gifted herself in many ways, Ella was a remarkable support to him, and he often referred to his marriage as one of the few real successes of his life (see Plates 4–7). His mother's sister, always referred to as 'Aunty Clara', remained a much-loved fixed point in his life until her death in 1944. As a whole, the Aldridge family gave Percy a sense of stability and orientation. Several of them remember him to this day with fondness and some wonder.[33] As a family, they were not musicians, and Percy never expected them to attend his concerts. Belatedly, they realised and were proud of his success. But the story of his wealthy and successful Uncle Jim (known as 'JH') illustrates how things were in his childhood. An impoverished Rose asked her brother if he could possibly help with buying a piano for his young prodigy of a nephew. 'A *piano*? No! Now, if he wanted a *horse* . . . well that would be a different matter!'

Grainger's, perhaps surprising, assertion that his music could only be understood as 'a pilgrimage to sorrow' is no more than the truth. He had a lifelong preoccupation with the tragedies of life and death, well concealed by his effervescent public and social manner. The story of his parentage makes clear why this was so. While feeling the sadness of it, one can only salute the way this extraordinary musician turned his experiences, good and bad, into a wealth of beautiful music.

---

[33] See Chap. 17, 'Reflection and Reminiscence'.

12

An Australian Composer?

Roger Covell

GRAINGER'S AUSTRALIANISM is aggressive, persistent, and from some points of view probably irritating, perhaps even counting as one of his irrational fixations such as his taste for flagellation or his persistence in placing Delius and even Cyril Scott among the greatest masters of music. After all, he left Australia when he was not quite thirteen, established his careers as pianist and composer in Britain and continental Europe, and then, immediately after the onset of World War I, moved to the United States, where he joined the US Army's band section, became a master of writing for American wind ensembles and a US citizen, and found in that country his most enthusiastic and faithful audience, a long-delayed but essentially happy marriage, a secure if sometimes querulous retirement, modest but mostly reliable prosperity, and as reconciled a death, despite his final cancer, as was possible for such an ardently unappeasable and self-critical spirit. If life choices were held to speak louder than words, America would have every right to claim him in absolute terms.

Nations whose existences have been defined in recent centuries by immigration, such as the United States and Australia, have long been aware, however, that the only tenable criterion for whether a composer, painter, author, or any other artist is an American or Australian embodiment of that art is the self-identification elected by that person. A composer who arrives in Australia from Britain as recently as the 1970s but who decides that he wishes to be counted as an Australian composer, as for example Roger Smalley has done, cannot be denied his right to do this, despite his birth, professional training, and earlier career in Britain and elsewhere. As older national identities in Europe, the Americas, Asia, Africa, or Oceania become increasingly extended in the present age by large-scale immigration, the same, seemingly arbitrary, choices are likely to be made by their most recently acquired adult citizens. The new identity that may be prompted by a change of residence can be withheld or denied, of course, in later years; yet in the years immediately before his death, Grainger expressed to some of his oldest, most sympathetic professional associates and in response to general inquiries about his artistic purposes his unaltered belief that one of the reasons he wrote music was 'in the hopes of bringing honor and fame to my native land: Australia'.[1]

---

[1] Gillies and Clunies Ross (eds.), *Grainger on Music*, 375–6, from a response to a 1955 Questionnaire.

Was this merely a form of words, repeated with variations to countless correspondents and inquirers until it became a habit and then maintained because any denial of it would have seemed the action of a turncoat? (We know how sensitive Grainger was to British accusations of unpatriotic cowardice after his sudden journey to the United States in September 1914 and how bitterly he flayed himself in words for this action.[2]) There are at least two bodies of evidence that argue against this rather cynical interpretation of Grainger's motives for emphasising a fundamental Australian allegiance. The first and most concrete is represented by an examination of his seven visits to Australia between August 1903 and June 1956. A positive interpretation of these visits in terms of Grainger's claimed commitment to an Australian identity does not rest on their frequency or duration: collectively they lasted less than five years, even if we take the most generous view of their extent and include visits to New Zealand and at least part of the substantial time necessarily spent at the time in sea travel.[3] The first two visits, in 1903–4 and 1908–9, in which Grainger travelled as an associate artist of the Australian contralto Ada Crossley, were part of the tradition of the triumphant return home after success in Europe and the United States that was a rite of passage for Australian singers and instrumentalists. It was what Australian performers did when they had made it abroad. Grainger, like Crossley, was contributing to the same kind of homecoming as Nellie Melba (Helen Porter Mitchell), Grainger's wary and (by him) disliked colleague,[4] made repeatedly from 1902. Such visits were usually very rewarding financially, and it would have been unlike Grainger or his mother, Rose, to pass up an opportunity to add significantly to their still very uncertain finances at this time. The fact that Grainger took part in these two tours cannot be cited as evidence in itself of any lasting commitment to Australia.

The five return visits he made after World War I are in a different category. These allowed him to measure his reactions to the country of his birth and its people, after a further absence (contributed to by the war) of fifteen years and against his now much more developed knowledge of many of the pre-eminent centres of Western concert music and the character and customs of their people. Many expatriates might have felt irrevocably sundered from their relationship with their natal country after such a passage of time and the changes in social and cultural organisation inevitably apparent to them within the principal cities. Certainly Grainger's recent adoption of American citizenship — and this at a time when the combination of this identity with any other comparable national status was impossible — would have given him the perfect excuse, had he chosen to invoke it, to decide to withdraw from his stated wish in earlier years to do honour to his birthplace through his career and creative activities. Cyril Scott, whose friendship with Grainger went back to their student days

---

[2] See his 'remarks on Rose Grainger's letters of May 12, 1917 & June 26, 1917 to Cecil J. Sharp', included as an 'Epilogue' in Dreyfus (ed.), *The Farthest North of Humanness*, 527–9.

[3] One reason for doing this is the fact that Grainger enlarged his knowledge of Australia and Australians through his shipboard encounters with Australians previously unknown to him; see, for example, n. 15 below.

[4] Gillies and Pear (eds.), *Portrait of Percy Grainger*, 81, reproducing a passage quoted in Thérèse Radic, *Melba: The Voice of Australia* (Melbourne, 1986), 146.

in Frankfurt, recorded in 1936, at the time when the Australian was in the thick of planning and establishing his museum in Melbourne, how surprised he was at the persistence of Grainger's strongly proclaimed patriotism: 'When I first met Grainger, some forty years ago, I regarded this exaggerated patriotism as merely a youthful enthusiasm to be out-grown as the years went by. But I was doomed to be wrong. Although Grainger has in the interim become an American citizen, his love for Australia and its enrichment is as passionate as when he was but fourteen years old.'[5]

Perhaps these visits also made it seem to a restlessly touring Grainger that nowhere else, despite his international renown, could he call on national, civic, and family networks so effectively to support the idea of establishing a museum devoted to his life and music and to the lives and music of his friends and associates. If he did believe that he would be advantaged in this way, no one could have blamed him for feeling disillusioned in later years.[6] It is true that he secured the agreement of the University of Melbourne for placing his museum on its grounds near the University Conservatorium premises, an agreement loudly regretted in later years by some university administrators. Yet the responsibility of finding the money to erect the museum's red-brick building in squashed Art Deco style (without the hoped-for additional floor) and to bring back to Melbourne the clothes, scores, letters, photographs, instruments, and other implements that belonged to Grainger and his friends fell almost entirely on him. Despite the delays occasioned by limited finances, the priorities of World War II, and official indifference and hostility, the Grainger Museum was eventually made to function spasmodically and with undoubted usefulness and even distinction on occasion during the second half of the twentieth century.

It must also be admitted that many of those Australians who were sufficiently aware of the existence of the Grainger Museum to have an opinion about it in this period were inclined to wonder why such an institution should be devoted to a musician whom they knew of mainly as the composer of *Country Gardens*, banged out remorselessly at end-of-year student recitals, and such neat, pleasing, and (as it has proved) indestructible miniatures as *Shepherd's Hey*, *Molly on the Shore*, *Handel in the Strand*, and *Mock Morris*. Grainger's unconventional behaviour (including his exploits in running to concerts) and his espousal of strange causes such as a belief in the innate superiority of 'Nordic' music had given him in his native country a reputation for eccentricity that was not unhelpful to him in attracting audiences. In return, his use of the newly established national radio system of the Australian Broadcasting Commission (now Corporation) during his 1933–5 and 1938 visits to plead the causes of music well outside the standard repertories suggested that he cared sufficiently about the people he regarded as his fellow Australians to want to educate and enlighten them.[7]

---

[5] Cyril Scott, 'Grainger and Frankfurt', in Lewis Foreman (ed.), *The Percy Grainger Companion* (London, 1981), 51: passages from an 83-page unpublished manuscript dated October 1936.

[6] Roger Covell, 'Australianism: Grainger and Tate', in Covell, *Australia's Music: Themes of a New Society* (Melbourne, 1967; repr. Lyrebird Press, 2016), 102.

[7] See Percy Grainger, *Music: A Commonsense View of All Types*, synopsis of lectures delivered for the Australian Broadcasting Commission (Sydney, 1934), 32 pp.

12. AN AUSTRALIAN COMPOSER?

The proposal to establish a museum devoted to his life, times, and music, in contrast, seemed to many people to go beyond eccentricity and to disclose a monumental ego. It was probably at about this time that the idea of Grainger as a lovable eccentric began to morph into something less endearing and more dismissive. Australians have a special word for a person whose crankiness seems to them to stop just short of certifiable delusion. It is *ratbag*. American dictionaries such as Merriam-Webster acknowledge it as Australian and place its origin as *c*.1890. British general dictionaries, including the latest Shorter Oxford, usually omit it entirely. In Australia it is sometimes credited with a complex range of meanings. The revised third edition of the Macquarie Dictionary gives as its first meaning rascal or rogue, but this, I feel, is a mistake. Its second and third options contain the essence of the word's general and widespread usage, defining a ratbag as a person of eccentric or nonconforming ideas or behaviour or as a person whose preoccupation with a particular theory or belief is seen as obsessive or discreditable. A ratbag can be lovable and can be admired for those aspects of his or her beliefs or behaviour that are not classified (rightly or wrongly) as ratbaggery. In certain moods Grainger might have come to like his honorary designation as a great Australian ratbag.

Fortunately perhaps, the Grainger Museum seems to have been rescued permanently from academic denigration and belittlement by the work of restoration and enhancement taking place in 2009 and by the commitment of Melbourne University to it implied in that work. It will take longer for the public at large to understand that the museum's planning and realisation are not to be dismissed out of hand as the proclamation of a deepening ego in the later years of an artist who is afraid that he will be forgotten and misunderstood. They are consistent in every respect with the eagerness of the young, folk-song-collecting Grainger of the first decade of the twentieth century to note every detail of the performances of the singers with whom he collaborated; documenting through a pioneering use of cylinder recording or on paper the individual singer's character, nuances of pronunciation and musical timing and inflection, variations in delivery, use of ornamentation or other embellishment, and expressive changes of vocal timbre and intensity. It was an approach diametrically opposed to the belief of most of the leading members of the English Folk-Song and Dance Society at the time that it was their mission to retrieve from the inconsistencies and inadequacies of the singers they consulted a collection of ur-versions: paradigmatic or ideal representations of songs in danger of being lost to view through the faults of memory and taste of the singers. When H. G. Wells accompanied Grainger on a folk-song-collecting trip in Gloucestershire in 1908 he was astonished at the detail noted by the collector and memorably observed, as recalled by Grainger, 'You are trying to do a more difficult thing than record folk-songs; you are trying to record life.'[8] That is exactly the scale of the challenge Grainger set himself in planning his museum, not least in ensuring that everything that might be thought discreditable to him should be included without reservation and, indeed, at times with a vehement overemphasis. Far from being the product of

---

[8] Gillies and Pear (eds.), *Portrait of Percy Grainger*, 53, quoting from Grainger, 'The Impress of Personality in Unwritten Music', *Musical Quarterly*, 1 (1915), 420.

an ego grown fearful through advancing years of the prospect of personal extinction, the museum represents in its principles of collection the life-long practice of a man whose creative intentions were nearly all conceived or defined during the first thirty-five years of his life.

The second body of evidence seeming to contradict a possible view that Grainger's utterances in support of his Australian identity are simply a habitual mantra, maintained beyond actual belief, is less concrete but surprisingly varied. It consists of remarks and actions attributed to him over a period of many years. Its combined effect is strongly to suggest that not only did he think of himself as an Australian but his views and behaviour are in several ways strikingly representative of an Australian of his time.[9] He acts like a typical Australian while also affirming his exceptional status.

It would be reasonable as well as easy, of course, to assume that Grainger's Australianism amounts to little more than a personal idealisation of this necessarily vague and selectively variable quality, based as it seems to be on an association with his native country limited in scope and duration. His hothouse education, based at home in Melbourne and increasingly directed by his mother, might well seem likely to have cut him off from the everyday realities of growing up and mingling with his generation of young Australians. On the other hand, the special tutors chosen for him by his parents and the friends they introduced him to brought him into typically precocious contact with leading practitioners in diction, music, and visual art in Melbourne. Frederick McCubbin, his drawing master, was to become one of the leading Australian artists of his day, though at the time he coached Grainger he had yet to arrive, it appears, at the fresh understanding of Australian light celebrated in the 2009 retrospective exhibition devoted to his paintings. Grainger responded to his coaching with a talent that vied for a time with his aptitude for music. His awareness of the work of highly gifted artists concerned with capturing truthful images of the Australian landscape was amplified by his parents' friendships with other members of the 'Heidelberg' school of Victoria-based artists,[10] sometimes referred to as 'Australian Impressionists'. Thomas Sisley, member of a family that was still teaching drama and speech in Australia half a century later, discovered in his charge much less talent for the theatre, according to Grainger himself,[11] but remained a friendly elder guide to literature and music, as did a family friend and physician, Dr Robert Hamilton Russell. Practical instruction from the virtuoso pianist Louis Pabst, resident in Melbourne since 1884, followed on the grounding provided by Grainger's mother, Rose. It gave the boy access to a piano tradition derived from Pabst's European teachers (Anton Rubinstein reportedly among them), representing both German and Russian streams of piano teaching and performance.

These opportunities for high-level instruction were not remarkable for families who had taken part in the great burst of development, building on the riches of

---

[9] See, for example, his delight in Australian sporting prowess, as recorded by Ernest Thesiger, cited in Gillies and Pear (eds.), *Portrait of Percy Grainger*, 39–40, and by Grainger himself, cited in Dreyfus (ed.), *The Farthest North of Humanness*, 223: Letter 208, 28 August 1908.

[10] Bird, *Percy Grainger* (1976), 16.

[11] Ibid., 18, 16–25.

the gold rushes, that had turned Melbourne into the largest and wealthiest city in Australia and brought it to the peak of its nineteenth-century prosperity in the first nine years of Percy Grainger's life. His father, John Grainger, was a cultivated man in many respects and a gifted architect who had won the competition to build the Princes Bridge over the Yarra River and had designed notable buildings, some of them still extant, for prosperous Melbourne. Among John Grainger's professional associates was the successful builder David Mitchell, whose daughter became Nellie Melba and who recalled the collaboration of the two men.[12] She received her seven-year grounding in singing from a Melbourne-based teacher, the Roman-born Pietro Cecchi, who arrived in the city with a professional vocal quartet in 1871 and probably deserves the main credit for the vocal guidance that was part of the basis of Melba's career and fame.

David Walker's Chapter 10 in this book provides a much more wide-ranging impression of the wealth and resources of Melbourne in this period;[13] but enough has been said here, particularly about the standard of training given there to Grainger and Melba to make it seem a careless gaffe on the part of that engaging writer and scholar Wilfrid Mellers to refer to Percy Grainger as the 'Boy from the Bush' in his study of him.[14] Mellers, as it happens, was defending Grainger in the relevant passage against the dismissive comments of Beecham — the 'Grand Seigneur' as Mellers called him — on Grainger's vastly yearning *Colonial Song* and was no doubt looking for a telling metaphorical antithesis. In one sense, however, Mellers was not so far off the mark. He correctly knew or divined that there was in Grainger an empathy with the broadest, even roughest strands of Australian feeling[15] that could not be deduced from his apparently sheltered, 'un-Australian' education by members of Melbourne's metropolitan elite.

Anyone adding up the duration of Grainger's absences from Australia could be tempted to wonder whether he had seen enough of the country to know what was special or unusual about it; but inspection of his letters from his tours in most of the Australian states and many of the cities reminds us of the vividness and surprising comprehensiveness of his observations. There is no doubt that he was remembering what he had seen and felt when, in letters written late in life to the conductors Sir Bernard Heinze and Basil Cameron, he expressed his preference for music that was 'unclear and monotonous' and invoked the Australian landscape to explain his belief that Australian composers should have a 'continental conception' of form based on the 'grandly monotonous, uneventful and unbroken-up' nature of Australian

---

[12] Gillies and Pear (eds.), *Portrait of Percy Grainger*, 81.

[13] Grainger, however, was never more Australian than when he expressed, during his 1908 return visit, some disenchantment with the legend of 'Marvellous Melbourne': 'Well, Melbourne looked the same as ever. It's a snobby, coldhearted, dusty, barren place; small-spirited, I feel.' Quoted in Dreyfus (ed.), *The Farthest North of Humanness*, 228: Letter 211 to Karen Holten, 27 September 1908.

[14] Wilfrid Mellers, *Percy Grainger* (Oxford, 1992), 47.

[15] See his extraordinarily frank and eloquent summary of revulsion and attraction in the presence of a domineering Australian loudmouth: Dreyfus (ed.), *The Farthest North of Humanness*, 21: Letter 17, 22 August 1903.

topography.[16] His belief, expressed in letters at least as late as 1957, that Australia 'as a leader in social experimentation' should also lead 'in musical go-aheadness'[17] displayed an informed citizen's pride in the early dates at which Australian state and federal governments had introduced such electoral and social novelties as the secret ballot, women's right to vote, an eight-hour day, and a basic or minimum wage.

It was one thing for Grainger to assign his career and achievements to Australia; it has been quite another for Australia to accept these assignments in a whole-hearted way. Grainger seems to have been disconnected by his own originality and absence from at least two generations of Australians, causing his intended national legacy to seem unearned by Australians and, to a degree, unassimilated. Composer-educators who worked in Australia in the late nineteenth century and the early part of the twentieth century, after thorough training elsewhere, like the Melbourne-born traditionalist Alfred Hill (1870–1960) and the Nietzschean Englishman, George William Marshall-Hall (1862–1915), were Grainger's seniors and produced in their music, despite the well-meaning interest in New Zealand Maori and Australian Aboriginal music of Hill and the rebellious or free-standing instincts of Marshall-Hall, reruns of nineteenth-century idioms. The London-born Fritz Hart (1874–1949), Marshall-Hall's successor at the Albert Street Conservatorium in Melbourne, was a friend of Holst and Vaughan Williams and to some extent their artistic colleague. Hart drew on the folk-song repertory of the British Isles when it suited him but in ways understandably remote from Grainger's practice. None of these three men, arguably the leading creative figures in music of their time in Australia, was in a position to go beyond enthusiastic commendation of Grainger as a greatly gifted young pianist. The music he created in the decades leading up to and including World War I, much of it kept from public inspection until a later date, would not be known widely until years beyond these men's own formative periods in style and outlook or, in the case of Marshall-Hall, beyond his lifespan.

When Grainger conducted his own educational mission in Australia in the early to middle 1930s, co-opting the new resource of radio, he spoke on behalf of so many ideas that were bewildering or incredible to most music-loving Australians of the time — the importance and relevance of non-European and medieval musics, for example — that his own creative aesthetic must have seemed to them dubiously grounded. Two Australian women, Margaret Sutherland (1897–1984) and Peggy Glanville-Hicks (1912–1990), with a stronger interest in new musical ideas than most of their colleagues, would be too preoccupied making their way in a man's world in the 1930s and 1940s to be ready to go beyond their immediate creative tasks: Sutherland heroically working her way in relative isolation towards a sharply outlined neo-classical idiom, Glanville-Hicks pursuing textural clarity and rhythmic gaiety in New York (though her later works took inspiration from the melodic-rhythmic self-sufficiency of elements of Greek and Indian music). Arthur Benjamin (1893–1960), firmly based in London's musical milieu, and Roy Agnew (1893–1944), some-

---

[16] Letter to Sir Bernard Heinze, 13 November 1949 (Grainger Museum file 421), 1; Letter to Basil Cameron, 9 June 1952 (file 363), 2; quoted in Covell, *Australia's Music*, 97.

[17] Letter to Basil Cameron, 2 May 1957 (Grainger Museum file 363), 3; quoted ibid.

times applying Australian titles to sub-Debussyan or sub-Skryabinesque music, went through the processes of echoing or rejecting the prominent styles of European music without betraying the slightest stylistic awareness of Grainger. Katharine Parker (1886–1971), a Tasmanian pianist and composer who sought out Grainger in London and studied with him there before World War I, wrote at least one piano piece, *Down Longford Way* (taking its title from her Tasmanian home), which in its hymnlike spaciousness and nostalgic cadences shows the influence of Grainger in his *Colonial Song* mood. Grainger evidently recognised the affinity, as he suggested to Parker that she orchestrate it and, when she despaired of her efforts, did the orchestration himself.[18]

By the time Australia was ready to give some more than limp recognition of its possession of a diverse group of young and not-so-young composers in the 1950s and 1960s, many of them taking advantage of the new surge in the international accessibility of recordings and scores to achieve a personal version of stylistic up-to-dateness, Grainger's life was coming to an end, and his most daring visions of a music untrammelled by instrumental limitations or academic tradition were being pursued with the aid of new developments in electronics. Australian composers encountered these visions in the form of technical news from their national[19] and international contemporaries rather than as messages from a home-grown prophet. Lacking the sustained personal input of Grainger as teacher and exemplar, Australian music experienced the rediscovery of his significance largely as a classroom lesson, a matter of repute, rather than a looming personal influence, though the young composer Keith Humble expressed his admiration in unmistakably warmer terms when he unsuccessfully proposed Grainger as a composer to be commissioned for music for the opening ceremony of the 1956 Melbourne Olympic Games.[20] Australian musicologists have contributed to the Grainger literature, and Australian, Australian-based, or Australian-affiliated performers have helped to swell significantly the now formidable array of Grainger recordings, though it seems almost eerie that most of these performers were born in the United Kingdom. The only living Australian musician known to me, for example, who has worked in a professional way in the idiom of Grainger — even to arranging English traditional tunes in a comparably robust manner — is the horn player, pianist, and conductor David Stanhope, who physically left behind his origins in Sutton Coldfield in the English Midlands as a child of early school age when his family emigrated to Australia.

---

[18] Ian Munro, notes (1977) for a disc of Parker's piano pieces and songs performed by Munro (piano) and Jane Edwards (soprano), *Down Longford Way: The music of Katharine Parker*, Tall Poppies TP174, 2005.

[19] The Fairlight CMI (Computer Musical Instrument), designed in Sydney by Peter Vogel and Kim Ryrie in 1979 and brought to unprecedented levels of effectiveness as a digital composing medium by the mid 1980s, was for some years the first choice internationally of many concert-music and film composers, sound production organisations (including the BBC's Radiophonic Workshop) and leading rock and pop groups. It provided musicians with the means to determine the characteristics of sound by a 'sculptural' tweaking of wave patterns. Grainger would probably have loved it.

[20] Bird, *Percy Grainger* (1976), 245.

Grainger's major project in his later years ('It is my only important contribution to music', he declared at the time) was an attempt, in collaboration with Burnett Cross, to realise mechanically and then electronically something of the *Free Music*, as he called it, that he remembered imagining as a boy. The means used for this experimental process passed through several phases and included reed boxes, hill-and-dale brown-paper rolls, pneumatic pressure from a vacuum cleaner, lengths of string, and what Grainger called the 'Kangaroo-pouch' method of synchronising and activating eight oscillators. In comparison with present-day digital manipulation of sound, this suggests something devised by Heath Robinson or the comic role of the vacuum cleaner in Greene's *Our Man in Havana*. I would argue that it also represents in moderately updated form a kind of outback ingenuity common to the older traditions of Australia and the US. Remote settlements and holdings in Australia required the development of a resourceful use of available materials summed up in story and song in the phrase 'stringybark and greenhide' ('the mainstay of Australia'), to which we could add fencing-wire from more recent times. Perhaps we could describe Grainger in all his aspects, without impugning his superlative standards of professionalism, as a stringybark, greenhide, and fencing-wire composer. I believe he would have quite liked that.

13

The Grainger Museum: Then, Now, and In the Future

A Museum for the Twenty-First Century
Brian Allison

IN A 1930 LETTER to his wife, Ella, Percy Grainger tussled with the idea of whether he was a genius — in his word, a 'lifemaster'. 'The Museum idea I see as follows: . . . it is the wont of our mindtilth [culture] to teach mankind by means of museums and to anchor museums to the houses and leavings of lifemasters. Thus we have museums and "houses" based on Goethe, Wagner, Beethoven, Dickens, Carlisle,[1] H. C. Andersen, Grieg, Leighton, Watts & many others. If I am a lifemaster I have the same "right" to a museum as these other men and have a full right to foreready for it while I am alive'.[2]

Quite early in his career he had conceived the advanced concept that in preserving the ephemera and minutiae of his life, together with the clothes he wore and the furniture upon which he sat, as well as his musical compositions — he would aid future scholars to build a more complex and detailed understanding of his thinking. Context and provenance were of paramount importance.

The Grainger Museum in the grounds of the University of Melbourne was the result of this 'lifemaster' vision. For sixty-five years, until October 2003, scholars and musicians, artists and Grainger enthusiasts from all around the world have travelled to see the Museum's uniquely designed gallery spaces, to view the extraordinarily diverse collection, and to study in the dimly-lit reading room. Though quite an advanced and inspired design in the 1930s, by the end of the millennium the building was no longer viable as a cultural heritage institution without a program of extensive building maintenance. Fractured storm-water plumbing and inadequate damp coursing meant that some galleries and store rooms were exposed to extensive rising damp. The building was originally designed to have a second storey, so that more than half the roof area is actually a simple ten-centimetre concrete slab, the planned floor to the second storey. Over the years, numerous leaks occurred through inevitable cracks in this unsuitable surface.

The Museum's internal climate was unstable. Temperatures ranged across the

---

[1] Probably Thomas Carlyle, whose house in Cheyne Row, London, well known to Grainger, opened as a museum in 1896.
[2] Letter from Percy Grainger to Ella Grainger, 15 July 1930. Grainger Museum Collection, the University of Melbourne.

seasons from as low as 6° Celsius in winter to as high as 34° Celsius in summer, with corresponding dramatic shifts in relative humidity. These climate variations, combined with the moisture problems, were ultimately destined to have highly destructive effects on a collection made up of a broad spectrum of media.

Leading Melbourne conservation architects Lovell Chen were commissioned to write a detailed conservation management plan identifying all major building works. Concurrently, the decision was made to relocate the collections to secure storage areas.

All archival material — the printed music and manuscript collections, some 50,000 items of correspondence, 15,000 photographs, extensive business documents, and autobiographical writings — the very valuable core of the Museum's research material — was rehoused in a purpose-built space in the University's Baillieu Library. A climate-controlled space was built into one of the University's storage centres to house the three-dimensional material. The collection is now far better protected than it has been at any time in its past history and is still accessible to researchers and interested parties.

The Grainger Museum entered a new era when it opened its doors again in 2010. It is now solely engaged in interpreting the many-faceted aspects of Percy Aldridge Grainger's creative life. Without being hampered by the need to store collection items, exhibition space has been almost doubled in comparison with the building's previous configuration. Two professional designers, working with Museum staff, have created five galleries that investigate this highly creative and omnivorous mind.

The visitor starts with an introduction to Grainger's early years in Melbourne and later at the Hoch Conservatory in Frankfurt, followed by his phenomenal successes as a young colonial, performing in London.

The next gallery is dedicated to the expansion of Grainger's creative ideas and the interconnectedness of the passions that drove him. For example, the gallery documents the way his pioneering work as a folk-song collector informed his composing and arranging. It reveals his love of ethnographic art and artefacts and his need to master the intricacies of native bead-work fabrication (an almost material equivalent of his often-preferred contrapuntal compositional style). This gallery also poses some of his more controversial ideas as a social commentator.

Grainger intended his Museum to house a so-called 'London Room' — a memorial to those halcyon years shared with his mother when her health was relatively stable, and when he began pushing the boundaries of his strengths, creatively and intellectually. The visitor will now experience Grainger's concept as a series of vignettes or tableaux, showcasing the rich furniture and decorative arts, and art collections dating from that era.

A gallery examining Grainger's experimental music houses the massive *Kangaroo Pouch Free Music Machine* and documents and drawings that contributed to Grainger's research and experimentation into a music that broke conventions of western musical composition and performance. The Grainger Museum has always been viewed as a 'sacred site' by many experimental musicians around the world because of Grainger's pioneering work with what was effectively proto-electronic music.

The Museum also houses a temporary exhibition space with regularly changing themes. The first exhibition focusses on 'Making the Museum' — an investigation into what motivated Grainger to collect and an illustration of the very disparate nature of his collection. This space presents as a veritable *Wunderkammer*.

Grainger's wish for a second storey to the Museum was, in part, motivated by his desire to divide his Museum between contextualising his own creative output and presenting a history of Australian musical composition from the 1880s to the present. Although this did not eventuate, a gallery in the Museum is allocated to building a picture of aspects of the history of musical culture in Melbourne. This includes material acquired by Grainger from the estate of G. W. L. Marshall-Hall, the highly influential composer, poet, and first Ormond Professor of Music at Melbourne University, who assisted Grainger in his desire to study in Frankfurt.

The University of Melbourne has acknowledged the cultural significance of the Grainger collection by embodying it into the infrastructure of the University's management systems for valuable cultural material. Now the Grainger scholar sits in the comfort of the University's Secure Reading Room and has research material brought to his or her desk, as in any contemporary world-class university or collecting institution. How unlike those pioneering days described below by Kay Dreyfus, when curators worked in an environment akin to an archaeological dig (may they be praised), aided by an arcane cataloguing system. Today, archival material sits in acid-free containers on dust-free shelves and is tracked using an electronic database and three published music catalogues.

The Museum is dedicated to articulating the many threads of Grainger's life, hopefully satisfying this 'lifemaster's' desire to explain his world and to engage in a dialogue with generations to come about the nature of the creative process in music.

Treasures of the Grainger Museum
Astrid Britt Krautschneider

A postgraduate student here at the University of Melbourne recently asked me what defines a treasure. She was studying Percy Grainger's *The Warriors* manuscript as a part of her Master of Cultural Materials Conservation degree and wanted to know exactly why this manuscript was considered one of the Grainger Museum's 'treasures'.[3] I replied that all the music manuscripts in the Museum's collection are precious as they were not only written in Percy Grainger's own hand and are therefore irreplaceable, but also because they offer musicians, musicologists, and researchers unique insights into his creative *modus operandi*. Being Grainger's most complex and ambitious work, I told her, the *Warriors* manuscript is especially noteworthy as it features many rewritten bars, pasted in over the originals, extra staves drawn freehand onto the page, as well as myriad other notes and markings that conductors and musicians can benefit from when considering performing the piece.

---

[3] See Plate 13.

Her question was a good one, and it set me thinking. The Grainger Museum collection is much more than the individual objects contained within it; it is the story of Percy Grainger himself. The story is very important for a collection such as this, because while the significance of some of the objects within it can be understood separately and in their own right — as objects on a 'white wall', so to speak — others are sometimes difficult to comprehend. The presence of Grainger's music manuscripts in the collection makes perfect sense, for example, because that is what one would expect to find in a museum dedicated to a renowned composer. However, there are many other items in the Grainger Museum (for instance a mastodon's tooth nestling in a little box![4]) that are much less readily recognisable as being of significance until they are contextualised within the collector's narrative and looked upon as part of a unified whole.

For Percy Grainger, an object was considered valuable and therefore worthy of placement in his Museum not just because it was worth a lot of money, or was rare or beautiful, but because it meant something to him on a personal level. He often attached the word 'relic' to items in the collection that he felt strongly about — especially in the case of his mother Rose. After Rose's death in 1922, he carefully preserved everything he could find that had belonged to her. Particularly poignant is the handbag Rose was carrying on the day she died. Grainger meticulously inventoried the bag's contents before sending it to the museum.[5]

Percy Grainger's use of the term 'relic' carries with it — oddly enough for someone who was not religious — a sort of modern-day kinship with the medieval practice of prizing the personal effects or bodily remains of a saint. A good illustration of this sort of thing in Grainger's collection is a lock of Hans Christian Andersen's hair, sewn onto one of his visiting cards. Wiry and slightly grey, it was given to Grainger by a member of the Melchior family, who had looked after Andersen (1805–1875) during his last years.[6] Another example is a box once owned by the composer Franz Liszt (1811–1886) and given to Percy Grainger by his friend and patron William Gair Rathbone. Rathbone explained that when he bought the box at Weimar he was told that Liszt had kept his private letters in it. Grainger took great pleasure in owning Liszt's box — he kept it proudly displayed atop his piano and stored his own documents in it for many years.[7]

The Grainger Museum also contains material that is considered significant to people from a variety of different interest groups. Melbourne's orchestral community, for example, currently seem to cherish Percy Grainger's 1930s Mayland metal marimba[8] — if one judges the frequent requests to borrow it for performances as an

---

[4] Grainger was influenced by and had a great respect for the native cultures of New Zealand, USA, Pacific Islands, and Scandinavia. His collection included numerous ethnographic artefacts. The mastodon tooth forms part of a small collection of primitive stone tools and other artefacts Grainger acquired during his travels between the years 1907 and 1916.

[5] See Plate 36.

[6] Given to Grainger by Harriet Melchior in 1908.

[7] See Plate 34.

[8] Manufactured by R. H. Mayland & Son, Brooklyn, New York, c.1930. See Chap. 3, p. 35 above.

indication of the instrument's rarity and importance. And experimental musicians and contemporary sound artists are perennially fascinated by Grainger's experiments with the concept of 'Free Music' and the strangely beautiful Heath Robinson-like designs for his Free Music machines held in the Museum's collection.[9]

Art buffs find the Grainger Museum's collection of late-nineteenth- and early-twentieth-century fine and applied art to be highly significant. The collection features works by the prominent Australian painters and printmakers Rupert Bunny, Tom Roberts,[10] Norman Lindsay, Mortimer Menpes, and Noel Counihan. It also carries art works by well-known British and European artists such as Francis Derwent Wood, Augustus John, and Jacques-Émile Blanche. The decorative arts and furniture collection is extensive and includes an interesting selection of Arts and Crafts items collected by Rose Grainger, such as hand-beaten silver and copperware by the leading American firms Lebolt and Jos. Heinrichs, and a pair of ladder-back chairs thought to be by the English architect/craftsman Ernest Gimson. Those interested in fashion and design might value Rose Grainger's exquisite Edwardian gowns or Percy Grainger's extraordinary towelling clothes outfits above all else.

Finally, Grainger's collection of manuscripts and published music by composers other than himself — often overlooked by visitors and researchers — is unquestionably of major significance. A crucial work in this collection is the original 1887 manuscript of *Florida*, the first orchestral work composed by Frederick Delius (1862–1934). Grainger met Delius in 1907, probably at the home of the painter John Singer Sargent. The two got along immediately and soon discovered that they shared similar ideas about composition and harmony. In 1938, Grainger informed the University of his plan to include in his Museum an exhibit of Delius's music, correspondence and other mementos. The *Florida* manuscript, according to an accompanying note by Grainger, duly arrived at the Grainger Museum in 1948.

An Experience Revisited
Kay Dreyfus

My intellectual encounter with Grainger and his Museum changed my life. I came to the Museum after spending six months in New York studying Schenkerian analysis at City College, Queens College, and the Mannes School of Music. Frank Strahan, the University Archivist, had contacted me in New York and asked me to apply for the job. Although I had been a student at the University of Melbourne for over a decade before I went to work at the Museum, I had never been inside. Grainger did not feature in my musical education (but then neither did Australian composers, musicians generally, or women).

The Museum transformed the way I think about music, enriching my perspectives and teaching me new research techniques. My love of textual analysis expanded into a passion for archival research, and music, for me, became embedded

---

[9] See Plate 33 for one example.
[10] See Plate 23.

in biography and social history. From that moment in time, and like so many others, I fell into a fascination with Percy Grainger.

When I came to the Grainger Museum in July 1974, I entered a Percy-dominated universe poised between two extremes of intellectual stimulation and physical discomfort. God may have said 'Let there be light!' (Gen 1:3), but Grainger said, 'I will not have electricity in my Museum!' Fortunately, the University's Faculty of Music had requisitioned one wing of the Museum as its electronic music studio. No electronics without electricity; power was connected. But the strain of extra bodies (two and then three full-time) and extra spaces requiring minimal winter heating resulted in many outages in those early days. Uncovered cement floors and brick walls combined with rising damp to create an atmosphere of extreme chill. I often wondered what I had got myself into. I became a great champion of the idea of the Museum as autobiography, but were Percy's workers expected to share his robust constitutional disregard for cold?

On the second day of creation, God separated the water that was under the space from the water that was above the space (Gen. 1:6). Grainger's water-management strategies left something to be desired. There was no running water in the Museum; all physical needs involving water required a trip to an adjacent building. The credit for surviving the installation of a washroom in the mid 1980s goes to the then Curator, Rosemary Florrimell. On the other hand, the building's flat roof and arcane drainage system made it prone to flooding whenever we experienced those then not infrequent Melbourne downpours. (Global warming has been kind to the Museum; it doesn't rain in Melbourne any more.) It was not until decades later that Rosie discovered that no provision had been made to connect the down pipes to the stormwater drains in the street. In Percy's place, the water collected under the floor of the foyer — an oddity that goes far to explain the staff's susceptibility to bronchitis and other respiratory-tract infections.

Pest control was another significant physical challenge. Left unmoderated, silverfish ate the paper while moths feasted on fabrics. The solutions — liberal applications of naphthalene and regular fumigations with toxic dioxins — were well in breach of modern health-and-safety regulations for staff working in a building without ventilation. Grainger was unquestionably a visionary in many ways, but he knew very little about museology.

The challenges of the collections were at once conceptual, physical, and technical. The great variety of materials called for a wide range of skills, but the first appointments comprised a musicologist, a librarian, and a historian, supplemented by another part-time librarian and another part-time historian. The bias towards the paper documentation was pretty clear, so we started with the paper. We instantly confronted a most fundamental conceptual challenge: Grainger's classification system.

Grainger had devised a numbering system for the materials he collected for the Museum that was essentially autobiographical. It was also incomplete, both in terms of its categories and in terms of his arrangement of the materials within them. It was also, in the end, probably unmanageable since it could not easily be expanded. Some of the approximately fifty thousand items of correspondence were sorted into envelopes bearing his classification numbers and descriptions. Thousands of letters remained tied up in small bundles, many of them by Rose Grainger, and bearing labels like 'letters from friends April–May 1906,' or 'letters from Roger, 1901.' How were these bundles to be dealt with? They told their own story, it is true, but this method of storage or arrangement was no basis for organizing the whole collection. Cataloguing the correspondence was a task of decades, especially after the transfer of the Library of Congress holding doubled the size of our own. The era was, of course, pre-digital.

When Percy looked at his Museum, even though it was not finished when he died, he saw that it was good. When the University looked at the Museum, it saw an opportunity for redevelopment: a prime piece of land occupied by a low-functioning building that a former Vice-Chancellor (Sir John Medley) had once compared to a public toilet. Efforts to preserve the Museum building, and its integrity as the appropriate repository for Grainger's collection, have exercised a number of dedicated people over a number of decades. Idealism, commitment, and reputation lined up against the University's formidable financial resources and hierarchical power structures. In one corner, in 1974, we had a cluster of prominent British musicians testifying to the Museum's worth; in the other, the University's legal heavyweights defending its right to pull the building down.

In the end it was local perseverance and initiative that saw the Museum included on the State Heritage Council's register of historic buildings, and listed by the National Trust of Australia. The late George Tibbits, conservation architect and architectural historian, was instrumental in effecting a change in the University's attitude towards historic buildings on campus and in articulating an appreciation of the Museum's distinctive architectural features.[11] The Museum's heritage listings mean that the fabric of the building is well protected; the Heritage Council's discussion of proposed renovations, 16 March 2009, may be found linked to the Council's website.[12] The Museum's status as the proper home for Grainger's collections is perhaps not so well settled.

My life was enriched by the many wonderful people who were drawn to Grainger and his Museum: people he knew and people he did not know, musicians, colleagues, donors, and visitors. There were some spine-tingling moments linked to some of these people. As, for example, when John Semmens, a steadfast friend to the Museum who came every Friday afternoon to 'tinker' with Percy's reproducing piano, finally got it to play. Or the moment when Burnett Cross, with the help of an over-stressed vacuum cleaner, coaxed sound from the Reed-Box Tone-Tool (one of the Free Music machines), accidentally set off the fire alarm, and summoned

---

[11] See, for example, George R. Tibbits, *Grainger and the Build-Wrights: A Past-Hoard-House in the Making* (The Percy Grainger Lecture 1997 on the history of the Museum), University of Western Australia, 1998 (38 pp.); George R. Tibbits, *The Grainger Museum, University of Melbourne: History and Conservation Guidelines*, The University of Melbourne, 1996 (63 pp.); George R. Tibbits, *The Planning and Development of the University of Melbourne: An Historical Outline*, The University of Melbourne, 1996 (74 pp.).

[12] http://www.heritage.vic.gov.au/admin/file/content2/c7/Grainger%20Decision%20 Report%20_Final_.pdf (accessed 22 July 2010).

the fire brigade. The firemen stayed for a lecture on Free Music. Or the time when Elinor Wrobel's daughter, returning home as her mother was conserving some of Percy's and Rose's clothing, detected the presence of two dead people in the house. Dead presences were strong in that inward-turning building, especially at night. Burnett Cross swore he once heard Percy's voice.

My universe no longer revolves around Grainger, but he has left an indelible imprint on my life.

14

The Pursuit of Nordic Music

Bruce Clunies Ross

IN THE CLOSING PHASE of his life, Percy Grainger suggested that 'most of my music... should be conceived as a Nordic revolt against civilization'.[1] He was given to making such unqualified statements, which often seem exaggerated and sometimes implicitly paradoxical. Overstatement was a characteristic mode of expression, but his tone and style varied according to whether he was developing his ideas in notebooks, letters, lecture notes, museum legends, memoirs, or essays intended for publication.[2] He was an expressive rather than a reflective writer, and rarely paused to analyse or qualify his ideas.

The brief summary of his composing career as a 'Nordic revolt' was made in an undated typescript of questions and answers prepared for a Norwegian volume entitled *Musikkens Verden* (The World of Music). The book was first published in Oslo in 1951, so it can be assumed that the questionnaire was completed a year or two previously.[3] Although most of the information it contains can also be found in letters and personal writings from Grainger's later years, the typescript sets it out in a distinctly challenging manner. There are implicit inconsistencies among the answers, and some introduce clues which invite further investigation. For example, he described his creed as 'musical democracy' and explained that 'the ideal of "equality" is the keystone of my musical endeavours'. Yet in the following paragraph he declared: 'The driving force behind my work as a composer is racialism & nationalism: I would not write any music at all if it were not to express the unity of the Nordic (blue-eyed) race, wherever found; to express the tragic position of the Nordic race (out-numbered in a hostile world).'[4]

Expressions of this kind are scattered throughout Grainger's personal writings,

---

[1] The works Grainger cited to illustrate this revolt were '*Kipling Jungle Book Cycle, Hill-Songs I & II, English Dance,* etc.'

[2] In his personal writings, Grainger used English and Danish spontaneously, as well as the Nordic, or Blue-eyed, English which he created on the basis of his knowledge of Nordic philology. There are occasional passages in other languages, such as German, Dutch, and the Polynesian language he called 'Maori'.

[3] The questionnaire is included in Gillies and Clunies Ross (eds.), *Grainger on Music*, 373–6, where I incorrectly identified the author and date of *Musikkens Verden*. It was compiled and edited by Kjell B. Sandved; published 1951. There are a number of subsequent editions and translations, some revised by other authors.

[4] Gillies and Clunies Ross (eds.), *Grainger on Music*, 375-6.

particularly in his later years. They certainly need to be explained, but it does not explain them to designate them as racist in the sense that the word is understood today. They relate to Grainger's comprehensive idea of race and the Nordic world which developed through his reading and studies in the 1890s and was fully formed before the First World War. This was integrated into his creativity as a complex impulse, rather than developed intellectually as a view of the world. It was racial, not racist, and allowed for attitudes which may now seem contrary. For example, Grainger had both a strong sense of racial affiliation and a belief in equality and democracy. It might be argued that these are not incompatible if democracy is restricted to the Nordic, or white, race, but this was not Grainger's view. In the first section of the questionnaire, he identified, as a significant early influence on his personality: 'A. E. Aldis (an English painter in Melbourne, Australia) who boarded at our house for a time (when I was eight or nine), who often spoke in the Maori (New Zealand) language & started a "native" (non-white) view of life & art in me.'

Grainger's ideas about Nordic culture and race began to develop very early. They were already forming at the age of thirteen, when he first met Cyril Scott and other members of the Frankfurt Group — and, crucially, the Danish cellist Hermann Sandby — at the Hoch Conservatorium in Frankfurt in 1895. In the following decade he began to visit Scandinavia regularly. He became acquainted with the fertile developments in Scandinavian literature and the arts, generally referred to as *det moderne gennembrud* (the modern breakthrough), but was particularly attracted to local and regional arts, and acquired a deep knowledge of some of them. During the same period, he was extending his knowledge of different forms of music, partly in his wider travels as a concert pianist, and this formed a context for his thinking about Nordic music.

By the end of *The Vertigo Years*,[5] as a recent historian has called the period of intellectual ferment before the First World War, his creative ideas were fully formed. He lived on through the world wars and the accelerating changes of the first half of the twentieth century, with ideas which were progressive at the time they were formed, but which, to an extent, were marginalized by subsequent events. Some, though, came into their own. For example, his distinctive idea of universalism in music, elaborated in his New York University lectures[6] and radio talks in Australia, put forward the idea that all races were equally musical in their own way.[7] However, he did not modify the concept on which it was based: that race was the fundamental determinant of musical (and other) difference. Paradoxically, Grainger is generally admired as ahead of his time in proclaiming that all races were equally musical (though the word 'race' would now be replaced with 'ethnicity' or one of its cognates), whereas his resort to race to explain human differences has become suspect. In the course of his life this concept, which circulated freely in his early creative

---

[5] See the book of that title by Philipp Blom (New York, 2008).

[6] 'A General Study of the Manifold Nature of Music', delivered at NYU between Sept. 1932 and May, 1933. Synopsis in Gillies and Clunies Ross (eds.), *Grainger on Music*, 223–31.

[7] See Gillies and Clunies Ross (eds.), *Grainger on Music*, 223–31, and Blacking, 'A Commonsense View of All Music', passim.

period and was fundamental to his ideas, was revealed by subsequent world events to be poisonous. Grainger himself, however, was not infected. For him, there was no contradiction between envisaging culture in terms of race, and continuing to work with and befriend people of diverse racial and cultural affiliations, as he had always done.

Grainger used the word 'Nordic' in various ways, sometimes idiosyncratically, as his comprehensive engagement with the Nordic world developed. On his own account, the 'Nordic revolt' to which he referred in the last decade of his career can be traced back to his reading, around the age of nine, ten, or eleven, an English paraphrase of the Icelandic saga *Grettir the Strong*.[8] At the same age he also read versions of the Old English epic *Beowulf*, which is set in the Nordic world, and the *Anglo-Saxon Chronicle*. It may seem remarkable reading for a ten-year-old, but the first decade of his life coincided with the peak of Victorian enthusiasm for Norse mythology, literature, and philology.[9] The fact that Grainger encountered it as a child in Melbourne in the early 1890s is an indication of its pervasiveness.

What is even more remarkable is that the stories Grainger read as a child remained strong in his memory and imagination for the rest of his life, and had a profound influence on his art and ideas. Even as a child in Melbourne he composed a piano duet entitled *Beowulf*[10] and sketched Viking swords and boar helmets in the margins. A few years later, three notebooks he kept around the turn of the nineteenth into the twentieth century, between the ages of eighteen and twenty-one, include ideas for compositions inspired by reading Norse stories.[11] They are mixed up with extensive transcriptions of Old English and Old Icelandic verse and prose, along with translations and philological notes, which indicate that he was enthusiastically learning the languages and already developing the ideas that would lead to the form of English he called variously 'Nordic', 'Blue-eyed', 'Rosey-Racy', 'Pinkman's', or 'Pinky'. By 1908, it appears from a letter to his Danish lover Karen Holten that he was reading Old Icelandic fluently: 'I gave myself the pleasure, a few days ago, of taking an Icelandic Saga (Grettir) with me in the train. It was like being embraced and caressed by some specially loved thing. That language! How it moves me!'

Allusions to *Grettir's Saga* are pervasive in the extensive documents which survive from Grainger's life, for, as he inscribed on one of the eight copies in various languages he deposited in the Museum, 'This is the book that had the greatest influence on my human and artistic life. Grettir was to me what Christ is to many Christians.' The tone is typical, and probably intended to shock. Grettir is an antitype to Christ, and a figure for whom modern readers are unlikely to feel sympathy, even though he is understandable in the context of early Nordic, or Viking, culture. Grainger's hero

---

[8] Grainger's later identification of the source was inaccurate. He probably read the paraphrase of the saga in *Tales of the Teutonic Lands* (1872) by G. W. Cox and E. H. Jones or in a later (1880) edition of their *Popular Romances of the Middle Ages*.

[9] Comprehensively described in Andrew Wawn, *The Vikings and the Victorians: Inventing the Old North in Nineteenth-Century Britain* (Cambridge, 2000).

[10] Part of the collection of Childhood Works, 1893.

[11] See for example his *Norse Dirge*, *The Wraith of Odin*, *The Crew of the Long Serpent*, *Saxon Twi-Play*, and other youthful tone-works.

was an outlaw, headstrong and impatient. He sought quarrels and made enemies, whom he killed ruthlessly, sometimes using underhand trickery which was hardly heroic. Grettir's saga is, amongst other things, a catalogue of brutal fights and killings by a man feared — and rarely admired — as the strongest and most violent of his time. Occasionally he used his strength to right injustice. He could be generous, and he quoted verses appositely, but violence was his dominant trait.

The influence of Grettir worked on Grainger's imagination and inspired the process of artistic creation. He himself wondered, in a letter to his mother, 'why . . . the bright echo of mainly sordid lives [of the saga heroes] haunt and inspire and satisfy such spiritualists as W. Morris & me almost beyond all other literature?'[12] His answer, in the same letter: 'These chaps *really lived their lives out*, & the tale of their deeds stands in relation to their personal instincts like a *fuldbesat*[13] orchestral performance does to a score.' This complex idea suggests that it was not the Viking culture depicted in the sagas, but its sublimation in their art, which was the source of inspiration. For Grainger, *Grettir's Saga* was an 'ideal example of what Nordic art should be: shapely yet "formless", many-sided yet monotonous, rambling, multitudinous, drastic, tragic, stoical, ruthlessly truth-proclaiming'. This no doubt influenced his ideas about unrecapitulating 'large form' and continually developing melody, which are put into practice in his *Hill-Songs*.[14]

In the letter quoted above, Grainger associates himself with William Morris, one of the key figures in the recovery, or (some have suggested) invention, of the Nordic past in the nineteenth century. Yet although that movement provided the initial impulse for Grainger's Nordic revolt, he took it much further than Morris, and the scale and depth of his preoccupation with the Nordic world set him apart. The Norwegian composer Sparre Olsen begins his memoir with the claim that no other foreign artist was more closely involved (*knytt*) in Norway than Percy Grainger,[15] and what he says of Norway could be extended to the whole region — Iceland, the Faeroes, Norway, Denmark, and Sweden — where the Scandinavian languages are spoken. Grainger knew all these languages, with some of their dialects, and spoke several of them fluently. He travelled extensively in Norway, Denmark, and Sweden, occasionally on foot, and was intimately familiar with some regions, such as the Jutish heath, where he collected folk songs with Evald Tang Kristensen.

On these visits he made friends with people at all levels of society, and he maintained a voluminous correspondence with many of them. The degree to which he was absorbed in this world is evident from various Scandinavian writings, such as the memoirs of Alette Schou and Sparre Olsen, along with Evald Tang Kristensen's account of their work together in his lengthy *Minder og Oplevelser* (1923–8) and the

---

[12] 10 February 1910. William Morris (1834–1896), artist, poet, a founder of the Arts and Crafts movement.

[13] Danish: an idiosyncratic compound, meaning something like 'fully realised'.

[14] For a fuller discussion of this, see my '"For the Glory of Australian Music, for the Glory of Nordic Music"', *Australian Studies*, 5 (April 1991), 43–6.

[15] Sparre Olsen, *Percy Grainger* (Oslo, 1963).

poem in the East Jutish dialect of Vejle, 'Percy Grainger (famous piano virtuoso and composer from America' by Anton Berntsen.[16]

What distinguishes Grainger more than anything else, though, is that he devoted his genius as a musician and linguist to a comprehensive project, inspired by his early reading of the Norse sagas and Eddic poems, along with Old English verse and prose. Grainger envisaged these as belonging to an interconnected North Atlantic world which was disrupted by the Norman Conquest.[17] A persistent idea throughout his life was to return English to its rightful place in that North Atlantic world, among speakers of Scandinavian languages who inherited Nordic traditions and values quite distinct from those deriving from classical civilization. This explains the proclamation displayed in the Grainger Museum: that his aim as a composer was to reverse the catastrophe of the Norman Conquest. The idea did not originate with Grainger; it had a limited currency among enthusiasts for the North in the nineteenth century, and can probably be traced back to the earliest efforts to purge English of its classical and romance elements in the Renaissance. Grainger, however, adopted it as a guiding principle, and took it further than anyone else.

As a young man, Grainger had been kept awake at night, worrying about the deplorable condition of the English language, and excited by the wish to restore it. For the rest of his life, he devoted a large amount of energy, and money, to rooting out romance and classical words, and recreating the language as it might have developed from Old English without these infections. The result reads something like transliterated Danish. Grainger preferred to compare it to modern Icelandic or the movement in Norway to create a national language distinct from the 'Dano-Norwegian' which reflected the nation's subjection for over four hundred years (until 1814) to Denmark. The chief feature of Nordic English was the introduction of transparent, or self-explanatory, compounds, some of which are delightful, such as 'sponge-guest' (parasite), while a few are risky tongue-twisters, such as 'fury-feel-thily' (passionately).

Nordic English was a quixotic project, but the time Grainger used on it was not wasted, for it probably provided a model for the pursuit of Nordic music. He regarded it as his duty as a composer to celebrate 'all seemingly Old English . . . and Norse characteristics' in his music. The difficulty is that whereas Old English and Old Norse are very rich philological sources, there are virtually no comparable musical sources. Grainger supplied this lack by speculating on how music might have evolved in early Nordic cultures, and by tracing Nordic characteristics in Scandinavian folk music.

He envisaged Nordic music as having its origins in the songs and movements of individuals isolated in wild natural surroundings. The notes for his lecture on 'Nordic Characteristics in Music', given at Yale in March 1921, mention

---

[16] See my 'Percy Grainger's "Nordic Revolt against Civilization"', *Musicology Australia*, 9 (1986), 53–65, for a fuller account of these writings. Grainger's English version of Berntsen's poem is quoted on p. 58.

[17] See Chap. 11, n. 4.

pioneer life, lonely pursuits, farms... wide apart, athletic tastes, cold weather and chilly dwellings: Results — individualistic melody of superlative quality, lack of harmony in folk music, jigs, reels and body warming dances... work music of all sorts. Later on in Nordic musical culture the lonely tunes ... come to be used in art music for the expression of nature moods ... inspired by contact with, contemplation of wide expanses and VIRGIN NATURE, rather than the landscapes of villages and semi-urban life.

In 'Characteristics of Nordic Music', broadcast by the New York radio station WEVD in July 1933, he described 'typical Nordic music' as 'the voice of the wide open spaces, the soul of virgin nature made manifest, and this is as true of our greatest art music (such as *Song of the High Hills* by Frederick Delius) as it is of our most primitive folk-songs'. Grainger went on to explain the attributes of this music as 'solemn or spiritual unadorned melodies with long sustained notes, or at least clearly defined intervals, gapped scales,[18] and a marked tendency to some kind of underlying harmonic or polyphonic thot'.

Identifying these attributes cornered Grainger in an awkward argument which led him to consider the music of Duke Ellington or George Gershwin, for example, as 'Nordic'. He did not regard this as a problem. On the contrary, it opened up possibilities. In the radio broadcast just mentioned, he actually played a recording of Duke Ellington's magnificent *Creole Love Call* to illustrate 'gliding tones' and imagined a future where

> Nordic composers will push these nature-inspired sounds so far that we will soon be able to compose entirely in soaring, floating sonorities ... and dispense with the slavish imitation of set intervals, which are perhaps merely a remnant of music's infancy ... Nordic music will no longer be chained to the present arbitrary limitations of scale, rhythm and harmony but will be able to freely tally in music the freedom and irregularity of nature as we sense it in us and around us.

Grainger is outlining in this passage the 'Free Music' he had been imagining since early in his career and which he was notating experimentally on graph paper around the time he wrote this lecture. Ultimately Grainger envisaged 'Nordic Music' as the whole innovative project by which he aimed to transform the art of composition.

While philology was central to Grainger's Nordic ideas and identification of himself as a Nordic artist, the concept fundamental to all his thought was race. He went even further, and claimed that race was something he felt as the deepest force driving his life and art. In *The Love-Life of Helen and Paris*, the candid account of his courtship with the Swedish Ella Ström, whom he married in 1928, he explained: 'My feelings for my race — for the Nordic race — are deeper and stronger than my

---

[18] 'Since I thought that close intervals (diatonic and chromatic) were characteristic of the European continent, while "gapped scales" (3-tone, 4-tone, 5-tone, 6-tone scales) were typical of Britain & the other North Sea islands, I strove to make my melodic intervals as wide as possible.' Grainger, 'Remarks on *Hill-Song I*' (1949), 2.

feelings for myself. I lose myself in my race as god-loving men lose themselves in the thought of god. My art is only my toplayer;[19] but my race is at the very heart of me.'[20] It is difficult to come to terms with Grainger's conception of race, because he lived through a period when events exposed racism as one of the greatest evils. Grainger continued to write explicitly about racial matters throughout this period and to the end of his life, and there are passages, particularly in his later letters and autobiographical writings, that lay him open to the charge of anti-Semitism. He was not alone in this: similar expressions can be found in the writings of a number of artists of Grainger's generation, including, remarkably, the Jewish composers Arnold Schoenberg and Ernest Bloch, according to books recently reviewed.[21]

Where Grainger differed from most of his contemporaries was that, to him, race was not so much an idea as *felt experience*, openly expressed at every opportunity. His constant idealisations of the Nordic race to which he felt he belonged were not expressions of prejudice. On the contrary, Grainger delighted in racial differences, in arts and crafts, dress, languages, and above all in music. His continuing exploration of these differences influenced his own music, for example in pieces such as *In Dahomey*, *Random Round*, and *Beautiful Fresh Flower*, and more generally in his pioneering work in what is now called 'ethnomusicology'. Interestingly, although he cultivated a kind of linguistic purism, he responded positively to blended, or creolized, music. His enthusiasms included ragtime and the Afro-American music he heard at the Clef Club in New York (described in his important article 'The Impress of Personality in Unwritten Music'[22]), as well as Rarotongan improvised part-singing and the music of Duke Ellington.

Grainger's way of classifying music according to 'racial characteristics' disregarded *qualitative* distinctions between different types of music and implicitly put Austro-Germanic music on a par with other types of music defined by 'racial characteristics'. This undermined its pretensions as *the* classical system of composition. Grainger did not reject it. His favourite composer was always Bach, and he performed music by other composers in that tradition, but he regarded its defining characteristics as Germanic, just as other kinds of music were defined by Latin, Slavonic, Hispanic, or Hungarian characteristics. Significantly, though he admired Wagner, he never regarded him as a Nordic composer. The Nordic music he spent his life defining and creating can be seen, in this light, as consistent with the projects of some of his contemporaries around the edges of Europe, in Spain, France, Hungary, and Russia, who were composing music based on national or regional traditions which Grainger would have defined as racially distinct. He certainly regarded his own art as the expression of a deep Nordic racial consciousness, but he admired these other composers, whose work seemed to him to be similarly inspired by other

---

[19] The blue-eyed compound 'toplayer' = top layer.
[20] P. 11 of manuscript dated 5 Nov. 1927, in Grainger Museum, Melbourne.
[21] Marina Frolova-Walker, review of Klára Móricz, *Jewish Identities: Nationalism, Racism and Utopianism in Twentieth-Century Music*, and Karen Painter, *Symphonic Aspirations: German Music and Politics, 1900–1945*, in the *Times Literary Supplement*, no. 5542 (19 June 2009), 26.
[22] Published in *The Musical Quarterly*, 1 (1915); repr. in Gillies and Clunies Ross (eds.), *Grainger on Music*, 43–64.

racial feelings. Grainger idealised the Nordic world in many ways, but he did not believe in the supremacy of any particular race,[23] and he was not a racist in the sense which that word has acquired.

Inevitably, though, his ideas collided with those of racial supremacists. He had some of their books in his library, yet it is difficult to trace any direct influence of them in his writings.[24] One exception is a passage in *The Love-Life of Helen and Paris* where he describes how the Nordic ardour of his passion for Ella Ström was intensified by his reading of Houston Stewart Chamberlain's notorious *Die Grundlagen des neunzehnten Jahrhunderts*.[25] Even so, Grainger is likely to have disagreed with Chamberlain's assertion of Teutonic superiority, and the assumption that it was indistinguishable from 'Nordic'. It was Grainger's normal practice to maintain a distinction between the two, not least because his pursuit of Nordic music was directed *against* what he regarded as Germanic practices of composition.

Two other references show Grainger dissociating himself from the racist views of these writers. The notes for his lecture on 'Nordic Characteristics in Music', given at Yale on 5 March 1921, begin disingenuously with the claim that he had never heard of the word 'Nordic' until he read it in Madison Grant's *The Passing of the Great Race*.[26] After critically outlining some of Grant's arguments, Grainger went on to differentiate his ideas from those of Nordic racists:

> I am not personally a believer in the magic of 'blood' . . . if I lay emphasis upon the artistic advantages of racial and local traits in art it is because I am thinking of what racial traits and the fostering of local traits can do to enrich the art of the world, of all the world, including China and the Islands of the South Sea, Europe, and all the rest. However it may appear to my listeners, I wish to assure them in advance that I do not believe in special artistic privileges for any race; I do not believe in special artistic superiorities in any race; I do not believe in the special artistic favouring of any race.[27]

What the notes for the Yale lecture suggest is that the circulation of the word 'Nordic' in racist writings was beginning to obscure Grainger's ideas, and that he was intent on clarifying them to prevent misrepresentation.

The second reference is just an allusion, but it is significant. Grainger's late description of his music as 'a Nordic revolt against civilization' turned the title of a book by the vociferous eugenicist Lothrop Stoddard, *The Revolt Against Civilization*,[28]

---

[23] See 'Nordic Characteristics in Music', in Gillies and Clunies Ross (eds.), *Grainger on Music*, 132.

[24] Grainger had books by leading figures in this movement in his library, but when I inspected them in the 1980s they were in mint condition (except for an inscription from his mother in one) and hardly appeared to have been opened. Apart from the dissociative reference and allusion discussed here, they are barely mentioned directly in Grainger's writings.

[25] 'The Love-Life of Helen and Paris', manuscript, pp. 8–9. Chamberlain's book was published in 1899.

[26] (New York, 1916). Grainger's copy was the revised edition of 1919, which his mother had presented him for Christmas that year.

[27] Gillies and Clunies Ross (eds.), *Grainger on Music*, 132.

[28] (New York, 1922).

on its head. Whereas Stoddard argued in defence of white civilization, which he claimed was threatened by the rise of coloured races, Grainger saw his whole creative endeavour as working against civilization, which he did not consider a condition for art. On the contrary, he regarded it as an unacceptable constraint on imaginative freedom. He worshipped Grettir precisely because he was an outlaw, and the Nordic world he envisaged of 'Scandinavians in their Western settlements'[29] around the North Sea, extended beyond the reaches of civilization and inspired art in which untamed nature played the prominent role. This was a fundamental impulse in his music. From the early design of a 'beatless-notation machine' in 1902–3 to the music machines he was building to the end of his life, he was impelled by an idea of music embodying the sounds in nature with the minimum interference of the civilized artifices of composition. The innovations in notation, irregular rhythm, instrumentation, large form, unresolved harmony, and free polyphony in most of his music, such as the examples mentioned in the contribution to *Musikkens Verden*, were working towards the same end: a music unconstrained by civilization.[30]

---

[29] 'Why "My Wretched Tone-Life"?', the final section of Grainger's 'Anecdotes', 423–89, 13 July 1953.

[30] It is worth mentioning in this connection that Grainger was an enthusiastic follower of Huckleberry Finn. See letters to Karen Holten, 15 and 20 March 1907, in Dreyfus (ed.), *The Farthest North of Humanness*, 100, 103.

15

At Home in New York

Stewart Manville

In 1962 Stewart Manville was invited to help Percy Grainger's widow, Ella, in the task of organizing a vast collection of music manuscripts, letters, essays, old concert programmes, photographs, and home recordings at the White Plains house. In 1972 Stewart and Ella were married, continuing their 'missionary work' of promoting Grainger's music both in the USA and abroad until Ella's death in 1979, aged 90. Nearly fifty years after that first beginning, Stewart is still active as curator of the Grainger house and archivist of the Grainger Estate.

WHAT LED TO PERCY'S taking up residence in White Plains, New York? This is one of the questions most frequently asked by visitors to the Grainger home and studio at 7 Cromwell Place.[1] The answer, quite simply, was his need for a place to practise the piano sufficiently for maintaining performing standards, often for hours at a time and, as was his wont, at 'all hours'. Such constant application must certainly have disturbed his neighbours in a multiple dwelling, evidenced by the various changes of address as one follows Percy and his mother Rose around New York during 1914–21. When he resorted to the use of a silent keyboard, one irate neighbour (the noted actor Lionel Barrymore) asked him to get back to his usual piano sessions because the clacking of the keyboard contraption was even more disconcerting.

Ultimately his concert manager Antonia Sawyer suggested a move to a single dwelling in White Plains, where she had her own summer place. The community was only a 35-minute express train ride from mid-Manhattan and offered relief in the hot, humid summer weather to those who could afford a second *pied-à-terre*. (One of them was the journalist Nelly Bly, who had gone 'around the world in eighty days'.) Here at last Percy could hold forth to his self-determined limits. Eventually there would be three pianos in the music room, one with what is called a 'heavy action', demanding extra effort. Local lore describes the congregating of young people on their way home from school, listening on the sidewalk in warm weather when the windows would be open. The author was amongst the audience — wheeled there in his perambulator by a music-loving mother!

The house had been built by the Cromwell family. David Cromwell (1838–1926) was one of the civic leaders of White Plains, and for a time his family occupied No. 7. It is a substantial 'American four-square' house with redwood shingles stained

---

[1] See Plate 3.

brown. It is early for its type (1893), with wider than common eaves, reflecting its Italianate predecessors. Angled corners in some of the downstairs rooms indicate the handiwork of an architect, although public records offer no clue as to his identity. Cast-iron columns support the cellar beams, and there are various other unique features such as a two-way cupboard on the outside wall of the kitchen pantry for milk delivery. The kitchen still has its iron stove. Dual lighting fixtures accommodated both gas and electricity, besides which there is a gas-fuelled fireplace in the music room. Three of the windows are of stained glass, utilising the richly marbled variety favoured by Tiffany; the largest such window adorns the stair landing. There is a back staircase.

While the rear porch is a mere stoop, the front verandah extends the full width of the building. When Percy and his mother took up residence in 1921, she installed an electric power point so that they could take their meals on the front verandah. Percy enjoyed working there, and when the Graingers were in residence, the view looked out to the hills. The outside cellar steps are of bluestone and covered with a pair of slanting wooden doors. Protruding bay windows look out on a lawn that is appropriately nineteenth-century, more meadow than putting green (woe betide any misguided gardener who seeks to 'suburbanize' it, in the manner Eric Fenby bewails when writing of the Delius property at Grez).

The International Percy Grainger website[2] offers a selection of views of the Grainger house interiors: a music room to the left of the entrance hall, living room, dining room — dominated by the trestle table on which Percy composed or scored — a serving pantry, the kitchen to the left-rear, its pantry, and a back entry.

Upon descending the cellar stairs, one discovers a darkroom (more about this later) and two fireproof storage rooms (having somewhat the character of an archaeological 'dig'), as well as another storage closet mainly of shelves, an open area with a carpenter's worktable (beneath which resides his famous wheelbarrow), and a full bathroom. Owing to the elevated situation of the building, the basement floor is actually higher than the level of the street out front. Natural humidity keeps paper from drying out and going brittle, while at the other extreme, dehumidifiers are employed in summer to deter mustiness.

Returning back upstairs and climbing to the next level above, we find four bedrooms off a square, central hall, and the main bathroom. Two of the rooms have one clothes closet apiece, which, according to Percy's wife, Ella, would have accommodated the Cromwell men, father and son. Percy occupied one on the front, street side, with a wide window opening onto the front-porch roof. Each of the ladies' bedrooms was provided with two closets. In the room occupied by Rose, one of the closets is equipped as an en-suite bathroom. This bedroom later became the 'study', with its large flat-top desk as another work area and various cabinets and bookshelves. Ella's room — at the back rear above the kitchen — looks out on a house which had been converted from the original carriage barn for 7 Cromwell Place.

The top floor consists of a full attic with three rooms converging on an open hallway. The full house-width front room is called the 'box room' and has assorted

---

[2] http://www.percygrainger.org/.

furniture, luggage, and the front-porch swing on which Percy and Rose were photographed. Two main rooms must have been intended for servants, but in Percy and Ella's time they provided living quarters for the American composer Henry Cowell (1897–1965) at the time of his parole (a situation similar to Oscar Wilde's). In this attic can be found a few items of furniture abandoned by the Cromwell family when, in 1905, they moved into another house nearby.

It is interesting to note that David Cromwell was a banker and the developer of the then-residential neighbourhood surrounding Cromwell Place. The period of his occupancy of what later became the Grainger house coincided almost precisely with the years in which he held office as president of the corporate village of White Plains — so as an official residence, prominently situated, the structure enjoyed 'standing' right from its beginning, if for quite another reason than as home of a world-famous musician. (Once White Plains had become a city, it was governed instead by a mayor.)

In the matter of home furnishing, Percy's writings mention that 'in buying old furniture my mother had no yearnings for the house beautiful, no wish to surround herself with beautiful things. She simply thought that the society people who took lessons from me and engaged me to play at their "At Homes" would be more impressed and therefore more likely to employ me if we had nice old furniture.' A number of these English antiques eventually found their way into the White Plains house. They were augmented by a few items of American provenance from their New York years during and following the Great War (the London furniture couldn't be sent until war's end). Certain pieces were subsequently shipped to the Grainger Museum in Melbourne.[3] And further, when Ella disposed of her English house at Pevensey Bay in 1961, she brought home a selection from that residence, including one of Cyril Scott's pianos, an upright Steck. Attempting to define a 7 Cromwell Place style is difficult, but Edwardian would be close.

The house was a crossroads of musical activity during the four decades of Percy Grainger's occupancy. Not only did it facilitate his sitting alone at a piano keyboard. Acetate home recordings bear witness to busy sessions with other musicians either rehearsing or trying out new material — a sequence from the six-hands two-piano edition of *The Warriors*, for instance, with Percy, Dorothy Payne from Cincinnati, and celebrity radio performer 'Ramona' (i.e. Mrs Helfer, familiar to Paul Whiteman audiences). We learn from these discs that Ella was a proficient pianist herself.

In the basement Percy converted the laundry room into a darkroom where, in pre-Xerox times, he could run off duplicate copies of scores and parts of as yet unpublished compositions, working from transparency originals. A substantial library of performing material was the result of his labours and is still much in use — not infrequently as an 'emergency' source in the face of bureaucratic inertia or orneriness.

Over time I was able to edit the acetate archive into a series of reel-to-reel tapes with such titles as *Grainger at Home, Grainger in Rehearsal*, etc. (In response to a Christmas greeting from Benjamin Britten and Peter Pears about 1964, Ella and

---

[3] Cf. Lewis Foreman's remarks (Chap. 16) about the 'London Music Room' in the Grainger Museum.

I forwarded a copy of the *Grainger at Home* tape to Aldeburgh, some of which repertory found its way into the Grainger concerts given there in 1966, 1968, and 1970.) Clearly, the inquiring mind, the insatiable curiosity of our restless Australian was functioning well before the period of his Free Music experiments. Evidence indicates that there were concerns other than his efforts to produce gliding tones. That digresses into another topic altogether, the main point here being that the White Plains house filled a multiplicity of purposes as studio, laboratory, music warehouse, business office (which it remains), and certainly in providing the comfort and stability of a permanent residence. When you compare this with the uprooting suffered by so many eminent European musicians in consequence of events of the 1930s, the contrast gives pause.

Ella had already settled Percy's estate by the time of my arrival on the scene in 1962, with most of the house contents in reasonable order as far as I, a newcomer, could determine. As our work commenced, it became clear that a list or catalogue of Grainger's compositions was of paramount importance, so this became our first major undertaking. Putting together such a compilation was a daunting challenge and took several years. Nearly everything was represented in one form or another and just needed to be brought to light, as when one explores uncharted territory. A master plan had existed in Percy's mind, with categories grouped appropriately to serve diverse needs and purposes, but Ella and I surely did Sherlock Holmes proud, emerging with not only an index but also a map — a treasure map. If we hadn't been able to go about our effort in a methodical fashion, the result could have been similar to the vandalism perpetrated by those who first dug into Herculaneum in the eighteenth century. By now you will have fathomed why we call 7 Cromwell Place a library. Some of the original Grainger 'matrix' yet remains and needs to be handled with care. (I joke about admonishing visitors not to disturb any of the 'original dust', but there is some truth in that.)

Over the years since Percy left this life we have hosted at least three dozen researchers. Most have been concerned with aspects of Grainger — whether folkloric, compositional, biographical, experimental, with a few seeking collateral data pertaining to Dom Anselm Hughes, Arnold Dolmetsch, the Frankfurt group of composers, Sousa, Goldman, British music hall, the polymath capabilities of Ella, and much else. It seems as if Percy had identified too many avenues of inquiry for one individual to pursue, but others have joined the hunt — vastly more than one mere 'hunter in his career'.

Visitors wishing to tour the house are frequent (if, thankfully, not overwhelming in numbers) and consist mainly of musicians having an understanding of Grainger's place in musical history. For some of them the visit is a pilgrimage. They want to sit at the Steinway grand piano or photograph interiors and objects. Some like to jot down titles of books on shelves. Many comment on their sense of having entered into a 'twilight zone' or special atmosphere, in which time has become suspended and a quality of reassuring calm prevails. Another kind of caller enjoys its echoes of old White Plains, going back to days of their grandparents. In recognition of our antiquity, the city has just installed street lighting of an early style in Cromwell Place. They had wanted to change the name of the block to Grainger Place until persuaded that 7 Cromwell Place has as much resonance as 10 Downing Street. Anyone fearing that Percy's name might otherwise be forgotten need only look it up in the Oxford Dictionary.

What of the future? Some have questioned the practicality of maintaining the place, more particularly after the income from performing royalties will have ceased as copyrights expire. This, by the way, is a question faced by other musicians' houses in the region — Aaron Copland's in Peekskill, N.Y., as well as Kurt Weill's and Louis Armstrong's on Long Island. Practicality? Various of the same people think nothing of spending substantial sums on publicity and public relations, whereas the fact is that the existence of the Grainger house generates an enormous amount of good will not only in the local community but nationwide, something 'money can't buy'. Think of past instances where such homes were dismantled only to precipitate a reversal — as when the Norwegian government retrieved the contents of Edvard Grieg's home — or the dilemma faced by the Hungarian authorities in their efforts to reconstitute the Béla Bartók household. Even the Copland property was nearly lost. Financial realities underlie all such matters; and when income is derived from music royalties destined to end, alternative sources of funding need to be developed. Needed for the Cromwell Place situation are endowment trusts to take care of overhead and maintenance on the one hand, and a curatorial stipend. Our outlay for utilities and periodic upkeep seldom exceed $10,000; it is merely a dwelling house, not a substantial public structure. We hear of vast sums being raised by other organizations, whereas our recent roofing bill amounted to $8,000. Landmark status exempts the property from taxation.

As curator and archivist I was able to manage on a part-time basis until Ella's final years demanded full attention. My personal resources played a role. My home (since 1930) has been deeded to the International Percy Grainger Society as a possible residence for my successor; it is eight blocks away.

What role does a cultural resource play other than, in our situation, a place of pilgrimage? How will we be using our holdings in the future? It may sound somewhat perplexing when I compare our activities to farming, unless one is familiar with the many demands made upon any reference library. Enquiries are of sufficient frequency, and complexity, that no land lies fallow for long. Researchers aren't the only oncomers, either. A favourite pursuit among the bandsmen of our country seems to be the preparation of band versions of Grainger material — and let's not overlook the necessary commercial aspect of that! There is no fermata to all that confronts us (oh, did Percy invent a blue-eyed word for that musical term which I should have used?).

A postscript: I actually heard Percy Grainger live in 1941 when students in the White Plains school system, active in either an orchestra, band, or chorus, were invited to a special assembly programme in one of the school auditoriums to attend a Grainger piano recital. (In the same year I also heard Rachmaninov in a White Plains concert.) And a final vignette: my single personal contact with Grainger was musical rather than verbal. I can whistle pretty well and was doing so on a train platform when Percy was standing nearby. I was actually doing this for his benefit, and he smiled: '. . . the arrival platform, I take it?'

Plate 32. The Grainger Museum, 2010

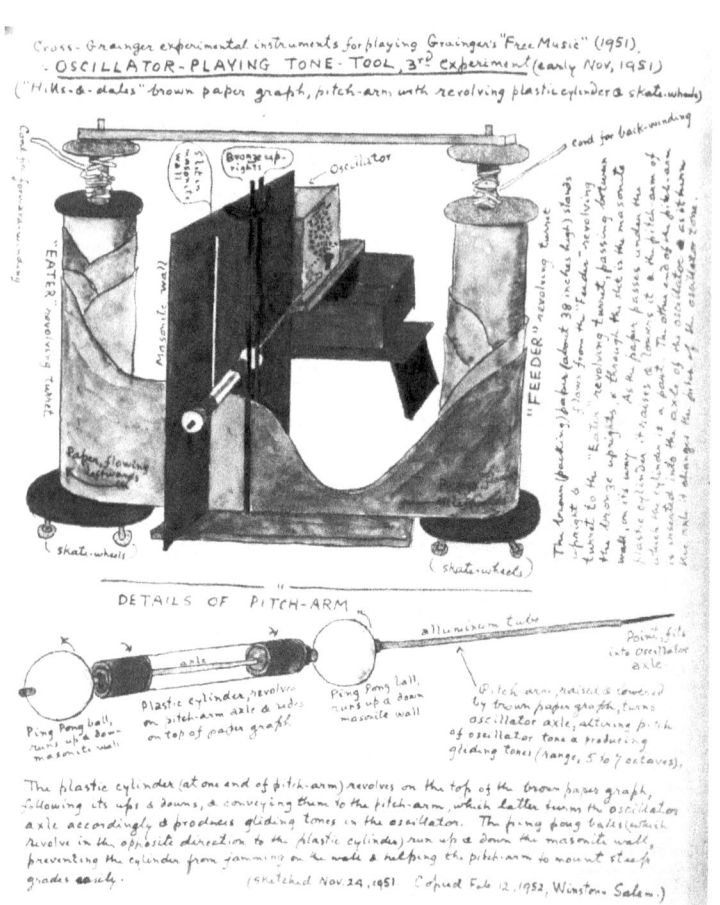

Plate 33. Oscillator-playing tone-tool: Grainger's design for one of his Free Music machines

Plate 34. Liszt's box for letters, given to Grainger in 1910 by his patron, William Gair Rathbone

Plate 35. The Butterfly piano, tuned in sixth-tones for Grainger's Free Music experiments

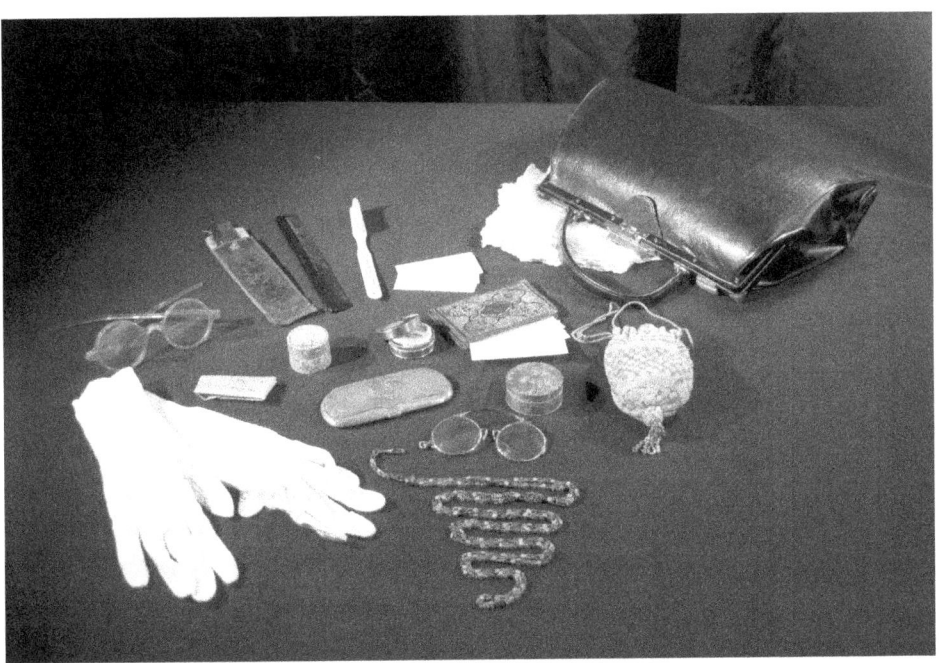

Plate 36. The contents of Rose Grainger's handbag on the day she died, 30 April 1922

Plate 37. Building the Grainger Museum, 1938

Plate 38. The family headstone of Percy Grainger's great-grandfather Jacob Grainger (1796–1880), Heighington, Co. Durham

Plate 39. Denton Chapel, Co. Durham, 2010, where Percy Grainger's grandfather John and his siblings were baptised

Plate 40. The family headstone of Grainger's great-uncle Jacob Grainger jr (1830–1871), Heighington, Co. Durham

Plate 41. Heighington village, 2010

16

Grainger and his Contemporaries

Lewis Foreman

PERCY GRAINGER'S ACTIVITIES in England and Europe, the USA, Australia, and the Pacific brought him into contact with a variety of musical communities across the world. His close creative contemporaries were therefore more varied than most, even if many of them were on the periphery of the concert life of the time. His unusually far-reaching concerns suggest an artistic sympathy with a variety of musicians, arising not only from his composing and his career as a touring piano virtuoso, but also with the folk-music world, both in England and Denmark.

It is arguable that his dream of a continuous and pulseless music, which led to his experiments and trials with 'free-music' machines, was not helpful in developing his acceptance as a mainstream composer. Although he wrote a large catalogue of music, for so long little of it was performed. For many of us Grainger was only the composer of *Handel in the Strand*, *Country Gardens*, *Molly on the Shore*, *Shepherd's Hey*, and *Mock Morris*. From that perspective, the 1970 Grainger Festival in London was a considerable ear-opener. Notable revelations came with the all-Grainger orchestral programmes conducted by Bryan Fairfax at the Queen Elizabeth Hall on 13 March[1] and at the Festival Hall on 20 March,[2] and an electrifying performance of *The Warriors* remains an exciting memory.

Grainger's closest — and most enduring — musical friends were those composers with whom he associated as a student in Frankfurt, as well as those with whom he came in contact in London before the First World War, especially those involved with folk song. Our best clue to Grainger's personal assessment of these contemporaries comes in the Grainger Museum catalogue of *Grainger's Collection of Music by Other Composers*.[3] This is a collection that has ensured the preservation of a number of works which their composers might well have allowed to be destroyed or lost, and yet have now been revealed, in recordings using the Grainger Museum copies, to be delightful music. Possibly the three most interesting examples to the present author are Frederic Austin's Symphony and Cyril Scott's First and Third

---

[1] The programme included: *Green Bushes, My Robin is to the Greenwood Gone, Scotch Strathspey and Reel, Random Round, Hill-Song I*.
[2] The programme included: *English Dance*, the suite *In a Nutshell, To a Nordic Princess*, and the English premiere of *The Warriors*, 54 years after its completion.
[3] Phil Clifford, *Grainger's Collection of Music by Other Composers*, Percy Grainger Music Collection, 1; Grainger Museum, University of Melbourne, Catalogue 1 (Parkville, Vic., 1983).

Symphonies, the recordings of which proved such a find: the Austin with the Royal Liverpool Philharmonic conducted by Douglas Bostock, the Scott by the BBC Philharmonic and Martyn Brabbins.[4]

In her Foreword to the *Music by other Composers* catalogue Kay Dreyfus wrote:

> In establishing the 'Music Museum and Grainger Museum' as it was originally called, Grainger wished to emphasise the creative rather than the executant side of music, to throw light upon the processes of musical composition as distinct from performances. Within this general aim, a geographical frame is provided by his particular championship of the so-called 'Nordic Group' of composers: British, Irish, American, Australian, Scandinavian. The chronological frame is roughly the period covered by his own lifetime: 1882–1961. The preference is for unknown or less known compositions.
>
> In pursuit of this end, Grainger asked composer friends to donate music manuscripts and published editions of their own works to the Museum. Cyril Scott, Balfour Gardiner, Roger Quilter and Herman Sandby, Grainger's fellow-students at Frankfurt, were the chief contributors. But in the course of a long and varied musical career Grainger attracted numerous gifts of published and manuscript music from composers whom he met as he travelled about in the United States of America, Europe and Australia. Some of these composers are still remembered today; others are now forgotten. The inscriptions bear witness to the range of his acquaintance and activities, the variety of motives for the gifts. Finally, there is that music which Grainger collected because he admired it, was interested in it or wished to promote it. In this latter category one might also include his assemblage of largely ephemeral popular vocal, piano and band music of the early twentieth century.
>
> It was also part of Grainger's intention that the Museum's collections should demonstrate the way in which the creative personality is moulded by what he called 'culturizing influences': propitious circumstances or fructifying personalities. Accordingly, the private collections of friends and relations, including his father John Grainger and his manager Antonia Sawyer, find their place in his collection. He believed that these collections reflected the musical tastes of the donors and that, as he was influenced by his friends and relations, their tastes must have some bearing on the formation of his own musical preferences.

Further evidence of Grainger's pre-war London circle (and his mother's part in promoting his career) was a reconstruction of a room from one of their residences. I remember it, when I visited in 1999, as the most vivid aspect of an extremely personal collection. Hanging on the wall was a panel bearing a narrative by Grainger himself (box on next page).[5] The composers that Grainger names here are now seen as very variable in terms of stature, yet at the time they might well have been viewed

---

[4] The Austin was issued on CD by RLPO Live on CLASSICO 1501, the Scott by Chandos in their Cyril Scott series (Symphony no. 1, CHAN 10452; no. 3, CHAN 10211).

[5] Transcribed from a photograph of the panel taken by the present author in 1999.

> **FROM LONDON MUSIC ROOM**
>
> THE CONTENTS OF THIS SECTION WERE PART OF A MUSIC ROOM IN LONDON IN WHICH CHORAL REHEARSALS & MUSICAL EXPERIMENTS WERE CONDUCTED BY RALPH VAUGHAN WILLIAMS, CYRIL SCOTT, ROGER QUILTER, FREDERICK AUSTIN, HERMAN SANDBY, MYSELF & OTHER COMPOSERS.
>
> In buying the old furniture my mother had no yearnings for 'The House Beautiful' — no wish to 'surround herself with beautiful things'. She had no social interests or ambitions.
>
> She simply wanted to help me as a composer. She thought that the 'Society people' who took lessons from me & engaged me to play at their 'at homes' would be more impressed (& therefore more likely to employ me) if we had some nice old furniture in our house.
>
> At the same time my mother did admire the roundness & shapeliness often seen in our furniture. Also, she thought old furniture was better value.
>
> Percy Aldridge Grainger, March 23, 1956.

as having considerable potential. The key words here, as far as we are concerned, are 'musical experiments'.

The use of folk music and folk elements to re-energise concert music inspired Grainger. He was a notable pioneer in taking tunes collected by himself and others into his music. Probably it was the example of Grieg that first inspired him. Grieg's collection of *Norwegian Peasant Dances*, also known as *Slåtter*, Op. 72, was published in London in December 1903. Lionel Carley tells us, 'Among the London musical fraternity, it was left to Percy Grainger first to discover this extraordinary collection. He accepted the challenge with gratitude and was soon to play them — together with some of his similarly favoured pieces from Op. 66[6] — whenever he had the opportunity.'[7] Grainger wrote to Grieg, his first letter dated 14 April 1905, and must have impressed the senior man by writing in Norwegian.[8] Carley notes: 'Herman Sandby, a young Danish cellist and one of Grainger's closest friends, had shown Grainger's first publications to Grieg and in doing so had opened a path to a new friendship . . . Grainger and Sandby had recently given a concert at the Bechstein Hall in London, where they had played *La Scandinavie* — Grainger's arrangements of Scandinavian folk-music.'[9]

Grainger met the Norwegian composer in London on 15 May 1906 and visited him at Troldhaugen in July 1907; a celebrated photograph with the Griegs and Julius Röntgen is dated 25 July. Grieg died on 4 September 1907, but before that he had written to Grainger on 11 August, celebrating Grainger's folk-song arrangements:

---

[6] *Nineteen Norwegian Folk Songs*, Op. 66.
[7] Lionel Carley, *Edvard Grieg in England* (Woodbridge, 2006), 340.
[8] Carley reproduces a facsimile of the first page, ibid., 347.
[9] Ibid., 348.

'I have once again immersed myself in your folk-song arrangements and it is becoming ever more clear to me how brilliant they are. You have given here a very important indication of the way in which the English folk song (in my opinion so very different from both the Scotch and the Irish) has the relevant qualities to be elevated to the level of art, thereby creating an English music that stands on its own.'[10]

Immediately before and just after the First World War similar influences in the music of composers such as Stravinsky, Bartók, Kodály, and various Scandinavian composers must have given them all at least a passing interest to Grainger. On the surface Bartók and Grainger had particular interests in common, and it is unfortunate that Delius's efforts in brokering a dialogue between them ran into the sand when the world changed on the outbreak of the First World War and Bartók and Grainger found themselves on opposing sides. Bartók had written to Delius in September 1910 asking him to 'mention me to Grainger when you have the opportunity; I should like to write to him on the subject of folklore'.[11] Nearly a quarter-century later Grainger published an article entitled 'Melody versus Rhythm' in the Chicago journal *Music News*,[12] and three months later the journal secured a scoop with 'Béla Bartók Replies to Percy Grainger',[13] in which the Hungarian composer offered two observations about the 'primitive state of music' which he had seen during his ethno-musicological research. Grainger did not take up the baton offered.

Clearly Grainger occupied a central place in the use of recently-collected folk song in concert music, as exemplified in the music of Vaughan Williams, Holst, and even Delius in a few works. Yet this was a development which took time to be felt by the general public, and although these early folk-song works started to appear around 1906, their wider performance and acceptance into the standard repertoire took place *after* rather than before the First World War. Percy Grainger was thus very much of his time when his popular folk-song encores started appearing, but he continued to work on them, arranging and re-arranging them for many years. In his folk-music collecting Grainger was not just gathering tunes or words, but people. Wilfrid Mellers noted that

> H. G. Wells, accompanying Percy on a folk-song hunt in Gloucestershire, observed that Grainger noted down not merely 'the music and dialect of the songs, but also many characteristic scraps of banter that passed between the old agriculturalists'. When he remarked that Percy seemed to be notating not merely songs, but a way of life, the musician retorted that there was no distinction.[14]

Balfour Gardiner, composer and forester, was a significant figure in Grainger's life — an older man in his Frankfurt circle — and a wealthy one, whose twin concerns of musical promotion and patronage impinged on Grainger at key moments.

---

[10] Carley, *Edvard Grieg in England*, 420.
[11] Béla Bartók, *Letters*, ed. János Demény (New York, 1971), 105.
[12] 29 September 1933.
[13] 19 January 1934, repr. in Béla Bartók, *Essays*, ed. Benjamin Suchoff (London, 1976), 224–5.
[14] Mellers, *Percy Grainger*, 75. The Wells quote is taken from from Elwes and Elwes, *Gervase Elwes*.

Balfour was such a self-critical composer that he destroyed both his symphonies, but not before they had been performed, leaving us intriguing musical examples in the printed programmes. (What a pity Grainger did not add them to his hoard for his later museum, for which in the mid-thirties Balfour provided emergency funding when Grainger ran out of money.) A key event in Grainger's early performance history were the Balfour Gardiner Concerts, eight choral and orchestral concerts of new music at Queen's Hall promoted by Balfour between March 1912 and March 1913. For a composer who had received few orchestral performances, it must have been eye-opening. In effect Balfour Gardiner gave him the first-ever Grainger-fest, for his music appeared in six of the eight concerts. His music was surrounded by the music of his friends who had gathered in that Chelsea music room: Bax, Austin, Vaughan Williams, Cyril Scott, Norman O'Neill, Holst, Quilter, and Balfour Gardiner himself. The music by Grainger was as follows (using the nomenclature of the programmes):

13 March 1912: *Irish Tune from County Derry* (for unaccompanied wordless choir); Faeroe Isles Dance: *Father and Daughter*; *Morning Song in the Jungle*; *Tiger, Tiger*; *We Have Fed Our Seas*.
17 April 1912: *Mock Morris* (for seven-part string orchestra).
1 May 1912: *English Dance*.
11 February 1913: *The Inuit*; *Green Bushes*.
25 February 1913: *Hill-Song I* (for 15 winds, 8 brass, and 5 percussion); *Colonial Song*.
4 March 1913: *Irish Tune from County Derry* (for unaccompanied wordless choir); *Sir Eglamore*.

Grainger had long championed his friends who had been his student contemporaries in Germany, all members of the 'Frankfurt Gang'. If Cyril Scott was the one to whom he seems to have been closest, it was Roger Quilter, the least secure artistically and emotionally, who offered to assist Grainger by subsidising publication and introduced him to Willy Strecker of Schott, Mainz, whose London branch was then, as now, in Great Marlborough Street. The members of the 'Gang' turned up at the Harrogate Festival in 1929, when their music was performed and Grainger was supportive in eulogising about Quilter's contribution to the Festival: 'I was very much impressed by yr conducting — steady, safe, nice to look at & getting ideal results . . . "I Arise"[15] is perfect in every way, and Children's Overture is richer & more stalwart & better knit under yr stick, than I have ever heard it.'[16]

Grainger's life was lived in a variety of milieux, and the role of his contemporaries in one 'life' was not necessarily reflected in others. Can we ascribe nationality to him? Was he a British composer by virtue of his life before the First World War? Or an American because of his adopted nationality and almost fifty years' residence? Or an Australian by virtue of his birth, allegiance, and later intended domicile? David Tunley wrote: 'In striking contrast to the music of another early radical, the

---
[15] A work by Quilter for tenor and orchestra.
[16] Valerie Langfield, *Roger Quilter: His Life and Music* (Woodbridge, 2002), 82.

American Charles Ives, Grainger's far-sighted concepts when realized in his own music often result, to modern ears, in a period ring because of the musical idiom in which he chose to write. Yet is it precisely because [some of][17] his compositions were so accessible in their day that the ideas underlying the most original of them might have quickly stimulated the emergence of a school of Australian composition striking new paths appropriate to a young country.'[18]

By including their manuscripts in his museum, Grainger has given some of his contemporaries musical life, because in a number of cases these are the only surviving copies. Looking through the list of manuscript music,[19] the composers of whom he preserved more than five manuscripts are few: Henry Cowell, Frederick Delius, Balfour Gardiner, Mabel Harris, Josef Holbrooke, Albert Jordan, Herman Sandby, and Cyril Scott. But the catalogue also shows a substantial holding of photoprinted music,[20] including photostats, dyelines, etc., incorporating another dozen works by Scott. Thus when Chandos, in co-operation with Scott's son Desmond, launched their recordings of Scott's symphonies, now completed, they would not have been able to record Symphonies no. 1 and 3 (*The Muses*) without Grainger's collection. This is a case of a substantial figure suddenly revealed, for now that that series is complete it is clear that not only was Scott's First Symphony a distinctive and delightful voice in his time — even if he withdrew the symphony in youthful insecurity and rage — but the Third with its choral finale is an imposing score. It was only forgotten because it appeared just before the Second World War and it was consigned to the critical junk heap with all Scott's later works, impossible to reassess in Scott's lifetime and needing fine performances and the perspective of time. In this Grainger did well by his memory. What becomes apparent in Scott's later works is his success in developing some of Grainger's musical concerns. Grainger's lifelong friendship with Cyril Scott included a mutual fascination with multiple time signatures and unbarred music. Indeed some of Scott's later works exemplify Grainger's interests in pulseless music and his 'free music' experiments.

While the importance of his Frankfurt years is well known, particularly for the British musical friends he made then, perhaps even more important though less remembered by commentators was the role of Karl Ferdinand Klimsch, whom Grainger described as his 'only composition teacher'. In fact Grainger's nominal teacher at the Hoch Conservatorium was Ivan Knorr.[21] But the young composer resented authority and was unsympathetic to the model of Tchaikovsky that Knorr placed in front of his pupils, and so rejected him.

Karl Klimsch came into the Grainger orbit around 1896. Klimsch had just retired from his business with a considerable fortune, and, as Grainger tells us, 'He violently threw himself upon riding, bicycling, painting, music.'[22] Klimsch had built

---

[17] My insertion.

[18] David Tunley, 'Australian Composition in the Twentieth Century: A Background', in *Australian Composition in the Twentieth Century*, ed. Frank Calloway and David Tunley (Melbourne, 1978), 1.

[19] Clifford, *Grainger's Collection of Music by Other Composers*, 223–43.

[20] Ibid., 245–60.

[21] For Knorr see Moritz Bauer, *Iwan Knorr: Ein Gedenkblatt* (Frankfurt am Main, 1916).

[22] Our main source for Klimsch is Percy Grainger's account dated 25 April 1956 at the Grainger

up one of the world's leading photographic, lithographic, and three-colour-process businesses. From this he had become a Marks millionaire. So when the Graingers knew him he was a wealthy patron of music. Percy summed it up in these words: 'He (an amateur) was my only composition teacher; & I (a wild Australian) was his only composition pupil.' The Graingers, both Percy and his mother, responded to Klimsch's fiery persona, Percy writing,

> Karl Klimsch had the nature of an angel, expressed in the manners of a fiend. His family thought him wonderful but insisted that living with him was mental torture. Almost everything everybody did was wrong in his eyes & though he was never violent bodily he was violent with his tongue. The fact was that everything he did himself, everything he wanted others to do, was pure goodness, pure generosity, pure rightness, pure wisdom. When my mother was threatened with paralysis, late 1899, in Frankfurt, he came to her bedside with a sum of money, saying: 'This will keep you & Percy in the Riviera for six months. It is your duty to accept it and get well. But I give it to you on the understanding that we never mention this money again.' He was an ardent Anglophile, having English governesses for his children and spending the summer holidays in Scotland (which he adored) with his family.

Grainger recalled that he used to have a weekly date with Klimsch's son Eugen and a friend to play piano trios, but on one occasion his mother sent apologies because they had been offered tickets for *Die Meistersinger*, an opera they had never heard. Klimsch was violently anti-Wagnerian and did not approve. As Percy remembered,

> my mother dashed off a hasty note to the Klimsches, telling the good news about our coming *Meistersinger* treat & putting off my Trio-appointment. The next time we saw the Klimsches mother said 'Well when is the next Trio evening?' Karl Klimsch said 'Mrs. Grainger, there's not going to be any Trio-evening. If your son, aged 13, is going to put off two elder players just to hear the *Meistersinger*, there won't be any more Trio-playing.' My mother said: 'I *am* disappointed in you. I thought you wanted Percy to have every possible opportunity to improve himself musically & I thought you would be delighted that we were given a chance to hear the *Meistersinger*. But I see what it is: You are just prejudiced against Wagner. Do you think Percy & I came all the way from Australia just for him to play Trios with what are, after all, amateurs?' Mr. Klimsch stormed up & down, with his hands locked behind his back, while devoted Mrs. Klimsch kicked my mother under the table & whispered 'He will have a Blutstürz (a stroke)!' But not at all. After a moment he turned to my mother with: 'Mrs Grainger, you are right & I am wrong. *Of course* Percy should hear the *Meistersinger*.' My mother's frank Australianism worked perfectly with a downright Frankfurter, like Karl Klimsch.

Not being a product of institutional German musical education, Klimsch had

---

Museum, *The Museum Legends*. All the following quotes attributed to Grainger are from this source.

views about composition that must have been very radical at the time, but were just what Percy wanted to hear. His advice to Percy was: 'If you have no theme or melody in your head, don't compose at all. If you have a theme or melody, start off with it right away, & the moment your melodic inspiration gives out, stop your piece. No prelude, no interlude, no postlude. Just the pith of music, all the time.' Percy said that he had tried to live up to that scheme, ever since. 'Sharply as he criticised most things I must admit that he really, at last, approved of my compositions—such as my Australian piece "Colonial Song" for instance. He listened to it with silent satisfaction. Perhaps he was the only friend my music satisfied.'

But perhaps Klimsch's most important influence on the music of Percy Grainger was his interest in Scottish folk song. Before Grainger met Grieg, and long before he collected English folk song, it was Karl Klimsch who first revealed to Grainger the beauty of folk song when he introduced him to Scottish traditional songs. This was in Macleod and Boulton's *Songs of the North, Gathered from the Highlands and Lowlands of Scotland*.[23] In the late Victorian period this was an enormously popular collection, first published in 1885 and within ten years going through eight editions. Not only did it show Grainger the possibilities of folk song but also the reality of collecting before the prevalence of the English Folk-Song Society. Might it also have set a seed in his mind of the dangers of providing such songs with conventional accompaniments?

We need to remember Grainger's special relationship with Frederick Delius. Grainger and his mother came to know Delius in April 1907 when Delius visited London. The 24-year-old Grainger seems to have found a replacement relationship for that with Grieg, who would die within a few months. He had known nothing of Delius until this meeting, and the composer's wider reputation in England only began in that year. Grainger found that Delius's works and his technique reflected his own aspirations, and they both had an aversion to the classical repertoire. Grainger had collected the folk song 'Brigg Fair' and set it chorally, and Delius asked his permission to base upon it his own orchestral variations. The mutual admiration lasted until Delius's death in 1934, and Grainger was called upon, from time to time, to help as Delius's incapacity grew worse. Ken Russell in his BBC film about Delius's last years, *Song of Summer*, cast David Collings as Percy Grainger,[24] who is made to perform Grainger's trick of throwing a ball over the house then running through fast enough to catch it on the other side. Even more evocative was their re-enactment of the episode of carrying the almost blind Delius up a Norwegian mountain to see the sunset from the peak for the last time.

Grainger's interest in Danish and Scandinavian music was enhanced by his brief friendship with Grieg and given context by his long friendships with Herman Sandby and Karen Holten. But it was brought into a particular musical focus by his journeys with the aged Danish folk-collector Evald Tang Kristensen. They travelled through Jutland with Grainger's phonograph in the summer of 1922 and collected

---

[23] Ed. A. C. Macleod and Harold Boulton; music arranged by Malcolm [Leonard] Lawson. (London, 1885; 8th edn, 1895).

[24] *Bfi* BFIVD518.

80 melodies. A further trip in 1925 added another 92, and there was a third expedition in 1927. These gave rise to folk-music settings in Grainger's most poignant vein, assembled as a concert work in 1928 as *Danish Folk-Music Suite*. Revised in 1941, it was recorded by Leopold Stokowski on 15 July 1945.[25]

A later Scandinavian member of the Grainger circle was the Norwegian composer Sparre Olsen.[26] Olsen wrote, 'Fate led to my meeting in my young years with Percy Grainger, and I will try to tell you about our friendship for 32 years. During our get-togethers, not the least on hiking trips, I gathered quite a lot of information and made notes. They form the background for this little biographical sketch.' From Olsen we know of Grainger's championship of the American composer Arthur Fickenscher, 'in his opinion the greatest of all American composers'. His complaint was that great music went unheard.

A pioneering exposition of 'Percy Grainger and his Circle' took place at London's Purcell Room on 18 May 1973. The pianist and composer Ronald Stevenson played an enormously wide-ranging programme: in addition to such Grainger works as *'The Gum-Suckers' March* and *Colonial Song*, he played music by Cyril Scott, Roger Quilter, Norman O'Neill, Balfour Gardiner, Frederick Delius, Eugene Goossens, Herman Sandby, Sparre Olsen, Grieg, Nathaniel Dett, Duke Ellington, Henry Cowell, and Gershwin. Grainger's transcripton of Gershwin's song *The Man I Love* came near the end, and at the climax, Stevenson's own transcription of *Hill-Song 1* (one of Grainger's favourites among his works).

While Grainger certainly made ambitious claims for his technical and compositional experiments, he never really produced an innovation that achieved widespread currency in his lifetime. Yet he certainly exemplified new ideas in music, and embraced the new. Richard Franko Goldman reminisced: 'I am happy to record the fact that I was first directed to the works of both Schönberg (*Five Orchestral Pieces*) and Stravinsky (Piano Concerto) by Mr Grainger in the 1920s when I was a young student.'[27] Grainger's experiments pre-date those of Charles Ives, but neither was a significant practical influence in their lifetimes. 'Grainger and Ives had more than a little in common, both working in an atmosphere as close to wilful independence as possible, and both anticipating later practices.'[28] Grainger also would have us note technical parallels between his *Hill-Song I* and Schoenberg's first Chamber Symphony and Stravinsky's *L'Histoire du soldat*. As early as 1915 he is quoted as saying: 'If Bach were living today I feel he would include ragtime, Schönbergisms, musical

---

[25] With the addition of Grainger's suite, *In a Nutshell*, this recording could be said to have cemented Grainger's place on the accepted concert platform.

[26] Olsen does not appear in *New Grove 2*. Carl Gustav Sparre Olsen (1903–1984) was a noted choral composer and conductor, who when Grainger met him was associated with Norwegian folk song. He was later celebrated as a critic. He published an illustrated account of his association with Grainger, *Percy Grainger* (Oslo, 1963). That book is only published in Norwegian, but fortunately when I acquired my copy soon after it was published I wrote to the author, who sent me an unofficial English translation, from which I quote.

[27] Richard Franko Goldman, 'Percy Grainger's "Free Music"', *Juilliard Review*, 2 (Fall 1955) 41, quoted by Thomas Carl Slattery, 'The Wind Music of Percy Aldridge Grainger' (PhD thesis, University of Iowa, 1967).

[28] Goldman, 'Percy Grainger's "Free Music"', 38.

comedy, Strauss, and all the grades in between.'[29] In truth Grainger was experimenting with things which were of their time. His technical and artistic concerns find their final summation in his wind-band scores and notably his *Lincolnshire Posy*.

In a letter to Stewart Deas (who was later Professor of Music at Edinburgh) written in 1931, Grainger addressed the practical problems of performing his orchestral music. This may go some way to explain why most of these works did not enter the regular repertoire — in the 1930s it was not possible routinely to obtain the performing materials.

> I am sending you today *Lord Peter & The Nightingale*. The 3rd number of this suite (*Jutish Medley*) will be sent to you from Schott London. *Green Bushes* will be sent to you from Schott, Mainz.
>
> The Danish Suite runs:
> (a) *Lord Peter*
> (b) *The Nightingale*
> (c) *Jutish M.*
> (*The Power of Love* is not out yet).
>
> In all of these works use <u>at least</u> 2 pianos. Use 2 harmoniums if you have not got a pipe organ. And double or treble all woodwind & double brass, where possible. Thus in *Lord Peter* let <u>all</u> the trombones play the trombone part in unison, etc. . . . You see I try to get as nearly as I can a balance between the various groups: woodwind, percussion (piano, marimbas, etc) strings, brass, etc.[30]

The creative world of Grainger as we have begun to understand it during the last fifty years has been dependent on increasing numbers of recordings and performances. Historically important in articulating this understanding was the band conductor Frederick Fennell (1914–2004).[31] His recording of *Lincolnshire Posy* not only launched that work to the wider musical world for the first time, but it also promoted Grainger to the world of wind bands of which, especially in the USA and Japan, there are an enormous number. When the celebrated Tokyo Kosei Wind Orchestra took up the work in their recording programme with conductor Douglas Bostock in 2003,[32] they were keen to document the background in the notes for a Japanese audience. In the preface to this most mature and integrated work, Grainger writes that he is celebrating the folk singers from Lincolnshire 'who sang so sweetly to me'. He would surely have been delighted by such a cross-cultural conjunction.

---

[29] D. C. Parker, *Percy Aldridge Grainger: A Study* (New York and Boston, 1918), 26. Parker goes on to remark: 'He is not among those who regard Schönberg as a madman. On the contrary, he rejoices in the fact that that modern prophet has pointed the way of escape from the inevitability of harmony.'

[30] Letter dated 'Aug. 31, 1931', author's collection.

[31] Fennell's own Eastman Wind Ensemble recording of Grainger's *Lincolnshire Posy*, 1958, was selected by *Stereo Review* magazine as one of the '50 Best Recordings of the Century of the Phonograph, 1877–1977'.

[32] Kosei KOCD 8011.

17

Reflection and Reminiscence

Desmond Scott

ONE OF THE LONGEST FRIENDSHIPS in musical history, lasting more than sixty years, began in 1895 when two boys, born half a world apart, met as students at the Hoch Conservatorium in Frankfurt. Percy Grainger was thirteen, my father, Cyril Scott, sixteen. Three years' difference at that age is huge, and when a composition of Grainger's was cruelly mocked by his teachers Scott's defence of it started a friendship that ended only with Grainger's death in 1961.

Even so, an 1899 letter from Scott sounds a little patronising (and ungrammatical): 'My dear boy, the true facility to composing is technique and unless you make up your mind to study that . . . you will be very long before you get that facility.'[1] Grainger must have been a quick study, because two years later, in 1901, Scott writes to Balfour Gardiner, 'After hearing Grainger's Cello piece (*Youthful Rapture*) all my work seems insipid. The boy is a genius of the first water . . . possessor of a strength, an originality, pathos and beauty which baffles all description.'[2]

At first glance they might seem an unlikely pair — the impetuous extrovert Australian and the sensitive refined Englishman — but opposites attract. As young men, they were equally eccentric, particularly in matters of dress. Cyril favoured black velvet jackets, check trousers, and flowing cravats with expensive tie-pins and was only too well aware of the impression he created. Clothes, at that time, were important to Percy too. Writing to Rose Grainger when his friend was staying with the Scotts in 1902, Cyril reports that Percy 'would rather go without his dinner than take less than fifty minutes to put on his dress clothes'.[3] Music was the bond that united them, and, amazingly, there is never the slightest hint of jealousy or rivalry between them. A work of Percy's performed and praised was as much a celebration for Cyril as it was for Percy and vice versa.

I have written elsewhere of Percy's amazing generosity to Cyril, giving him his English royalties during World War II and lending him Ella's little house in Pevensey Bay rent-free.[4] More important, he insisted on making copies at his own expense of a number of Cyril's major compositions for his Museum, hating the idea of single copies lying around and getting lost.

---

[1] 17 November 1899.
[2] 13 August 1901.
[3] Ibid.
[4] *In a Nutshell* [Friends of the Grainger Museum Newsletter] (April 2001).

Perhaps what endeared Cyril to Percy was Cyril's complete acceptance of him as a human being. Percy's biographer John Bird told me that of all the people he interviewed during his research it was my father who most helped him find the true self behind the thousand masks that Percy wore. I never had the good fortune to meet Percy, but reading over the correspondence again I agree about the masks, feeling that beyond the mass of contradictions, outrageous statements, bravado, and the obsessions there lies a very vulnerable, humane, and loveable man. His concern for his fellow composers is apparent. He worries over Quilter's 'mind troubles'[5] and Balfour Gardiner's health. He writes to him and Cyril (knowing his interest in alternative medicine) three times in 1947 expressing his concerns and enlisting Cyril's aid.[6] Percy had great faith in Cyril's homeopathic suggestions and felt he genuinely benefited from them.

They had their disagreements, of course. Percy thought Cyril lived in an ivory tower and never wanted to get out and be a practical musician — 'conducting and testing your own things, leaning how to write readable mss [manuscripts] . . . you never want to come out and learn yr craft (the craft of making music *performable*)'.[7] He felt Cyril was too self-critical, dismissing as juvenile so many of his early works: 'I have always resented in you that you always wanted to criticise your own music, wished to discard what you felt you had risen above. I am thankful for my lownesses as well as my heights, proud of my sins as well as my virtues.'[8]

The only serious falling out they had concerned Percy's mother, Rose. A short while after her death, Cyril was staying with Mrs Nelsa Chaplin, a clairvoyant, and her husband.[9] Apparently Rose appeared to Mrs Chaplin and asked Cyril to give a message to Percy. That, not surprisingly, distressed and angered Percy. If she were going to appear to anyone, surely it should be to her son! Cyril tried to explain, but Percy was aggrieved over Rose's apparent favouritism. Eventually they resolved it and the friendship resumed.

They saw each other less frequently after Percy moved to America but continued to write through good times and bad. World War II was a particularly hard time for Cyril. He was unwell, short of money, and so depressed he actually felt death to be near. Things improved after he took a 'biochemic' remedy he found in a book he'd asked Percy to send him: 'I had got into such a state that I could hardly bring myself to write a letter but all is different now.'[10] In the Eastbourne house where my father moved after the war I remember there were very few photos except in the music room, where there were two. One was of the German poet Stefan George, 'the awakener in me of all poetry', as Cyril said, and the other was of Percy Grainger.

Cyril writes, 'My beloved friend, as long as you and I are both alive we need each other's stimulus — at any rate I need yours.'[11] Percy writes: 'Darling Cyril . . . when

---

[5] 4 February 1947.
[6] 18 August 1947, Grainger to Balfour Gardiner, urging him to ask Scott's advice.
[7] 24 January 1947.
[8] Ibid.
[9] Cyril Scott, *Bone of Contention: Life Story and Confessions* (London, 1969), 158 ff.
[10] 7 April 1943.
[11] 23 November 1944.

I was sixteen you developed me from a Handelian composer to a modern composer and when I was on the brink of seventy you GAVE ME A NEW LEASE OF LIFE, THEREBY ENABLING ME TO REALISE MY FREE MUSIC.'[12] The 'new lease' is a further reference to Cyril's help concerning Percy's cancer. The latter would be delighted to know how crucial he has been to the current revival of Cyril's music. Many of the orchestral works exist solely in Grainger's Museum; had Percy not continually pestered Cyril for them there would have been very few scores available to be recorded!

In 1920 Percy made a two-piano arrangement of Cyril's Three Symphonic Dances, and in 1922 he and Cyril recorded no. 1.[13] It is a delight — two friends, both brilliant pianists, playing a work they thoroughly enjoy and having enormous fun playing together: for me, it is the perfect symbol of their remarkable and enduring friendship.

Scott/Grainger/Balfour Gardiner letters, Grainger Museum, Melbourne.
Grainger/Scott letters, Estate of Cyril Scott, Toronto and Grainger Museum, Melbourne.

Ronald Stevenson

Transcriber's Note:
Between 1957 and 1961 Grainger and the young Scottish pianist and composer Ronald Stevenson enjoyed a correspondence which grew to include 32 letters.[14] They covered a wide range of topics from Bach to folk music to the latest musical innovations. What follows are some of Stevenson's thoughts on Grainger, including a little-known aspect, culled from an interview given at his home in West Linton, Scotland, on 25 March 2009.
Teresa Balough

My correspondence with Grainger began in the wrong way because I was researching Busoni and contacting everybody I could who had known Busoni. Percy Grainger had been a Busoni student. That's how it began, on the wrong foot: it should have begun about Percy, not about Busoni; but it soon got round to Percy. There was certainly the theme of Marxism in the correspondence. (I was very interested in Shostakovich, so that linked up.) Percy's physician and close friend K. K. Nygaard told me that he knew that Percy had been a member of the American Communist Party for two years and Percy came out of it, decided to stop attending meetings, because he felt that it was a narrow view of Marxism that they had. Percy's friendship with the American composer Henry Cowell, I think, may have been part of this because, as is well known, Henry Cowell was certainly a member of the American Communist Party. I think possibly that Percy knew Cowell through Ruth Crawford Seeger, Pete Seeger's stepmother. In America I met Pete Seeger who remembered that his father, the musicologist Charles Seeger, knew Percy and spoke very often of him.

In our correspondence I questioned Percy about electronic music, Free Music,

---

[12] 13 October 1951.
[13] *Legendary Artists 4 Hands*, vol. 1, Klavier Records LP KS102; currently on YouTube.
[14] *Comrades in Art: The Correspondence of Ronald Stevenson and Percy Grainger*, ed. Teresa Balough (London, 2009).

folk music, folk-music collecting, the range of repertoire and the idea of transcribing. I transcribed his *Hill-Song*, and *The Warriors* for piano. Grainger himself was, of course, a tremendous transcriber. I don't differentiate between composition and transcription. I think every good transcription is an original composition and is sometimes better than the original material from which it was transcribed.

There was a kinship. I can't analyse what the kinship was. And then also personal appearance is so important to me. I think Percy had such a beautiful face and hair, and it means a great deal to me. I was very interested then in writing for wind band and I wrote one specific piece for wind band including the piano. Somebody said: 'Oh, you mustn't write for piano and wind band, that's not a good idea. The piano doesn't take any part of the wind band.' You know, this is concerto style, with a wind band instead of an orchestra and that is my work *Corroboree for Percy Grainger*. Percy, of course, wrote for piano and wind band and was a pioneer in that respect.[15]

The fact that he loved Scottish folk-song and wrote those early settings from *Songs of the North* and made his series of British Folk-Music settings was also very encouraging to me as a young Scottish composer. In fact, it was performances by folk singers that suggested to Percy the use of free rhythm in his original compositions.[16] His *Hill-Song* and *Train Music*, orchestral works both dating from the early years of the twentieth century, were notated in multiple time signatures: 4 beats to the bar followed by 3, 4 1/2, 2, 5, 7, and so on.

In regard to Grainger's influence on my own work, the orchestration, yes, but not the composition. I admired his orchestration so much, and for this reason: he played every instrument. I don't mean he played it as a virtuoso, but he borrowed an instrument from Boosey & Hawkes and would spend a month or two learning the principles of it. I admired that very much. I therefore learn as much from his orchestration as I can. I think there's only one other musician who did all that with the orchestra, and that was Mendelssohn. Mendelssohn played every instrument.

I think he was music's natural man at a time when there was so much unnatural and so much artificial stuff; Grainger was natural. One of my favourites — as time goes on more and more — I love his *My Robin is to the Greenwood Gone*.[17] I think it is so beautiful and there is the idea of taking only a fragment of Elizabethan music and out of that, fashioning a re-creation, an extension. It's not just variation, as the academic would have it. It's amazing. It's as though the whole composition is a kind of overtone technique from the basic tone of the Elizabethan music; it's marvellous. For me, I think that's maybe my favourite Grainger piece.

Much has been made of his nationalism but I think it's because he felt that the North, the northern culture, had been neglected; and then I think that, in order to make a point, he exaggerated. A concomitant of Grainger's nationalism was his folk-song collecting. Grainger was a racist in the non-pejorative sense. He was interested in races and made a profound study of music and peoples. One shouldn't have to

---

[15] See Grainger's *Children's March: Over the Hills and Far Away*. [Ed.]
[16] Amongst other things. [Ed.]
[17] A 'ramble' upon the first four bars of the old tune of that name for small chamber ensemble. [Ed.]

justify him because he's the justification of himself, his work is his own justification. His published articles give ample proof that he was totally open to American Jewish composers, for instance, and admiring of their work.

His whole work, the life work, should be known. It's all good. I think Percy never published anything that was bad or inferior. He was so careful. He wanted to hear the work practised to see how it went, and that was an insurance that it would be good.

Alan Woolgar

My first encounter with the music of Percy Grainger was as a member of a youth orchestra, but on joining the music publishers Schott & Co. Ltd in 1948, it became literally a hands-on experience. One of my early tasks was to collect large packages of music from a nearby warehouse depot, and this certainly included large parcels of *Country Gardens* and many others of his popular works in their piano versions.

Later on I was given the task of making up band sets of *Lincolnshire Posy*; the separate parts were laid out on a long bench and one walked along picking up one (or more) of each part as required, putting them into the cover folders. Usually some 25–30 sets were made up at a time, so some quite good exercise was achieved as well!

One event I do remember (painful on a toe at the time) was when Percy was over in London (in the early 1950s?) and wished to take back with him a set of handbells that had been especially made for him and left with Schott many years before. They were in a wooden travelling case, very awkward to get down the narrow staircases from the attic room in which they had been stored; there were quite a few bruises on the way down! Percy was lucky in that they had escaped unscathed during the war, as a German incendiary bomb had come through the roof. (It was perhaps ironic that the main casualties of that event were sets of orchestral parts to the Wagner operas; they had survived, but in a somewhat singed state.)

Grainger was an unusual composer in his dealings with Schott as his publisher, in that he paid half of all the printing costs for the production of his works. He fully realised that not all of them would be such instant best-sellers as *Country Gardens* turned out to be, and that many of them would possibly remain unsold on the shelves for some years. In a reciprocal gesture, Schott paid him a much higher than normal royalty rate on sales of his printed music. Often I had to look out various sets of printed parts for his use, and he always insisted that these were to be properly invoiced to him, and not merely supplied as 'freebies'.

On one of the last visits that Percy and Ella made to Schott's, our Managing Director, Max Steffens, asked Percy how he was, to which Percy replied — 'I can't jump over five-barred gates any more', which caused much laughter in the Trade department into which he always came, rather than wait in the front shop and then be shown upstairs to the Director's own office. I remember Percy presenting Max Steffens with one of his new LP records. One thing that does stay in my memory is that he had a very intense look — you had the feeling that he could read your very thoughts; perhaps, indeed, he could!

Vera Bradford
Attending Grainger's classes at the Chicago Music College 1930[18]

The millionaire college president engaged the best artists to teach at the Summer Schools, including Grainger, Leopold Auer — famous Russian teacher of Heifetz — Raab, Ganz and many others. The ten-storey building simply vibrated with the comings and goings of so many famous people, but the most fascinating and original person was Percy Grainger. I remember his lessons and master classes with gratitude. He was a formidable virtuoso, and a master of rhythm and pedalling. All this reflected in his teaching. The college president had suggested that he could have as many pianos as he wished, so Percy settled for twenty grands![19] Moving pianos up and down in the college lift for rehearsals created bedlam, but it was all part of the lively ensemble that Percy enjoyed. There were gongs, bells, marimbas, and mallets used on the strings of pianos (all influenced by his love of the exotic) with fantastic results.

Colin Cameron
Turning pages for Grainger in Mt Gambier, 27 February 1935[20]

I was a sixteen-and-a-half-year-old piano student when I was offered the opportunity by my piano teacher to turn for Mr Grainger during his solo performance. I can't recall whether he wore a dinner suit or a lounge suit but I can recall that he wore red socks. From what I gathered in later years, he was quite an eccentric. At rehearsal I sat on the left side of the bench whilst he quietly pointed out that he would nod when ready to turn, and that I was to use forefinger and thumb on the centre of the page to be turned. I had to keep my arm high so as not to cover his vision. I can't recall anything of his playing. I imagine my nerves about remembering what to do would have meant concentrating on the job in hand.

Gerald Gentry
Grainger's only television appearance, 29 May 1957
(recorded in the BBC Birmingham Studios)[21]

I was then the thirty-year-old staff conductor for the BBC. I had a small advantage over some other conductors, since I had already met Cyril Scott, Balfour Gardiner

---

[18] Extract from unattributed newspaper interview, sent to the Editor.
[19] See Plate 12. [Ed.]
[20] From a personal letter to the Editor. An enclosed review from the *Border Watch Newspaper* (28 Feb. 1935) describes a 'Great Reception for Visiting Artist'.
[21] Excerpt from Gerald Gentry, 'Grainger's Only Appearance on Television', *In a Nutshell* (March 2001), 9. The *Radio Times* (May 1957) shows that Grainger played *Handel in the Strand* and Grieg's *To the Spring*.

and Roger Quilter. With meeting Percy Grainger I could claim I had met four of the 'Frankfurt Gang'. I would like to remind readers that in 1957 all programmes were transmitted live. With his first piano entry all doubts were dispelled about how great a pianist Percy Grainger still was in his seventy-fifth year. After the concert there was a very touching moment when Percy informed me that with his fee he was going to buy the best record player and reproduction equipment, so that his friend Cyril Scott could listen to some good music in his old age. Cyril Scott was then seventy-eight years old.

Cara Aldridge Ham
The Aldridge Family

If you said something was black, Percy would be sure to say it was white. My husband Rod and I had many of our own paintings on the wall of our London studio. We remember Percy coming to see us, rushing around exclaiming: 'Ah! Picasso! Yes! Matisse!' We assumed he was pulling our legs. My father George (horse trainer and sometime jockey) was a cousin of Percy. The sport-loving Aldridge boys had been rather ashamed of their relation (the young piano prodigy) turning up to play in *white gloves*: 'bit of a sis' was their assessment. In adult life Percy revenged himself by attending another cousin's cocktail party dressed in one of his outfits made from colourful towelling. Conservative Adelaide was shocked. I well remember him arriving at our house on one of his Australian visits, vaulting the gate and going straight to the piano. *The Juba Dance* was one of his specialties, and the piano would rock to and fro with the force of his playing. My mother could play, and they sometimes performed duets, mother apologising for her small hand, Percy adapting to it. He had no snobbery. When his cousin Bill Morrish requested *Yes, We Have No Bananas*, Percy was happy to oblige.

My brother, James, was very keen on jazz and enjoyed his discussions with Percy on the subject. And he remembered how his cousin prepared for one of his long bush walks by putting up and spending some time in a tent on the front lawn of grandfather James Aldridge's house 'Richmond Park'. My sister Athalie was briefly inspired to vegetarianism, having met Percy. His favourite foods were bread, butter, cream, jam, fruits, and nuts. Another cousin, Jack Morrish, son of our 'Aunt Babs', remembered him staying with them in the 1920s and playing football for hours with the twelve-year-old and his friends. Percy would suddenly disappear to take the thirty-mile walk to Gawler and back. Jack recollects that Percy would 'look at you straight in the eye, with a kind of half smile.' When he attended a Grainger performance at the Adelaide Town Hall, he remembers him as a flamboyant showman — 'his hands flying over the keys, shaking his wavy hair'. All the family were delighted when Percy returned to Australia in 1933 with his wife Ella. She was a beautiful, artistic and generous woman.

Peter Sculthorpe

One of the great occasions of my childhood occurred in 1938.[22] On a visit to Melbourne with my mother, I met Percy Grainger. He was strolling in the Botanical Gardens with Professor W. A. Laver, who taught at the Conservatorium of Music. I'd come to know Professor Laver from his visits to Launceston as a music examiner for Trinity College, London. He always seemed enthusiastic about my early attempts at composition. I told Percy Grainger that, when I grew up, I, too, would be a composer. 'My boy,' he proclaimed, 'you must look North, to the islands!' At the time, I thought he was referring to the islands of Melanesia and Micronesia. Much later, it became clear that he really meant North-East Asia. As it turned out, I did follow his advice, without even realising it.

One of the first Australian works to employ an oriental melody is Percy Grainger's solo piano piece *Beautiful Fresh Flower* (1935). Based on a Chinese popular song, it was completed in Hobart at the Highfield Hotel, while Grainger was on a concert tour of my native Tasmania. When I was a boy, the hotel in Hobart most favoured by my parents was the Highfield and we often stayed there. It's not surprising that I should make an arrangement, for strings, of the Grainger arrangement. I did this in 1989, especially for a concert given by the Sydney Symphony Orchestra for my sixtieth birthday.

Grainger was once offered the honorary degree, Doctor of Music, from the New York College of Music. In declining it, he wrote: 'I feel myself closer to the music of the South Seas, China, Japan, Java, Africa, than to the music of Europe, and I would be insincere if I took upon myself a distinction that identified myself with the art, culture and opinions of the civilized world — my own trends being so very different.'

Percy Grainger died in 1961. If he'd lived until the end of the decade, he would have seen one of his dreams realised: the adoption of Asian and Pacific ideas into Australian music.[23]

---

[22] Sculthorpe was eight or nine at the time. This incident rather amusingly parallels the meeting between the young Percy and Frederic Cowen (see David Walker's Chap. 10). [Ed.]

[23] Author's self-quotations from *Sun Music: Journeys and Reflections from a Composer's Life* (Sydney, 1999).

18

The Spiritualising Influence of Music: Grainger's Philosophy of Life and Art

Teresa Balough

IF A PHILOSOPHER is a person who offers views or theories on the profound questions of life, then Grainger certainly qualifies as one of the twentieth century's most original thinkers. His extensive writings (more than fifty published articles) are almost always shot through with statements on the universality of art, the desirability of developing people creatively, the spiritualising influence of music, and the evolutionary need for tallying the freedom of nature within it. To include his name in the company of such great writers as Meister Eckhart, Marsilio Ficino, Goethe, Schopenhauer, Rudolf Steiner, and Benedetto Croce might seem implausible to some: yet his published writings demonstrate why he belongs in the circle of those vitally concerned with the philosophical and spiritual dimensions of art. Grainger's philosophy of music may be summed up in two statements made by him as a mature man:

> I cannot appreciate music without some sense of its relation to human progress . . . if music is not going to play its part in making mankind more loving, compassionate, understanding, thoughtful, restrained, scientific and concentrated, I don't know why we are giving so much time to it.[1]

> My musical creed is 'musical democracy' . . . a chance for all to shine in a starry whole.[2]

These were themes which he not only expounded but acted upon throughout his life. They were beliefs in which he never lost faith.

Even as a young boy Grainger appreciated the seriousness and importance of the arts, especially music. He wrote that he and his mother lived in the love of art as 'monks live in the love of God'.[3] Art was his religion. In later life he would write, 'I look on music as a religious art, a form of devotion, and essentially an art in which many different personalities blend into one harmonious whole.'[4] Music was for

---

[1] Percy Grainger to the music critic Olin Downes, 10 September 1942.
[2] *Musikens Verden*, ed. Kjell B. Sandved (Oslo, 1951).
[3] Percy Grainger, *The Aldridge-Grainger-Ström Saga*, unpublished manuscript dated September 1933 – January 1934, 17.
[4] Percy Grainger, *Percy Grainger to Broadcast*, undated press release in the Grainger Museum, c.1934.

Grainger a great unifying force for all humanity, but he also saw clearly that the way must be from the local, to the national, to the universal. For this reason he found folk music to be of great value, not only as a means of bringing music to the people but also as a vehicle for bringing the inherent freedom of folk music into concert music: 'Music should belong to the people, and we can best bring them to an understanding and enjoyment of the greatest music through folk music, the musical expression of the people.'[5] When he made his own folk-song collecting expeditions in Lincolnshire, England, he was intrigued by the individual variation present in the music which he collected and saw in it an example to be taken up into art music as well: 'Primitive music and folk-music encourage almost unlimited individuality in the performer, to such an extent that it is hard to say, with such music, where the creative and executive roles begin and end.'[6]

He felt it his inherent duty to champion not only British folk music but (as he saw it) the neglected music of English-speaking composers, detecting in it special qualities. In a *Broadcast to Australia* in 1943 he expressed the view that 'The very things that our peoples are fighting for in this war (as in the last war) are, also, the bulwarks of our music. Our music affirms and illuminates the ideals about which all English-speaking peoples are united . . . For the invariable characteristic of all English-speaking music, is brotherliness and freedom.'[7]

Yet he also felt keenly the imperative for each nation, each racial and ethnic group, to bring forward its own unique contribution. Writing to the distinguished African-American composer Nathaniel Dett in 1925, Grainger averred, 'Art should be one of the meeting places of all races, without racial, national or local prejudices, jealousies or smallnesses.'[8] Here he is independently echoing the words of the great Austrian philosopher, scientist, and educator Rudolf Steiner, who stated in a 1923 lecture,

> Every nation, even the smallest, has to contribute its share toward the whole evolution of humanity . . . Individuals belonging to the several peoples will only be able to bring their free, concrete contributions to this joint mission, if they have, first of all, an understanding of the folk to which they belong . . . What is given to all mankind, and must be given, can only spring up at a certain place; but it must be given to the whole of humanity.[9]

Grainger was an advocate of 'world music' education in a day in which the word 'ethnomusicologist' had not yet been coined and the concert repertoire was basically limited to the output of European composers from between the years 1700 and 1900. In 1924 he wrote, 'As I see it the greatest need of music today is the need of universalism in every aspect of the word. The only healthy thing today is to be able, as far

---

[5] Percy Grainger, 'Rare Music of Early English Age Restored', an interview with Edna Horton, *Musical Courier* (1 Oct. 1939).

[6] Percy Grainger, *Music: A Commonsense View of All Types*, a synopsis of lectures delivered for the Australian Broadcasting Commission in 1934 and 1935 (Sydney, 1934), 6.

[7] Percy Grainger, *Broadcast to Australia*, 21 October 1943.

[8] Percy Grainger to Nathaniel Dett, 6 March 1925.

[9] Rudolf Steiner, *The Mission of the Folk Souls* (Blauvelt, N.Y., 1989), 56, 3, 141.

as possible, to admire the products of all ages, all races, all styles, and all schools.'[10] In 1915 he advocated the formation of an International Musical Society 'for the purpose of making all the world's music known to all the world by means of imported performances, phonograph and gramophone records and adequate notations'.[11] As he wrote a few years later, 'What matters is that we, at last, make of music a universal language, a cosmopolitan experience, and (as far as possible) a timeless art.'[12] In the outline for his course entitled 'A General Study of the Manifold Nature of Music', taught during his tenure as head of the music department at New York University in 1932 and 1933, he stated, 'The main purpose of this course is to make the student familiar with the chief types of music of all periods and places (as far as they are known and available), to show the threads of unity, running through all kinds of music'.[13]

Over half a century later Grainger's far-sighted vision was still a dream. In his series of essays on '*A Commonsense View of All Music*': *Reflections on Percy Grainger's Contribution to Ethnomusicology and Music Education*, Professor John Blacking wrote,

> Grainger's idea of music as a universal language is still a vision of the future, and we continue to live in a world in which people's musical experience reflects divisions of wealth, creed, class and nation which breed poverty, ignorance and violence. [But] I am convinced that Grainger's plan is feasible, and that it can best be brought about by developments in music education and ethnomusicology.[14]

Hand in hand with Grainger's belief in the need for universalism in music was his feeling for 'musical democracy' — a call for community music in which individuals learned to create their own music: 'Every born creature is artistic',[15] and 'the main thing in music is that we make it an expression of our lives'.[16] Furthermore, 'I would like to see a condition in music where everybody in the community composed his own music. If we are really serious about democracy every individual should have a chance of expressing himself musically.'[17] From a twenty-first-century standpoint, Grainger's ideas emerge as prophetic. Much that he envisaged in education is now happening.

He took his idea of 'art for all' even further: 'A civilized wage-slave not only has laughably little time to be artistic but he is held back from the natural unreasoning

---

[10] Percy Grainger, 'Percy Grainger's Fighting Creed: His Guiding Principles as a Composer,' *The Australian Musical News* (1 Oct. 1924), 18.
[11] Percy Grainger, 'The Impress of Personality in Unwritten Music,' *The Musical Quarterly*, 1 (July 1915), 433.
[12] Percy Grainger, 'The Culturizing Possibilities of the Instrumentally Supplemented A Cappella Choir,' *The Musical Quarterly*, 28/2 (April 1942), 169.
[13] Percy Grainger, *A General Study of the Manifold Nature of Music*, typescript dated 1932.
[14] Blacking, '*A Commonsense View of All Music*', 3.
[15] Percy Grainger, quoted in Parker, *Percy Aldridge Grainger*, 22.
[16] Percy Grainger, 'The Fun that Lies in Making Music', a talk with Gertrude Kinscella in *The Musician* (May 1932), 7.
[17] Percy Grainger, quoted in *The Sun* [Melbourne] (3 Sept. 1938).

self-abandonment of art by a thousand and one ideals, ideas, rights and wrongs.'[18] He looked forward to the time when

> the bulk of civilized men and women will come to again possess sufficient mental leisure in their lives to enable them to devote themselves to artistic pleasures on so large a scale as do the members of uncivilized communities. Then the spectacle of one composer producing music for thousands of musical drones (totally uncreative themselves, and hence comparatively out of touch with the whole phenomenon of artistic creation) will no longer seem normal or desirable and then the present gulf between the mentality of composers and performers will be bridged.[19]

In his own compositions, such as *Marching Song of Democracy*, inspired by the poetry of Walt Whitman, Grainger strove to express a form of musical democracy in which each voice played an equal part. 'The ideal of "equality" is the keystone of my musical endeavours.'[20] 'I would like each voice, at all times throughout my music, to enjoy equal importance & prominence. If this cannot be realized, I would like each voice, at given moments, to have its moments of prominence & importance, no less than all other voices.'[21]

Grainger was concerned, above all, with the social and spiritual effects of music. For him the greatest significance of spirit in music was its ability to create new social forms and communications to uplift the human race. He made some specific suggestions in a 1942 letter to Olin Downes:

> If we are going to go on spending as much time (for instance, in the schools) as we do on music . . . at least a considerable part of that music should fit us to face the complicated facts and problems of modern life (cosmopolitanism, racial questions, aviation, chemistry, engineering and how other human forces and natural forces act and counteract). I can see
>
> > that music with long notes (sustained melody) may be construed as increasing man's devotion to sustained emotions and concentrations . . .
> >
> > that polyphonic music (whether Purcell's string *Fantasies* or Roy Harris's *American Creed*) with parts all equal in initiative and responsibility may be called a fine training for that awareness-of-what-happens-to-others that is the keystone of Christianity, democracy, socialism;
> >
> > that 'nature music' such as Delius's *Song of the High Hills*, Sandby's *Sea Mood*, V. Williams's *Pastoral Symphony*, Grieg's *Evening in the High Hills* and *Lost in the Hills* (*Den Bergtekne*) present a fine emotional springboard from which to launch a growing passion for the study of nature;
> >
> > that oriental art-music such as the Javanese and Balinese, and hybrid musics (half native, half European) such as the Rarotongan, Tahitian and Mad-

---

[18] Percy Grainger, quoted in Parker, *Percy Aldridge Grainger*, 22.
[19] Grainger, *The Impress of Personality*, 428.
[20] *Compositional Life of Percy Aldridge Grainger*, undated typescript in the Grainger Museum, Melbourne.
[21] Ibid.

agascan may be regarded as pointing the way to a more loving, harmonious-with-nature, gentle-nerved . . . view of life that may be truly needful to a further extension of the calm, fair, dispassionateness called for by our scientific age.[22]

Although Grainger created more than a hundred original compositions in addition to preparing over a hundred folk-music settings and producing more than a hundred and eighty arrangements, transcriptions, and editions of works dating from the tenth to the twentieth centuries, he felt that his most important contribution was in the area of what he termed 'Free Music'.[23] He was one of the few creative musicians of the twentieth century to give serious thought to the music of the future, setting it above the music of the past and the present: 'I clearly see another kind of progress running through every kind of known music . . . Just as human thought begins with superstition and leads through religion towards science, so does music start with highly artificial and rule-clad forms and works persistently towards ever greater freedom and irregularity.'[24]

He envisaged a future form of music in which 'the various tone-strands (melodic lines) may each have their own rhythmic pulse (or not), if they like.'[25] In this music,

> melody is as free to roam thru tonal space as a painter is free to draw and paint free lines, free curves, create free shapes. . . . In FREE Music there are no scales — the melodic lines may slide and glide to any depths and heights of (practical) tonal spaces just as they may hover around any 'note' without ever alighting upon it. In other words, they have freedom of melodic movement, as a bird has (compared with an airship, which does 'trips' between 'destinations.') . . . In FREE MUSIC harmony will consist of free combinations (when desired) of all free intervals. . . . It seems to me the only type of music that tallies our modern scientific conception of life (our longing to know life AS IT IS, not merely in a symbolistic interpretation), and clearly the kind of music to which all musical progress of many centuries has been working up.[26]

He likened this music to nature, remarking: 'The wish to capture in music . . . nature sounds and irregular rhythms led me to conceive my Free Music.'[27] The creation of such 'nature' sounds in music was a life-long quest, which began for Grainger when he was still a small boy, watching the movement of the water against the side of his boat on the Albert Park Lake in Melbourne. He was drawn in fascination to the free forms of the lapping waves, the swooping of birds in flight above the water, and in the Australian bush, the fractal patterns made by the leaves of ferns and lichens. He wondered, even at this early age, what music would sound like if it

---

[22] Grainger to Downes, 10 September 1942.
[23] See Appendix II.
[24] Grainger, *Music: A Commonsense View*, 11.
[25] Grainger to Downes, 10 September 1942.
[26] Ibid.
[27] Percy Grainger, quoted in Covell, *Australia's Music: Themes for a New Society*.

were to have the freedom enjoyed by such forms of nature. He seemed instinctively to understand with Schopenhauer that when man is artistically engaged with tone, he puts his ear to the very heart of nature itself.[28]

Grainger spent much of his creative life looking for a way to reproduce these sounds of nature heard in his head since childhood. In 1907, when he was twenty-five, he composed his first sketch in a beatless 'Sea-Songs' style and would later arrange it for solovoxes as well as for strings. Even before that, he was experimenting with irregular rhythms in works such as *Love Verses from 'The Song of Solomon'* (1899–1900) and *Hill-Song I* (1901–2). In 1909 he first heard recordings of South Sea Rarotongans singing microtonal polyphonic part-songs, which filled him with a desire to add such harmonious improvisation to his own works, as in *Random Round* (1912–14). In 1935 he composed his *Free Music No. 1* for four theremins or four strings.

After years of ineffective search for an existing instrument that could reproduce the sounds which he heard in his mind, Grainger had the good fortune in the early 1940s to meet the young physics teacher Burnett Cross, with whom he would subsequently spend nearly twenty years building various trial machines for the production of 'Free Music' (see Plates 33, 35). The early machines were mechanical, but by the year before Grainger's death in 1961 they had become almost entirely electrical. The final free-music machine was capable of producing seven-part polyphonic glides and instantaneous leaps, with complete control of dynamics and irregular or free rhythms. But as always, it was the spiritual content of this music which motivated him: 'The connection between such approximations to Free Music and the goals of human progress is obvious enough. Such musical procedures help to attune men's thoughts and feelings to a keener understanding of the processes of nature . . . the urge to know nature better, to live on closer terms with her and if need be, to master her'.[29]

Grainger took his own musical inspiration from extra-musical sources. Aside from nature, his major influences were literary: Walt Whitman, Rudyard Kipling, and the Icelandic Sagas, all of which came to him in his childhood. It was his discovery of Rudyard Kipling in 1898 that actually set Grainger on his path as a modernist composer as he strove to capture the words of Kipling's *Jungle Book* poems in expansive, chromatic, and experimental style. The first of his thirty-four Kipling settings was begun in 1898 and the last completed in 1947, encompassing virtually his entire compositional life.

In 1958 Grainger's *Jungle Book Cycle*, consisting of eleven settings, was published complete, and he wrote to his publisher: 'I AM SO GRATEFUL TO BE ABLE TO PUBLISH MY CYCLE COMPLETE. I consider it so important to the future to have this cycle available.'[30] The *Jungle Book Cycle* represents a concise statement of the philosophy of both Kipling and Grainger: a love of the natural

---

[28] Rudolf Steiner, *The Inner Nature of Music and the Experience of Tone* (New York, 1983).
[29] Percy Grainger, 'Grieg: Nationalist and Cosmopolitan', *The Etude* (June, July, and Aug. 1943), 492.
[30] Percy Grainger to Max Steffens, Schott & Co., 26 July 1957.

and the free, a belief in strength through courage and the observance of natural law, and a distrust of the forces in civilisation that lead to needless cruelty, oppression, and a severance from nature. Grainger foresaw a future world (already with us) in which such messages would be needed. He felt that this music of nature, developed through sliding intervals, irregular rhythms, and unrestricted harmonies, would be an important step in the direction towards freedom in music and a release of its spiritualising influence.

Walt Whitman, the great poet of democracy, inclusivity, and freedom was also a huge influence. In 1947, the same year in which he completed his *Jungle Book Cycle*, Grainger wrote to Cyril Scott: 'I am in the Walt Whitman business: trying to relish and tally the myriad attractiveness of a million different arts and experiences.'[31] Not only Whitman's ideas but his free rhythms appealed to Grainger, who, like Whitman, created many of his own works in freely flowing form. His *Marching Song of Democracy* bears the inscription 'For my darling mother, united with her in loving adoration of Walt Whitman.' Whitman was the unmet 'Camerado' with whom Grainger shared the love of democracy ('This is the meal equally set, this the meat for natural hunger'), demotic art ('What is commonest, cheapest, nearest, easiest, is Me'), universalism ('My spirit has pass'd in compassion and determination around the whole earth'), and love of many-voiced ensemble ('I will not make poems with reference to parts, But I will make poems, songs, thoughts, with reference to ensemble').[32] He was the musical corollary of Whitman's thought.

In later years, Grainger became embittered over what he saw as his failed attempts to awaken people to his messages of freedom in music, democratic polyphony, and the neglected 'spiritualising' repertoire which he championed. He wrote of his distress quite openly, even calling one unpublished manuscript *My Wretched Tone-Life*. His early career had met with a great deal of success: his original compositions as well as his folk-music settings were performed and acclaimed, he was in demand as a performer and speaker, his ideas were taken seriously. But following the First World War, a change came about in the musical climate, and he began to be looked upon as an eccentric. As early as 1933 his disappointment was obvious: 'It is our soul-fate to be soul-teachers to mankind; but as long as the manherd knows no better than to take us for magic-mongers we are powerless to reach their souls — unable to begin our truest life's work.'[33]

Rudolf Steiner wrote that 'the facts of human evolution are expressed in musical development more clearly than anywhere else'.[34] Grainger echoes this thought when he says,

> I do not mean to exalt music over the other arts when I say that it is, more largely than they are, an art of love. It even makes us love our fellow musicians, for whom we may cherish no great love at other moments; for in playing one sound yourself and hearing alongside it another sound of a different

---

[31] Percy Grainger to Cyril Scott, 19 November 1947.
[32] Walt Whitman, *Leaves of Grass*, the 1892 edn (New York, 1982), 37, 32, 118, 12.
[33] Grainger, *The Aldridge-Grainger-Ström Saga*, 78.
[34] Steiner, *The Inner Nature of Music and the Experience of Tone*, 70.

quality, thus generating a beautiful harmony or a difficult discord, is to love that person at that moment. At least, it is so with every true musician.[35]

In 1921, amidst the aftermath of World War I, he had expressed a more personal philosophy:

> the exact reaction needed most from the present world-wide immersion in strife and commercial enslavement and competition, the message that the seer, however, at all times has to proclaim to the empirical world (is) that the real gold dwells in the heart within, and is not to be captured in any other place, and that the real hero is he who, turning dissatisfied away from the outer world's illusionary shows of victory and defeat, finds contentment finally within himself . . . viewing in the mirror of his own contemplative soul the whole universe suffused in a glory of love and understanding.[36]

Nearly three decades later he was still writing in a similar vein: music should 'refine our emotional susceptibilities, thereby making music-lovers (and perhaps mankind in general) more receptive to all those delicate stirs that make for world-peace and for a gentler and happier life on this globe'.[37] He still believed in the words he had written in 1937: 'I want mankind to fulfil its wishes, reach its goals, and (if possible) lead a life of heavenly happiness upon earth.'[38]

In some future world which Grainger envisioned, perhaps this will be a reality.

---

[35] Percy Grainger, 'The Gregarious Art of Music: Australia Needs the Get-Together Spirit,' *The Australian Musical News* (1 April 1927), 13.
[36] Percy Grainger, 'Richard Strauss: Seer and Idealist,' *Musical Courier* (17 Nov. 1921), 6.
[37] Percy Grainger, 'The Saxophone's Business in the Band,' *The Instrumentalist*, 4 (Sept.–Oct. 1949), 7.
[38] Percy Grainger to Mrs Cowell (Henry Cowell's mother), 15 August 1937.

APPENDICES

APPENDIX I
To Conductors

AND TO THOSE FORMING, OR IN CHARGE OF, AMATEUR ORCHESTRAS, HIGH SCHOOL, COLLEGE AND MUSIC SCHOOL ORCHESTRAS AND CHAMBER-MUSIC BODIES

Elastic scoring

My 'elastic scoring' grows naturally out of two roots:

1. That my music tells its story mainly by means of *intervals* and the liveliness of the part-writing, rather than by means of tone-color, and is therefore well fitted to be played by almost any small, large or medium-sized combination of instruments, provided a proper *balance of tone* is kept.

2. That I wish to play my part in the radical experimentation with orchestral and chamber-music blends that seems bound to happen as a result of the ever wider spreading democratization of all forms of music.

As long as a really satisfactory balance of tone is preserved (so that the voices that make up the musical texture are clearly heard, one against the other, in the intended proportions) I do not care whether one of my 'elastically scored' pieces is played by 4 or 40 or 400 players, or any number in between; whether trumpet parts are played on trumpets or soprano saxophones, French horn parts played on French horns or E flat altos or alto saxophones, trombone parts played on trombones or tenor saxophones or C Melody saxophones; whether string parts are played by the instrument prescribed or by mandolins, mandolas, ukeleles, guitars, banjos, balalaikas, etc.; whether harmonium parts are played on harmoniums (reed-organs) or pipe-organs; whether wood-wind instruments take part or whether a harmonium (reed-organ) or 2nd piano part is substituted for them. I do not even care whether the players are skilful or unskilful, as long as they play well enough to sound the right intervals and keep the afore-said tonal balance — and as long as they play badly enough to *still enjoy playing* ('Where no pleasure is, there is no profit taken' *Shakespeare*).

This elastic scoring is naturally fitted to musical conditions in small and out-of-the-way communities and to the needs of amateur orchestras and school, high school, college and music school orchestras everywhere, in that it can accommodate almost any combination of players on almost any instruments. It is intended to encourage music-lovers of all kinds to play together in groups, large or small, and to promote a more hospitable attitude towards inexperienced music-makers. It is intended to play its part in weaning music students away from too much useless, goalless, soulless, selfish, inartistic solistic technical study, intended to coax them into happier, richer musical fields — for music should be essentially an art of self-forgetful, soul-expanding communistic cooperation in harmony and many-voicedness.

Orchestral experimentation

In our age orchestras and orchestral conditions are changing. In a few years an otherwise-put-together orchestra may replace the conventional 'symphony orchestra.' Rather than such a mere replacement of an old medium by a new I, personally, would prefer to see several different kinds of orchestras (included a revised, better balanced, more delicately toned 'symphony' orchestra) thriving side by side in friendly rivalry, none of them final as to make-up and with no hard-and-fast boundaries between them.

We might well look upon the present time as one well suited to bold experimentation with orchestral and chamber music sound-blends. Let us encourage all music-lovers, particularly those in their teens, to enter orchestras and other music bodies formed partly with the aim of trying new combinations of instruments. In such try-outs let us use copiously all instruments that young people like best — easy-to-play, characteristically-toned instruments such as saxophone, piano, harmonium (reed-organ), celesta, dulcitone, xylophone, wooden marimba, glockenspiel, metal marimba, staff bells (shaped like church bells or locomotive bells, having a very metallic, piercing tone), guitar, ukelele, banjo, mandolin, etc.

Let us not snub budding music-lovers because they have chosen instruments unwritten for in 'classical' music! Let us not banish thousands and hundreds of thousands of musically-inclined young people from the boon of orchestral experience simply because their taste runs to instruments (charming instruments, too) which did not happen to have been invented or perfected in Europe a hundred years ago and therefore did not come to form a part of the conventional 'symphony orchestra' as it grew up! Let us remember that at the time of the crystallization of the symphony orchestra most of our most perfect modern instruments (such as the saxophone, the sarrusophone, the harmonium, the modern piano, the modern pipe-organ, the celesta, the dulcitone, the ukelele, the marimbas) did not exist, or were not known in Europe! That, in most cases, sufficiently explains their absence from older symphony orchestrations. But it does not justify their absence from present and future orchestras!

What we need in our composers and in our leaders of musical thought is an attitude like Bach's. He seems to have been willing enough to experiment with all the instruments known to him and to arrange and rearrange all kinds of work for all sorts of combinations of those instruments. It is easy to guess what liberal uses he would have made of the marvellous instruments of to-day.

Let us rid ourselves of aesthetic snobbery, priggishness and prejudice when orchestra-building! Let us take full advantage of the great richness of lovely new instruments, using them together with the lovely old instruments sanctioned by 'classical' usage where it proves effective to do so. Let us build better-balanced, clearer-toned, more varied-coloured orchestras than ever before. Above all, let us press into orchestral playing as many young music-lovers as possible. Whether they are to become laymen or professionals, they need some experience of musical team-work before they can become *practical* musicians, *real* musicians sensing the inner soul of their art.

In addition to getting to know some of the world's best music the budding musician needs the inspiration of hearing a grand cooperation of myriad sounds surging around him, to which he joins his own individualistic voice. This is the *special experience* of music, without which mere lonely practising to acquire soloistic skill must always remain esthetically barren and unsatisfying.

Orchestral use of keyboard-players

Let us use in our orchestras the vast mass of keyboard players (pianists, organists, etc.) that preponderate everywhere in our musical life. Pianists — with their alarming lack of rhythmic neatness, their inability to follow a conductor's beat, their inability to listen while they play — are in more need of some kind of musical team-work (to offset their all too soloistic study activities) than almost any other class of musicians. Use pianists 'massed,' in smaller or larger groups, in experimental and study orchestras, letting them play on small, light, cheap, easily-moved upright pianos (where grand pianos are not easily available) and on harmoniums (reed-organs). These instruments are readily found and handled anywhere — in village or city; only laziness prompts a contrary belief! It is my personal experience, in many lands, that serviceable harmoniums (reed-organs) can be found in every community — by advertising in the newspapers, if not otherwise. By this latter means a really good instrument can sometimes be picked up, second-hand, for as low a figure as five dollars. In selecting a harmonium (reed-organ) for orchestral use, be sure that it carries continuous 8 foot, 16 foot and 4 foot stops throughout its full range.

Harmonium (reed-organ) playing gives to piano students the legato-ear and legato-fingers they otherwise usually so sadly lack. Moreover, massed harmoniums (reed-organs) add a glowing, clinging resonance to the orchestral tone, while massed pianos (the more the mellower) provide brilliance, rhythmic snap and clearness of chord-sound. In determining how many pianos and harmoniums (reed-organs) should be used in a given orchestra we must really use our ears, our sense of balance: It is absurd to use only one piano, only one harmonium, in a large orchestra (having 16 first violins, for instance), when common sense listening tells us at once that three or six or eight pianos, and the same number of harmoniums, would be required to keep the proper tonal balance in such a big tone-body!

If I were forced to choose one instrument only for chamber-music — forced to discard all other instruments than the one chosen — I would choose the harmonium (reed-organ) without hesitation; for it seems to me the most sensitively and intimately expressive of all instruments. Its gusty, swelling emotionality resembles so closely the tides of feeling of the human heart. No other chord-giving instrument is so capable of extreme and exquisitely controlled *pianissimo*. It is unique as a refining musical influence, for it tempts the player to tonal subtleties of gradation as does no other instrument. Both in chamber-music and in the orchestra it provides the ideal background to the individualistic voices of the woodwinds. For all these reasons, let us spread the use of this glorious little instrument to ever wider fields.

Abuses in the percussion section

One of the stupidest of stupid abuses in the orchestra is the unwarrantable habit of ignoring the composer's intentions with regard to percussion instruments. Conductors who would think twice before they left out 2 horns or a harp called for in a given score think nothing of essaying with 2 percussion players a work needing 4 or 8 percussion players — think nothing of leaving out important passages in glockenspiel, celesta or tubular chimes. I ask myself: Has my orchestral *Shepherd's Hey* ever been performed with the full complement of intended percussion players? If not, then this piece — despite thousands of performances — has never been completely played or heard! This indifference to percussion instruments is the more absurd in the case of amateur and student orchestras; as instruments such as cymbals, bass drum, glockenspiel, xylophone, tubular chimes, dulcitone and celesta are almost the easiest of all instruments to play without special training and are specially well suited to 'breaking in' players to orchestral routine, counting rests, following the beat, etc.

'Tuneful percussion' instruments

And what are we to think of the lack of vision, lack of innate musicality, shown by 'high-brow' composers and conductors in their neglect of the exquisite 'tuneful percussion' instruments invented and perfected in America and elsewhere during the last 30 or 40 years — metal and wooden marimbas, staff bells, vibraphones, nabimbas, dulcitone, etc.? Yet these same 'classicists' — who probably consider these mellow and delicate-toned instruments too 'low-brow' to be admitted into the holy precincts of the symphony orchestra — endure without protest the everlasting thumping of kettle-drums (which with brutal monotony wipes out all chord-clearness) in the Haydn-Mozart-Beethoven orchestrations! The truth is that most 'high-brows' are much more 'low-brow' than they themselves suspect!

In this connection it is interesting to note that it is only the most harsh-toned tuneful-percussion instruments (glockenspiel, xylophone, tubular chimes) that have found a place in the symphony orchestra thus far. Can it be that the symphony orchestra prizes stridence of tone *only* in such instruments? If not, why has no place been found for the mellow-toned metal marimba (the continuation downwards of the glockenspiel) and the gentle-toned wooden marimba (the continuation downwards of the xylophone)? Perhaps because their quality of tone is too refined to be heard amidst the harsh sound-jumble of the symphony orchestra? If so, it is high time that we revised our symphony orchestrations in the direction of a delicacy and refinement that can accommodate the subtler creations of modern instrument-building geniuses such as Deagan and others.

To use, orchestrally, a glockenspiel without a metal marimba, a xylophone without a wooden marimba, is just as absurd and incomplete as it would be to use piccolo without flute, violins without lower strings, the two top octaves of the piano without the lower octaves. Let us get rid of this barbarism as soon as we can!

Young people love such colourful, easy-to-play instruments as staff-bells, marimbas, dulcitone, etc. Let us use such tuneful-percussion enthusiasts 'with both hands'. Every orchestra should sport at least 20 such players; 2 on 1 glockenspiel, 4 on 1 metal marimba, 2 on 1 xylophone, 4 on 1 wooden marimba, 4 or more on 1 staff bells, 2 on 1 tubular chimes, 1 on celesta, 1 on dulcitone. (If the metal and wooden marimbas could be used in twos, threes, fours or fives it would be still better.) Apart from the luscious sounds thus produced — think how many 'low-brow' beginners would be enticed into a knowledge of, and a love for, 'high-brow' music by such means? Salvation Army Booth objected to the devil having all the good tunes. I object to jazz and vaudeville having all the best instruments! Let us find a place in highbrow music for the *gentler* instruments — ukelele, guitar, harmonium, saxophone, sarrusophone, marimbas, etc. There is no reason why the symphony orchestra should be given over *exclusively* to loud and strident sounds.

Why do so many of our high-brow composers, our virtuoso conductors, our 'leaders of musical thought' *lag so very far* behind commercial instrument-makers, jazz-musicians and vaudeville artists in musical imagination, refinement and vision? Because they are ignorant or lazy. They do not *know* the wonderful world of tone created by American and other musical instrument-makers or they cannot be bothered adapting it to their own fields. Such ignorance and laziness are dangerous. The public ear, trained to the orchestration refinements of Paul Whiteman, Grofé, jazz and vaudeville music, may get tired of the dullness and coarseness of the sound of the conventional symphony orchestra: It may move on, gently but irresistibly, to better things.

Orchestral use of saxophones

If the saxophone (the crowning achievement of Adolphe Sax, that outstanding genius among wind-instrument creators and perfectors) is not the loveliest of all wind-instruments it certainly is *one* of the loveliest — human, voice-like, heart-revealing. It has been used in symphonic music by Bizet, Vincent D'Indy, Richard Strauss and others with lovely results. It has been used in jazz orchestras with excellent effect. Yet it has not yet been taken up into the symphony orchestra. Why not? What are we waiting for? Apart from its glorious orchestral possibilities *as a saxophone*, it is a most useful substitute for trumpet, French horn, bassoon — even for trombone.

The average amateur, school and music school orchestra usually holds artistically unsatisfying rehearsals because of gaping holes in its wood-wind and brass sections. These missing melodies, missing chords, lessen the musical benefits of such rehearsals to those taking part in them. Those in charge of such orchestras should make every effort *never* to rehearse with incomplete texture (with important voices left out). Texture and balance are, musically speaking, much more important than tone-colour!

The complete wood-wind parts should always be arranged (an excellent task for the more musical members of the orchestra to tackle) for harmonium (reed-organ) or pipe-organ and played on those instruments if one or more wood-wind players are absent at rehearsal or concert.

All the brass instruments can be replaced or supported by saxophones — always for study rehearsals and often with effect for concerts also. Generally more than one saxophone will be needed to replace each brass instrument with correct balance.

Let it be admitted that there are many passages originally written for French horn that sound better on that instrument than they do on E flat alto or alto saxophone. On the other hand, there are other passages, also originally written for French horn, that happen to sound as well, or better, on E flat alto or alto saxophone as they do on French horn. Let us experiment widely with all such cases, using E flat altos and alto saxophones on French horn parts until we have substituted experience for prejudice.

How to achieve tonal balance in string sections

In the symphony orchestra of to-day the clearness of the part-writing, the richness of the lower voices of the harmony and the balance of tone are all sacrificed to a cloying, over-sensuous over-weight of violin tone. I know of no good reason for using more violins to a part than violas or 'cellos to a part: I have yet to discover that the higher members of an instrumental family have more difficulty in making themselves heard than the lower members. In performing such a work as Bach's *Brandenburg Concerto no. 3* (for 3 violins, 3 violas, 3 'cellos, 'violone e continuo') with single strings one soon finds that the violas and 'cellos have some difficulty in holding their own, in tonal prominence, with the violins. The top-heaviness of the string section of the symphony orchestra was natural at a time when the melody mostly floated on the top of the musical texture like oil on water — at a time when harmonic expressiveness and subtle many-voicedness were not greatly valued. But our musical tastes are richer, more many-sided, to-day than they were at the time of the up-growing of the symphony orchestra and we now need properly balanced string sections that can do justice to the best many-voiced music of all periods, be it Purcell and Bach or Vaughan Williams and Cyril Scott. Our conductors are too apt to lag behind public taste and the taste of our best composers; our conductors are wedded too closely to the *banal* simplicities of the 18th and 19th centuries; they are too ignorant of the deeper, grander music of the 17th and 20th centuries. String orchestras and conductors should feed their musical souls on Purcell's sublimely beautiful three-, four-, and five-part *Fantasias for Strings*, recently edited by Peter Warlock and André

Mangeot (Curwen edition). This volume should be to string-quartet players and to string orchestras what Bach's 'Well-tempered Clavier' is to pianists. There is no reason why conductors should put up with such bad tonal balance (top-heaviness) as exists in the string sections of most amateur, school and study orchestras. Suppose your string section consists of 34 violins, 2 violas, 3 'cellos and 1 bass; you can still achieve perfect tonal balance, if you want to. Transcribe the viola part for third violin, either transposing up one octave such notes as lie below the violin range or leaving them out entirely where it seems more desirable to do so. (It is a good musical exercise for orchestral players, especially music students, to transpose and copy their own parts. Being able to read music is not enough; every musician should aim at writing music as freely as he writes his own language.)

Then divide up your violins as follows:

> 1st violins, 12 players.
> 2nd violins, 12 players.
> 3rd violins (as substitute for violas) 10 players
> violas, 2 players
> = (12 players on viola part)

Arrange the 'cello and double-bass parts for piano and have this piano part played on about 3 or 4 pianos — also on harmoniums, if available. By such means the tonal balance is preserved, though the tone-colour is, of course, distorted. But tonal balance is vastly more important than tone-colour in most worth-while music. (In this connection, consult the 3 viola parts transcribed for 4th, 5th and 6th violins, the 'cello and double-bass parts transcribed for piano 2 in my edition of Bach's *Brandenburg Concerto no.* 3; also my edition for strings of Scarlatti's *'The Quiet Brook'*; both published by G. Schirmer, Inc.)

Let our orchestras grow naturally

The symphony orchestra uses many strings because string players abounded at the time of its formation. That was a good reason. Let us, in forming the orchestras of the present and the future, try using large numbers of the instruments that abound most to-day: The mere fact that they abound (that they are widely liked and therefore draw many beginners into musical habits) should be recommendation enough. If these instruments, under ample experimentation, prove orchestrally ineffective in massed usage, let us then discard such usage. But do not let us discard any instrument or usage of it without a fair trial.

Percy Aldridge Grainger, Dec. 2, 1929.

[from the Preface to *Spoon River*, AFMS2 (Schott, 1930)]

APPENDIX II
Free Music
Percy Aldridge Grainger

Music is an art not yet grown up; its condition is comparable to that stage of Egyptian bas-reliefs when the head and legs were shown in profile while the torso appeared 'front face' — the stage of development in which the myriad irregular suggestions of nature can only be taken up in regularized or conventionalized forms. With Free Music we enter the phase of technical maturity such as that enjoyed by the Greek sculptures when all aspects and attitudes of the human body could be shown in arrested movement.

Existing conventional music (whether 'classical' or popular) is tied down by set scales, a tyrannical (whether metrical or irregular) rhythmic pulse that holds the whole tonal fabric in a vice-like grasp and a set of harmonic procedures (whether key-bound or atonal) that are merely habits, and certainly do not deserve to be called laws. Many composers have loosened, here and there, the cords that tie music down. Cyril Scott and Duke Ellington indulge in sliding tones: Arthur Fickenscher and others use intervals closer than the half tone; Cyril Scott (following my lead) writes very irregular rhythms that have been echoed, on the European continent, by Stravinsky, Hindemith, and others. Schönberg has liberated us from the tyranny of conventional harmony. But no non-Australian composer has been willing to combine *all* these innovations into a consistent whole that can be called Free Music.

It seems to me absurd to live in an age of flying and yet not be able to execute tonal glides and curves — just as absurd as it would be to have to paint a portrait in little squares (as in the case of mosaic) and not be able to use every type of curved lines. If, in the theatre, several actors (on the stage together) had to continually move in a set metrical relation to one another (to be incapable of individualistic, independent movement) we would think it ridiculous; yet this absurd goose-stepping still persists in music. Out in nature we hear all kinds of lovely and touching 'free' (non-harmonic) combinations of tones; yet we are unable to take up these beauties and expressiveness into the art of music because of our archaic notions of harmony.

Personally I have heard free music in my head since I was a boy of eleven or twelve in Auburn, Melbourne. It is my only important contribution to music. My impression is that this world of tonal freedom was suggested to me by wave movements in the sea that I first observed as a young child at Brighton, Victoria, and Albert Park, Melbourne. Yet the matter of Free Music is hardly a personal one. If I do not write it someone else certainly will, for it is the goal that all music is clearly heading for now and has been heading for through the centuries. It seems to me the only music logically suitable to a scientific age.

The first time an example of my Free Music was performed on man-played instruments was when Percy Code conducted it (most skilfully and sympathetically) at one of my Melbourne broadcasting lectures for the Australian Broadcasting Commission in January, 1935. But Free Music demands a non-human performance. Like most true music, it is an emotional, not a cerebral, product and should pass direct from the imagination of the composer to the ear of the listener by way of delicately controlled musical machines. Too long has music been subject to the limitations of the human hand, and subject to the interfering interpretations of a middle-man: the performer. A composer wants to speak to his public direct. Machines (if properly constructed and properly written for) are capable of niceties of emotional expression impossible to a human performer. That is why I write my Free Music for theremins — the most perfect tonal instruments I know. In the original scores each voice (both on the pitch-staves and on the sound-strength staves) is written in its own specially coloured ink, so that the voices are easily distinguishable, one from the other.

Grainger's Statement on Free Music, 6 December 1938, Grainger Museum, University of Melbourne, Australia

APPENDIX III
The Family Trees and Family Groups
Rita Boswell and Penelope Thwaites

Important information about the British/Australian Aldridge family was collated by Percy Grainger from the records and recollections of his aunt, Clara Jane Aldridge (1856–1944). Known as *Aunty Clara's Aldridge History*, the six pages of facts and anecdotes give a framework to the story of his mother Rose's family. Individual members of the Aldridge family have kindly supplied additional material. We have been able to go one generation further back from George and Sarah Aldridge, the pioneers, and to gain more insight, for example, into the family expertise with horses.

John Harry Grainger, Percy's father, seems to have passed on to his son little about his Grainger relatives. It has been an absorbing exercise to start to piece together the jigsaw. Internet sources have transformed research possibilities since the earlier Grainger biographies, and the usual public record offices have played their part. Much use has been made of digitised parish registers of London, available on Ancestry.com, while a visit to Durham Record Office enabled us to gather personal dates of the Grainger family in that area.

Nevertheless, many dates (particularly of sisters, whose spouses, if any, are unknown) are still to be discovered. It has been our decision to provide the picture as it now stands, because, incomplete as it is, Jacob Grainger's family members have begun to emerge from the shadows and, in doing so, have played their part in making sense of many aspects of Percy Grainger's gifts, personality, and interests. Chapter 11, 'The Family Background', weaves some of these strands together, and the family trees and additional information can be read as a complement to it.

Superior numbers after names relate the family trees to the family tables following.

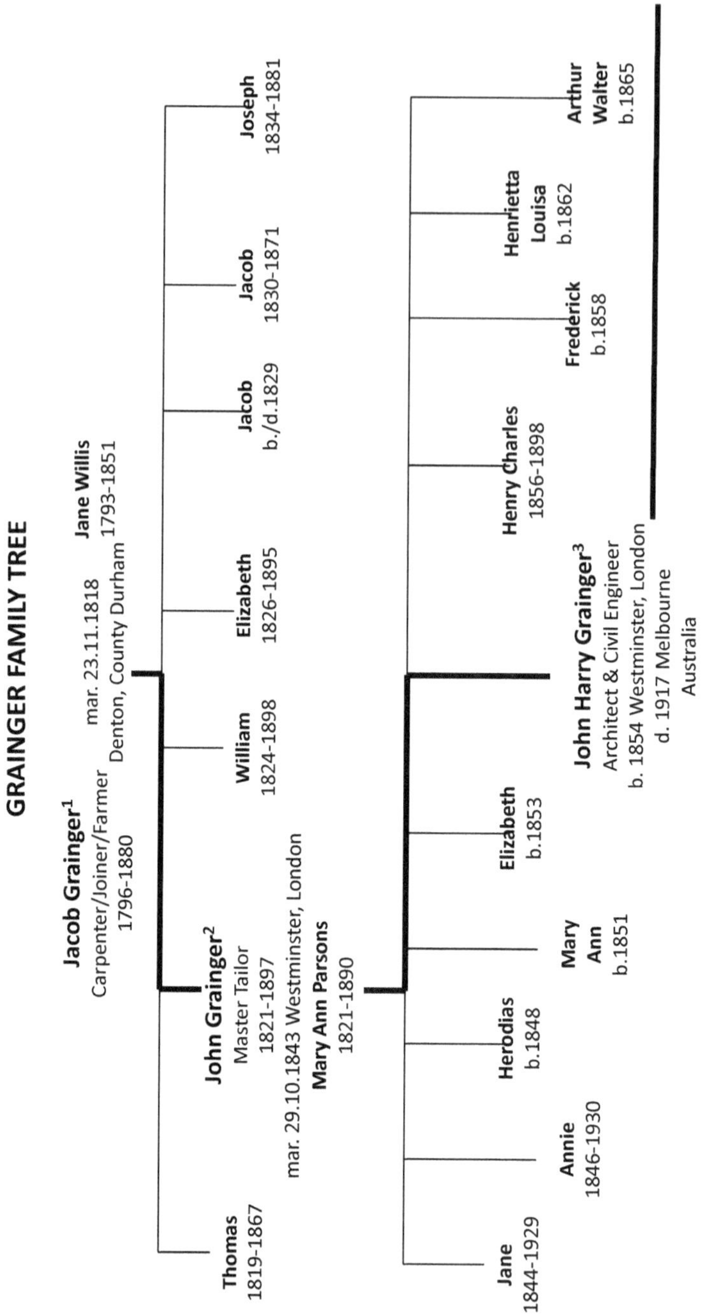

APPENDIX III

GRAINGER FAMILY TREE

Jacob Grainger[1]
Carpenter/Joiner/Farmer
1796-1880

mar. 23.11.1818
Denton, County Durham

Jane Willis
1793-1851

Children of Jacob Grainger and Jane Willis:
- Thomas 1819-1867
- **John Grainger**[2], Master Tailor, 1821-1897
- William 1824-1898
- Elizabeth 1826-1895
- Jacob b./d. 1829
- Jacob 1830-1871
- Joseph 1834-1881

John Grainger[2] mar. 29.10.1843 Westminster, London **Mary Ann Parsons** 1821-1890

Children of John Grainger and Mary Ann Parsons:
- Jane 1844-1929
- Annie 1846-1930
- Herodias b.1848
- Mary Ann b.1851
- Elizabeth b.1853
- **John Harry Grainger**[3], Architect & Civil Engineer, b. 1854 Westminster, London, d. 1917 Melbourne Australia
- Henry Charles 1856-1898
- Frederick b.1858
- Henrietta Louisa b.1862
- Arthur Walter b.1865

THE FAMILY TREES AND FAMILY GROUPS

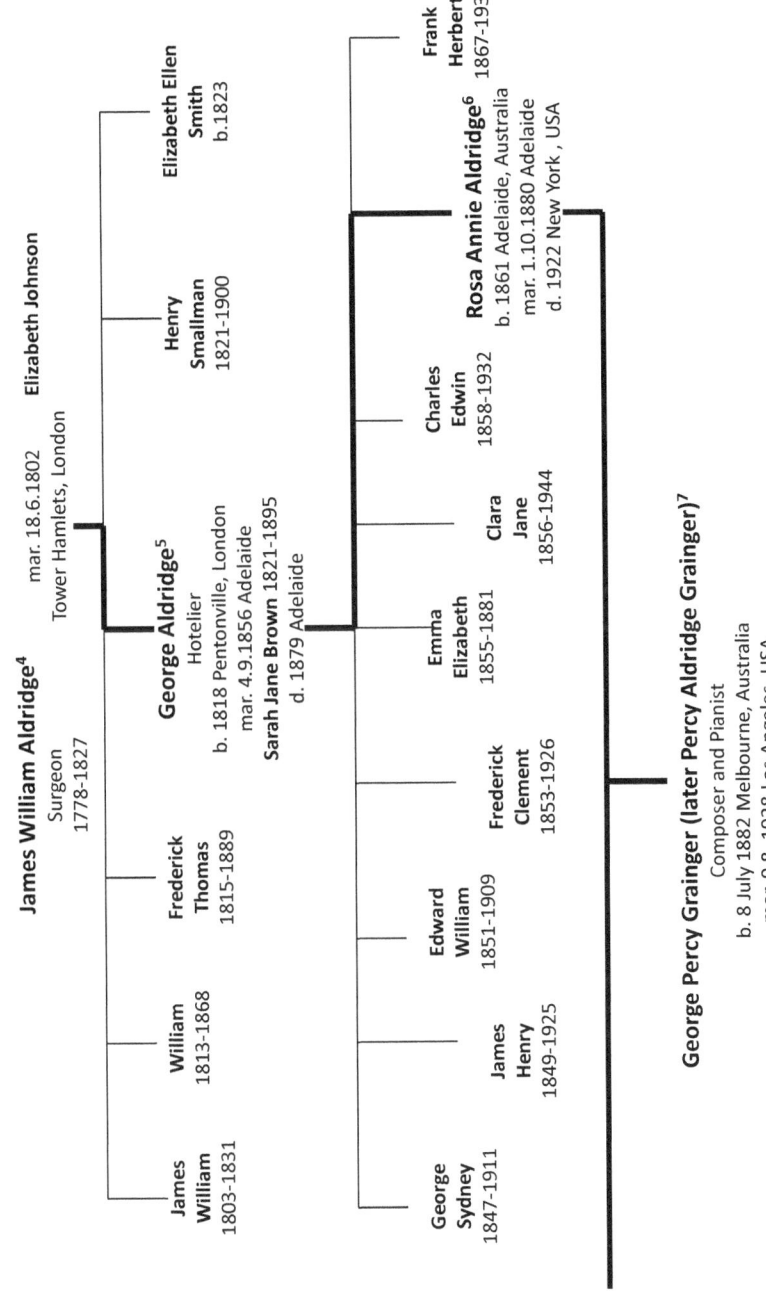

Family of Jacob GRAINGER[1] and Jane WILLIS

Husband   Jacob Grainger (1796–1880)
Wife   Jane Willis (1793–1851)
Marriage 23 Nov. 1818   Denton St Mary, County Durham

Husband: Jacob Grainger[1]

Father   Thomas Grainger (1752–1816) } Married 14 Aug. 1774, Auckland St Andrew
Mother   Ann Bradley (1766–1833)   }
Baptism   7 Sept. 1796   Gainford St Mary, County Durham
Occupation   Joiner/Carpenter, later farmer of 36 acres
Death   9 March 1880   Walworth Gate, Walworth, Darlington
Burial   17 March 1880   Heighington St Michael, County Durham

Sources:
Joiner Marriage Index
Census (1861)   Walworth Gate, Walworth, Durham; recorded as a Widower; aged 66. Occupation: Carpenter. Born in Bolam, County Durham
Census (1871)   Walworth Gate, Darlington, aged 74. Occupation: Carpenter & Farmer of 36 acres. Born: Gainford, County Durham
Death Certificate   Death recorded as 14 March 1880 but marked as 9 March 1880 on gravestone in St Michael's Churchyard, Heighington. Died at 84 years Walworth Gate, Walworth, County Durham. Cause: Senile decay. Son, Joseph Grainger, in attendance

Wife: Jane Willis

Birth   1793   Staindrop, County Durham
Death   24 April 1851
Burial   27 April 1851   Heighington St Michael, County. Durham

Sources:
Census (1841)   Walworth Gate, Walworth
Parish registers   Heighington St Michael
                      Gravestone in St Michael's Churchyard, Heighington

Child I: Thomas Grainger   Spouse: Sarah (1817-?)

Baptism   2 May 1819   Denton St Mary, County Durham
Death   7 May 1867   Walworth Gate, County Durham
Burial   12 May 1867   Heighington St Michael, County Durham

Sources:
Census (1841)   Walworth Gate, Walworth. Occupation: Joiner
Census (1851)   Heighington. Occupation: Carpenter Master
Census (1861   Heighington. Occupation: Joiner employing 2 boys
Parish registers   Denton St Mary
                      Heighington St Michael

Child 2: John Grainger[2] mar. Mary Ann Parsons (1821-1890) 29 Oct. 1843, Westminster

Baptism	3 June 1821	Denton St Mary, County Durham
Death	1897	St George, Hanover Square

Child 3: William Grainger mar. Elizabeth Cordell (1827-?) 1847, Stepney, London

Baptism	8 Feb. 1824	Denton St Mary, County Durham
Death	1898	Chester-le-Street, County Durham

Sources:

Census (1841)	Walworth Gate, Walworth
Census (1861)	2 Cocken Lodge, Cocken, County Durham. Occupation: Joiner & Cabinet Maker
Parish register	Denton St Mary
FreeBMD	Marriage: Oct.–Dec.1847, Stepney Vol. 2, p. 451
	Death: April–June 1898, Chester-le-Street, Vol. 10a, p. 269

Child 4: Elizabeth Grainger mar. Joseph Hindmarsh (1832-?) 1856, Heighington, Co. Durham

Baptism	27 Aug. 1826	Denton St Mary, County Durham
Death	1895	Darlington, County Durham

Sources:

Census (1841)	Walworth Gate, Walworth
Parish registers	Denton St Mary and Heighington St Michael
FreeBMD	Marriage: Jan.–March 1856, Darlington, Vol. 10a, p. 21
	Death: July–Sept. 1895, Darlington, Vol. 10a, p. 9

Child 5: Jacob Grainger

Baptism	8 March 1829	Denton St Mary, County Durham
Died	3 Aug. 1829	Denton St Mary, County Durham
Buried	18 Sept 1829	Denton St Mary, County Durham

Source:

Parish register	Denton St Mary

Child 6: Jacob Grainger mar. Elizabeth Ramshaw (1825-1866) 1854, Auckland, Co. Durham

Baptism	31 Oct. 1830	Denton St Mary, County Durham
Death	30 Aug. 1871	Walworth Gate, County Durham
Burial	3 Sept 1871	Heighington St Michael, County Durham

Sources:

Census (1841)	Walworth Gate, Walworth
Census (1871)	Walworth, Darlington. Widower. Occupation: Carpenter
Parish registers	Denton St Mary and Heighington St Michael
	Gravestone in St Michael's Churchyard, Heighington
FreeBMD	Marriage: Jan.–March 1854, Auckland, Vol. 10a, p. 161

Child 7: Joseph Grainger   mar. Mary Ann Wright (1830–1890) 1854, Darlington, Co. Durham

Baptism	26 Oct. 1834	Denton St Mary, County Durham
Death	12 Sept 1881	Accidentally killed at Darlington Market
Burial	16 Sept 1881	Heighington St Michael, County Durham

Sources:

Census (1841)	Walworth Gate, Walworth
Census (1871)	Walworth, Darlington. Occupation: Carpenter
Parish registers	Denton St Mary and Heighington St Michael
	Gravestone in St Michael's Churchyard Heighington
FreeBMD	Marriage: Oct.–Dec. 1854, Darlington, Vol. 10a, p. 21

Family of John GRAINGER[2] and Mary Ann PARSONS

Husband	John Grainger (1821–1897)	
Wife	Mary Ann Parsons (1821–1890)	
Marriage	29 Oct. 1843	St Margaret's Church, Westminster, London

Sources:

Marriage Certificate	Married on 29 Oct. 1843 in St Margaret's Church, Westminster, according to Rites of the Church of England
	Certificate signed by both. Witnessed by Henry Parsons and Mary Ann Vincent
	Fathers: Jacob Grainger, Joiner, and Henry Parsons, Compositor
	Both single and of full age. Residence at time of marriage Little Queen Street, Westminster
Census (1851)	Living at 1 New Street, St John, Westminster, London. Master Tailor employing 3 men
Census (1871)	Living at 135 Page Street, Westminster, St John, London
Census (1881)	Living at 25 Little Queen Street, St Margaret, Westminster. Master Tailor employing 5 men

Husband: John Grainger[2]

Father	Jacob Grainger (1795–1880)	
Mother	Jane Willis (1801–1851)	
Birth	3 June 1821	Denton St Mary, County Durham
Death	1897	St George, Hanover Square, London

Sources:

Parish register	Denton St Mary, County Durham
FreeBMD	Death: July–Sept. 1897, St George Hanover Square, Vol. 1a, p. 355

Wife: Mary Ann Parsons

Father	Henry Parsons (1809–?)	
Mother	Mary Ann Vincent (1808–?)	
Birth	1821	Westminster, London
Death	1890	St George Hanover Square, London

Sources:		
Census (1841)	Living at 47 New Compton St Giles in the Fields, London. Occupation: Shirtmaker	
FreeBMD	Death: July–Sept. 1890, St George Hanover Square, Vol. 1a, p. 374	

Child 1: Jane Grainger   mar. Phineas Henry Romanel (1826-1887) 5 July 1871, Westminster

Birth	1844	St Margaret's, Westminster, London
Died	1929	Brentford

Sources:	
Census (1861)	Staying with grandfather Jacob Grainger at Walworth Gate, Durham. Occupation: Housekeeper
Census (1871)	Visitor. Staying at 59 Haymarket, St James, Westminster, London with sister Annie Cave
Marriage Certificate	5 July 1871, St James's Church, Westminster. Phineas Romanel, Widower & Jane Grainger, Spinster.
Census (1881)	Married. Occupation: Assistant Caterer, Court of Probate. Living at 5 Champion Terrace, Camberwell, London
Census (1891)	Widow. Occupation: Refreshment Contractor. Living at 1 Springfield Villas, Newington St Mary, London
Census (1901)	Widow. Occupation: Coffee House proprietor — employer. Living at 22 Glazbury Road, Barons Court, Fulham
FreeBMD	Birth: July–Sept. 1844, Westminster, Vol. 1, p. 404
	Death: Oct.–Dec. 1929, Brentford, Vol. 3a, p. 222

Child 2: Annie Grainger   mar. (1)George Louis Cave 1867; (2)George Clark 1879, London

Birth	22 Feb. 1846	Westminster, London
Death	1930	Lambeth, London

Sources:	
Census (1841)	Living at 1 New Street, St John, Westminster, London
Census (1861)	Staying with grandfather Jacob Grainger at Walworth Gate, County Durham. Occupation: Dairymaid
Census (1871)	Married. Husband Licensed Victualler. Living at 59 Haymarket, St James, Westminster, London
FreeBMD	Birth: Jan.–March 1846, Westminster, Vol. 1, p. 446
	Marriages: Jan.–March 1867, Westminster, Vol. 1a, p. 589; April–June 1879, Camberwell, Vol. 1d, p. 1012
	Death: April–June 1930, Lambeth, Vol. 1d, p. 589

Child 3: Herodias Grainger

Birth	1848	St Margaret, Westminster, London

Sources:	
Census (1851)	1 New Street, St John, Westminster, London
FreeBMD	Birth: July–Sept. 1848, Westminster, Vol. 1, p. 425

Child 4: Mary Ann Grainger

Birth	1851	Westminster, London

Sources:
Census (1851)   1 New Street, St John, Westminster, London
Census (1871)   Visitor. Staying with sister Annie Cave at 59 Haymarket, St James Westminster, London
FreeBMD   Birth: Jan.–March 1851, Westminster, Vol. 1, p. 498

Child 5: Elizabeth Grainger

Birth	1853	Westminster, London

Sources:
Census (1871)   Visitor. Staying with sister Annie Cave at 59 Haymarket, St James Westminster, London
FreeBMD   Birth: Jan.–March 1853, Westminster, Vol. 1a, p. 225/8

Child 6: John Harry Grainger[3] mar. Rosa Annie Aldridge (1861–1922) 1 Oct. 1880, Adelaide

Birth	30 Nov. 1854	1 New Street, Westminster, London
Occupation		Architect & Civil Engineer
Marriage	1 Oct. 1880	Adelaide, Australia
Death	13 Apr 1917	71 Stevenson Street, Kew, Melbourne, Australia
		One son, George Percy Grainger[7]

Sources:
Birth Certificate   Parents: John Grainger, Master Tailor, and Mary Ann Grainger formerly Parsons. Living at 1 New Street, Westminster
Census (1871)   Occupation: Clerk living at 5 Princes Street, St Margaret, Westminster, London, with brother Henry

Child 7: Henry Charles Grainger   mar. Mary Ellenor Martin 1876, London

Birth	1856	Westminster, London
Death	1898	St George, Hanover Square, London

Sources:
Census (1881)   Living at 75 Ponsonby Place, St John's, Westminster, London. Occupation: Tailor
FreeBMD   Birth: Oct.–Dec. 1856, Westminster, Vol. 1a, p. 249
    Marriage: April–June 1876, St George, Hanover Square, Vol. 1a, p. 715
    Death: Jan.–March 1898, St George, Hanover Square, Vol. 1a, p. 415

Child 8: Frederick Grainger

Birth	1858	Westminster, London

Sources:
Census (1871)   Living at 135 Page Street, St James, Westminster, London
FreeBMD   Birth: Oct.–Dec. 1858, Westminster, Vol. 1, p. 252

Child 9: Henrietta Louisa E. Grainger   mar. James Stephens 1880, London

Birth	1862	Westminster, London

Sources:

Census (1871)	Living at 135 Page Street, St John, Westminster, London
Census (1881)	Staying with sister Jane Romanel at 5 Champion Terrace, Camberwell, London, Scholar
Census (1891)	Staying with older sister Jane Romanel at 1 Springfield Villas, Newington St Mary, London. Occupation: Waistcoat maker. Possible illegitimate daughter Mary A. Grainger, age 4
FreeBMD	Birth: April–June 1862, Westminster, Vol. 1a, p. 307
	Marriage: April–June 1880, St George Hanover Square, Vol. 1a, p. 592

Child 10: Arthur Walter Grainger   mar. Elizabeth Grainger (1861–?) 1886, London

Birth	1865	Westminster, London

Sources:

Census (1871)	Living with parents at 135 Page Street, St John, Westminster, London
Census (1881)	Living with parents at 25 Little Queen Street, St Margaret, Westminster, London
Census (1891)	Living at 22 Ponsonby Terrace, St John the Evangelist, London. Occupation: Tailor. With wife Elizabeth, who was born in Durham 1861, and nephew George, age 3 born in Westminster
FreeBMD	Birth: July–Sept. 1865, Westminster, Middlesex, Vol. 1a, p. 328
	Marriage: April–June 1886, St George Hanover Square, Vol. 1a, p. 796

Family of James William ALDRIDGE[4] and Elizabeth JOHNSON

Husband	James William Aldridge (1778–1827)	
Wife	Elizabeth Johnson	
Marriage	18 June 1802	St George in the East, Tower Hamlets, London

Source:

Parish register	Married by Licence at St George in the East, Tower Hamlets, London. Elizabeth a minor.
	Both single and signed their names. Witnessed by Maria and Oliver Johnson and John Bott, jr

Husband: James William Aldridge[4]

Birth	1778	Shadwell, London
Occupation		Surgeon
Death	1827	Clerkenwell, London
Burial	17 Feb. 1827	Clerkenwell St John the Baptist, London
		Family legend has it that he committed suicide

Source:

Parish register	Clerkenwell St John the Baptist

Wife: Elizabeth Johnson

Child 1: James William Aldridge

Birth	1803	
Death	1831	St John Street, Pentonville, London
Burial	13 May 1831	Pentonville Chapel, St James, Islington, London

Sources:
Parish register   Burial: Pentonville Chapel, St James, Islington, London

Child 2: William Aldridge   mar. Charlotte Amelia Briddon 1837, St Pancras, London

Birth	1813	St James, Pentonville, London
Baptism	10 Feb. 1813	Pentonville St James, London
Death	1868	Lambeth, London

Sources:
Parish register   Baptism: Pentonville, St James, Islington, London. Father: James William Aldridge, surgeon, living at Henry Street
FreeBMD   Marriage: July–Sept. 1837, St Pancras, Vol. 1, p. 328

Child 3: Frederick Thomas Aldridge   Spouse: Ann

Birth	14 July 1815	St James, Pentonville, London
Baptism	9 Aug. 1815	Pentonville St James, Islington, London
Death	1889	Camberwell, London

Sources:
Parish register   Baptism: Pentonville St James, Islington. Father: James William Aldridge, surgeon, living at Henry Street
Census (1851)   Frederick Aldridge living in Camberwell. Occupation: Journeyman Hatter
FreeBMD   Death: Jan.–March 1889, Camberwell, Vol. 1d, p. 580

Child 4: George Aldridge[5]   mar. Sarah Jane Brown (1821–1895) 4 Sept. 1856, Adelaide

Birth	7 May 1818	Henry Street, Pentonville, London
Baptism	10 June 1818	Pentonville St James, Islington, London
Marriage	4 Sept 1856	Adelaide, Australia,
Death	12 Dec. 1879	Adelaide, Australia

Source:
Parish register   Baptism: Pentonville St James, Islington. Father: James William Aldridge, surgeon, living at Henry Street

Child 5: Henry Smallman Aldridge   mar. Eliza Hamber 3 July 1841, St George Southwark, London

Baptism	30 Apr 1821	Clerkenwell St James, London
Death	1900	Steyning, Sussex

Sources:
Parish register   Baptism: Clerkenwell St James. Father: James William Aldridge, surgeon, living in Henry Street
Census (1851)   Henry Aldridge, living in Shoreditch. Occupation: Grocer and Cheesemonger
FreeBMD   Death: April–June 1900, Steyning, Sussex, Vol. 2b, p. 190

Child 6: Elizabeth Ellen Smith Aldridge   mar. George Frederick Hawkins 1842, St Luke, London

Birth	6 June 1823	Penton Street, Clerkenwell, London
Baptism	2 July 1823	Pentonville St James, London

Sources:

Parish register	Baptism: Pentonville St James, Islington. Father: James William Aldridge, surgeon, living in Penton Street
FreeBMD	Marriage: Jan.–March 1842, St Luke, London, Vol. 2, p. 237

Family of George ALDRIDGE[5] and Sarah Jane BROWN

Husband	George Aldridge (1818–1879)	
Wife	Sarah Jane Brown (1821–1895)	
Marriage	4 Sept. 1856	Free Presbyterian Church, Adelaide, Australia

Husband: George Aldridge[5]

Father	James William Aldridge (1778–1827)	Married 18 June 1802, St George in the East, Tower Hamlets, London
Mother	Elizabeth Johnson	
Birth	7 May 1818	Pentonville, London
Baptism	10 June 1818	St James, Pentonville, London
Death	12 Dec. 1879	Adelaide, Australia

Sources:

Parish register	Baptism: St James's Pentonville, London. Father: James William Aldridge, surgeon, living at Henry Street

Wife: Sarah Jane Brown

Father	Timothy Brown	Married 23 Jan. 1820, St John the Evangelist, Westminster, London
Mother	Sarah Butler	
Birth	27 May 1821	Westminster, London
Death	26 Nov. 1895	Claremont, Kensington, Australia

Child 1: George Sydney Aldridge   mar. Marion MacFie 20 Oct. 1880, Adelaide

Birth	23 July 1847	London
Death	21 Aug. 1911	Adelaide, Australia

Child 2: James Henry Aldridge   mar. Sarah Carr

Birth	4 July 1849	The Shop, corner of High and Bridge Streets, Kensington, Adelaide, Australia
Death	11 Nov. 1925	Richmond Park, nr Adelaide, Australia

Child 3: Edward William Aldridge   mar. (1)Clara; (2)Margaret Smith

Birth	24 July 1851	The Shop, corner of High and Bridge Streets, Kensington, Adelaide, Australia
Death	22 July 1909	Adelaide, Australia

Child 4: Frederick Clement Aldridge   mar. (1)Maria Morcombe, 7 Jan. 1875; (2)Alvina Klem

Birth	12 May 1853	The Shop, corner of High and Bridge Streets, Kensington, Adelaide, Australia
Death	1926	Geelong, Australia

Child 5: Emma Elizabeth Aldridge

Birth	3 Feb. 1855	The Shop, corner of High and Bridge Streets, Kensington, Adelaide, Australia
Death	Sept. 1881	Kensington, Australia

Child 6: Clara Jane Aldridge

Birth	15 Nov. 1856	High Street opposite The Shop, Kensington, Australia
Death	Oct. 1944	Claremont, Kensington, Adelaide, Australia

Child 7: Charles Edwin Aldridge   mar. (1)Annie Cairns, 1879; (2)Margaret Hislop

Birth	16 Dec. 1858	High Street opposite The Shop, Kensington, Australia
Death	21/2 April 1932	Melbourne, Australia

Child 8: Rosa Annie Aldridge[6]   mar. John Harry Grainger (1854–1917) 1 Oct. 1880, Adelaide

Birth	3 July 1861	The Shades, White's Rooms, King William Street, Adelaide
Death	30 Apr 1922	New York City
		One son, George Percy Grainger[7]

Child 9: Frank Herbert Aldridge

Birth	14 March 1867	The Prince of Wales Hotel, Angas Street, Adelaide, Australia
Death	17 Apr 1931	Claremont, Kensington, Adelaide

Note on occupations

The second generation of Aldridges tended to work in building, with horses, and in the hotel business. For example, the *South Australian Gazette* (17 April 1884) lists:

> *James Henry Aldridge*, Publican, Globe Hotel, Rundle Street Adelaide
> *Frederick Clement Aldridge*, Publican, Freemasons Tavern, Pine Street, Adelaide
> *Charles Edwin Aldridge*, Publican, Southern Cross Hotel, King William Street, Adelaide.

James Henry was the most successful, later building up his own horse-stud, having retired to live in some style at Richmond, outside Adelaide (see Plate 26).

Select Bibliography

ALLISON, Brian. 'Grainger Photographs', *University of Melbourne Library Journal*, 6/2 (2000), 20–23.
ALLISON, Brian, ed. *John Harry Grainger: Architect and Civil Engineer* (Melbourne, 2007).
ANDERSON, Peter James. 'The Innovative Music of Percy Grainger: An Examination of the Origins and Development of Free Music' (M.Mus. thesis, University of Melbourne, 1980).
BALOUGH, Teresa. *A Complete Catalogue of the Works of Percy Grainger*, Music monograph 2 (Nedlands, W.A., 1975).
——. 'Kipling and Grainger', *Studies in Music* [CIRCME, University of Western Australia], 11 (1977), 74–108.
——. 'The English Gothic Music of Dom Anselm Hughes and Percy Grainger', *Studies in Music* [CIRCME, University of Western Australia], 13 (1979), 63–5.
——. 'Percy Grainger as Music Educator and International Music Pioneer', *Australian Journal of Music Education*, 29 (October 1981), 3–8.
——. 'The Inner Fire: Spirit and Evolving Consciousness in the Work of Percy Grainger', *The Percy Grainger Lecture 1993*, CIRCME series no. 5, University of Western Australia (Perth, 1993).
BALOUGH, Teresa, ed. *A Musical Genius from Australia: Selected Writings by and about Percy Grainger* (Nedlands, W.A., 1982).
——, ed. *Comrades in Art: The Correspondence of Ronald Stevenson and Percy Grainger, 1957–61, with Interviews, Essays and Other Writings on Grainger by Ronald Stevenson* (London, 2009).
BARWELL, Graham. 'Percy Grainger and the Early Collecting of Polynesian Music', *Journal of New Zealand Studies*, ns 2–3 (Oct. 2003 – Oct. 2004), 1–17.
BEARMAN, C. J. 'Percy Grainger, the Phonograph, and the Folk Song Society', *Music & Letters*, 84/3 (2003), 434–55.
BIRD, John. *Percy Grainger* (London, 1976; repr. 1982).
——. *Percy Grainger* (Sydney, 1998).
——. *Percy Grainger*, new edn (Oxford, 1999).
BLACKING, John. *'A Commonsense View of All Music': Reflections on Percy Grainger's Contribution to Ethnomusicology and Music Education*, (Cambridge, 1987).
BLADES, James. *Percussion Instruments and Their History* (London, 1975).
BRIGGS, Asa. *Victorian Cities*, new edn (Harmondsworth, 1968).
BRISBANE, Katherine, ed. *Entertaining Australia: An Illustrated History* (Sydney, 1991).
CALLAWAY, Frank, ed. *Percy Grainger Centennial Volume*, Studies in Music, 16 (Nedlands, W.A., 1982; repr. Melbourne, 1997, as *Percy Aldridge Grainger Symposium*).
CANNON, Michael. *The Land Boomers*, new illus. edn (Melbourne, 1976).
CLIFFORD, Phil. *Grainger's Collection of Music by Other Composers*, Percy Grainger

Music Collection, 2; Grainger Museum, University of Melbourne, Catalogue 2 (Parkville, Vic., 1983).

CLUNIES ROSS, Bruce. 'Percy Grainger's "Nordic Revolt against Civilization"', *Musicology Australia*, 9 (1986), 53–65.

——. 'Percy Grainger in his Letters', *Meanjin*, 2 (1988), 233–42.

——. Introduction to *Percy Grainger's Personal Library*, Grainger Museum, University of Melbourne, Catalogue 3 (Parkville, Vic., 1990).

——. '"For the Glory of Australian Music, for the Glory of Nordic Music"', *Australian Studies*, 5 (1991), 36–49.

COOPE BOYES AND SIMPSON. *Triple Echo: Songs Collected by Ralph Vaughan Williams, George Butterworth and Percy Grainger.* (CD, No Masters NMCD22, 2005).

COVELL, Roger. *Australia's Music: Themes of a New Society* (Melbourne, 1967; repr. 2016).

DARIAN-SMITH, Kate, and Alessandro SERVADEI, eds. *Talking Grainger: Perspectives on the Life, Music and Legacy of Percy Grainger* (Melbourne, 1998).

DAVIES, Gwilym. 'Percy Grainger's Folk Music Research in Gloucestershire, Worcestershire, and Warwickshire, 1907–1909', *Folk Music Journal*, 6/3 (1992), 339–58.

——. *Grainger in Gloucestershire: Songs and Tunes collected by Percy Grainger in Gloucestershire and Warwickshire* (The Author, 1994; repr. 1995).

DAVISON, Graeme. *The Rise and Fall of Marvellous Melbourne* (Melbourne, 1984).

DEVAL, Dorothy. 'The Transformed Village: Lucy Broadwood and Folksong', in *Music and British Culture, 1785–1914: Essays in Honour of Cyril Ehrlich*, ed. Christina Bashford and Leanne Langley (Oxford, 2000), 341–66.

——. '"Fresh and Sweet like Wildflowers": Lucy Broadwood, Percy Grainger, and the Collecting of English Folksong', *Context*, 22 (2001), 125–34.

DORUM, Eileen. *Percy Grainger: The Man Behind the Music* (Melbourne, 1986).

DREYFUS, Kay, *Music by Percy Aldridge Grainger*, Percy Grainger Music Collection, 1; Grainger Museum, University of Melbourne, Catalogue 1 (Parkville, Vic., 1978).

——. *Percy Grainger's Kipling settings: A Study of the Manuscript Sources*, Music monograph 3, University of Western Australia (Perth, 1980).

——. *Supplementary List and Index: Music by Percy Aldridge Grainger*, Percy Grainger Music Collection, 3; Grainger Museum, University of Melbourne, Catalogue 4 (Parkville, Vic., 1995).

DREYFUS, Kay, ed. *The Farthest North of Humanness: Letters of Percy Grainger, 1901–14* (Melbourne and London, 1985).

EASTWOOD, Jill. *Melbourne: The Growth of a Metropolis* (Melbourne, 1983).

FAIRHURST, Tony. 'On The Record', *Folk News (East Yorkshire District)*, 100 (March/May 1996), 18.

FLANNERY, Tim, ed. *The Birth of Melbourne* (Melbourne, 2002).

FLOYD, James Michael, ed. 'An Interview with Percy Grainger', *Tempo* 61 (2007), 18–26.

FOREMAN, Lewis, ed. *The Percy Grainger Companion* (London, 1981).

GAROFALO, Robert J., ed. *Folk Songs and Dances in 'Lincolnshire Posy' by Percy Grainger*, Folk Songs/Dances Anthology, 4 (Silver Spring, Md., 2008).

GILLIES, Malcolm, and Bruce CLUNIES ROSS, eds. *Grainger On Music* (Oxford and New York, 1999).

GILLIES, Malcolm, and David PEAR, eds. *The All-Round Man: Selected Letters of Percy Grainger, 1914–1961* (Oxford, 1994).

——. *Portrait of Percy Grainger*, Eastman Studies in Music, 18 (Rochester, N.Y., 2002).

GILLIES, Malcolm, and Mark CARROLL, eds. *Australasian Music Research*, 5 (2000), Percy Grainger Issue.

GILLIES, Malcolm, David PEAR, and Mark CARROLL, eds. *Self-Portrait of Percy Grainger* (Oxford, 2006).
GRAINGER, Percy. 'Collecting with the Phonograph', *Journal of the Folk-Song Society*, 12 (1908), 147–242; repr. in Balough (ed.), *A Musical Genius from Australia*.
——. 'The Impress of Personality in Unwritten Music', *Musical Quarterly*, 1 (1915), 416–35; repr. in Gillies and Clunies Ross (eds.), *Grainger on Music*.
——. 'The Completion of the Percussion Family in the Orchestra' [original in German], *Pult und Taktstock*, 3/1 (1926); trans. in Gillies and Clunies Ross (eds.), *Grainger on Music*.
——. 'To Conductors', *Jutish Medley* (London, 1930); repr. in Balough (ed.), *A Musical Genius from Australia*.
——. 'A General Study of the Manifold Nature of Music', lecture notes, New York University, 1932; repr. in Gillies and Clunies Ross (eds.), *Grainger on Music*.
——. 'Can Music Become a Universal Language?' broadcast over Radio WEVD, New York, 20 June 1933; repr. in Gillies and Clunies Ross (eds.), *Grainger on Music*.
——. 'A Commonsense View of All Music', lectures broadcast and published by the Australian Broadcasting Commission, 1934; repr. in Blacking, 'A *Commonsense View of all Music*'.
GREIG, Ruairidh. 'Joseph Taylor from Lincolnshire: A Biography of a Singer', in *Folk Song: Tradition, Revival and Re-Creation*, ed. Russell and David Atkinson (Aberdeen, 2004), 386–92.
GROGAN, Christopher, 'Percy Grainger and the Revival of Early English Polyphony: The Anselm Hughes Correspondence', *Music & Letters*, 77 (1996), 425–39.
HARRIS, Amanda, 'The Nature of Nordicism: Grainger's "Blue-Gold-Rosy-Race" and his Music', *Musicology Australia*, 23 (2000), 19–48.
HORNBOSTEL, Erich Moritz von. Notes to *Music of the Orient: Dr EM von Hornbostel*, Ethnic Folkways Records FE 4157.
HUGHES, Charles W. 'Percy Grainger, Cosmopolitan Composer', *The Musical Quarterly*, 23/2 (1937), 127–36.
JEFFRIES, Dai. 'Tuning in to CBS', *Songbook 6* (2005), 36–40.
JOSEPHSON, David. 'The Case for Percy Grainger, Edwardian Musician, on his Centenary', in *Music and Civilization: Essays in Honour of Paul Henry Lang*, ed. Edmond Strainchamps and Maria Rika Maniates with Christopher Hatch (New York, 1984), 350–62.
LANGFIELD, Valerie. *Roger Quilter: His Life and Music* (Woodbridge, 2002).
LEWIS, Thomas P., ed. *A Source Guide to the Music of Percy Grainger*, Pro/Am General Music Series, 7 (White Plains, N.Y., and London, 1991).
LINZ, Rainer. 'The Free Music Machines of Percy Grainger', *Experimental Musical Instruments*, 3/1 (1997), 10–12.
LLOYD, Stephen. *H. Balfour Gardiner* (Cambridge, 1984; repr. 2005).
LOWE, Rachel. *A Descriptive Catalogue with Checklists of the Letters and Related Documents in the Delius Collection of the Grainger Museum, University of Melbourne, Australia* (London, 1981).
MELLERS, Wilfrid. *Percy Grainger* (Oxford, 1992).
NELSON, Kathleen E. 'Percy Grainger's Work for the Australian Broadcasting Commission, 1934–1935: Background and Reception', *Australasian Music Research*, 2–3 (1997–8), 99–110.
——. '"Living, Deathless, Timeless Music": Grainger and Early Music', *Australian Music Research*, 5 (2000), 83–104.

NEMEC, Belinda. 'The Grainger Museum in its Museological and Historical Contexts' (PhD Thesis, The University of Melbourne, 2006).
O'BRIEN, Jane. 'A Folk Music Pioneer: Percy Grainger', *English Dance and Song*, 44/2 (1982), 18–19.
——. *The Grainger English Folk-Song Collection*, Music Monograph 6, University of Western Australia (Perth, 1985).
Official Record of the Melbourne Centennial International Exhibition, 1888–89 (Melbourne, 1890).
O'SHAUGHNESSY, Patrick, ed. *Lincolnshire Folk Songs from the Manuscript Collection of Percy Grainger* (Oxford, 1966).
——. *Twenty-One Lincolnshire Folk-Songs from the Manuscript Collection of Percy Grainger* (Oxford, 1968).
——. *Yellowbelly Ballads: A Third Selection of Lincolnshire Folk-Songs, the Majority of them from the Collection of Percy Aldridge Grainger*, 2 parts (Lincoln, 1975).
——. *More Folk Songs from Lincolnshire*, 2nd edn (Lincoln, 1983).
PACEY, Robert W. *Folk Music in Lincolnshire* (D.Phil. thesis, University of Oxford, 1978).
——. 'Percy Grainger's Folk Song Collecting Tours in Lincolnshire', in *A Prospect of Lincolnshire, being Collected Articles on the History and Traditions of Lincolnshire in Honour of Ethel H. Rudkin*, ed. Naomi Field and Andrew White (Lincoln, 1984), 119–25.
PARKER, D. C. *Percy Aldridge Grainger: A Study* (New York, 1918).
PARROTT, Ian. *Cyril Scott and his Piano Music* (London, 1991).
PEAR, David. 'Walt Whitman and the Synthesis of Grainger's Manliness', *Australasian Music Research*, 5 (2001), 61–81.
PEAR, David, ed., *Facing Percy Grainger* (exhibition catalogue, National Library of Australia, 2006).
Percy Aldridge Grainger: List of Published Works (Mainz: Schott, 1996).
Percy Grainger and the Arts of the Pacific (exhibition catalogue, Grainger Museum, 1979).
PRESCOTT, A. M. *A Guide to the Grainger Museum* (Melbourne, 1975).
RAHKONEN, Carl. 'Special Bibliography: Natalie Curtis (1875–1921)', *Ethnomusicology* 42/3 (1998), 511–22.
REEVES, Helen. 'A Universalist Outlook: Percy Grainger and the Culture of the Non-Western Societies', *Studies in Music*, 16 (1982), 32–52.
ROBINSON, Suzanne, and Kay DREYFUS, eds. *Grainger the Modernist* (Farnham, 2015).
SANDFORD, Gordon. 'Percy Grainger and the Viol Consort', *The Consort*, 43 (1987), 35–7.
SERVADEI, Alessandro. 'Percy Grainger's *Hill-Songs*: The Culmination of his Early Musical Experiments' (BMus Special Studies paper, University of Melbourne, 1993).
——. 'A Critical Edition and Exploration of Percy Grainger's *The Warriors: Music to an Imaginary Ballet*' (MMus thesis, University of Melbourne, 1996).
SCOTT, Cyril. 'Percy Grainger: The Music and the Man', *The Musical Quarterly*, 2/3 (July 1916), 425–33.
SHARP, Cecil, et al. *Journal of the Folk-Song Society*, 5/20 (Nov. 1916).
SIMON, Robert. *Percy Grainger: The Pictorial Biography* (Troy, N.Y., 1983).
SLATTERY, Thomas C. *Percy Grainger: The Inveterate Innovator* (Evanston, Ill., 1974).
TALL, David. 'Grainger and Folksong', in Lewis Foreman (ed.), *The Percy Grainger Companion* (London, 1981), 55–71.
——. *Percy Grainger: A Catalogue of the Music* (Schott, London, 1982).
TESTRO, Ron. 'Lively Days in the Eastern Market', *The Argus* (25 March 1939).
The Many Faces of Percy Grainger (exhibition, Grainger Museum, in association with the 1997 Melbourne Festival and the Australian Centre, University of Melbourne, 1997).

THOMSON, Bob. Notes to *Unto Brigg Fair: Joseph Taylor and Other Traditional Lincolnshire Singers Recorded in 1908 by Percy Grainger* (LP, Leader LEA 4050, 1972).

TWOPENY, R. E. N. *Town Life in Australia* (London, 1883; facs. repr. Sydney, 1973).

WANG Zheng-Ting. *Chinese Music in Australia: Victoria, 1850s to mid-1990s* (Melbourne, 1997).

WATERMAN, R. A., et al. 'Bibliography of Asiatic Musics', *Notes*, 2nd ser., 5/1 (1947), 21–35.

YASSER, Joseph. *A Theory of Evolving Tonality*, American Library of Musicology, Contemporary Series, 1 (New York, 1932).

YATES, Michael. 'Percy Grainger and the Impact of the Phonograph', *Folk Music Journal*, 4/3 (1982), 265–75.

Select Discography

Barry Peter Ould

It is the nature of catalogues to be out of date as soon as they appear in print. Discographies are especially notorious as recordings are deleted, companies are taken over and recordings lost, especially their documentation. Grainger's original recordings on shellac (sections **A-D**) and some of the earlier LPs (sections **E-H**) are now difficult to obtain, although from time to time they can surface at auction sites on the internet — notably eBay. The same applies to the deleted CD issues included below (marked with a superior [d]).

The Discography is divided into two main sections: (*a*) historical performances by Grainger himself (further subdivided into acoustic and electric recordings, LP recordings, piano roll recordings and CD transfers)[1] and (*b*) recordings of Grainger's music performed by others. The selection under (*b*) is based on recent complete recordings and important repertoire not otherwise available. Hence a number of recordings mentioned in the text are not included. A complete discography is available from the Percy Grainger Society. For help in compiling these lists I wish to express my thanks to John Bird, Kees Kramer and Stephen Lloyd.

Since the 2010 publication of this Select Discography, many new Grainger releases have appeared. Space limitations preclude adding most, apart from those presenting hitherto unrecorded repertoire. However, all are listed on the Percy Grainger web site: http://www.percygrainger.org.uk/recordings

Performances by Percy Grainger

Acoustic and electric recordings
*An asterisk denotes 10" master. All others are 12".

(**A**) *The Gramophone Company, Limited, and Sister Companies* (recorded and issued in Great Britain only)[2]

GRIEG
  Piano Concerto in A minor, Op. 16: cadenza only from 1st mvt (78 rpm) 1908

LISZT
  Hungarian Rhapsody no. 12 (abridged) (80 rpm) 1908

STANFORD
  Four Irish Dances, Op. 89 no. 1: A March-Jig (McGuire's Kick) (arr. Grainger) 1908

---

[1] For further details of historical recordings, see John Bird, *Percy Grainger*, new edn (Oxford, 1999), 338–49.
[2] The Columbia Graphophone Company in the United States changed from the acoustic recording method to the Western Electric System of recording in March 1925.
  The Company changed from 80 rpm to 78 rpm recordings during September 1927.

(B) *His Master's Voice* (recorded and issued in Great Britain only)

DEBUSSY
  Toccata from *Pour le piano* (79 rpm) 1914

GRAINGER
  Mock Morris Dances (79 rpm) 1914
  *Shepherd's Hey (80 rpm) 1914

(C) *The Columbia Graphophone Company* (USA) (recorded in the United States and issued in the United States, Great Britain, Europe and Australia)

BACH
  Blithe Bells (Ramble on *Sheep may safely graze* arr. Grainger) 1931
  Gigue from *1st Partita* 1926
  Organ Fantasia and Fugue in G minor (arr. Liszt) 1931
  Organ Fantasia and Fugue in A minor (arr. Liszt) 1931
  Toccata and Fugue in D minor (arr. Tausig–Busoni–Grainger) 1931

BRAHMS
  *Cradle Song (arr. Grainger) 1922
  *Cradle Song (arr. Grainger) 1927
  Sonata in F minor, Op. 5 1926
  Waltz in A-flat, Op. 39 no. 15 1920
  Waltz in A-flat, Op. 39 no. 15 1926

CHOPIN
  Étude in B minor, Op. 25 no. 10 1928
  Étude in C minor, Op. 25 no. 12 1926
  Polonaise in A-flat, Op. 53 1918
  Prelude in A-flat, Op. 29 no. 17 1918
  Prelude in A-flat, Op. 29 no. 17 1926
  *Scherzo in B-flat minor, Op. 31 no. 2 1924
  Sonata No. 2 in B-flat minor, Op. 35 1928
  Sonata No. 3 in B minor, Op. 58 1925
  Valse in A-flat, Op. 42 1917

DEBUSSY
  *Golliwog's Cakewalk 1923
  Clair de Lune 1926
  Toccata from *Pour le piano* 1926

DETT
  Juba Dance 1920

GLUCK
  Gavotte (arr. Brahms) 1923

GRAINGER
  *Colonial Song (P. Grainger conducting orchestra with A. Atwater (sop), L. A. Sanchez (ten)) 1927
  Country Gardens 1918
  *Country Gardens 1927
  *'The Gum-Suckers' March 1921
  'The Gum-Suckers' March (with orchestra) 1927
  Irish Tune from Country Derry (P. Grainger conducting the Kasschau Solo Choir) 1925

Jutish Medley 1929
*Lord Peter's Stable-Boy (P. Grainger (pf), R. Leopold (harm), with Columbia Symphony Orchestra) 1927
Molly on the Shore 1920
*Molly on the Shore 1927
One More Day, My John 1919
The Power of Love (A. Atwater (sop), P. Grainger (harm), R. Leopold (pf) plus 11 instruments) 1927
Scotch Strathspey and Reel (the Grainger Singers and Players, conducted by Frank Kasshau, P. Grainger and R. Leopold (guitars)) 1925
Shepherd's Hey 1918
*Shepherd's Hey 1927
*Shepherd's Hey (P. Grainger conducting Columbia Symphony Orchestra) 1927
*Spoon River 1922

GRIEG
Norwegian Bridal Procession 1917
Norwegian Bridal Procession 1921
To the Spring 1919
To the Spring 1927
Wedding Day at Troldhaugen 1921
Wedding Day at Troldhaugen 1927

GUION
Sheep and Goat walkin' to the pasture 1926
*Turkey in the Straw 1921

HANDEL
*Hornpipe from Water Music (arr. Grainger) 1924

LISZT
Hungarian Fantasia (with orchestra) 1918
Hungarian Rhapsody no. 2 1917
Hungarian Rhapsody no. 12 1920
Liebestraum no. 3 1921
Liebestraum no. 3 1927
Polonaise no. 2 in E major 1921

MACDOWELL
*To a Water-Lily 1923

SCHARWENKA
Polish Dance in E-flat minor, Op. 3 no. 1 1919

SCHUMANN
Études symphoniques, Op. 13 1928
Romance in F-sharp, Op. 28 no. 2 1928
Sonata in G minor, Op. 22 1927
*Warum? Op. 12 no. 3 1924

SINDING
*Rustle of Spring 1923

STRAUSS, R.
*Ramble on the last love-duet in 'Der Rosenkavalier' 1929

TCHAIKOVSKY
Paraphrase on Tchaikovsky's Flower-Waltz (The Nutcracker) 1918

Unissued items made at Columbia Studios (USA)
CHOPIN
Étude in A-flat (unidentified)
DEBUSSY
Jardins sous la pluie from Estampes 1922
Toccata from Pour le piano 1919
GRAINGER
Colonial Song 1922
*'The Gum-Suckers' March (with 15th Band of Coast Artillery) 1917
*Eastern Intermezzo 1922
*Handel in the Strand 1930
*The Hunter in His Career 1930
*Irish Tune from County Derry 1917
*One More Day, My John 1918
*Shepherd's Hey 1918
GRIEG
*Norwegian Peasant Dance (unidentified) 1926
*To the Spring 1918
HANDEL
*Hornpipe from Water Music 1922
LISZT
Hungarian Rhapsody no. 15: Rákóczy March 1922
Liebestraum no. 3 1926
SCHUBERT
Marche militaire (arr. Tausig) 1921
SCHUMANN
Romance in F-sharp, Op. 28 no. 2 1926
STANFORD
*Four Irish Dances, Op. 89 no. 1: A March-Jig (McGuire's Kick) (arr. Grainger) 1917
Four Irish Dances, Op. 89 no. 4: A Reel (arr. Grainger) 1922

(D)   Decca Records Inc. (USA) (recorded and issued in the United States only). All sides 10″ (78 rpm).

DETT
Prelude (Night) excerpt from Suite 'In the Bottoms' 1945
Juba Dance excerpt from Suite 'In the Bottoms' 1945
GRAINGER
Country Gardens 1945
Irish Tune from County Derry 1945
Molly on the Shore 1945
One More Day, My John 1945
HORN
Cherry Ripe (arr. Scott) 1945

SCOTT
Danse Nègre 1945
Pierrot Triste (Lento), Op. 35 no. 1 of Pierrot Pieces 1945

Unissued items made at Decca Studios

ARNDT
Nola 1945

COWELL
The Aeolian Harp 1945
The Lilt of the Reel 1945

GERSHWIN
Love Walked In (arr. Grainger) 1945
The Man I Love (arr. Grainger) 1944
The Man I Love (arr. Grainger) 1945

GRAINGER
Country Gardens 1944
One More Day, My John 1944

GRIEG
Piano Concerto in A minor, Op. 16: concert transcription of main themes and episodes from 1st mvt (arr. Grainger) 1944
Piano Concerto in A minor, Op. 16: concert transcription of main themes and episodes from 1st mvt (arr. Grainger) 1945

LP recordings

(E) RCA Victor (USA). Recorded in 7th floor ballroom, Manhattan Center, 311 West 34th Street, New York, 31 May 1950 and 8 Nov. 1950. P. Grainger (pf) with L. Stokowski and his Orchestra. Issued in the United States and Great Britain (HMV).[3]

GRAINGER
Country Gardens
Early One Morning
Handel in the Strand (solo piano part)
Mock Morris
Molly on the Shore
Shepherd's Hey

Unissued items made at Manhattan Center (USA)
My Robin is to the Greenwood Gone

---

[3] In *Country Gardens* and *Shepherd's Hey* Grainger appears as instrumentalist within the orchestra and as a highlighted soloist only in *Handel in the Strand*. The remaining three orchestrations, which Grainger made especially for Stokowki, do not include a piano part. Grainger took the score and parts of his *My Robin is to the Greenwood Gone* to the sessions and it was duly recorded but never issued and sadly, has failed to survive. The Grainger items have now been issued on CD together with other Stokowski recordings by Cala Records. See CD Transfers section for further details.

(F) *The Vanguard Recording Society, Inc.* (USA).[4] Recorded from a 'live' performance in 'Scala' Hall, Aarhus, Denmark, 25 Feb. 1957, with P. Grainger (piano) and P. Dreier conducting the Aarhus Municipal Orchestra. Catalogue no. VRS 1098, 12" (33⅓ rpm)[5]

GRAINGER
Country Gardens (solo) 1957
Danish Folk-Music Suite (with orchestra) 1957

GRIEG
Piano Concerto in A minor, Op. 16 1957

STRAUSS, R.
Ramble on the last love-duet in 'Der Rosenkavalier') (solo) 1957

Other works performed at concert but not issued:

GRAINGER
Walter Børner, conductor; Inger Kynne Frandsen, mezzo-soprano; Torben Viskum Sørensen, tenor; Jydsk Academic Choir[6]
Love Verses from Song of Solomon 1957
Mowgli's Song Against People 1957
The Sea-Wife 1957

(G) *Decca Records, Inc.* (USA) (recorded and issued in United States only). Recorded at Pythian Temple, 135 West 70th Street, New York, 15 Aug. 1957, with P. Grainger (pf) and the Goldman Band conducted by Richard Franko Goldman. Catalogue no. DL 78633, 12" (33⅓ rpm)

GRAINGER
Children's March

(H) *International Piano Archives* (USA)

GRIEG
Piano Concerto in A minor, Op. 16. Recorded 15 July 1945. P. Grainger (pf) with L. Stokowski and the Hollywood Bowl Symphony Orchestra, 'live' performance at Hollywood Bowl.
Piano Concerto in A minor, Op. 16: cadenza only from 1st mvt. Recorded 16 May 1908.
Piano Concerto in A minor, Op. 16. Recorded 27 Oct. 1956. P. Grainger (pf) with Richard A. Morse and the Southeast Iowa Symphony Orchestra, 'live' performance.

---

[4] When this record was transferred to CD in 1998 by the Omega Record Group Inc., they were made aware of the unissued recordings listed above, but the CD was issued with only the tracks from the original LP. See CD Transfers section for further details.

[5] This recording was scheduled for release in United States but withdrawn shortly before date of issue, though a few copies reached the New York record shops, some of which were purchased by the then *Percy Grainger Library Society* now *The International Grainger Society*. Limited stocks are available. The LP was later transferred to CD Vanguard Classics (OVC 8205). See CD Transfers section for full details.

[6] The Percy Grainger Society Sound Archive has these recordings and can make copies available.

Four Norwegian Folksongs from Op. 17:[7] no. 4 'Nils Tallesfjorden'; no. 8 'The Suckling Pig'; no. 12 'Solfager and the Snake-King'; no. 16 'I Know a Little Maiden'. Recorded 31 Dec. 1950, 'live' at home (White Plains). Catalogue no. IPA 508, 12" (33⅓ rpm)

CD Transfers

Piano rolls

Masters of the Piano Roll
    Includes: SYMPHONIC DANCE NO. 1 FOR TWO PIANOS (Cyril Scott) [Grainger and Cyril Scott]; A MARCH-JIG (MAGUIRE'S KICK) (Stanford, *Four Irish Dances*, Op. 89 no. 1, arr. Grainger) [Grainger]
    Dal Segno Records DSPRCD006 (13 tracks; total time 73:07)

Masters of the Piano Roll, Volume 4: Percy Grainger
    MORNING (Grieg, *Peer Gynt Suite*, Op. 46); DEATH OF ÅSE (Grieg, *Peer Gynt Suite*, Op. 46); ANITRA'S DANCE (Grieg, *Peer Gynt Suite*, Op. 46); HALL OF THE MOUNTAIN KING (Grieg, *Peer Gynt Suite*, Op. 46); LOVE POEM Op. 43 (Grieg); NORWEGIAN FOLK SONGS Op. 66 nos. 1, 2, 10, 14, 16, 18 (Grieg); LOTUS LAND Op. 47 No. 1 (Cyril Scott); TOCCATA FROM 'POUR LE PIANO' (Debussy); NELL Op. 18 no. 1 (Fauré); LENTO Op. 36 no. 1 (Cyril Scott); MARCH (Tchaikovsky, *Nutcracker Suite*, Op. 71a); DANCE OF THE SUGAR PLUM FAIRY (Tchaikovsky, *Nutcracker Suite*, Op. 71a); RUSSIAN DANCE (Tchaikovsky, *Nutcracker Suite*, Op. 71a); ARABIAN DANCE (Tchaikovsky, *Nutcracker Suite*, Op. 71a); CHINESE DANCE (Tchaikovsky, *Nutcracker Suite*, Op. 71a); DANCE OF THE FLUTES (Tchaikovsky, *Nutcracker Suite*, Op. 71a); WALTZ OF THE FLOWERS (Tchaikovsky, *Nutcracker Suite*, Op. 71a); ÉTUDES SYMPHONIQUES Op. 13 (Schumann)
    Dal Segno Records DSPRCD020 (23 tracks; total time 74:12)

Tchaikovsky and Grieg: The Original Piano Roll Recordings
    MORNING (Grieg, *Peer Gynt Suite*, Op. 46); DEATH OF ÅSE (Grieg, *Peer Gynt Suite*, Op. 46); ANITRA'S DANCE (Grieg, *Peer Gynt Suite*, Op. 46); HALL OF THE MOUNTAIN KING (Grieg, *Peer Gynt Suite*, Op. 46); EROTIKON (LOVE POEM) Op. 43 no. 5 (Grieg); NORWEGIAN FOLK SONGS Op. 66 nos. 1, 2, 10, 14, 16, 18 (Grieg); MARCH (Tchaikovsky, *Nutcracker Suite*, Op. 71a); DANCE OF THE SUGAR PLUM FAIRY (Tchaikovsky, *Nutcracker Suite*, Op. 71a); RUSSIAN DANCE (Tchaikovsky, *Nutcracker Suite*, Op. 71a); ARABIAN DANCE (Tchaikovsky, *Nutcracker Suite*, Op. 71a); CHINESE DANCE (Tchaikovsky, *Nutcracker Suite*, Op. 71a); DANCE OF THE FLUTES (Tchaikovsky, *Nutcracker Suite*, Op. 71a); WALTZ OF THE FLOWERS (Tchaikovsky, *Nutcracker Suite*, Op. 71a)
    Dal Segno Records DSPRCD035 (21 tracks; total time 59:45)

Schumann (Grand Piano Project)
    Includes: ÉTUDES SYMPHONIQUES Op. 13 (Schumann); PIANO SONATA NO. 2 IN G MINOR Op. 22 (Schumann)
    Nimbus Records NI8804 (23 tracks; total time 71:57)

Debussy (Grand Piano Project)
    Includes: TOCCATA FROM 'POUR LE PIANO' (Debussy)

---

[7] The LP incorrectly states 3 *Norwegian Folksongs from op. 17*.

Nimbus Records NI8807 (15 tracks; total time 70:09)

Bach (Grand Piano Project)
Includes: ORGAN FANTASIA AND FUGUE IN G MINOR (Bach, transcribed by Liszt)
Nimbus Records NI8808 (21 tracks; total time 73:10)

Grainger Plays Grainger (Grand Piano Project)
SHEPHERD'S HEY; COUNTRY GARDENS; SUSSEX MUMMERS' CAROL; JUTISH MEDLEY; MOLLY ON THE SHORE; ONE MORE DAY, MY JOHN; SPOON RIVER; THE WARRIORS; RAMBLE ON THE LAST LOVE-DUET IN 'DER ROSENKAVALIER'; A MARCH-JIG (MAGUIRE'S KICK) (Stanford, *Four Irish Dances*, Op. 89 no. 1, arr. Grainger); THE LEPRECHAUN'S DANCE (Stanford, *Four Irish Dances*, Op. 89 no. 2, arr. Grainger); A REEL (Stanford, *Four Irish Dances*, Op. 89 no. 4, arr. Grainger); SHEEP AND GOAT WALKIN' TO THE PASTURE (trad. American, arr. Guion); TURKEY IN THE STRAW (trad. American, arr. Guion); 'THE GUM-SUCKERS' MARCH (duet with Lotta Hough); ZANZIBAR BOAT-SONG; COLONIAL SONG; WALKING TUNE; CHILDREN'S MARCH (duet with Lotta Hough)
Nimbus Records NI8809 (20 tracks; total time 76:24)

Percy Grainger Plays Grieg and Liszt
PIANO CONCERTO IN A MINOR Op. 16. (Grieg, arr. Grainger); BALLADE Op. 24 (Grieg); WEDDING DAY AT TROLDHAUGEN Op. 65 no. 6 (Grieg); EROTIKON (LOVE POEM) Op. 45 no. 3 (Grieg); TO SPRING Op. 43 no. 6 (Grieg); POLONAISE NO. 2 IN E (Liszt); HUNGARIAN RHAPSODY no. 12 (Liszt)
Klavier Records KCD-11075 (9 tracks; total time 71:21)

Percy Grainger plays Schumann, Strauss and Tchaikovsky
SONATA NO. 3 IN G MINOR Op. 22 (Schumann); ÉTUDES SYMPHONIQUES Op. 13 (Schumann); ROMANCE IN F-SHARP Op. 28 no. 2 (Schumann); ROMEO AND JULIET (FANTASY OVERTURE) (Tchaikovsky, arr. for four hands with Ralph Leopold); TILL EULENSPIEGEL'S MERRY PRANKS Op. 28 (R. Strauss, arr. for four hands with Ralph Leopold); SYMPHONIC DANCE (Scott, arr. four hands with Cyril Scott)
Klavier Records KCD-11081 (8 tracks; total time 68:30)

Edvard Grieg: Piano Concerto (Rolf Gupta, conductor; Kristiansand Symphony Orchestra; Rex Lawson, pianolist)
Includes: PIANO CONCERTO IN A MINOR Op. 16 (Grainger Duo-Art Rolls, 1921); TO SPRING Op. 45 no. 6 (Grieg – Percy Grainger Duo-Art Roll, 1919)
2L Records 60SABC, available as SACD and Blue-ray (11 tracks; total time 66:20)

Percy Grainger Archive Piano Rolls in the Grainger Museum[8]
MOLLY ON THE SHORE; THE WARRIORS A; BARBARA ALLEN; COUNTRY GARDENS; DUKE OF MARLBOROUGH, DUBLIN BAY; LORD BATEMAN; O MY LOVE; THE WHITE HARE; THE GOLDEN VAN-

---

[8] This compilation of Grainger's private piano rolls was transferred to Yamaha Clavierdisk by Denis Condon. The Clavierdisk files were then transferred to General MIDI and then converted to sound files by Sydney O'Connell. They are included here for readers' awareness but are not commercially available as the other discs shown. The *Warriors* A has been transcribed by John Lavender and published as *Bridal Lullaby Ramble* (see Catalogue of Works). *Seven Men from All the World* (see Catalogue of Works) has been similarly transcribed, and both pieces have been recorded by Penelope Thwaites (see 'Performances by other Performers' section of this discography).

ITY; THE WARRIORS B; PIANO CONCERTO (Delius; orchestral reduction only); TWO MUSICAL RELICS OF MY MOTHER; CAPTAIN WARD; PAUL JONES; KNIGHT AND SHEPHERD'S DAUGHTER; SEVEN MEN FROM ALL THE WORLD; TJUGUNDI BIIDIL; LETS DANCE GAY IN GREEN MEADOW; RIVAL BROTHERS; FRAGMENT

Pianola

The Aeolian Company: Original Compositions and Arrangements for Pianola (Rex Lawson, pianola)
   Includes: MOLLY ON THE SHORE; SHEPHERD'S HEY[9]
   NMC Records Archive Series NMC D136 (21 tracks; total time 79:57)

Piano

Percy Grainger (Percy Grainger, piano)
   PRELUDE AND FUGUE IN A MINOR (Bach); TOCCATA AND FUGUE IN D MINOR (Bach); FANTASY AND FUGUE IN G MINOR (Bach); SONATA NO. 2 IN B-FLAT MINOR Op. 35 (Chopin); ÉTUDE IN B MINOR Op. 25 no. 10 (Chopin); SONATA NO. 3 IN B MINOR Op. 58 (Chopin)
   Biddulph Recordings LHW 010^d (12 tracks; total time 76:08)

Percy Grainger (Percy Grainger, piano)
   SONATA NO. 2 IN G MINOR Op. 22 (Schumann); ROMANCE IN F-SHARP Op. 28 no. 2 (Schumann); WARUM? Op. 12 no. 3 (Schumann); ÉTUDES SYMPHONIQUES Op. 13 (Schumann); WALTZ IN A-FLAT Op. 39 no. 15 (Brahms); SONATA NO. 3 IN F MINOR Op. 5 (Brahms)
   Biddulph Recordings LHW 008^d (25 tracks; total time 69:27)

Percy Grainger in Performance (Percy Grainger, piano; Leopold Stokowski, conductor; Hollywood Bowl Orchestra)
   CONCERTO IN A MINOR Op. 16, 'live' (Grieg); MOLLY ON THE SHORE, 'live'; SUITE 'IN A NUTSHELL', 'live'; (Percy Grainger, piano) ROMANCE IN F-SHARP Op. 28 no. 2 (Schumann); ÉTUDES SYMPHONIQUES Op. 13 (Schumann)
   Music and Arts CD-1002 (22 tracks; total time 72:25)

Percy Grainger Plays (Percy Grainger, piano)
   TOCCATA AND FUGUE IN D MINOR (Bach); PRELUDE AND FUGUE IN A MINOR (Bach); FANTASIA AND FUGUE IN G MINOR (Bach); ICH RUF ZU DIR (Bach, arr. Busoni); SONATA NO. 2 IN G MINOR Op. 22 (Schumann); ÉTUDE IN B MINOR Op. 25 no. 10 (Chopin); ÉTUDE IN C MINOR Op. 25 no. 12 (Chopin); WEDDING DAY AT TROLDHAUGEN Op. 65 no. 6 (Grieg); TOCCATA FROM 'POUR LE PIANO' (Debussy); (Grainger talks about Debussy's *Pagodes*); GOLLIWOG'S CAKEWALK (Debussy); MOLLY ON THE SHORE
   Pearl (Pavilion Records) GEMM CD 9957 (19 tracks; total time 78:30)

Percy Grainger Plays, Volume II (Percy Grainger, piano)
   PIANO SONATA NO. 2 IN B-FLAT MINOR Op. 35 (Chopin); PIANO SONATA NO. 3 IN B MINOR Op. 58 (Chopin); ROMANCE IN F-SHARP Op. 28 no. 2 (Schumann); ÉTUDES SYMPHONIQUES Op. 13 (Schumann); (Grainger

---

[9] Grainger's special pianola versions were issued in 1914. Early copies of the rolls stated that they could be played with Grainger's other arrangements of the same folk songs.

lectures on William Byrd); 'THE CARMAN'S WHISTLE' (Byrd, arr. Grainger); A MARCH-JIG (MAGUIRE'S KICK) (Stanford, *Four Irish Dances*, Op. 89 no. 1, arr. Grainger)
    Pearl (Pavilion Records) GEMM CD 9013 (25 tracks; total time 76:57)

Edvard Grieg: The Piano Music in Historic Interpretations (3 CDs)
    Includes: PIANO CONCERTO IN A MINOR Op. 16 (cadenza only from 1st mvt (1908)); TO THE SPRING Op. 43 no. 6; NORWEGIAN BRIDAL PROCESSION Op. 19 no. 2; WEDDING DAY AT TROLDHAUGEN Op. 65 no. 6; I KNOW A LITTLE MAIDEN Op. 17 no. 16; THE SUCKLING PIG Op. 17 no. 8; SOLFAGER AND THE SNAKE-KING Op. 17 no. 12; NILS TALLEFJORDEN Op. 17 no. 4
    Simax Records PSC 1809 (1) Grieg: Historical Piano Recordings (Pt 1) (29 tracks; total time 74:21)

Grieg Performed by Percy Grainger (Percy Grainger, piano; Per Dreier, conductor; Aarhus Municipal Orchestra, 'live')
    PIANO CONCERTO IN A MINOR Op. 16 (Grieg); COUNTRY GARDENS; RAMBLE ON THE LAST LOVE-DUET IN 'DER ROSENKAVALIER' (R. Strauss, arr. Grainger); DANISH FOLK-MUSIC SUITE
    Vanguard Classics USA OVC 8205 (9 tracks; total time 53:57)

Rachmaninoff and Grieg Concerti (Percy Grainger, piano; Leopold Stokowski, conductor; Hollywood Bowl Symphony Orchestra, 'live')
    Includes: PIANO CONCERTO IN A MINOR Op. 16 (Grieg); SUITE 'IN A NUTSHELL'
    Biddulph Recordings LHW 041^d (10 tracks; total time 75:37)

Grieg and his Circle play Grieg (Various pianists including Percy Grainger)
    Includes: PIANO CONCERTO IN A MINOR Op. 16 (cadenza only from 1st mvt) (Grieg); NORWEGIAN BRIDAL PROCESSION Op. 19 no. 2 (Grieg); WEDDING DAY AT TROLDHAUGEN Op. 65 no. 6 (Grieg)
    Pearl (Pavilion Records) GEMM CD 9933 (16 tracks; total time 76:10)

A Grainger/Stokowski Collaboration (Percy Grainger, piano; Leopold Stokowski, conductor; Hollywood Bowl Symphony Orchestra, 'live')
    PIANO CONCERTO IN A MINOR Op. 16 (Grieg); SUITE 'IN A NUTSHELL'; DANISH FOLK-MUSIC SUITE
    Archive Documents ADCD 2003 (10 tracks; total time 62:44)

Stokowski conducts Percy Grainger Favourites (*Percy Grainger, piano; Leopold Stokowski and his Symphony Orchestra)
    Includes: COUNTRY GARDENS*; EARLY ONE MORNING; HANDEL IN THE STRAND*; IRISH TUNE FROM COUNTY DERRY; MOCK MORRIS, MOLLY ON THE SHORE; SHEPHERD'S HEY
    Cala Records CACD0542 (16 tracks; total time 77:58)

Percy Grainger: The Complete 78-rpm Solo Recordings (1908–1945) [5 CDs] (Percy Grainger, piano)
    Appian Publications & Recordings APR 7501 (104 tracks; total time 390:05)

Performances by Others

Piano

Percy Grainger, Dished up for Piano: The Complete Piano Music (Volumes 1–5) (Martin Jones, piano)

Volume 1: Original Works: HANDEL IN THE STRAND; BRIDAL LULLABY; ENGLISH WALTZ; MOCK MORRIS; TO A NORDIC PRINCESS; ARRIVAL PLATFORM HUMLET; GAY BUT WISTFUL; PASTORAL; 'THE GUM-SUCKERS' MARCH; PEACE; SAXON TWI-PLAY; ANDANTE CON MOTO; CHILDREN'S MARCH; THE IMMOVABLE DO; SAILOR'S SONG; COLONIAL SONG; WALKING TUNE; HARVEST HYMN; IN DAHOMEY

Nimbus Records NI 5220 (19 tracks; total time 71:35)

Volume 2: Arrangements: OPENING OF B-FLAT MINOR CONCERTO (Tchaikovsky); CRADLE SONG (Brahms); LOVE WALKED IN (Gershwin); SECOND PIANO CONCERTO (3rd mvt) (Rachmaninov); NOW, O NOW, I NEEDS MUST PART (Dowland); NIMROD (Elgar); RAMBLE ON THE LAST LOVE-DUET IN 'DER ROSENKAVALIER' (R. Strauss); BEAUTIFUL FRESH FLOWER (Chinese trad.); PARAPHRASE ON TCHAIKOVSKY'S FLOWER WALTZ; LULLABY FROM 'TRIBUTE TO FOSTER' (Foster); THE RAG-TIME GIRL (Emerson); BLITHE BELLS (Bach); FUGUE IN A MINOR (Bach); THE MAN I LOVE (Gershwin)

Nimbus Records NI 5232 (14 tracks; total time 58:56)

Volume 3: Folksongs: COUNTRY GARDENS; THE MERRY KING; MOLLY ON THE SHORE; IRISH TUNE FROM COUNTY DERRY; KNIGHT AND SHEPHERD'S DAUGHTER; THE NIGHTINGALE AND THE TWO SISTERS; JUTISH MEDLEY; SUSSEX MUMMERS' CHRISTMAS CAROL; THE RIVAL BROTHERS; NEAR WOODSTOCK TOWN; WILL YE GANG TO THE HIELANDS, LIZZIE LINDSAY; THE BRISK YOUNG SAILOR; ONE MORE DAY, MY JOHN (both versions); RIMMER AND GOLDCASTLE; SPOON RIVER; THE WIDOW'S PARTY; THE HUNTER IN HIS CAREER; MY ROBIN IS TO THE GREENWOOD GONE; DIED FOR LOVE; SCOTCH STRATHSPEY AND REEL; BRISTOL TOWN; HARD-HEARTED BARB'RA (H)ELLEN; MO NINGHEAN DHU; LISBON (DUBLIN BAY); STALT VESSELIL; O GIN I WERE WHERE GADIE RINS; SHEPHERD'S HEY

Nimbus Records NI 5244 (28 tracks; total time 68:26)

Volume 4: Arrangements and Original Works: FOUR IRISH DANCES Op. 89 (Stanford); NELL Op. 18 no. 1 (Fauré); APRÈS UN RÊVE (Fauré); PIANO CONCERTO (1st mvt) (Schumann); AIR AND DANCE (Delius); HORNPIPE (Handel); TOCCATA AND FUGUE IN D MINOR (Bach); LULLABY FROM 'TRIBUTE TO FOSTER' (2nd version) (Foster); ANGELUS AD VIRGINEM (anon.); KLAVIERSTÜCK IN E; EASTERN INTERMEZZO; THE BIGELOW MARCH (Ella Grainger); PIANO CONCERTO (1st mvt) (Grieg); AT TWILIGHT; KLAVIERSTÜCK IN A MINOR; KLAVIERSTÜCK IN B-FLAT; KLAVIERSTÜCK IN D

Nimbus Records NI 5255 (21 tracks; total time 77:19)

Volume 5: Arrangements and Original Works for up to Six Hands (with Philip Martin, Richard McMahon, pianos): CHILDREN'S MARCH; UP-COUNTRY SONG; ENGLISH DANCE; YE BANKS AND BRAES; SPOON RIVER; TRAIN MUSIC; ZANZIBAR BOAT SONG; 'PAGANINI VARIATIONS' no. 12

(Brahms); GREEN BUSHES; THE CARMAN'S WHISTLE (Byrd); A DANCE RHAPSODY (Delius); EMBRACEABLE YOU (Gershwin); THE WARRIORS
Nimbus Records NI 5286 (13 tracks; total time 78:13)

Percy Grainger: Piano Music for Four Hands, Volume I (Penelope Thwaites and John Lavender, pianos)
SUITE 'IN A NUTSHELL'; SPOON RIVER; WHEN THE WORLD WAS YOUNG; MOLLY ON THE SHORE; HILL-SONG II; COUNTRY GARDENS; MOWGLI'S SONG AGAINST PEOPLE; EASTERN INTERMEZZO; ENGLISH WALTZ; THE WRAITH OF ODIN; ALWAYS MERRY AND BRIGHT; THE DUKE OF MARLBOROUGH FANFARE; LINCOLNSHIRE POSY
Pearl (Pavilion Records) SHE 9611 (21 tracks; total time 77:01); re-released on Heritage Records HTGCD 403

Percy Grainger: Piano Music for Four Hands, Volume II (Penelope Thwaites and John Lavender, pianos)
CHILDREN'S MARCH; SHEPHERD'S HEY; HILL-SONG I; HANDEL IN THE STRAND; HARVEST HYMN; THE WIDOW'S PARTY; THE LONELY DESERT-MAN SEES THE TENTS OF THE HAPPY TRIBES; THE RIVAL BROTHERS; THE WARRIORS II; TWO MUSICAL RELICS OF MY MOTHER; LET'S DANCE GAY IN GREEN MEADOW; BLITHE BELLS; PRITTELING, PRATTELING, PRETTY POLL PARROT
Pearl (Pavilion Records) SHE 9623 (13 tracks; total time 66:27); re-released on Heritage Records HTGCD 403

Percy Grainger: Piano Music for Four Hands, Volume III (Penelope Thwaites and John Lavender, pianos)
THREE SYMPHONIC DANCES (Cyril Scott, arr. Grainger); RONDO; THE CREW OF THE LONG SERPENT (DRAGON); DANCE RHAPSODY no. 1 (Delius, arr. Grainger); KNUT LURASEN'S HALLING II Op. 72 no. 11 (Grieg, arr. Grainger); FESTIVAL (Addinsell, arr. Grainger); LA BEL' ARONDE (Le Jeune, arr. Grainger); EARLY ONE MORNING; YE BANKS AND BRAES; TIGER, TIGER; WALKING TUNE; LA BEL' ARONDE (Le Jeune, arr. Grainger, 2nd version); EMBRACEABLE YOU (Gershwin, arr. Grainger); FANTASY ON 'PORGY AND BESS' (Gershwin, arr. Grainger)
Pearl (Pavilion Records) SHE 9631 (14 tracks; total time 78:15); re-released on Heritage Records HTGCD 403

Percy Grainger: Piano Music for Four Hands, Volume IV (Penelope Thwaites and Timothy Young, pianos)
ENGLISH DANCE (Balfour Gardiner, arr. Grainger); KONZERTSTÜCK [1896]; MORI QUASI IL MIO CORE (Palestrina, arr. Grainger); SIX PART FANTASY AND AIR (Lawes, arr. Grainger); THE MAIDEN AND THE FROG (Danish folksong, arr. Grainger); SONG OF THE HIGH HILLS (Delius, arr. Grainger); FUGUE IN C MAJOR [WTK Book 1 no. 1] (Bach, arr. Grainger); FUGUE IN D-SHARP MINOR [WTK Book 2 no. 8] (Bach, arr. Grainger); WALKING TUNE [extended version]; NIMROD (Elgar, arr. Grainger); PASTORAL (FROM SUITE 'IN A NUTSHELL'); WARSAW CONCERTO (Addinsell, arr. Grainger)
Heritage Records HTGCD 403 (10 tracks; total time 69:36); issued as part of a boxed set with Volumes I–III

Chandos Grainger Edition, Volume Ten: Works for Pianos (Penelope Thwaites, John

Lavender, Wayne Marshall, Rhondda Gillespie, Antony Gray, Barry Peter Ould, pianos)
GREEN BUSHES; LET'S DANCE GAY IN GREEN MEADOW; IN BRISTOL TOWN; ENGLISH DANCE; ZANZIBAR BOAT SONG; THE WIDOW'S PARTY MARCH; YE BANKS AND BRAES; JUTISH MEDLEY; HARVEST HYMN; COUNTRY GARDENS; RANDOM ROUND; THE KEEL ROW; THE WARRIORS
Chandos Records CHAN 9702 (13 tracks; total time 68:55)

Chandos Grainger Edition, Volume Sixteen: Works for Solo Piano 1 (Penelope Thwaites, piano)
PRELUDE IN G; PRELUDE IN C; GIGUE; ANDANTE CON MOTO; KLAVIERSTÜCK IN D; KLAVIERSTÜCK IN E; KLAVIERSTÜCK IN A MINOR; KLAVIERSTÜCK IN B-FLAT; PEACE; SAXON TWI-PLAY; EASTERN INTERMEZZO; ENGLISH WALTZ; AT TWILIGHT; TRAIN MUSIC; SAILOR'S SONG; WALKING TUNE; THREE SCOTTISH FOLK-SONGS; SCOTCH STRATHSPEY AND REEL; SEVEN MEN FROM ALL THE WORLD; PARAPHRASE ON TCHAIKOVSKY'S FLOWER WALTZ; IRISH TUNE FROM COUNTY DERRY; NEAR WOODSTOCK TOWN; IN DAHOMEY
Chandos Records CHAN 9895 (25 tracks; total time 78:01)

Chandos Grainger Edition, Volume Seventeen: Works for Solo Piano 2 (Penelope Thwaites, piano)
TIGER, TIGER; THE HUNTER IN HIS CAREER; THE SUSSEX MUMMERS' CHRISTMAS CAROL; THE RIVAL BROTHERS; AUSTRALIAN UP-COUNTRY SONG; HARVEST HYMN; THE MERRY KING; LISBON; PASTORAL; THE WIDOW'S PARTY; DIED FOR LOVE; HORKSTOW GRANGE; THE BRISK YOUNG SAILOR; HARD-HEARTED BARB'RA (H)ELLEN; BRISTOL TOWN; SEA SONG SKETCH; MOLLY ON THE SHORE; ARRIVAL PLATFORM HUMLET; SHEPHERD'S HEY; COUNTRY GARDENS; MOCK MORRIS; 'THE GUM-SUCKERS' MARCH; COLONIAL SONG; THE TENTS OF THE HAPPY TRIBES; GAY BUT WISTFUL; HANDEL IN THE STRAND; MY ROBIN IS TO THE GREENWOOD GONE
Chandos Records CHAN 9919 (27 tracks; total time 74:29)

Chandos Grainger Edition, Volume Nineteen: Works for Solo Piano 3 (Penelope Thwaites, piano)
LULLABY FROM 'TRIBUTE TO FOSTER'; ONE MORE DAY, MY JOHN; A BRIDAL LULLABY; KNIGHT AND SHEPHERD'S DAUGHTER; CHILDREN'S MARCH; BRIDAL LULLABY RAMBLE; SPOON RIVER; RAMBLE ON THE LAST LOVE-DUET IN 'DER ROSENKAVALIER' (R. Strauss, arr. Grainger); DANISH FOLK-MUSIC SUITE; TO A NORDIC PRINCESS; BLITHE BELLS; WALKING TUNE; LULLABY FROM 'TRIBUTE TO FOSTER' (simplified version); PROUD VESSELIL; RIMMER AND GOLDCASTLE; IRISH TUNE FROM COUNTY DERRY; COUNTRY GARDENS; THE IMMOVABLE DO; BEAUTIFUL FRESH FLOWER; NOW, O NOW, I NEEDS MUST PART (Dowland, arr. Grainger)
Chandos Records CHAN 10205 (22 tracks; total time 75:49)

Percy Grainger: Chosen Gems for Piano (Penelope Thwaites, piano)
DANISH FOLK-MUSIC SUITE (THE POWER OF LOVE) (transcribed Thwaites); THE NIGHTINGALE AND THE TWO SISTERS; JUTISH MEDLEY; ONE MORE DAY, MY JOHN; KNIGHT AND SHEPHERD'S

DAUGHTER; NEAR WOODSTOCK TOWN; COUNTRY GARDENS; THE SUSSEX MUMMERS' CHRISTMAS CAROL; SHEPHERD'S HEY; TO A NORDIC PRINCESS; LOVE AT FIRST SIGHT (Ella Grainger, arr. Stevenson); BRIDAL LULLABY; HANDEL IN THE STRAND; COLONIAL SONG; NELL Op. 18 no. 1 (Fauré, arr. Grainger); PARAPHRASE ON TCHAIKOVSKY'S FLOWER WALTZ; NOW, O NOW, I NEEDS MUST PART (Dowland, arr. Grainger)

Unicorn-Kanchana DKP(CD) 9127 (re-issued on Regis RRC1107) (18 tracks; total time 69:21)

Piano Music by Percy Grainger (Marc-André Hamelin, piano)
JUTISH MEDLEY; COLONIAL SONG; MOLLY ON THE SHORE; HARVEST HYMN; A REEL (Stanford, *Four Irish Dances*, Op. 89 no. 3, arr. Grainger); SPOON RIVER; COUNTRY GARDENS; WALKING TUNE; MOCK MORRIS; RAMBLE ON THE LAST LOVE-DUET IN 'DER ROSENKAVALIER' (R. Strauss, arr. Grainger); SHEPHERD'S HEY; IRISH TUNE FROM COUNTY DERRY; HANDEL IN THE STRAND; A MARCH-JIG (MAGUIRE'S KICK) (Stanford, *Four Irish Dances*, Op. 89 no. 1, arr. Grainger); THE HUNTER IN HIS CAREER; SCOTCH STRATHSPEY AND REEL; 'THE GUM-SUCKERS' MARCH; THE MERRY KING; IN DAHOMEY

Hyperion Records CDA 66884 (19 tracks; total time 73:11)

Rambles and Reflections (Piers Lane, piano)
THE CARMAN'S WHISTLE (Byrd, arr. Grainger); NOW, O NOW, I NEEDS MUST PART (Dowland, arr. Grainger); HORNPIPE (Handel, arr. Grainger); HANDELIAN RHAPSODY (Scott, arr. Grainger); AIR AND DANCE (Delius, arr. Grainger); FOUR IRISH DANCES Op. 89 (Stanford, arr. Grainger); BEAUTIFUL FRESH FLOWER (Chinese trad., arr. Grainger); RAMBLE ON THE LAST LOVE-DUET IN 'DER ROSENKAVALIER' (R. Strauss, arr. Grainger); CRADLE-SONG (Brahms, arr. Grainger); APRÈS UNE RÊVE (Fauré arr. Grainger); NELL (Fauré, arr. Grainger); PARAPHRASE ON TCHAIKOVSKY'S FLOWER WALTZ; THE MAN I LOVE (Gershwin, arr. Grainger); LOVE WALKED IN (Gershwin, arr. Grainger); LULLABY FROM 'TRIBUTE TO FOSTER'

Hyperion Records CDA67279 (18 tracks; total time 75:20)

Orchestra
* works applicable under this section (when not the entire disc)

Chandos Grainger Edition, Volume One: Orchestral Works 1 (Richard Hickox, conductor; BBC Philharmonic Orchestra)
THE DUKE OF MARLBOROUGH FANFARE; COLONIAL SONG; ENGLISH DANCE; SHEPHERD'S HEY; THERE WERE THREE FRIENDS; FISHER'S BOARDING HOUSE; WE WERE DREAMERS; HARVEST HYMN; BLITHE BELLS; WALKING TUNE; SUITE 'IN A NUTSHELL'; GREEN BUSHES

Chandos Records CHAN 9493 (15 tracks; total time 72:28)

Chandos Grainger Edition, Volume Six: Orchestral Works 2 (Richard Hickox, conductor; BBC Philharmonic Orchestra)
YOUTHFUL SUITE; MOLLY ON THE SHORE (version for Stokowski); IRISH TUNE FROM COUNTY DERRY (version for Stokowski); SHEPHERD'S HEY (version for Stokowski); COUNTRY GARDENS (version for Stokowski); EARLY ONE MORNING (version for Stokowski); HANDEL IN THE STRAND (version for Stokowski); MOCK MORRIS (version for Stokowski); DREAMERY; THE WARRIORS

Chandos Records CHAN 9584 (14 tracks; total time 74:35)

Chandos Grainger Edition, Volume Fifteen: Orchestral Works 3 (Richard Hickox, conductor; BBC Philharmonic Orchestra)
GREEN BUSHES (1905/6 version); HILL-SONG II; THE MERRY KING; EASTERN INTERMEZZO; COLONIAL SONG (1919 version); SPOON RIVER; LORD MAXWELL'S GOODNIGHT; THE POWER OF ROME AND THE CHRISTIAN HEART; THE IMMOVABLE DO; IRISH TUNE FROM COUNTY DERRY; YE BANKS AND BRAES; ENGLISH DANCE no. 1
Chandos Records CHAN 9839 (12 tracks; total time 70:25)

Chandos Grainger Edition, Volume Three: Works for Chorus and Orchestra 1 (Richard Hickox, conductor; City of London Sinfonia; Joyful Company of Singers; Mark Padmore, tenor; Stephen Varcoe, baritone; Penelope Thwaites, piano)
SHALLOW BROWN; MARCHING TUNE; I'M SEVENTEEN COME SUNDAY; SHENANDOAH; STORMY; MOLLY ON THE SHORE*; BRIGG FAIR; EARLY ONE MORNING; AFTERWORD; THERE WAS A PIG WENT OUT TO DIG; THE LONELY DESERT-MAN SEES THE TENTS OF THE HAPPY TRIBES; THOU GRACIOUS POWER; COUNTY DERRY AIR; HANDEL IN THE STRAND*; SIX DUKES WENT A-FISHIN'; ANCHOR SONG; YE BANKS AND BRAES
Chandos Records CHAN 9499 (17 tracks; total time 60:44)

Chandos Grainger Edition, Volume Five: Works for Chorus and Orchestra 2 (Richard Hickox, conductor; City of London Sinfonia; Joyful Company of Singers)
THE WIDOW'S PARTY; THE SEA-WIFE; THE RUNNING OF SHINDAND*; WE HAVE FED OUR SEA FOR A THOUSAND YEARS; TIGER, TIGER*; THE LOVE SONG OF HAR DYAL; COUNTRY GARDENS (1952 version)*; THE IMMOVABLE DO*; MOCK MORRIS*; COLLEEN DHAS*; SCOTCH STRATHSPEY AND REEL; DREAMERY*; COLONIAL SONG; MY ROBIN IS TO THE GREENWOOD GONE*; HARVEST HYMN; HANDEL IN THE STRAND (1952 version)*; LORD MAXWELL'S GOODNIGHT; THE LOST LADY FOUND
Chandos Records CHAN 9554 (18 tracks; total time 66:57)

Chandos Grainger Edition, Volume Nine: Works for Chorus and Orchestra 3 (Richard Hickox, conductor; Susan Gritton, soprano; Pamela Helen Stephen, mezzo; Mark Tucker, tenor; Stephen Varcoe, baritone; Tim Hugh, cello; City of London Sinfonia; Joyful Company of Singers)
MOCK MORRIS*; THE POWER OF LOVE; DIED FOR LOVE; LOVE VERSES FROM 'THE SONG OF SOLOMON'; SHEPHERD'S HEY*; EARLY ONE MORNING; THE THREE RAVENS; SCHERZO*; YOUTHFUL RAPTURE*; RANDOM ROUND (set version); THE MERRY KING*; O GIN I WERE WHERE GADIE RINS; SKYE BOAT SONG; DANNY DEEVER; IRISH TUNE FROM COUNTY DERRY*; DOLLAR AND A HALF A DAY; MOLLY ON THE SHORE*
Chandos Records CHAN 9653 (17 tracks; total time 62:34)

Chandos Grainger Edition, Volume Eleven: Works for Chorus and Orchestra 4 (Richard Hickox, conductor; Jesper Grove Jørgensen, conductor; Pamela Helen Stephen, mezzo; Johan Reuter, baritone; Danish National Radio Choir; Danish National Radio Symphony Orchestra)
FATHER AND DAUGHTER; KLEINE VARIATIONEN FORM*; A SONG OF VERMELAND; TO A NORDIC PRINCESS*; THE MERRY WEDDING; STALT VESSELIL*; THE RIVAL BROTHERS; DALVISA; THE

CREW OF THE LONG SERPENT (DRAGON)*; UNDER A BRIDGE; DANISH FOLK-MUSIC SUITE*
 Chandos Records CHAN 9721 (14 tracks; total time 64:35)

Percy Grainger: In A Nutshell (Simon Rattle, conductor; City of Birmingham Symphony Orchestra)
 SUITE 'IN A NUTSHELL'; TRAIN MUSIC; COUNTRY GARDENS (version for Stokowski); LA VALLÉE DES CLOCHES (Ravel arr. Grainger); LINCOLNSHIRE POSY; PAGODES (Debussy arr. Grainger); THE WARRIORS
 EMI Classics 72435 56412 29 (15 tracks; total time 69:59)

Music of Percy Aldridge Grainger (Geoffrey Simon, conductor; The Melbourne Symphony Orchestra)
 THE WARRIORS; BEAUTIFUL FRESH FLOWER (Chinese trad., arr. Sculthorpe); HILL-SONG no. 1; IRISH TUNE FROM COUNTY DERRY (BFMS 29); HILL-SONG no. 2; COLLEEN DHAS; THE POWER OF LOVE; LORD PETER'S STABLE-BOY; THE NIGHTINGALE AND THE TWO SISTERS; JUTISH MEDLEY
 Koch International 3-7003-2 (10 tracks; total time 66:41)
 ABC Classics ABC 426989-2 (10 tracks; total time 66:50)
 Cala Records CACDS4033 (10 tracks; total time 66:46)

Percy Grainger: The Power of Love (Keith Brion, conductor; Slovak Radio Symphony Orchestra)
 DANISH FOLK-MUSIC SUITE; COLONIAL SONG; COUNTRY GARDENS (arr. Schmid); IRISH TUNE FROM COUNTY DERRY; GREEN BUSHES; YE BANKS AND BRAES; SHEPHERD'S HEY; MY ROBIN IS TO THE GREENWOOD GONE; TO A NORDIC PRINCESS
 Naxos Records 8.554263 (12 tracks; total time 58:38)

Wind Band

Chandos Grainger Edition, Volume Four: Works for Wind Orchestra 1 (Timothy Reynish, conductor; Clark Rundell, conductor; Royal Northern College of Music Wind Orchestra)
 HILL-SONG II; YE BANKS AND BRAES; FAEROE ISLAND DANCE; 'THE LADS OF WAMPHRAY' MARCH; IRISH TUNE FROM COUNTY DERRY; SHEPHERD'S HEY; THE MERRY KING; MOLLY ON THE SHORE; COUNTRY GARDENS; COLONIAL SONG; 'THE GUM-SUCKERS' MARCH; LINCOLNSHIRE POSY
 Chandos Records CHAN 9549 (17 tracks; total time 60:58)

Chandos Grainger Edition, Volume Eight: Works for Wind Orchestra 2 (Timothy Reynish, conductor; Clark Rundell, conductor; Royal Northern College of Music Wind Orchestra)
 THE POWER OF ROME AND THE CHRISTIAN HEART; CHILDREN'S MARCH; BELL PIECE; BLITHE BELLS; THE IMMOVABLE DO; HILL-SONG I (Original scoring); HILL-SONG II (1929 version); IRISH TUNE FROM COUNTY DERRY (County Derry Air BFMS 29); MARCHING SONG OF DEMOCRACY
 Chandos Records CHAN 9630 (9 tracks; total time 65:04)

To The Fore: Percy Grainger's Great Symphonic Band Music (Keith Brion, conductor; Kenneth Bloomquist, director of bands; Michigan State University Symphonic Band)
MOLLY ON THE SHORE; COUNTRY GARDENS (arr. Grainger); THE IMMOVABLE DO; COLONIAL SONG; 'THE GUM-SUCKERS' MARCH; TUSCAN SERENADE (Fauré, arr. Grainger); CHORALE no. 2 (Franck, arr. Grainger); MARCH (Bach, arr. Grainger); O MENSCH, BEWEIN' DEIN' SÜNDE GROSS (Bach, arr. Grainger); COUNTRY GARDENS (arr. Sousa); YE BANKS AND BRAES; CHILDREN'S MARCH
Delos Records DE 3101 (12 tracks; total time 56:44)

The Music of Percy Grainger, Volume One (University of Houston Wind Ensemble; Eddie Green, conductor)
MOLLY ON THE SHORE; LINCOLNSHIRE POSY; COLONIAL SONG; BLITHE BELLS; IRISH TUNE FROM COUNTY DERRY; SHEPHERD'S HEY; THE DUKE OF MARLBOROUGH FANFARE; COUNTRY GARDENS; THE POWER OF ROME AND THE CHRISTIAN HEART
Mark Custom Recording Service, Inc. MCD-1086 (special order only) (14 tracks; total time 53:41)

The Music of Percy Grainger, Volume Two (University of Houston Wind Ensemble; Eddie Green, conductor)
'THE LADS OF WAMPHRAY' MARCH; HANDEL IN THE STRAND; SPOON RIVER; WALKING TUNE; FAEROE ISLAND DANCE; THE SUSSEX MUMMERS' CHRISTMAS CAROL; YE BANKS AND BRAES; EASTERN INTERMEZZO; THE IMMOVABLE DO; SCOTCH STRATHSPEY AND REEL (arr. Osmon)
Mark Custom Recording Service, Inc. MCD-1350 (special order only) (10 tracks; total time 44:00)

The Music of Percy Grainger, Volume Three (University of Houston Wind Ensemble; Eddie Green, conductor)
CHILDREN'S MARCH; HILL-SONG II; DOWN LONGFORD WAY (Parker, arr. Grainger); MOCK MORRIS (arr. Simpson); AUSTRALIAN UP-COUNTRY TUNE (arr. Bainum); BELL PIECE (Dowland, arr. Grainger); MARCHING SONG OF DEMOCRACY
Mark Custom Recording Service, Inc. MCD-1523 (special order only) (7 tracks; total time 35:00)

The Music of Percy Grainger, Volume Four (University of Houston, Moores Wind Ensemble; Tom Bennett, conductor)
'THE GUM-SUCKERS' MARCH; TUSCAN SERENADE (Fauré, arr. Grainger); PRELUDE IN THE DORIAN MODE (Cabezón, arr. Grainger); CHORALE no. 2 (Franck, arr. Grainger); THE MERRY KING; O MENSCH, BEWEIN' DEIN' SÜNDE GROSS (Bach, arr. Grainger); THE WARRIORS (arr. Pappajohn)
Mark Custom Recording Service, Inc. MCD-4835 (special order only) (7 tracks; total time 53:28)

Grainger at the National Library of Victoria (Grainger Wind Symphony; Roland Yeung, conductor)
MOLLY ON THE SHORE; BLITHE BELLS (Bach/Grainger, arr. Jager); O MENSCH, BEWEIN' DEIN' SÜNDE GROSS (Bach, arr. Grainger); HANDEL IN THE STRAND (Grainger, arr. Goldman); SIX DUKES WENT A-

FISHIN' (Grainger, arr. Kreines); I'M SEVENTEEN COME SUNDAY (Grainger, arr. Daehn); EARLY ONE MORNING (Grainger, arr. Kreines); YE BANKS AND BRAES; ENGLISH WALTZ (Grainger, arr. McKinney); AUSTRALIAN UP-COUNTRY SONG (Grainger, arr. Bainum); 'THE GUM-SUCKERS' MARCH; LINCOLNSHIRE POSY; COUNTRY GARDENS
Move Records MCD 196 (19 tracks; total time 61:37)

The Composer's Collection: Percy Aldridge Grainger (North Texas Wind Symphony; Eugene Milgiaro Corperon, conductor)
CHILDREN'S MARCH; IRISH TUNE FROM COUNTY DERRY; SHEPHERD'S HEY; COLONIAL SONG; THE IMMOVABLE DO; PRELUDE IN THE DORIAN MODE (Cabezón, arr. Grainger); THEME FROM 'GREEN BUSHES' (Grainger, arr. Daehn); DOWN LONGFORD WAY (Parker, arr. Grainger, arr. Osmon); THE SUSSEX MUMMERS' CHRISTMAS CAROL (Grainger, arr. Kreines); YE BANKS AND BRAES; SIX DUKES WENT A-FISHIN' (Grainger, arr. Kreines); EARLY ONE MORNING (Grainger, arr. Kreines); LINCOLNSHIRE POSY; 'THE LADS OF WAMPHRAY' MARCH; IRISH TUNE FROM COUNTY DERRY (Grainger, arr. Kreines); MOLLY ON THE SHORE; AUSTRALIAN UP-COUNTRY SONG (Grainger, arr. Bainum); HANDEL IN THE STRAND (Grainger, arr. Goldman); O MENSCH BEWEIN' DEIN' SÜNDE GROSS (Bach, arr. Grainger); COUNTRY GARDENS (Grainger, arr. Clark); SHENANDOAH (Grainger, arr. Osmon); 'THE GUM-SUCKERS' MARCH; HARVEST HYMN (Grainger, arr. Kreines); THE WARRIORS (Grainger, arr. Pappajohn)
GIA Composer's Collection GIA CD-656 (2 CDs, 29 tracks; total time 126:44)

Transcriptions for Wind Orchestra (Royal Northern College of Music Wind Orchestra; Ivan Hovorun, piano; Clark Rundell, conductor)
ANGELUS AD VIRGINEM (anon., arr. Grainger); BALLADE no. 17 (Machaut, arr. Grainger); LA BERNARDINA (Josquin des Prez, arr. Grainger); PRELUDE IN THE DORIAN MODE (Cabezón, arr. Grainger); THE FOUR NOTE PAVAN (A. Ferrabosco II, arr. Grainger); FIVE PART FANTASY no. 15 (Jenkins, arr. Grainger); MARCH (Bach, arr. Grainger); SEE WHAT HIS LOVE CAN DO (Bach, arr. Grainger); O MENSCH, BEWEIN' DEIN' SÜNDE GROSS (Bach, arr. Grainger); HUNGARIAN FANTASY (Liszt, arr. Grainger); CHORALE No. 2 (Franck, arr. Grainger); TUSCAN SERENADE (Fauré, arr. Grainger); FOLK-TUNE (Goossens, arr. Grainger); DOWN LONGFORD WAY (Parker, arr. Grainger)
Chandos Digital CHAN 10455 (14 tracks; total time 60:51)

A Tribute to Percy Grainger (United States Military Academy Band; Lt. Col. Timothy J. Holtan, Cpt. Treg Ancelet, conductors)
THE SUSSEX MUMMERS' CHRISTMAS CAROL; THE DUKE OF MARLBOROUGH FANFARE; THE MERRY KING; YE BANKS AND BRAES; LISBON; DIED FOR LOVE; MARCH (Bach, arr. Grainger); BLITHE BELLS; TUSCAN SERENADE (Fauré, arr. Grainger); HANDEL IN THE STRAND; COLONIAL SONG; 'THE GUM-SUCKERS' MARCH; CHILDREN'S MARCH; SHEPHERD'S HEY; THE IMMOVABLE DO; FAEROE ISLAND DANCE; ENGLISH WALTZ; HILL-SONG II; COUNTRY GARDENS
USMA WPPG07 (19 tracks; total time 67:32)

Percy Grainger's Lincolnshire Posy (Dallas Wind Symphony; Jerry Junkin, conductor)
THE DUKE OF MARLBOROUGH FANFARE; LINCOLNSHIRE POSY; THE MERRY KING; CHILDREN'S MARCH; COLONIAL SONG;

MOCK MORRIS; 'THE GUM-SUCKERS' MARCH; MOLLY ON THE SHORE; SPOON RIVER; AFTERWORD; 'THE LADS OF WAMPHRAY' MARCH; IRISH TUNE FROM COUNTY DERRY; SHEPHERD'S HEY
Reference Recordings RR-117 HDCD (17 tracks; total time 73:43)

Vocal / Choral
* works applicable under this section (when not the entire disc)

Chandos Grainger Edition, Volume Three: Works for Chorus and Orchestra 1 (Richard Hickox, conductor; City of London Sinfonia; Joyful Company of Singers; Mark Padmore, tenor; Stephen Varcoe, baritone; Penelope Thwaites, piano)
SHALLOW BROWN*; MARCHING TUNE*; I'M SEVENTEEN COME SUNDAY*; SHENANDOAH*; STORMY*; MOLLY ON THE SHORE; BRIGG FAIR*; EARLY ONE MORNING*; AFTERWORD*; THERE WAS A PIG WENT OUT TO DIG*; THE LONELY DESERT-MAN SEES THE TENTS OF THE HAPPY TRIBES*; THOU GRACIOUS POWER*; COUNTY DERRY AIR*; HANDEL IN THE STRAND; SIX DUKES WENT A-FISHIN'*; ANCHOR SONG*; YE BANKS AND BRAES*
Chandos Records CHAN 9499 (17 tracks; total time 60:44)

Chandos Grainger Edition, Volume Five: Works for Chorus and Orchestra 2 (Richard Hickox, conductor; Geoffrey Tozer, piano; City of London Sinfonia; Joyful Company of Singers)
THE WIDOW'S PARTY*; THE SEA-WIFE*; THE RUNNING OF SHINDAND; WE HAVE FED OUR SEA FOR A THOUSAND YEARS*; TIGER, TIGER; THE LOVE SONG OF HAR DYAL*; COUNTRY GARDENS (1952 version); THE IMMOVABLE DO; MOCK MORRIS; COLLEEN DHAS; SCOTCH STRATHSPEY AND REEL*; DREAMERY; COLONIAL SONG*; MY ROBIN IS TO THE GREENWOOD GONE; HARVEST HYMN*; HANDEL IN THE STRAND (1952 version); LORD MAXWELL'S GOODNIGHT*; THE LOST LADY FOUND*
Chandos Records CHAN 9554 (18 tracks; total time 66:57)

Chandos Grainger Edition, Volume Nine: Works for Chorus and Orchestra 3 (Richard Hickox, conductor; Susan Gritton, soprano; Pamela Helen Stephen, mezzo; Mark Tucker, tenor; Stephen Varcoe, baritone; Tim Hugh, cello; City of London Sinfonia; Joyful Company of Singers)
MOCK MORRIS; THE POWER OF LOVE*; DIED FOR LOVE; LOVE VERSES FROM 'THE SONG OF SOLOMON'*; SHEPHERD'S HEY; EARLY ONE MORNING; THE THREE RAVENS*; SCHERZO; YOUTHFUL RAPTURE; RANDOM ROUND (SET VERSION)*; THE MERRY KING; O GIN I WERE WHERE GADIE RINS*; SKYE BOAT SONG*; DANNY DEEVER*; IRISH TUNE FROM COUNTY DERRY; DOLLAR AND A HALF A DAY*; MOLLY ON THE SHORE
Chandos Records CHAN 9653 (17 tracks; total time 62:34)

Chandos Grainger Edition, Volume Eleven: Works for Chorus and Orchestra 4 (Richard Hickox, conductor; Jesper Grove Jørgensen, conductor; Pamela Helen Stephen, mezzo; Johan Reuter, baritone; Danish National Radio Choir; Danish National Radio Symphony Orchestra)
FATHER AND DAUGHTER*; KLEINE VARIATIONEN FORM; A SONG OF VERMELAND*; TO A NORDIC PRINCESS; THE MERRY WEDDING*; STALT VESSELIL; THE RIVAL BROTHERS*; DALVISA*;

THE CREW OF THE LONG SERPENT(DRAGON); UNDER A BRIDGE*; DANISH FOLK-MUSIC SUITE
Chandos Records CHAN 9721 (14 tracks; total time 64:35)

Chandos Grainger Edition, Volume Eighteen: Works for Unacccompanied Chorus (Academy of St Martin-in-the-Field Chorus, Richard Hickox, conductor)
MY LOVE'S IN GERMANIE; SIX DUKES WENT A-FISHIN'; O MISTRESS MINE (Morley, arr. Grainger); MARY THOMPSON; EARLY ONE MORNING; IRISH TUNE FROM COUNTY DERRY; AGINCOURT SONG; AUSTRALIAN UP-COUNTRY SONG; RECESSIONAL; AT TWILIGHT; THE GIPSY'S WEDDING DAY; MO NIGHEAN DUBH; YE BANKS AND BRAES; SOLDIER SOLDER; NIGHT SONG IN THE JUNGLE; LUKANNON; HUNTING SONG OF THE SEEONEE PACK; TIGER, TIGER; NEAR WOODSTOCK TOWN; LOVE AT FIRST SIGHT
Chandos Digital CHAN 9987 (20 tracks; total time 53:33)

Chandos Grainger Edition, Volume Two: Songs for Baritone (Stephen Varcoe, baritone; Penelope Thwaites, piano)
WILLOW WILLOW; SIX DUKES WENT A-FISHIN'; BRITISH WATERSIDE; THE PRETTY MAID MILKIN' HER COW; THE LOST LADY FOUND; CREEPING JANE; BOLD WILLIAM TAYLOR; LEEZIE LINDSAY; BONNIE GEORGE CAMPBELL; DROWNED; WILLIE'S GANG TO MELVILLE CASTLE; LUKANNON; MERCIFUL TOWN; RIDE WITH AN IDLE WHIP; NORTHERN BALLAD; THE MEN OF THE SEA; SOLDIER, SOLDIER; HARD-HEARTED BARB'RA (H) ELLEN; THE SECRET OF THE SEA; SAILOR'S CHANTY; SHALLOW BROWN
Chandos Records CHAN 9503 (21 tracks; total time 64:50)

Chandos Grainger Edition, Volume Seven: Songs for Tenor (Martyn Hill, tenor; Penelope Thwaites, piano)
DEDICATION (2nd setting); ANCHOR SONG; THE SEA-WIFE; GANGES PILOT; THE FIRST CHANTEY; THE WIDOW'S PARTY; SOLDIER, SOLDIER; THE YOUNG BRITISH SOLDIER; DEDICATION I; YON WILD MOSSY MOUNTAINS; EVAN BANKS; AFTON WATER; MY FAITHFUL FOND ONE; THE WOMAN ARE A GANE WUND; O'ER THE MOOR; FAIR YOUNG MARY; THE POWER OF LOVE; THE TWA CORBIES; A REIVER'S NECK-VERSE; LORD MAXWELL'S GOODNIGHT
Chandos Records CHAN 9610 (20 tracks; total time 69:12)

Chandos Grainger Edition, Volume Twelve: Songs for Mezzo (Della Jones, mezzo; Mark Padmore, tenor; Stephen Varcoe, baritone; Penelope Thwaites, piano; George Black, guitar)
DAVID OF THE WHITE ROCK; DIED FOR LOVE; THE SPRIG OF THYME; WILLOW WILLOW; NEAR WOODSTOCK TOWN; EARLY ONE MORNING; IN BRISTOL TOWN; WEAVING SONG; THIS IS NO MY PLAID; SKYE BOAT SONG; TURN YE TO ME; THE BRIDEGROOM GRAT; THE LAND O' THE LEAL; PROUD VESSELIL; UNDER A BRIDGE; HUSBAND AND WIFE; THE LONELY DESERTMAN SEES THE TENTS OF THE HAPPY TRIBES; COLONIAL SONG; THE ONLY SON; THE LOVE SONG OF HAR DYAL; A SONG OF AUTUMN; FIVE SONGS OF ELLA GRAINGER (TO ECHO; HONEY POT BEE; FAREWELL TO AN ATOLL; CRYING FOR THE MOON;

LOVE AT FIRST SIGHT); O GLORIOUS GOLDEN ERA (Corteccia, arr. Grainger); LITTLE OLE WITH HIS UMBRELLA (Peter Lemche, arr. Grainger; text by Ella and Percy Grainger); VARIATIONS ON HANDEL'S 'THE HARMONIOUS BLACKSMITH'; HARVEST HYMN; AFTERWORD
   Chandos Records CHAN 9730 (31 tracks; total time 73:49)

Chandos Grainger Edition, Volume Fourteen: Works for Chamber Ensemble 2 (Della Jones, mezzo; Martyn Hill, tenor; Stephen Varcoe, baritone; Academy of St. Martin-in-the-Fields Chamber Ensemble)
   LORD PETER'S STABLE-BOY; THE SHOEMAKER FROM JERUSALEM; HUSBAND AND WIFE*; THE ONLY SON; YE BANKS AND BRAES; LISBON; THE BRIDEGROOM GRAT*; THE LAND O' THE LEAL*; WALKING TUNE; WILLOW WILLOW*; HARVEST HYMN; THE OLD WOMAN AT THE CHRISTENING*; THE NIGHTINGALE; THE TWO SISTERS; SEA SONG; BOLD WILLIAM TAYLOR*; THE POWER OF LOVE; LORD MAXWELL'S GOODNIGHT*; COLONIAL SONG*; FREE MUSIC; THE TWA CORBIES*; DIED FOR LOVE*; MOLLY ON THE SHORE
   Chandos Records CHAN 9819 (23 tracks; total time 67:49)

Jungle Book (Stephen Layton, conductor; Libby Crabtree, soprano; John Mark Ainsley, tenor; David Wilson-Johnson, baritone; Polyphony; Polyphony Orchestra)
   JUNGLE BOOK CYCLE; SHALLOW BROWN; GOOD-BYE TO LOVE (BRIDAL LULLABY, arr. Gibbs); DIED FOR LOVE; THE POWER OF LOVE; THE RIVAL BROTHERS; SIX DUKES WENT A-FISHIN'; THE SPRIG OF THYME (arr. Perna); WILLOW WILLOW; RECESSIONAL; LORD MAXWELL'S GOODNIGHT (arr. Tall); THE THREE RAVENS; THE RUNNING OF SHINDAND; EARLY ONE MORNING (ed. Tall); THE LOVE SONG OF HAR DYAL; MY LOVE'S IN GERMANIE
   Hyperion Records CDA 66863 (26 tracks; total time 73:57)

At Twilight: The Choral Music of Grainger and Grieg (Stephen Layton, conductor; David Wilson-Johnson, baritone; Polyphony)
   Includes: IRISH TUNE FROM COUNTY DERRY (BFMS6); A DOLLAR AND A HALF A DAY; SHENANDOAH; STORMY; THE GYPSY'S WEDDING DAY; BRIGG FAIR; MO NIGHEAN DUBH; O MISTRESS MINE (Morley, arr. Grainger); SOLDIER, SOLDIER; MARY THOMPSON; YE BANKS AND BRAES; DALVISA; AUSTRALIAN UP-COUNTRY SONG; NEAR WOODSTOCK TOWN; THE SUSSEX MUMMERS' CAROL; A SONG OF VERMELAND; AT TWILIGHT
   Hyperion Records CDA 66793 (22 tracks; total time 75:13)

Grainger Choral Works: Danny Boy (John Eliot Gardiner, conductor; The Monteverdi Choir and Orchestra (English Country Gardiner Orchestra))
   I'M SEVENTEEN COME SUNDAY; THE LOST LADY FOUND; LOVE VERSES FROM 'THE SONG OF SOLOMON'; THE THREE RAVENS; TRIBUTE TO FOSTER; MO NIGHEAN DUBH; BRIGG FAIR; IRISH TUNE FROM COUNTY DERRY (BFMS 6); SHALLOW BROWN; SCOTCH STRATHSPEY AND REEL; FATHER AND DAUGHTER; DANNY DEEVER (world premiere recording); THE BRIDE'S TRAGEDY (world premiere recording); THE MERRY WEDDING (world premiere recording)
   Philips Classics CD 446 657-2 (re-issued on Philips Classics CD 475 213-2) (14 tracks; total time 74:58)

Percy Grainger: Works for Large Chorus and Orchestra (Sir Andrew Davis, conductor; Melbourne Symphony Orchestra and Chorus; Sydney Chamber Choir)
  KING SOLOMON'S ESPOUSALS; DANNY DEEVER; MARCHING SONG OF DEMOCRACY; THE WRAITH OF ODIN; THE HUNTER IN HIS CAREER; SIR EGLAMORE; THE LADS OF WAMPHRAY; THE BRIDE'S TRAGEDY; TRIBUTE TO FOSTER; THANKSGIVING SONG
  Chandos Digital CHSA 5121 (20 tracks; total time 72:39)

Miscellaneous

Chandos Grainger Edition, Volume Fourteen: Works for Chamber Ensemble 1 (Academy of St Martin-in-the-Fields Chamber Ensemble)
  MOLLY ON THE SHORE; MY ROBIN IS TO THE GREENWOOD GONE; SHEPHERD'S HEY; HARVEST HYMN; ARRIVAL PLATFORM HUMLET; HANDEL IN THE STRAND; LA SCANDINAVIE; THE NIGHTINGALE AND THE TWO SISTERS; THE MAIDEN AND THE FROG; THE SHOEMAKER FROM JERUSALEM; MOCK MORRIS; THE SUSSEX MUMMERS' CHRISTMAS CAROL; THEME AND VARIATIONS; YOUTHFUL RAPTURE; COLONIAL SONG
  Chandos Digital CHAN 9746 (19 tracks; total time 73:00)

Grainger Tuneful Percussion (Michael Lichnovsky, conductor; WOOF!; Vaughan McAlley, tenor; Kirsten Boerema, mezzo; Clifford Plumpton, bass; members of the Ormond College Choir; Linden String Quartet; Mark Knoop, piano; Wendy Clarke, flute; Mary Anderson, harp; Sylvia Hosking, double bass) [* instrumental only]
  SHEPHERD'S HEY*; GAMELAN ANKLUNG*; IRISH TUNE FROM COUNTY DERRY (arr. Ragsdale)*; THE LONELY DESERT-MAN SEES THE TENTS OF THE HAPPY TRIBES; BLITHE BELLS*; EASTERN INTERMEZZO*; CRYING FOR THE MOON (Ella Grainger); ARRIVAL PLATFORM HUMLET*; PAGODES (Debussy, arr. Grainger)*; BAHARIYALE V. PALANIYANDI*; LONDON BRIDGE (Gardiner, arr. Grainger)*; LA VALLÉE DES CLOCHES (Ravel, arr. Grainger)*; SEKAR GADUNG; UNDER A BRIDGE; COUNTRY GARDENS (arr. Woof!)*
  Move Records Move MD 3222 (16 tracks; total time 54:15)

Music from The Ether: Original Works for Theremin (Lydia Kavina, theremin)
  Includes: FREE MUSIC no. 1 (for 4 theremins)
  Mode Records MODE 76 (12 tracks; total time 67:24)

Spellbound! Original Works for Theremin (Lydia Kavina, theremins; Ensemble Sospeso; Charles Peltz, conductor; Burkhard Stangl, electric guitar)
  Includes: FREE MUSIC no. 1; FREE MUSIC no. 2; BEATLESS MUSIC
  Mode Records MODE 199 (20 tracks; total time 63:17)

Catalogue of Works

Barry Peter Ould

In preparing this catalogue, I am indebted to Thomas Slattery (*The Instrumentalist* 1974), Teresa Balough (University of Western Australia 1975), Kay Dreyfus (University of Melbourne 1978–95) and David Tall (London 1982) for their original pioneering work in cataloguing Grainger's music.[1] My ongoing research as archivist to the Percy Grainger Society (UK) has built on those references, and they have greatly helped both in producing catalogues for the Society and in my work as a music publisher. The Catalogue of Works for this volume lists all Grainger's original compositions, settings and versions, as well as his arrangements of music by other composers. The many arrangements of Grainger's music by others are not included, but details may be obtained by contacting the Percy Grainger Society.[2] Works in the process of being edited are marked ‡.

Key to abbreviations used in the list of compositions

Grainger's generic headings for original works and folk-song settings

AFMS	American folk-music settings
BFMS	British folk-music settings
DFMS	Danish folk-music settings
EG	Easy Grainger [a collection of keyboard arrangements]
FI	Faeroe Island dance folk-song settings
KJBC	Kipling *Jungle Book* cycle
KS	Kipling settings
OEPM	Settings of songs and tunes from William Chappell's *Old English Popular Music*
RMTB	Room-Music Tit Bits
S	Sentimentals
SCS	Sea Chanty settings
YT	Youthful Toneworks

Grainger's generic headings for transcriptions and arrangements

CGS	Chosen Gems for Strings
CGW	Chosen Gems for Winds

---

[1] See Bibliography above.
[2] See Main Grainger Contacts below.

CT Concert Transcriptions of Favourite Concertos
DC Dolmetsch Collection of English Consorts
EGM English Gothic Music
FS Free Settings of Favourite Melodies
GV Guide to Virtuosity
WTK Well-Tempered Klavier (Bach)

Key to the scoring symbols

Instrumental scoring follows five groups:
WOODWIND — SAXOPHONES — BRASS — PERCUSSION AND KEYBOARD — STRINGS

WOODWIND: flutes · oboes · clarinets · bassoons

SAXOPHONES: The symbols s, ms, a, t, β, b, indicate: soprano · mezzo-soprano · alto · tenor · baritone · bass

BRASS: horns · trumpets · trombones · [euphoniums · baritones] · tubas
(The bracketed instruments indicate Grainger's preferred scoring for concert brass)

PERCUSSION AND KEYBOARD: T = timpani · s = side-drum · b = bass-drum · t = tambourine · w = woodblock · Δ = triangle · c = cymbals · k = castanets · g = gong · h = 'Shaker' chimes · G = glockenspiel · X = xylophone · M = metal marimba · W = wooden marimba · N = nabimba · S = staff bells (Swiss hand bells) · B = tubular bells · V = vibraphone or vibraharp · C = celesta · D = dulcitone · A = harp · H = harmonium (or reed organ) · O = organ · p = pipe-organ · R = reed-organ · P = piano · E = electric organ

STRINGS: Where figures are given, they indicate the number of parts for violins, violas, violoncellos and double basses, e.g. 4 · 2 · 2 · 1 indicates a string ensemble of 4 violins, 2 violas, 2 violoncellos, and 1 double bass.

Further sub-divisions of groups are given in the usual way, using standard nomenclature, with an asterisk prefixed to indicate an optional instrument. For example, the woodwind section, scored thus (piccolo · flute · oboe · cor anglais · *bass oboe · *E-flat clarinet · clarinet · *alto clarinet · bass clarinet · bassoon · double bassoon) is listed as (piccolo · 1 · 1 · cor anglais · *bass oboe · *E-flat clarinet · 1 · *alto clarinet · bass clarinet · 1 · double bassoon).

Alternative instruments are given in brackets, following the preferred instruments, thus: O(H) indicates organ, or harmonium in lieu. Similarly, alternatives used in later compositions are: for trumpets, soprano saxophones (s); for horns, alto saxophones (a); for trombones, tenor saxophones (t); for bassoons, baritone saxophones (β). Other substitutes are possible (e.g. cornets for trumpets). For full details, consult the appropriate score.

Optional numbers of instruments are indicated within parentheses: e.g. 4(2) indicates 4 instruments, of which 2 are optional (usually parts 3 and 4). In some cases these are shown with #, indicating which number of part is optional: e.g. 4(#1#3) indicates 4 instruments, of which nos. 1 and 3 are optional.

ADDITIONAL PLAYERS AND INSTRUMENTS

The notation P^2 indicates 2 players at 1 piano, whilst 2P or PP indicates 2 pianos with 1 player each. A plus sign following an instrument code (A+) indicates that the instruments may be massed: in this case the harp part.

CATALOGUE OF WORKS · 251

ELASTIC SCORING

Works with elastic scoring (a Grainger device, allowing for greater flexibility of instrumentation) are denoted by a dagger (†). Earlier scores, for instance *Mock Morris* or *Molly on the Shore*, published as being for theatre orchestra, in fact have many possible instrumental permutations. These are elastically scored in all but name.

ROOM-MUSIC

Grainger used this term for ensembles with one player to a part, up to twenty-four players.

CHORAL WORKS

S = soprano, mS = mezzo-soprano, A = contralto, T = tenor, β = baritone, B = bass
 Capital letters indicate solo; small letters indicate chorus (satβb); a letter with a small number after it indicates the number of divisions within the basic part: e.g. s^2s^2 indicates two soprano lines of which each is divided, whilst $s^2a^2t^2b^2$ indicates a eight-part mixed voice chorus. Unison voices are indicated thus: uc = (mixed) unison chorus, um = unison men's chorus, uw = unison women's chorus.

Original works and folk-music settings

Afterword (1900–1901, 1957) [S3] 3'51"
 1. uc † and brass (3 · 3(cornets) · 3 · euphonium — P) [Bardic Edition]
 2. uc + P [Bardic Edition]

Afton Water (see also *Three Burns Songs*) 5'58"
 voice and piano [Bardic Edition]

Agincourt Song (1907) [BFMS] 2'00"
 chorus (satβb) a cappella (ed. Gibbs) [Bardic Edition]

Always Merry and Bright (see also *Mock Morris*) (1910) 3'30"
 2 pianos (4 hands) [Bardic Edition]

Anchor Song (1899, 1905, 1915, 1921) [KS6] 3'30"
 1. baritone solo + male chorus (t^3b^2 [or T^3B^2]) + P [Schott]
 2. voice and piano [Bardic Edition]

Andante con moto (c.1897) [YT] 3'24"
 piano solo [Bardic Edition]

Arrival Platform Humlet (1908, 1910, 1912, 1916) [RMTB7: 1st mvt of *In a Nutshell*]
 2'30"
 1. orchestra, piano and tuneful percussion (piccolo · 2 · 2 · cor anglais · 2 · *bass clarinet · 2 · double bassoon — 4 · 3 · 3 · 1 — Tsbcg*GXM²W¹(²)*S*NCAP — strings 2 · 1 · 1 · 1) [Schott]
 2. piano solo [Schott]
 3. 2 pianos (4 hands) [Schott]
 4. solo viola or massed violas [Schott]
 5. solo violin or massed violins [Bardic Edition]
 6. solo oboe or massed oboes [Bardic Edition]

As Sally Sat a-Weeping (1908–12) [BFMS: no. 1 of *Two Musical Relics of my Mother*] 1′00″
    2 pianos (4 hands) [Schott]

At Twilight (adapted from *The Rhyme of the Three Sealers*) (1900–1909) 3′00″
1. tenor solo and mixed chorus (s²a²tβ²β²b²) [Schott]
2. piano solo [EG] [Bardic Edition]

Australian Marching Song (see also *Marching Song of Democracy*) (1930) 7′15″
1. mixed chorus (s³a³t²b²) and room-music (o · o · o · o — 1 · 1 · 1(euphonium) · o — 2P · p¹(H²) — strings 2 · 1 · 1 · 1) + *4T*b*c*G*M³(or *bar-piano or *dulcitone)*S³(⁴)*B¹(²)*A [Bardic Edition]
2. orchestra (all the above + 2 · 2 · 2 · bass clarinet · 2 — ssmsatβ — 1 · E-flat horn · 2 · 2 · 2 euphoniums · o — strings 2 · 1 · 2 · o) [Bardic Edition]

Australian Up-Country Song 2′00″
1. mixed chorus (s²a²t²β²b²) a cappella (1928) [Schott]
2. piano solo (1932) [Bardic Edition]

The Ballad of the 'Bolivar' (1901) [KS] 4′15″
    men's chorus (t²b³) and orchestra (4 · 4 · 4 cor anglais · 8 · 2 · 2 double bassoon — 4 · 3(cornet) · o · o — T — banjos — strings 16 · 8 · 8 · 8) [Bardic Edition] ‡
    [Grainger sets only two stanzas from Kipling's poem beginning 'Seven men from all the world'.]

Ballad of the 'Clampherdown' (1899) [KS] (incomplete) [Grainger Society]

The Beaches of Lukannon (see also *Lukannon*) (1941–2) [KS20: 5th mvt of KJBC] 2′30″
    mixed chorus (s³a³t²b²) and room-music (*H — strings 4 · 2 · 2 · 1) [Schott]

Beatless Music (see also *Sea Song*) (1907–37) 0′33″
    six Theremins (graph score only) [Bardic Edition]

Beautiful Fresh Flower (Chinese Melody) (1935) 1′55″
    piano solo [Bardic Edition]

Bell Piece (after Dowland) (1951–3) 5′30″
    tenor solo and wind band (1 · 1 · 3 · alto clarinet · bass clarinet · 1 — aatβ — 4 · 4 · 3 · euphonium · baritone · 1 — GBVOAP — string bass) (ed. Duffy and Ould) [Bardic Edition]

Blithe Bells (free ramble on Bach's *Sheep may safely graze* from Cantata 208) (1930–32) 3′35″
1. orchestra (2 · 1 · 2 · 2(1) — 1(ms or a) · 2(ss) · 1(t) · o — GP²H(p)M(V)WC(D or P)A — strings 2 · 1 · 1 · 1) [Schott]
2. small orchestra (1 · 1 · 1 · 1 — 1 · 1 · 1 · o — GP² — strings 2 · 1 · 1 · 1) [Schott]
3. theatre orchestra or †elastic scoring (any or all of the orchestral parts with the version for 2 pianos (4 hands) [Schott]
4. large room-music (2 · 1 · 2 · 1 — 1(ms or a) · 1(s) · o · o — GP² — strings 2 · 1 · 1 · 1) [Schott]
5. piano and military band (piccolo · 2 · 2 · E-flat clarinet · solo clarinet · 3 · alto clarinet

· bass clarinet · 2 — *satβb* — 4 · 2 · 2 cornets · flugelhorn · 3 · baritone · euphonium · 2 — GMW*AP — string bass) (ed. Ould) [Bardic Edition]
6. piano solo (concert and easy versions) [Schott]
7. 2 pianos (4 hands) [Schott]

Bold William Taylor (1908) [BFMS43] 3′45″
1. voice (mezzo-soprano or baritone) and room-music (1 or 2 clarinets — H(p or reed-organ or concertina or accordion) — strings 2 · 1 · 2 · 1) [Schott]
2. voice and piano [Schott]

A Bridal Lullaby (1916) 2′16″
   piano solo (ed. Stevenson) [Bardic Edition]

Bridal Lullaby Ramble (1918) (see also *Warriors* A) 6′47″
   piano solo (transcr. from piano roll and ed. John Lavender and Penelope Thwaites) [Bardic Edition]

The Bridegroom Grat (1902) [YT] 1′34″
   voice and strings (0 · 2 · 3 · 0) (ed. Ould) [Bardic Edition]

The Bride's Tragedy (1908–9, 1913–14) 9′16″
   double (satb + um) or single chorus (satb) and orchestra (piccolo+ · 2+ · 2+ · 2+ · bass clarinet+ · 2+ · double bassoon+ — *s*a*t*β — 4 · 3 · 3 · 1 — 3TcgR(H) — strings 2 · 1 · 1 · 1) [Schott]

Brigg Fair (1906) [BFMS7] 3′45″
   tenor solo and mixed chorus (satbβb) [Schott]

The Brisk Young Sailor 1′40″
1. piano solo [EG] [Bardic Edition]
2. wind band (piccolo · 2 · 2 · cor anglais · E-flat clarinet · 3 · alto clarinet · bass clarinet · 2 · double bassoon — *saatβb* — 4 · 3(cornets) · 3 · baritone · euphonium · 2 — Tsbc — string bass) [Schott UK; Ludwig Masters USA]
   (in this version it is the 4th mvt of *Lincolnshire Posy*)

Bristol Town (see *In Bristol Town*)

British Waterside (*The Jolly Sailor*) (1920) [BFMS26] 1′45″
1. high voice and piano [Schott]
2. low voice and piano [Schott]

The Camp (*Y Gadlys*) (1904) [BFMS: Welsh Fighting Song no. 1] 2′00″
1. mixed chorus (satβb + um) and piano [Bardic Edition]
2. mixed chorus (satβb + um) and band (0 · 0 · 0 · 0 — 4 · 3 · 3 · 1 · euphonium — 2 guitars) (realised Ragsdale) [Bardic Edition]

Charging Irishrey (1901–7) (see also *Train Music*)
   orchestra (2 · 2 · cor anglais · 3 · 2 · double bassoon — 3 · 0 · 0 · 0 — T — strings 3 · 2 · 4 · 1) (ed. Rathburn) [Bardic Edition]

Childhood Works (*Birthday Gift to Mother*) (1893)
   [Bardic Edition; various piano and choral pieces in the process of being edited and published] ‡

Children's March: 'Over the Hills and Far Away' (1916–20) [RMTB4] 6'30"
 1. wind band with or without chorus (satb or ttbb) + (piccolo · 3(1(E-flat clarinet)) · 2 · bass oboe(cor anglais) · E-flat clarinet · 4 · alto clarinet · bass clarinet · 2 · double bassoon(contrabass clarinet or contrabass sarrusophone) — s(a)atβb(contra-alto clarinet) — 4 · 4 cornets(trumpets) · euphonium · 2 — TsbcgkwΔSXB*P — string bass) (ed. Rogers) [Bardic Edition UK; Southern Music USA]
 2. orchestra (piccolo · 2 · 2 · bass oboe(cor anglais) · *E-flat clarinet · 3 · *alto clarinet · bass clarinet · 2 · double bassoon — *s*a*t — 4 · 4 cornets(trumpets) · 3 · *euphonium · 2 — TsbcgkwΔSXB*P — strings 0 · 0 · 0 · 1) [Bardic Edition UK; Southern Music USA]
 3. theatre orchestra or †elastic scoring (any or all of the wind, percussion and double bass parts with the version for 2 pianos (4 hands)) [Bardic Edition UK; Southern Music USA]
 4. room-music (flute · oboe · 2 clarinets · bassoon — 2 horns · cornet(trumpet) · euphonium — bells · 2 pianos (4 hands) — double basses) [Bardic Edition UK; Southern Music USA]
 5. small room-music (flute · oboe · clarinet · bassoon(bass clarinet) — horn — 2 pianos (4 hands)) [Bardic Edition UK; Southern Music USA]
 6. large room-music (piccolo · oboe · 2 clarinets · alto clarinet · bass clarinet · bassoon · double bassoon — sa — horn · cornet(trumpet) — scBX · 2 pianos (4 hands)) [Bardic Edition UK; Southern Music USA]
 7. small orchestra (piccolo · flute · oboe · bass oboe(cor anglais) · 2 clarinets · bass clarinet · bassoon · double bassoon — sa — 2 horns · 2 cornets (trumpets) · 2 trombones · euphonium · tuba — TsbcΔBX · 2 pianos (4 hands)) [Bardic Edition UK; Southern Music USA]
 8. 2 pianos (4 hands) [Schott]
 9. piano solo (excerpt) [Schott] 2'00"

Colleen Dhas ('The valley lay smiling' in Moore's *Irish Melodies*) (1907) [BFMS] 3'31"
 small room-music (flute · cor anglais — guitar(A) — strings 2 · 1 · 1 · 1) [Bardic Edition]

Colonial Song (1911–60) [S1] 6'00"
 1. soprano and tenor soli and orchestra (piccolo · 2 · 2 · 2 · 2 — 4 · 3 · 3 · 1 — TcA*A*P — strings 2 · 1 · 1 · 1) [Schott]
 2. orchestra with or without ST voices (piccolo · 2 · 2 · *cor anglais · 2 · *bass clarinet · 2 — 4 · 2(cornets) · 3 · 1 — A*A*P — strings 2 · 1 · 1 · 1) [Bardic Edition]
 3. orchestra (piccolo · 2 · 2 · 2 · 2 — 4 · 3 · 3 · 1 — TcA*A*P — strings 2 · 1 · 1 · 1) [Schott]
 4. soprano solo and orchestra (piccolo · 2 · 2 · cor anglais · 2 · bass clarinet · 2 — 4 · 3 · 3 · 1 — TcA*A*P — strings 2 · 1 · 1 · 1) [Bardic Edition]
 5. orchestra (1919 version) (piccolo · 2 · 2 · cor anglais · 2 · bass clarinet · 2 · double bassoon — 4 · 3(2) · 3 · euphonium · 1 — TcA*A*P — strings 2 · 1 · 1 · 1) [Bardic Edition]
 6. theatre orchestra or †elastic scoring (any or all of the instrumental parts with the version for piano solo) [Schott]
 7. wind band (2 piccolos · 2 · 2 · E-flat clarinet · solo clarinet · 3 · alto clarinet · bass clarinet · contra-alto clarinet · 2 · double bassoon — atβ — 4 · solo cornet(trumpet or flugelhorn) · 3(cornets) · 3 · baritone · 1 — TscgGAP — string bass) (ed. Topolewski) [Carl Fischer USA]

8. military band (2 piccolos · 3(#3E-flat clarinet) · 2 · E-flat clarinet · 4 · alto clarinet · bass clarinet · contra-alto clarinet(contrabass clarinet) · 2 · double bassoon(contra-alto clarinet or contrabass clarinet or contrabass sarrusophone) — s(a)atβ — 4(E-flat) · 2(cornets) · 2 flugelhorns(trumpets or cornets) · 3 · euphonium · 2 — TscgB*A*P — string bass) (ed. Rogers) [Southern Music USA]
9. soprano and tenor soli and piano trio (P — violin · violoncello) [Schott]
10. soprano and tenor soli, piano and string quartet (P — 2 · 1 · 1 · 0) [Bardic Edition]
11. soprano and tenor soli and piano [Schott]
12. violin, violoncello and piano [Schott]
13. piano solo (2 versions) [Schott]

Country Gardens (English Morris Dance Tune) (1908–47) [BFMS22] 1'45"
1. piano solo [Schott]
2. piano solo (easy version) [Schott]
3. piano solo (very easy version) [Schott]
4. 2 pianos (4 hands) [Schott]
5. 1 piano (4 hands) [Schott]
6. 2 pianos (8 hands) [Schott]
7. descant and treble recorder [Bardic Edition]
8. for 2 instruments in C [Bardic Edition]
9. wind band (piccolo · 2 · 2 · E-flat clarinet · solo clarinet · 3 · alto clarinet · bass clarinet · 2 — s(a)atβb — 4 · 4 E-flat horns(altos) · 2 · 2 cornets · *flugelhorn · 3 · euphonium · baritone · 2 — TsbcBX) (ed. Clark) [Schirmer]
10. orchestra (as no. 9 above + A — string bass (or any of the instrumental parts from Adolf Schmid's arrangement with piano conductor part (*piccolo · 2(1) · 2(1) · 2 · 2(1) — 4(2) · 2 · 3(2) · 1(1) — TsbcBX*A — strings (solo and obbligato violin in lieu of violin I part · 2 · 1 · 1· 1) [Schott]

It seems strange that Grainger himself made no orchestral or room-music version of this version of perhaps his most popular piece. There are two orchestral arrangements in print, one by Leo Artok (d. 1935) and another by Adolf Schmid (1858–1958), both published by Schott. They are not listed here as they come under the category of arrangements by others, although Grainger himself mentions in a radio interview towards the end of his life that most of his popular pieces, including 'Country Gardens', were in fact orchestrated by himself and adapted by others at the instigation of his publishers. [B.P.O.]

Country Gardens (2nd version) (1949, 1950–53) 1'30"
1. orchestra (ed. Perna) (version for Stokowski):
versions A & B (piccolo · 2 · 2 · cor anglais · 2 · bass clarinet · 2 · double bassoon — 4 · 3 · 3 · 1 — TswGVCAP — strings 2 · 1 · 1 · 1) [Schott UK; Ludwig Masters USA]
2. wind band (piccolo · 2 · 2 · cor anglais · 3 · alto clarinet · bass clarinet · 2 · *double bassoon — aatβ — 4 · 3 cornets(trumpets) · 3 · baritone(euphonium) · 2 — Tsw*CGVMAP — string bass) (ed. Brion) [Schirmer]
3. large room-music (1952 version) (piccolo · 1 · 1 · 1 · 1 — a — 1 · 1 · 0 · 0 — GVHP — strings 2 · 1 · 1 · 1) (ed. Ould) [Bardic Edition]
Can be performed as 1st mvt of a suite for piano and orchestra (with link to *Bridal Lullaby*, arr. John Pickard).

County Derry Air (see *Irish Tune from County Derry*, 2nd version)

Creeping Jane (1920–21) [BFMS] 4'08"
voice and piano [Bardic Edition]

The Crew of the Long Serpent (Dragon) (1898) [YT] 4'47"
1. orchestra (piccolo · 2 · 2 · 3 · 2 · double bassoon — 2 · 2 · 3 · 0 — strings 2 · 1 · 1 · 1) [Bardic Edition]
2. 2 pianos (4 hands) [Bardic Edition]

Dalvisa (Swedish folk song) (1904) 1'08"
mixed chorus (satβb or sat²b) a cappella (ed. Ould) [Bardic Edition]

Danish Folk-Music Suite (see separate titles for full scoring and other versions): 'The Power of Love' [DFMS2] 3'15"; 'Lord Peter's Stable Boy' [DFMS1] 2'45"; 'The Nightingale and The Two Sisters' [DFMS10] 4'00"; 'Jutish Medley' [DFMS9] 7'15"
orchestra (†elastic scoring) [Schott]

Danny Deever (1903, 1922–4) [KS12] 3'15"
1. double men's chorus (um + t²b²) and orchestra (piccolo · 2 · 2 · 3 · bass clarinet · 2 · double bassoon — *s*a*t*β — 4 · 2 · 3 · euphonium · 1 — Tsbc — strings 2 · 1 · 1 · 1) [Schott/Bardic]
2. baritone solo, men's chorus (t²b²) and piano [Schott/Bardic]
3. men's chorus (t²b²), piano and harmonium [Bardic Edition]
4. baritone solo, men's chorus (t²b²), piano and harmonium [Bardic Edition]

Death Song for Hjalmar Thuren (1916–17)
1. bartitone solo, chorus (satb) and orchestra (unfinished composition, but sketches survive)
2. mixed chorus (satb) and harp(s) (Tail-piece) (ed. Ould) [Bardic Edition] ‡

Dedication (1901) [KS1] 1'42"
1. voice and piano [Schott]
2. voice and piano (1st setting) [Bardic Edition]

Died for Love (1906–7) [BFMS10] 1'42"
1. voice and piano [Schott]
2. voice and instrumental trio (flute · clarinet · bassoon) or (violin(flute) · viola · violoncello) [Schott]
3. string orchestra (2 · 1 · 1 · *1) [Bardic Edition]
4. string quartet (2 · 1 · 1 · 0) [Bardic Edition]
5. piano solo [Bardic Edition]
6. violoncello(violin) and piano (ed. Welsh) [Bardic Edition]

Dollar and a Half a Day (1908–9) [SCS2] 3'30"
male chorus (β solo + T²B² + um + t³β²b²) [Schott]

Dreamery (slow tween-play from *The Power of Rome and the Christian Heart*) (1939, 1942–3)
1. orchestra (2 · 2 · 2 · bass clarinet · 2 — 4 · 3 · 3 · 1 · baritone — aatβ — pVWP — strings 3 · 2 · 2 · 1) 6'32" [Bardic Edition]
2. string orchestra (2 versions) 2'24" [Bardic Edition]
   a) strings 2 · 2 · 2 · 1 (C Major)
   b) strings 2 · 2 · 3 · 1 (A-flat Major)

Dublin Bay (see *Lisbon*)

CATALOGUE OF WORKS · 257

Duke of Marlborough Fanfare (1939) [BFMS36] 2′15″
1. orchestral brass and woodwind (0 · 0 · 0 · *2 — *a*t — 4 · 4(4 cornets(#4 at will)) · 3 · *baritone · *euphonium · tuba — c — *string bass) (ed. Ould) [Bardic Edition]
   minimum orchestration (0 · 0 · 0 · 0 — 4 · 3 · 3 · 1 — c — 0 · 0 · 0 · 0)
2. orchestral brass and woodwind (0 · 0 · 0 · *2 — *a*t — 4 · 4(4 cornets(#4 at will)) · 3 · *baritone · *euphonium · tuba — c — *string bass) (ed. Simon) [Ludwig Masters USA]
   minimum orchestration (0 · 0 · 0 · 0 — 4 · 3 · 3 · 1 — c — 0 · 0 · 0 · 0)
3. 2 pianos (4 hands) + c (ed. Ould) [Bardic Edition]

Early one morning (1899, 1901, 1939, 1950) [BFMS] 2′55″
1. orchestra (2 · 1 · 2 · bass clarinet · 2 · double bassoon — 2 · 1 · 1 · euphonium · 1 — strings 2 · 2 · 2 · 1) (version for Stokowski) [Schott]
2. string orchestra (2 · 2 · 3 · *1) [Bardic Edition]
3. soprano solo(baritone solo) + uw and orchestra (2 · 0 · 0 · 1 · double bassoon) — 1 · 1 · 0 · 1 — strings 2 · 2 · 3(2) · 2(1) or 3 · 2 · 2 · 2) (1940 version) [Bardic Edition]
4. room-music (1(solo violin) · 0 · 0 · 1 · *double bassoon — *s — 1 · *1 · 0 · *baritone · 1 — strings 2 · 2 · 3(2) · 1(1) or 3 · 2 · 2 · 2) (1940 version) [Bardic Edition]
5. soprano solo and mixed chorus (s²a²t²b²) + um a cappella (realised Tall) [Bardic Edition]
6. high voice and piano [Bardic Edition]
7. harmonium(P) duet [EG] [Bardic Edition]
8. reed organ and 2 solovoxes [Bardic Edition]

Early Settings of Folksongs and Popular Tunes (from Augener's *The Minstrelsy of England*, ed. Duncan): 'The Vicar of Bray'; 'Drink to me only'; 'The Leather Bottel'; 'Sally in our Alley'; 'The British Grenadiers'; 'Near Woodstock Town'; 'Oh! The Oak and the Ash'; 'My lodging it is on the cold ground'; 'The Plough-boy'; 'The Girl I've Left Behind Me'; 'The Bailiff's Daughter of Islington'; 'Come lasses and lads'; 'Early one morning'; 'A-hunting we will go'; 'Jockey to the Fair'; 'Barbara Allen'; 'There was a jolly miller once'; 'A poor beggar's daughter'; 'The Three Ravens'; 'The Hunt is Up'; 'Jog on, jog on'; 'It was a maid of my country'; 'Begone, dull care!'; 'The Banks of Allan Water'; 'The Lass of Richmond Hill'
voice and piano (1899) [Bardic Edition] ‡

Eastern Intermezzo (1898/9, 1922, 1933, 1950) [RMTB5: 4th mvt of *Youthful Suite*] 2′00″
1. orchestra (piccolo · 2 · 2 · 2 · 2 — 4(#3) · *1 · *3 · *1 — TsbctGXMWSBHPA — strings 2 · 1 · 1 · 1) or (piccolo · 2 · 2 · 2 · 2 — 2 · 0 · 0 · 0 — strings 2 · 1 · 1 · 1) [Schott]
2. small orchestra (2 · 2 · 2 · 2 — 2 · 0 · 0 · 0 — strings 2 · 1 · 1 · 1) [Bardic Edition]
3. piano solo [Schott]
4. 2 pianos (4 hands) [Schott]
5. percussion ensemble (*h*GBDSM⁴X²W²P²P²⁻³H — string bass) [Bardic Edition]

English Dance (1898, 1901–2, 1924–9, 1952) 12′00″
1. orchestra (2 versions):
   a) (piccolo · 3 · 4 · 2 cor anglais · 3 · bass clarinet · 4 — 4 · 2 · 3 · 0 — Tc — strings 4 · 2 · 2 · 1) [Bardic Edition]
   b) (piccolo · 2 · 2 · cor anglais · E-flat clarinet · 3 · bass clarinet · 2 · double bassoon — 6 · 3 · 3 · euphonium · 1 — TscGA — strings 2 · 1 · 1 · 1 [Bardic Edition]

2. orchestra with organ (piccolo · 2 · 2 · cor anglais · E-flat clarinet · 3 · bass clarinet · 2 · double bassoon — 4 · 3 · 3 · euphonium · 1 — TsbcGP+O — strings 2 · 1 · 1 · 1) [Schott]
3. theatre orchestra or †elastic scoring (any or all of the instrumental parts from 2 above with the edition for 2 pianos, 6 hands (which also may be massed to any extent)) [Schott]
4. 2 pianos (6 hands) [Schott]
5. room-music (p(electric organ) · H · solovox · P — strings 2 · 1 · 1 · 1) (1952 version) [Bardic Edition]
6. 2 pianos (6 hands) and room-music (1 · 0 · 0 · 0 — sa — 0 · 0 · 0 · 0 — R — strings 1 · 0 · 1 · 0) (completed Kramer) [Bardic Edition]

English Dance no. 4 (see *Rustic Dance*)

English Waltz (1899, 1901, 1940–45, 1948–50) [5th mvt of *Youthful Suite*] 4′23″
1. orchestra (piccolo · 2 · 2 · cor anglais · 2 · bass clarinet · 2 · double bassoon — 4 · 3 · 3 · 1 — TsbcΔtGXM(V)WSBP+A+ — strings 2 · 1 · 1 · 1) or (piccolo · 2 · 2 · cor anglais · 2 · bass clarinet · 2 · double bassoon — 4 · 3 · 3 · 1 — TsbcΔtP+A+ — strings 2 · 1 · 1 · 1) [Schott]
2. 2 pianos (4 hands) [Schott]
3. piano solo [Bardic Edition]

Evan Banks (see *Three Burns Songs*)

Faeroe Island Dance (*Let's Dance Gay in Green Meadow*) (1954) 3′00″
concert band (piccolo · 2 · 2 · cor anglais · 4 · alto clarinet · bass clarinet · 2 · double bassoon — aatβb — 4 · 3(cornets) · 3 · euphonium(baritone) · 2 — TsbWX — string bass) [Faber Music]

The Fall of the Stone (1901–4, 1923, 1941–2, 1958) [KS16: 1st mvt of KJBC] 2′00″
1. βB soli + chorus (satβb) + TT²β²B² soli and room-music (0 · 0 · 2 cor anglais · 0 — ββ — 3 · 0 · 0 · 0 — strings 0 · 0 · 4 · 1) [Bardic Edition]
2. βB soli + chorus (satβb) + TT²β²B² soli and room-music (0 · 0 · *cor anglais · 0 · 2(β) — 2(a) · 0 · 0 · euphonium — strings 0 · 2 · 3 · 1) [Bardic Edition]
3. chorus (satβb) + *T²*β²*B² soli and room-music (0 · 0 · *cor anglais · 2 · 2 — 4 · 0 · 3 · 0 — HP — strings 2 · 2 · 3 · 1) [Bardic Edition]
4. chorus (sat²β²b²) + *T²*β²*B² soli and room-music (0 · 0 · cor anglais(clarinet) · 0 · 2(β) — 2(a) · 0 · *2 · 0 — *M(*V*A)*H(*p)*P — strings 2 · 2 · 2 · 1) [Schott]

Father and Daughter (*Fadir og Dottir*) (1908–11) [FI1] 2′38″
1. TTββBB solo voices, double mixed chorus (satβ²b² + s²atβ²b) + brass (4 · 0 · 3 · euphonium ·1), percussion (Tsc) and strings (*mandolins · 4 guitars(P²) · 2 · 1 · 1 · 1) [Schott]
2. voices as above + 2 pianos, 2 harmoniums

The First Chanty (1899, 1903) [KS] 4′00″
1. voice and piano [Bardic Edition]
2. β solo(um) and brass [incomplete]

Fisher's Boarding House (1899) [YT] 6′36″
orchestra (2 · 2 · 2 · 2 — 2 · 0 · 0 · 0 — strings 2 · 1 · 1 · 1) [Bardic Edition]

Free Music No. 1 (1935–7)
   1. string quartet or string orchestra (2 · 1 · 1 · 0) [Bardic Edition]
   2. strings (1 · 1 · 1 · 1) [ed. Stout] 0'59" [Bardic Edition]
   3. four theremins (graph score only) 1'33" [Bardic Edition]

Free Music No. 2 (1935–7)
   1. strings 0 · 3 · 0 · 3 [ed. Stout] 1'50" [Bardic Edition]
   2. six theremins (graph score only) 1'19" [Bardic Edition]

Ganges Pilot (1899) [KS] 2'26"
   voice and piano [Bardic Edition]

Gay but Wistful (1912, 1915–17) [2nd mvt of *In a Nutshell*] 2'30"
   1. orchestra, piano and tuneful percussion (piccolo · 2 · 2 · cor anglais · 2 · *bass clarinet · 2 · *double bassoon — 4 · 3 · 3 · 1 — 3T¹scGM²ACP — strings 2 · 1 · 1 · 1) [Schott]
   2. piano solo [Schott]
   3. 2 pianos (4 hands) [Schott]

Gigue (1893) (from *Childhood Works*) [YT] 0'50"
   piano solo (ed. Thwaites) [Bardic Edition]

Green Bushes (1905–6, 1919–21) [BFMS] 9'00"
   1. small orchestra (piccolo · 2 · 2 · cor anglais · 2 · bass clarinet · 2 — 4 · 2 · 2 · 0 — TsbcΔG — strings 2 · 1 · 1 · 1) (1905/6 version) [Bardic Edition]
   2. orchestra (*piccolo · 1 · 1 · 1 · 1 · *double bassoon — s(trumpet II or clarinet II)β(bassoon II) — 2(or E-flat alto horns or 2a) · 1 · 0 · 0 — TsbcXH(p)P — strings 3 · 2 · 2 · 1) [Schott]
   3. large room-music (*piccolo · 1 · 1 · 1 · 1 · *double bassoon — s(trumpet II or clarinet II)β(bassoon II) — 2(E-flat alto horns or 2a) · 1 · 0 · 0 — TsbcXH(p)P — strings 3 · 2 · 2 · 1) [Schott]
   4. theatre orchestra (†elastic scoring) (any or all of the above instruments with the version for 2 pianos (6 hands) [BFMS12] [Schott]
   5. 2 pianos (6 hands) [BFMS25] [Schott]

Grettir the Strong (see *Sea Song*)

'The Gum-Suckers' March (1905–7, 1914–17, 1942) [4th mvt of *In a Nutshell*] 3'45"
   1. orchestra, piano and tuneful percussion (piccolo · 2 · 2 · 2 · *bass clarinet · 2 · *double bassoon — 4 · 3 · 3 · 1 — T¹sbcg*GM²*SXW¹(²)*NCP — strings 2 · 1 · 1 · 1) or (piccolo · 2 · 2 · 2 · 2 — 4 · 3 · 3 · 1 — TsbcGCP — strings 2 · 1 · 1 · 1) [Schott]
   2. piano solo [Schott]
   3. 2 pianos (4 hands) [Schott]
   4. military band, tuneful percussion and piano (piccolo · 3(#3E-flat clarinet) · 2 · cor anglais · E-flat clarinet · 4 · alto clarinet · bass clarinet · 2 · double bassoon(contra-alto clarinet or contrabass clarinet) — s(a)aattβ — 4 · 4(cornets) · 3 · euphonium · 2 — TsbcM²W²*N*SBXCP — string bass) (ed. Rogers) [Bardic Edition UK; Southern Music USA]

The Gypsy's Wedding Day (1906) [BFMS] 2'30"
   mixed chorus (satb²) a cappella [Bardic Edition]

Handel in the Strand (Clog Dance) (1911–12, 1930, 1947, 1952) [RMTB2] 4′00″
1. piano+ and strings 2 · 1 · 2 · 1 [Schott]
2. orchestra (piccolo · 1 · 1 · 2 · 2 · double bassoon — 4 · 2 · 3 · 1 — TsbcGXWAP — strings 2 · 1 · 1 · 1) (version for Stokowski) [Schott]
3. large room-music (1 · 1 · 1 · 1 — 1 · 1 · 0 · 0 — GXHP — strings 2 · 1 · 2 · 1) (1952 version) [Bardic Edition]
    (also 3rd mvt of an interpolated suite for piano and orchestra)
4. piano solo [Schott]
5. 2 pianos (4 hands) [Schott]

Hard-hearted Barb'ra (H)Ellen (1906–14, 1932, 1946) [BFMS] 6′45″
1. piano solo (2 keys) [EG] [Bardic Edition]
2. voice and piano [Bardic Edition]

Harvest Hymn (1905, 1932–8) 3′30″
1. massed orchestra (1 · 1 · 2 · bass clarinet · 2(2β) — 1(E-flat horn or *a*) · 1(cornet or *s*) · 1(baritone or euphonium or *t*) · 0 — H(p or E)P — strings 2 · 1 · 2 · 1) [Schott]
    (all instruments may be massed at will, and all substitute instruments may be used together with the instruments they are substituting for)
2. large room-music (1 · 1 · 2 · bass clarinet · 0 — sat(β)ββ — 1 · 1 · 1 · 0 — H(p)P — strings 2 · 1 · 2 · 1) or (1 · 1 · 2 · bass clarinet · 2 — *a* — 0 · flugelhorn · 0 · euphonium · 0 — H(p)P — strings 2 · 1 · 2 · 1) [Schott]
3. string sextet (2 · 1 · 2 · 1) + *H(p or E)*P
4. string orchestra (2 · 1 · 2 · 1) + *H(p or E)*P
5. string quartet (2 · 1 · 1 · 0) + P(H(p or E)
6. violin, violoncello and piano(or harmonium or pipe-organ or electric organ) [Schott]
7. violin(violoncello) and piano [Schott]
8. 1 piano (4 hands) [Schott]
9. piano solo [Schott]
10. voice (single voice or voices or uc or um or uw) and piano duet [Schott]
11. 1 piano (6 hands) [Bardic Edition]
12. 2 pianos (8 hands) [Bardic Edition]
13. wind ensemble (1 · 1 · 2 · bass clarinet · 2 — satβ — 1(E-flat horn) · 1 · cornet · flugelhorn · 1 · euphonium · baritone · 0 — H(p or electric)P — string bass) [Schott]
    (All the above versions are interchangeable and may be used together freely. The voice part of no. 10 above may be added to any of the other versions.)

Hermunder Illi (*Hermund the Evil*) (1905–11) [FI: no. 2 of *Two Musical Relics of my Mother*] 2′15″
   2 pianos (4 hands) [Schott]

Hill-Song I (1901–2, 1921–3) 15′00″
1. orchestra woodwind ensemble (2 piccolos/flutes · 2 · 6 · 6 cor anglais · 0 · 6 · double bassoon) (ed. Stout) [Bardic EditionUK; Southern Music USA]
2. large room-music (piccolo · 1 · 1 · cor anglais · 0 · 1 · doubles bassoon — *sa* — 1 · 1 · 0 · euphonium · sopranino sarrusopone · tenor sarrusophone · 0 — TcHP — strings 2 · 2 · 2 · 1) or (piccolo · 1 · 2 · cor anglais · E-flat clarinet · 2 · bass clarinet · 0 — 1 · 1 · 0 · 0 — TcHP — strings 2 · 2 · 2 · 1 or (piccolo · 1 · 2 · cor anglais ·1 · 1 · double bassoon — TcHP — strings 2 · 2 · 2 · 1) [Universal Edition]
3. 2 pianos (4 hands) [Schott]

CATALOGUE OF WORKS

Hill-Song II (1901–7, 1911, 1940–46, 1950) 5'30"
1. solo wind ensemble (piccolo · 2 · 3(#3) · cor anglais · E-flat clarinet · 3 · alto clarinet · bass clarinet · 2 · double bassoon — satβ — 2(E-flat) · 2(cornets) · o · o — c) or (piccolo · 2 · *1 · cor anglais · E-flat clarinet · 6 · bass clarinet · 2 · double bassoon — atβ — 2(E-flat) · 3(cornets) · o · o — c) [Bardic Edition UK; TRN USA]
2. wind band (piccolo · 3 · 3(#3) · cor anglais · E-flat clarinet · 3 · alto clarinet · bass clarinet · 2 · double bassoon — satβ — 2(E-flat) · 2(cornets) · 3 · baritone piccolo · 2 · 3(#3) · cor anglais · E-flat clarinet · 3 · alto clarinet · bass clarinet · 2 · *double bassoon — satβ — 2(E-flat) · 2(cornets) · 3 · baritone · euphonium · 2 — c — string bass) [Bardic Edition UK; TRN USA]
(consult full score for other instrumental combinations)
3. orchestra (piccolo · 2 · 3(#3) · cor anglais · E-flat clarinet · 3 · bass clarinet · 2 · *double bassoon(tuba) — 2(E-flat) · 3(cornets) · 3 · 1 — c — strings o · 2 · 2 · 1) [Bardic Edition UK; TRN USA]
4. large room-music (1929) (piccolo · 2 · 1 · cor anglais · 2 · bass clarinet(or bassoon II) · 1 — 1 · 2 · 1 · o — cH*RP2) [Bardic Edition UK; Ludwig Masters USA]
5. 2 pianos (4 hands) [Schott]

Horkstow Grange (1937–8) [2nd mvt of *Lincolnshire Posy*] 3'24"
1. wind band (piccolo · 2 · 2 · cor anglais · E-flat clarinet · 3 · alto clarinet · bass clarinet · 2 · double bassoon — saatβbb — 4 · 3(cornets) · 3 · baritone · euphonium · 2 — Tsbc — string bass) 3'24" [Schott UK; Ludwig Masters USA]
2. piano solo (ed. Thwaites) 1'19" [Bardic Edition]

The Hunter in his Career (1903, 1929–30) [OEPM] 2'30"
1. double men's chorus (um + t²β²b) + P(or band) [instrumental parts lost — realisation by Ragsdale available]
2. chorus (um(uc)) and orchestra (piccolo · 1 · 1 · 2 · 1 — 4 · 3 · 3 · 1 — TbcGPPO — strings 2 · 1 · 1 · 1) [OEPM3] [Bardic Edition]
3. chorus (um(uc)) and 2 pianos [OEPM3] [Schott]
4. piano solo [OEPM4] [Schott]

The Hunting Song of the Seeonee Pack (1898–1942) [KS] 1'00"
1. male chorus (t²b²) a cappella (1898) [Bardic Edition]
2. male chorus (t²t²b²b²) and strings *(2 · 1 · 2 · 1) [KS8; 8th mvt of KJBC] [Schott]
3. male chorus (t²t²b²b²) and large room-music (o · o · 2 · 2 — 4 · 3 · o · o — strings 2 · 2 · 2 · 1) [Bardic Edition]

The Hunt is Up (1901) [OEPM]
1. chorus (um) and piano (4 hands) [Bardic Edition]
2. chorus (um) and room-music (o · o · 4 · 3 — 3 · 2 · o · o — strings o · o · 1 · 1) [Bardic Edition]

Husband and Wife (*Hubby and Wifey*) (1923) [DFMS5] 1'15"
1. 2 voices (CB(ST)) or chorus (um and uw) + (2 guitars(P), violoncello and *timpani)) or (2 guitars(P), string bass and *timpani) [Bardic Edition]
2. 2 voices (CB(ST)) or chorus (um and uw) and piano [Bardic Edition]
3. room-music (*piccolo · clarinet · bassoon — s(a) — 2 guitars(P) · *timpani — violoncello) [Bardic Edition]

The Immovable Do (or **The Ciphering C**) (1933–40) 4′45″
1. orchestra (2 piccolos(#2) · 2 · 2 · *cor anglais · 2 · bass clarinet · 2 · *double bassoon — 4 · 3 · 3 · 1 — TsbcΔ*O — strings 4 · 2 · 2 · 1) [Schott]
2. string nonet (4 · 2 · 2 · 1) [Schott]
3. string orchestra (4 · 2 · 2 · 1) [Schott]
4. mixed chorus ($s^3a^2t^2b^2$) a cappella [Schott]
5. mixed chorus ($s^3a^2t^2b^2$) + organ(or pipe-organ or electric organ or reed organ or harmonium) 2 players required if played on reed-organ or harmonium [Schott]
6. saxophone choir (saattβb) [Bardic Edition]
7. clarinet choir (E-flat clarinet · 7 · alto clarinet · bass clarinet) [Bardic Edition]
8. woodwind choir [Bardic Edition]
9. wind band [Bardic Edition UK; Schirmer USA]
10. piano solo [Schott]
11. pipe-organ(or electric organ or reed-organ or harmonium) [Schott]
(All versions may be performed together in any combination. The mixed chorus score, no. 4 above, may be used with any or all of the other editions of this piece.)

I'm Seventeen Come Sunday (1905–12) [BFMS8] 3′00″
1. mixed chorus (sat^{2}b^2), percussion and brass (4 horns · 3 trumpets(cornets) · 3 trombones · *euphonium · 2 tubas — TsΔ) [Schott]
2. mixed chorus (sat^{2}b^2), percussion and strings (TsΔ — strings 2 · 1 · 1 · 1) [Bardic Edition]

In a Nutshell (Suite) (see separate titles for full scoring and other versions): 'Arrival Platform Humlet' [RMTB7] 2′30″; 'Gay but Wistful' 2′30″; 'Pastoral' 6′45″; '"The Gum-Suckers" March' 3′45″
1. orchestra [Schott]
(see under titles for full details of instrumentation)
2. piano solo [Schott]
3. 2 piano (4 hands) [Schott]

In Bristol Town (1906, 1947–51) [BFMS] 0′47″
1. piano solo [EG] [Bardic Edition]
2. piano (6 hands) [EG] [Bardic Edition]

In Dahomey (Cakewalk Smasher) (1903–9) 4′27″
piano solo (ed. Stevenson) [Peters Edition]

The Inuit (1902) [KS5: 4th mvt of KJBC] 1′30″
mixed chorus($s^2a^2t\beta^2\beta^2b^2$) a cappella [Schott]

Irish Tune from County Derry (1902, 1911–18, 1949–52) 4′00″
1. chorus (sa^{2}t$^2\beta^3$b^2) a cappella [BFMS5] [Schott]
2. 10 single strings or string orchestra with or without 2 horns (strings 4 · 2 · 2 · 1) [BFMS15]
3. orchestra (2 · 1 · 2 · 2(1) — 2 · 1 · 0 · euphonium · 0 — c — strings 2 · 2 · 1 · 1) (version for Stokowski) [Schott]
4. large room-music (1 · 1 · 0 · 0 — 0 · 1 · 0 · 0 — a — cH · solovox — strings 2 · 1 · 2 · 1) (1952 version) [Bardic Edition]
5. military band (1 · 1 · E-flat clarinet · 4 · alto clarinet · bass clarinet · 1 — s(a)atβ — 4 · 4(cornets) · 3 · baritone · 1 — c — string bass) (ed. Clark/Schmidt) [BFMS20] [Carl Fischer USA]

6. military band (1 · 1 · E-flat clarinet · 4 · alto clarinet · bass clarinet · 1 — satb — 4 · 4(cornets) · 3 · euphonium · 2 — c — string bass) (ed. Rogers) [BFMS20] [Southern Music USA]
7. piano solo [BFMS6] [Schott]
8. piano solo [EG] 1'26" [Bardic Edition]

Irish Tune from County Derry (2nd version, *County Derry Air*) (1919–20) [BFMS29] 5'15"
1. orchestra (2 · 1 · 3 · alto clarinet · bass clarinet · contrabass clarinet · 2 · double bassoon — satβ — alto sarrusophone · tenor sarrusophone · baritone sarrusophone · contrabass sarrusophone — 4(4 E-flat horns or 4 E-flat alto horns) · 1 · 3 · baritone · euphonium · 1 — H(p) — strings 5 · 1 · 1 · 1) (all parts may be played singly or massed) [Schott]
2. 4 women's single voices or women's small chorus (ssaa) and room-music (H(p) — strings 5 · 1 · 2 · 1) [Schott]
3. 4 women's single voices or women's small chorus (ssaa) + *um and orchestra (2 · 1 · 3 · alto clarinet · bass clarinet · contrabass clarinet · 2 · double bassoon — satβ — alto sarrusophone · tenor sarrusophone · baritone sarrusophone · contrabass sarrusophone — 4(4 E-flat horns or 4 E-flat alto horns) · 1 · 3 · baritone · euphonium · 1 — p(H) — strings 5 · 1 · 1 · 1) (all parts may be played singly or massed) [Schott]
4. 4 women's single voices or women's small chorus (ssaa) + *um and 2 pianos [Bardic Edition]
5. small room-music (4 women's single voices or women's small chorus (ssaa) + *um + bass clarinet(bassoon or baritone saxophone or violoncello) · euphonium(tenor saxophone or Trombone) · contrabass sarrusophone(double bassoon or double bass) — p(H) — strings *3 · 1 · 0 · 0) [Schott]
6. military band (*2 · *2 · alto clarinet · *3 · bass clarinet · *contrabass clarinet · 2 · double bassoon — *satβ — *alto sarrusophone · *baritone sarrusophone · *contrabass sarrusophone — 4 E-flat horns(4 E-flat alto horns) · *1 · 2 · baritone · euphonium · 0 — p(H) — string bass) (all parts may be played singly or massed) [Bardic Edition]
7. 4 women's single voices or women's small chorus (ssaa) + *um + military band (*2 · *2 · alto clarinet · *3 · bass clarinet · *contrabass clarinet · 2 · double bassoon — *satβ — *alto sarrusophone · *baritone sarrusophone · *contrabass sarrusophone — 4 E-flat horns(4 E-flat alto horns) · *1 · 2 · baritone · euphonium · 0 — p(H) — string bass) (all parts may be played singly or massed) [Bardic Edition]
8. †elastic scoring (6 or more single instruments (many possible combinations) — p(H)) [Schott]

The Jolly Sailor (see *The Brisk Young Sailor*)

Jungle Book Cycle (see separate titles for full scoring and other versions): 'The Fall of the Stone' [KS16] 2'11"; 'Morning Song in the Jungle' [KS3] 2'50"; 'Night Song in the Jungle' [KS17] 0'48"; 'The Inuit' [KS5] 2'17"; 'The Beaches of Lukannon' [KS20] 3'23"; 'The Red Dog' [KS19] 1'11"; 'The Peora Hunt' [KS14] 0'40"; 'Hunting Song of the Seeonee Pack' [KS8] 1'19"; 'Tiger, Tiger' [KS4] 1'19"; 'The Only Son' [KS21] 4'40"; 'Mowgli's Song against People' [KS15] 3'41"
chorus and large room-music or piano(s)

Jutish Medley (1923, 1927–30) [4th mvt of *Danish Folk-Music Suite*] 7′30″
1. orchestra (piccolo · 2 · 2 · 2 · bass clarinet · 2(2β) · double bassoon — 4(4a) · 3(3s) · 3 · *euphonium · 1 — TsbcwG*M*W*S*BX*C*DAP²H(p) — strings 2 · 1 · 1 · 1) [DFMS9] [Schott]
2. †elastic scoring (any or all of orchestral parts of no. 1 with the edition for 2 pianos (6 hands), no. 4)
3. piano solo (in this version *Lord Peter's Stable-boy* is included) [DFMS8] [Schott]
4. 2 pianos (6 hands) [DFMS9] [Schott]

The Keel Row (1901) [BFMS] 2′55″
1. chorus (uc + whistlers) and orchestra (piccolo · 1 · 2 · 2 · 2 — 2 · 1 · 1 · 1 — strings 3 · 2 · 2 · 1) (ed. Ould) [Bardic Edition]
2. 2 pianos (6 hands) (ed. Ould) [Bardic Edition]
3. 2 pianos (10 hands) (ed. Ould) [Bardic Edition]

King Solomon's Espousals (Song of Solomon, Part V) (1899–1900) 8′45″
1. chorus (satb) and orchestra (2 piccolo · 4 · 8 · 2 cor anglais · 8 · 2 bass clarinets · 4 · 2 double bassoon — 6 · 2 · 3 · 0 — strings 2 · 1 · 1 · 1) (ed. Ould) [Bardic Edition]
2. chorus (satb) and piano (ed. Ould) [Bardic Edition] ‡
3. 2 pianos (4 hands) (ed. Ould) [Bardic Edition] ‡

Klavierstück in A minor (1898) [YT] 5′46″
piano solo (ed. Thwaites) [Bardic Edition]

Klavierstück in B-flat (1898) [YT] 1′39″
piano solo (ed. Thwaites) [Bardic Edition]

Klavierstück in D (1898) [YT] 3′38″
piano solo (ed. Thwaites) [Bardic Edition]

Klavierstück in E (1898) [YT] 6′44″
piano solo (ed. Thwaites) [Bardic Edition]

Kleine Variationen-Form (1898) [YT] 5′17″
small orchestra (2 · 2 · 2 · 2 — 2 · 2 · 0 · 0 — strings 2 · 1 · 1 · 1) [Bardic Edition]

Knight and Shepherd's Daughter (1918) [BFMS18] 2′35″
piano solo [Schott]

The Lads of Wamphray (Scots Border Ballad) (1904–7, 1951) 7′45″
1. men's chorus (t²β²b²)* and orchestra (piccolo · 2 · 2 · cor anglais · E-flat clarinet · 3 · alto clarinet · bass clarinet · 2 · double bassoon — 6 · 2 E-flat horns · 3 · 3 cornets · 3 · 2 euphoniums · 1 — Tsbcg — strings 2 · 1 · 2 · 1) [Bardic Edition/Schott]
2. men's chorus (t²β²b²)* and orchestra revised scoring (piccolo · 2 · 2 · cor anglais · E-flat clarinet · 3 · alto clarinet · bass clarinet · 2 · double bassoon — 4 · 2 E-flat horns(2a) · 3 · 3 cornets(3s) · 3 · 2 euphoniums(tβ) · 1 — Tsbcg — strings 2 · 1 · 1 · 1) [Bardic Edition/Schott]
3. men's chorus (t²β²b²)* and 2 pianos (4 hands)+ [Bardic Edition/Schott]
   * Also written for female chorus (material located in The National Library of Scotland).

The Lads of Wamphray March (1905, 1937–8) 8′30″
wind band (piccolo · 3(#3 E-flat clarinet) · 2 · E-flat clarinet · 3 · alto clarinet · bass

clarinet · 2 · double bassoon — *saatβb*(contrabass clarinet) — 4 · 2 · 3 cornets · 3 · baritone · euphonium · 1 — Tsbc · rattle · string bass) (ed. Kreines) [Carl Fischer USA]

The Land o' the Leal (1901) [YT] 2'06"
    voice and strings (1 · 2 · 2 · 0) (ed. Ould) [Bardic Edition]

Leezie Lindsay (see also *Songs of the North*; *Three Scottish Folk Songs*) (1900)
1. voice and piano [Bardic Edition]
2. piano solo [Peters Edition]

Let's Dance Gay in Green Meadow (see also *Faeroe Island Dance*) (1905, 1932, 1943) 3'15"
1. piano (4 hands) [EG] [Faber Music]
2. piano (6 hands) [EG] [Bardic Edition]
3. harmonium or reed organ (6 hands) [EG] [Bardic Edition]

Lincolnshire Posy (1935–7) [BFMS] (see separate titles for full scoring and other versions): 'Lisbon (Dublin Bay)' 1'24"; 'Horkstow Grange' 3'24"; 'Rufford Park Poachers' 4'36"; 'The Brisk Young Sailor' 1'37"; 'Lord Melbourne' 3'25"; 'The Lost Lady Found' 2'44"
1. wind band [Schott UK]
2. 2 pianos (4 hands) [Schott]
3. wind band (ed. Fennell) [Ludwig Masters USA]

Lisbon (*Dublin Bay*) (1906, 1932–7, 1943) [BFMS40] 1'24"
1. wind quintet (flute · oboe · clarinet · bassoon — horn) [Schott]
2. wind band (piccolo · 2 · 2 · cor anglais · E-flat clarinet · 3 · alto clarinet · bass clarinet · 2 · double bassoon — *saatβb* — 4 · 3(cornets) · 3 · baritone · euphonium · 1 — T — string bass) [Schott UK; Ludwig Masters USA]
(in this version it is the 1st mvt of *Lincolnshire Posy*)
3. recorders (2 descant and 1 treble) [Bardic Edition]
4. piano solo (2 versions) [EG] [Bardic Edition]
5. saxophone quintet (*saatβ* or *s(a)at(a)tβ*) [Bardic Edition]
6. brass quintet (1(E-flat horn) · 2(cornets) · baritone(trombone I) · euphonium(trombone II)) [Bardic Edition]

The Lonely Desert-Man Sees the Tents of the Happy Tribes (1911–49) [RMTB9] 2'32"
1. TSβ soli(uw + um chorus) and room-music (*2 clarinets · *1 bassoon — 2 guitars — WW*V(*A)P — strings 2 · 1 · 1 · *1) [Bardic Edition]
2. TSβ soli(uw + um chorus) and room-music (2 guitars — WW*V(*A)*P) [Bardic Edition]
3. TSβ soli(uw + um chorus) and room-music (*V(*A)P — strings 2 · 1 · 1 · *1) [Bardic Edition]
4. TSβ soli(uw + um chorus) and room-music (*W*W*V(*A)P) [Bardic Edition]
5. TSβ soli(uw + um chorus) and piano [Bardic Edition]
6. room-music (*2 clarinets(or *clarinet and *bassoon) · trumpet · 2 guitars · WW*V(*A)*P — strings 2 · 1 · 1 · *1) or (2 clarinets(or clarinet and bassoon) · trumpet · 2 guitars · WW*V(*A)*P) or (2 clarinets(or clarinet and bassoon) · trumpet · V(*A)*P — strings 2 · 1 · 1 · *1) or (2 clarinets(or clarinet and bassoon) · trumpet · WW*V(*A)*P) [Bardic Edition]

7. large room-music (o · o · 4 · 2 — a(trumpet) — *W*W*V(*A)*P — strings 2 · 1 · 1 · 1) [Bardic Edition]
8. piano duet [EG] [Bardic Edition]
9. alto saxophone and piano (ed. Krieger) [Bardic Edition]
    NB: The wooden marimba parts (WW) in nos. 1–4 and 6–7 can be played by 3–12 players. (There are many more possible combinations, too numerous to list here.)

Lord Maxwell's Goodnight (1904–58) 3'38"
1. voice and string quartet (1 · 1 · 2 · 0) or (2 · 1 · 1 · 0) [BFMS42] [Bardic Edition]
2. solo voice or chorus (um) and strings (4 · 2 · 2 · 1) [BFMS14] [Bardic Edition]
3. orchestra (piccolo · 2 · 2 · 2 · bass clarinet · 2 — 2 · 2 · 2 · 0 — strings 4 · 2 · 2 · 1) (ed. Ould) [BFMS14] [Bardic Edition]
4. baritone solo or chorus (um) and strings (2 · 2 · 2 · 0 soli + 2 · 1 · 1 · 1) [BFMS42] [Bardic Edition]
5. voice and piano [Bardic Edition]

Lord Melbourne (1935–7) [5th mvt of Lincolnshire Posy] 3'25"
wind band (piccolo · 2 · 2 · cor anglais · E-flat clarinet · 3 · alto clarinet · bass clarinet · 2 · double bassoon — saatßb — 4 · 3(cornets) · 3 · baritone · euphonium · 2 — Tsbc — string bass) [Schott UK; Ludwig Masters USA]

Lord Peter's Stable Boy (1922–7, 1930) [DFMS1: 2nd mvt of Danish Folk-Music Suite] 2'45"
1. orchestra (o · o · 1+ · o — 1(E-flat or a)+ · 1(cornet or s)+ · 1(euphonium or t)+ · *euphonium+ — TcB*G*M*(*V)*W*S*XP2(P)+H(R or p)+ — strings 2 · 1 · 1 · 1) [Schott]
2. violin, violoncello, piano (2 or 4 hands) and H [Schott]
3. †elastic scoring #1 (instruments as no. 2 above + any or all of the following (clarinet — horn(E-flat or a) · trumpet(s) · trombone(or euphonium or t) — T — violin II · viola · double bass) [Schott]
4. †elastic scoring #2 — single instruments (instruments as no. 2 above + any or all of instruments from no. 1 above [Schott]
5. chorus and room-music (unfinished arrangement, but sketches survive)

The Lost Lady Found (1910–38) [BFMS33] 2'45"
1. uw + men's chorus (tβb) and small orchestra (o · o · o · o — 3(#3 trombone) · 2(cornets) · o · o — T*s*c*G*W*M*B*S*X*H — strings 3 · 2 · 2 · 1) [Schott]
2. uw + men's chorus (tβb) and large room-music (o · o · o · o — o · o · o · o — *T*s*c*G*W*M*B*S*X*H — single strings 3 · 2 · 2 · 1) [Schott]
3. solo voice(um or uw or uc) and small orchestra (o · o · o · o — 3(#3 trombone) · 2(cornets) · o · o — T*s*c*G*W*M*B*S*X*H — strings 3 · 2 · 2 · 1) [Schott]
4. solo voice(um or uw or uc) and large room-music (o · o · o · o — o · o · o · o — *T*s*c*G*W*M*B*S*X*H — single strings 3 · 2 · 2 · 1) [Schott]
5. solo voice(um or uw or uc) and piano [Schott]
6. wind band (piccolo · 2 · 2 · cor anglais · E-flat clarinet · 3 · alto clarinet · bass clarinet · 2 · double bassoon — saatßb — 4 · 3(cornets) · 3 · baritone · euphonium · 2 — TsbcGBSX — string bass) [Schott UK; Ludwig Masters USA]
    (in this version it is the 6th mvt of Lincolnshire Posy)

The Love Song of Har Dyal (1901, 1957) [KS11] 2′30″
1. voice and piano [Schott]
2. soprano solo(uw) and room-music (0 · 1 · 0 · 1 — AHP — strings 3 · 2 · 2 · 1) [Bardic Edition]
3. soprano solo(uw) and piano [Bardic Edition]

Love Verses from the 'Song of Solomon' (Song of Solomon, Part II) (1899–1931) 6′45″
1. soprano solo, chorus (sa^{2}t^{2}b^2) or and orchestra (2 · 2 · cor anglais · 4 · bass clarinet · 2 · double bassoon — 2 · 0 · 0 · 0 — strings 2 · 1 · 1 · 1) (1st setting) [Bardic Edition]
2. mST soli, chorus (s^{2}a^{2}t^{2}b^2 or soli) and large room-music (1 · 1 · 1 · 1 — 1 · 1 · 0 · 0 — H(p)+ — strings 2 · 1 · 1 · 1) (1931 revision) [Oxford University Press]
3. mST soli, chorus (s^{2}a^{2}t^{2}b^2 or soli) and small room-music (H(p)+P^2 — strings 2 · 1 · 1 · 1) (+ any of the instruments from no. 2 above) (1931 revision) [Oxford University Press]
4. mST soli, chorus (s^{2}a^{2}t^{2}b^2 or soli) and small room-music (H(p)+P^2) (1931 revision) [Oxford University Press]
5. mST soli, chorus (s^{2}a^{2}t^{2}b^2 or soli) and piano (4 hands) (1931 revision) [Oxford University Press]
6. mST soli, chorus (s^{2}a^{2}t^{2}b^2 or soli), H(p or electric or R) and 2 solovoxes [Bardic Edition]

Lukannon (1898) (see also *The Beaches of Lukannon*) [KS] 5′35″
1. men's chorus (t^{2}b^2) [Bardic Edition]
2. voice and piano (transcr. Ould) [Bardic Edition]

Lullaby from *Tribute to Foster* (1915, 1932) 3′40″
1. piano solo [Schott]
2. piano solo (simplified version) [EG] [Bardic Edition]

The Maiden and the Frog (1925) [DFMS] 1′00″
1. 2 pianos (4 hands) [Bardic Edition]
2. violoncello and piano (ed. Ould) [Bardic Edition]

March of the Men of Harlech (Welsh Fighting Song no. 2) (1904) 2′00″
double chorus (um + st^{2}βb) and drums (T + 4 or more military drums) [Bardic Edition]

Marching Song of Democracy (see also *Australian Marching Song*) (1901, 1908, 1915–17, 1948–53) 7′30″
1. chorus (s^{2}a^{2}t^{2}b^2) and orchestra (piccolo · 2 · 2 · 2 · bass clarinet · 2 · double bassoon — 4 · 3 · 3 · euphonium · 1 — TbcMGG(electric)SBPOA — strings 2 · 1 · 1 · 1) [Universal Edition]
2. wind band (2 piccolo(#2) · 2 · 2 · cor anglais · E-flat clarinet · 3 · alto clarinet · bass clarinet · 2 · *double bassoon — s(a)atβ*b — 4 · 2 · 3(cornet) · 3 · baritone · euphonium · 2 — TbcgGB*S^3*W*M(V)^3*A+*P+ — string bass) (ed. Brion) [G. Schirmer/Hal Leonard USA]

Marching Tune (1905) [BFMS9] 4′30″
1. chorus (satβb) and brass (4(tenor or baritone horns) · 3(#3) · 3(#3 euphonium) · 1(E-flat or B-flat bass) — Tsc)) [Schott]
2. chorus (satβb) and piano [Schott]

Mary Thomson (1909–10) [BFMS] 2′43″
SATB soli or chorus (satb) [Bardic Edition]

The Men of the Sea (1899) [KS10] 1′29″
voice and piano [Schott]

The Merchantmen (1902–3) [KS]
men's chorus (t²βb³ + whistlers) and orchestra (0 · 0 · 0 · 0 · double bassoon — 4 · 0 · 0 · 0 — strings 5 · 4 · 4 · 1) [Bardic Edition] ‡

Merciful Town (1899) [KS] 3′04″
voice and piano [Bardic Edition]

The Merry King (1905–6, 1936–9) 3′45″
1. piano and 9 (or 10, or 11) single wind instruments (*piccolo · flute · 3 clarinets · alto clarinet · bass clarinet(bassoon I) · double bassoon(string bass) — β(bassoon II) — 1(E-flat or a) · 1(cornet or s) · 0 · 0 — *H(*p)) [BFMS39] [Bardic Edition UK; Southern Music USA]
2. small orchestra (piccolo · 1 · 0 · 3 · alto clarinet · bass clarinet · 2 · double bassoon — 1(a) · 1(s) · 0 · 0 — H(p)P — strings 2 · 1 · 2 · 1) [BFMS 39] [Bardic Edition UK; Southern Music USA]
3. large room-music (piccolo · 1 · 0 · 2 · 2 — 1(a) · 1(s) · 0 · 0 — P — strings 2 · 1 · 2 · 1) [BFMS39] [Bardic Edition UK; Southern Music USA]
4. piano and single strings (2 · 1 · 2 · 1)or string orchestra (2 · 1 · 2 · 1) (*flute — *H(*p)) [Bardic Edition UK; Southern Music USA]
(for other instrumental possibilities consult full score)
5. piano solo [BFMS38] [Schott]

The Merry Wedding (Bridal Dance) (1912–15) [FI] 5′45″
1. S²A²T²βB²soli, chorus (s²a²t²b²) and orchestra (*2 · 0 · *2 · *2 — 4 · 2 · 3 · *1 — Tc*O — strings 2 · 1 · 1 · 1) [Oxford University Press]
2. S²A²T²βB²soli, chorus (s²a²t²b²) and piano [Oxford University Press]
3. S²A²T²βB²soli + P and single strings (2 · 1 · 1 · 1) [Oxford University Press]

Mo Nighean Dubh (*My dark-haired maid*) (see also *Songs of the North*; *Three Scottish Folk Songs*) (1900) 4′27″
1. chorus (sa²t²b²) [Bardic Edition]
2. piano solo [Bardic Edition]
3. piano solo [Peters Edition]

Mock Morris (1910, 1950–52) [RMTB1] 3′30″
1. orchestra (piccolo · 2 · 2 · 2 · 2 · double bassoon — 4 · 3 · 3 · 1 — TsbcΔWX — strings 3 · 1 · 2 · 1) (version for Stokowski) [Schott UK; Ludwig Masters USA]
2. orchestra (2 · 1 · 2 · 1 — 2 · 2 · 1 · 0 — sbcX — strings 3 · 1 · 2 · 1) [Schott]
3. †elastic scoring #1 (strings 3 · 1 · 2 · 1 + any or all of the instruments of no. 2 above) [Schott]
4. †elastic scoring #2 (violin and piano + any or all of the instruments of no. 2 above) [Schott]
5. domestic orchestra (piccolo · 2 · 1 · 1 · 0 — 0 · 1 · 1 · 0 — sbcXPH — strings (violin obbligato · 1 · 0 · 1 · 1)) [Schott]
6. large domestic orchestra (piccolo · 2 · 1 · 2 · 1 — 2 · 2 · 1 · 0 — sbcXPH — strings (violin obbligato · 2 · 1 · 1 · 1)) [Schott]

7. large room-music (piccolo · 1 · 1 · 1 · 1 — 1 · 1 · 0 · 1 — H(p)P — strings 3 · 1 · 2 · 1) (1952 version) [Bardic Edition]
8. single strings or string orchestra (3 · 1 · 2 · 1) [Schott]
9. piano solo (concert version) [Schott]
10. piano solo (popular version) [Schott]
11. 2 pianos (4 hands) (see also *Always Merry and Bright*) [Bardic Edition]
12. violin and piano [Schott]
13. string quartet and piano [Bardic Edition]

Molly on the Shore (1907–49) [BFMS] 3'30"
1. orchestra (piccolo · 2 · 1 · cor anglais · 2 · 2 · double bassoon — 4 · 2 · 3 · 1 — TscGV — strings 2 · 1 · 1 · 1) (version for Stokowski) [Schott UK; Ludwig Masters USA]
2. orchestra (piccolo · 2 · 2 · 2 · 2 — 4 · 2 · 3 · 1 — TsbcGMBXC — strings 2 · 1 · 1 · 1) [BFMS1] [Schott]
3. †elastic scoring #1 (string quartet (2 · 1 · 1 · 0) + any or all of the instruments from no. 2 above) [BFMS1] [Schott]
4. †elastic scoring #2 (piano solo + any or all of the instruments from no. 2 above) [BFMS1] [Schott]
5. salon orchestra (1 · 1 · 1 · 0 — 0 · 0 · 2 · 0 —TsbcGXPH — strings (violin obbligato · 1 · 1 · 0 · 1)) [Schott]
6. domestic orchestra (1 · 1 · 2 · 1 — 2 · 2 · 1 · 0 —TsbcGXPH — strings (violin obbligato · 2 · 1 · 1 · 1)) [Schott]
7. large domestic orchestra (piccolo · 2 · 2 · 2 · 2 — 2 · 2 · 3 · 0 —TsbcGCPH — strings (violin obbligato · 2 · 1 · 1 · 1)) [Schott]
8. pianola + any or all of the instruments from no. 2 above [BFMS1] [Schott]
9. string quartet (2 · 1 · 1 · 0) [Schott]
10. string orchestra (2 · 1 · 1 · 1) [BFMS1] [Schott]
11. military band (piccolo · 3(#3 E-flat clarinet) · 2 · E-flat clarinet · 4 · alto clarinet · bass clarinet · double alto clarinet · double bass clarinet · 2 · double bassoon(double alto clarinet or double bass clarinet) · double bass sarrusophone — s(a)atβ — 4(E-flat) · 4(cornets) · 3 · euphonium · 2 — TsbcM(V)B*W*X*C — string bass) (ed. Rogers) [BFMS23] [Southern Music USA]
12. concert band (piccolo · 1 · 1 · E-flat clarinet · 4 · alto clarinet · bass clarinet · 1 · double bassoon —satb — 4 · 4 · 3 · euphonium · 1 — TsbcMG — string bass) (ed. Clark) [BFMS23] [Carl Fischer USA]
13. piano solo [BFMS19] [Schott]
14. 2 pianos (4 hands) [BFMS1] [Schott]
15. violin and piano [Schott]
16. alto saxophone and piano (ed. Cohen) [Bardic Edition UK; To the Fore Publishers USA]

Morning Song in the Jungle (1903–56) [KS3: 2nd mvt of KJBC] 2'50"
chorus (s²a²t²β²b²) a cappella [Schott]

Mowgli's Song Against People (1903, 1941–2, 1956) [KS15: 11th mvt of KJBC] 3'41"
1. Tβ²B soli + chorus (s²a²t²β²b) and large room-music (0 · *2 · *cor anglais · 0 · 0 — *1 · *2 · 0 · 0 — *H(*p)P — strings 1 · 2 · 3 · 1) [Schott]
2. Tβ²B soli + chorus (s²a²t²β²b) and large room-music (0 · 2 · cor anglais · 0 · 0 — 4 · 3 · 3 · 0 — H(*p)P — strings 2 · 2 · 3 · 1) or (0 · 1(#2) · *cor anglais · 0 · 0 — 0 · 0 · 0 · 0 — H(p)P — strings 1 · 2 · 3 · 1) [Bardic Edition]

3. 2 pianos (4 hands) [Bardic Edition]

My Love's in Germanie (1903) [BFMS] 3'52"
S²AT²B soli + chorus (s²a²a²t³β²b²) a cappella [Bardic Edition]

My Robin is to the Greenwood Gone (1912) [OEPM2] 4'57"
1. room-music (flute · cor anglais — strings 1 · 2 · 2 · 1) [Schott]
2. violin, cello, piano [Schott]
3. piano solo [Schott]

Near Woodstock Town (1903, 1942) [BFMS] 2'11"
1. chorus (sa²t²β²b²) a cappella [Bardic Edition]
2. piano solo [EG] [Bardic Edition]

The Nightingale (1925–6) 2'04"
1. violin (or viola or cello) and harmonium (pipe-organ) [Bardic Edition]
2. violin, cello and pipe-organ [Bardic Edition]

The Nightingale and The Two Sisters (1922–30, 1949) [DFMS10: 3rd mvt of *Danish Folk-Music Suite*] 4'00"
1. orchestra (*piccolo · *2 · 2 · 2 · bass clarinet · 2(2β) · *double bassoon — 4(4 E-flat horns) · 2(s) · 2(t) · bass trombone · 1 — APH(R or p) — strings 2 · 1 · 1 · 1) [Schott]
2. violin, violoncello and piano [Schott]
3. †elastic scoring #1 (No. 2 above + *H(*p) — violin II · viola · double bass) [Schott]
4. clarinet · bassoon(β) — horn(E-flat or *a*) — H(p) [Schott]
5. †elastic scoring #2 (No. 4 above + flute · oboe — trumpet(s) — strings 2 · 1 · 1 · 1) [Schott]
6. string orchestra and keyboard(s) (2 · 1 · 1 · 1) + pipe-organ(H+ or P) [Schott]
7. military band (*piccolo · 2 · 2 · 3 · bass clarinet · 2(β) · *double bassoon — 4(E-flat or *a*) · 2(s) · 2(t) · bass trombone · 1(E-flat or B-flat bass) — pAP — string bass) [Schott]
8. piano solo (ed. Smith) [Bardic Edition]

Night-Song in the Jungle (1898, 1905 -1924) [KS17: 3rd mvt of KJBC] 0'48"
1. men's chorus (t²b²) [Schott]
2. men's chorus (t²b²) (1898 setting) [Bardic Edition]

Norse Dirge (1899, 1942–3) [3rd mvt of *Youthful Suite*] 8'56"
orchestra (2 piccolo(#1) · 2 · 2 · cor anglais · 2 · bass clarinet · 2 · double bassoon — 4 · 3 · 3 · 1 — TscGM²(V²)W²S²BXH(p)P+A — strings 2 · 1 · 1 · 1) or (piccolo · 2 · 2 · cor anglais · 2 · bass clarinet · 2 · double bassoon — 4 · 3 · 3 · 1 — TscH(p)P+A — strings 2 · 1 · 1 · 1) [Schott]

Northern Ballad (1898–9) [KS] 1'03"
voice and piano [Bardic Edition]

Northern March (1899–1901, 1950) [1st mvt of *Youthful Suite*] 6'36"
orchestra (piccolo · 2 · 2 · bass clarinet · 2 · double bassoon — 4 · 3(#3) · 3 · 1 — TsbcG — strings 2 · 1 · 1 · 1) [Schott]

Now, O now, I needs must part (after Dowland) (1937) (see also *Bell Piece*) 4'28"
1. piano solo (easy version) [FS5] [Schott]
2. piano solo (concert version) [FS6] [Schott]

O gin I were where Gadie rins (see also *Songs of the North*; *Three Scottish Folk Songs*) (1900) 1'43"
1. piano solo [Peters Edition]
2. S solo, chorus (sat²b) a cappella [Bardic Edition]
3. S solo, chorus (sat²b) and piano [Bardic Edition]

Old Irish Tune (see *Irish Tune from County Derry*)

The Old Woman at the Christening (1925) [DFMS 11] 2'42"
voice, piano and harmonium [Bardic Edition]

One More Day, My John (1915, 1932) [SC1] 1'47"
1. piano solo [Schott]
2. piano solo (simplified) [EG] [Bardic Edition]

The Only Son (1945–7, 1953) [KS21: 10th mvt of KJBC] 4'40"
1. ST soli, *chorus (s²a²tβb²) and room-music (o · *1 · *cor anglais · *3 · *bass clarinet · *2 — *2(a) · o · *3 · o — *T*AH(p) — strings 2 · 1 · 2 · 1) [Schott]
2. ST soli, *chorus (s²a²tβb²) and piano [Schott]
3. small room-music (H(P) — strings 2 · 1 · 1 · o) (ed. Ould) [Bardic Edition]

Pastoral (1915–17) [3rd mvt of *In a Nutshell*] 10'16"
1. orchestra, piano and tuneful percussion (piccolo · 2 · 2 · cor anglais · 2 · *bass clarinet · 2 · *double bassoon — 4 · 3 · 3 · 1 — TcgM²*S²ACP — strings 2 · 2 · 2 · o + soli 2 · 1 · 1 · 1) [Schott]
2. orchestra, piano and tuneful percussion (piccolo · 2 · 2 · cor anglais · 2 · 2 — 4 · 3 · 3 · 1 — TcgGM²CAP — strings 2 · 2 · 2 · o + soli 2 · 1 · 1 · 1) [Schott]
3. piano solo [Schott]
4. 2 pianos (4 hands) [Schott]

Peace (1898) [YT] 2'50"
piano solo [Bardic Edition]

The Peora Hunt (1901, 1941–2, 1958) [KS14: 7th mvt of KJBC] 0'40"
1. chorus (s²a²t²β²b) and large room-music (o · o · o · 2 · double bassoon — o · o · o · o — H(p)P — strings 2 · 1 · 2 · 1) [Schott]
2. chorus (s²a²t²β²b) and room-music (o · o · o · 2 — β — H(p)P — strings 2 · 2 · 2 · 1) [Bardic Edition]
3. chorus (s²a²t²β²b) [Bardic Edition]
4. chorus (s²a²t²β²b) + H(p)P [Bardic Edition]
5. chorus (s²a²t²β²b) + 2 bassoon(2 violoncello) and piano (*H) [Bardic Edition]
6. chorus (s²a²t²β²b) + P*H(*p) — strings (2 · 2 · 2 · 1) [Bardic Edition]
7. chorus (s²a²t²β²b) + 2 bassoon(#1β) — strings (2 · 2 · 2 · 1) — P*H(*p) [Bardic Edition]
8. six-part men's chorus (contraltino + tβb²b) a cappella [Bardic Edition]

Piano Concerto (1896) [YT] (**Konzertstück** 1896) [1 mvt] 9'29"
2 pianos (4 hands) (ed. Lavender and Thwaites) [Bardic Edition]

The Power of Love (1922, 1941) [DFMS 2: 1st mvt of *Danish Folk-Music Suite*] 4'00"
1. orchestra (piccolo · 2 · 2 · 2 · bass clarinet · 2 · *double bassoon — 4(E-flat or a) · 3(s) · 3(t) · 1 — TscW*MVA*AP*H(*R(p or E)) — strings 2 · 1 · 1 · 1) [Schott]

2. †elastic scoring #1 — 4 or more single instruments (violin · violoncello — *W*VH(R)P*p(*E)) [Schott]
3. †elastic scoring #2 — 12 or more single instruments (clarinet · bass clarinet · bassoon — horn(E-flat or *a*) · trumpet(s) — *WH(R)P*p(*E) — strings 2 · 1 · 1· *1) [Schott]
4. †elastic scoring #3 — H(p)P + any or all of the instrumental parts of no. 1 above [Schott]
5. string orchestra, piano and organ (Pp(E)*W*V*H(*R) — strings 2 · 1 · 1 · 1) [Schott]

The Power of Love (1922) [DFMS4] 4'00"
1. Soprano solo + uw and room-music (*2 horns — HP — strings 1 · *1 · 1 · 1) [Bardic Edition]
2. Soprano solo(uw) — HP — violin · viola · violoncello · *double bass [Bardic Edition]
3. Soprano solo(uw) + HP [Bardic Edition]
4. violin · *violin II · *viola · violoncello · *double bass, harmonium and piano [Bardic Edition]
5. *violin · viola · violoncello · *double bass, harmonium and piano [Bardic Edition]
6. room-music (0 · 0 · 0 · 0 — *2 · 0 · 0 · 0 — HP — strings 2 · 1 · 1 · 1) [Bardic Edition]
7. voice and piano [Bardic Edition]

The Power of Rome and the Christian Heart (1918, 1943) 12'06"
1. orchestra (2 piccolo(#2) · 2 · 2 · cor anglais · E-flat clarinet · 3 · alto clarinet · 2 — 4 · 3 · 3 · euphonium · baritone · 0 — *saatβb* — TsbcgO(P)GBSWM(V)CDP+A+ — strings 2 · 1· 1 · 1) [Bardic Edition UK; Edwin Kalmus USA]
2. military band (2 piccolo(#2) · 2 · 2 · cor anglais · E-flat clarinet · 3 · alto clarinet · bass clarinet · 2 — s(trumpet)*aatβb* — 4 · 3(cornets) · 3 · baritone · euphonium · 1 — Ts bcg*B*S²*W⁴+*M⁴(*V⁴)+*G*X*C*Dp(E or P)*A+*P+ — string bass) [Bardic Edition UK; Edwin Kalmus USA]

Prelude in C (see also *Childhood Works*) (1893) 0'45"
piano solo (ed. Thwaites) [Bardic Edition]

Prelude in G (see also *Childhood Works*) (1893) 2'57"
piano solo (ed. Thwaites) [Bardic Edition]

The Pretty Maid Milking Her Cow (1920) [BFMS27] 1'22"
1. high voice (original version) and piano [Schott]
2. low voice and piano [Schott]

Pritteling, Pratteling, Pretty Poll Parrot (*c*.1911) 4'37"
1. 2 pianos (4 hands) (ed. Ould) [Bardic Edition]
2. 2 guitars and wind [Bardic Edition] ‡

Proud Vesselil (see *Stalt Vesselil*)

Random Round (1912–14, 1943, 1954) [RMTB8] 6'00"
1. voices and room-music (random version) (a join-in when-you-like Round for a few voices & instruments accompanied by a gut-strung guitar) [Bardic Edition]
 a) †elastic scoring #1 (ST soli(uw + um) + oboe(viola) — *t* — gut-strung guitar — W — strings 1 · 0 · 1 · 0)
 b) †elastic scoring #2 (SmST soli(sa + um) + oboe(s) — gut-strung guitar — WX — strings 1 · 1 · 0 · 0)

    c) †elastic scoring #3 (SmST soli(sa + um) + flute · oboe — t — gut-strung guitar · steel-strung guitar · mandolin · *mandola — WXP — strings 1 · 1 · 1 · 0)
    d) many other combinations possible (too numerous to list here)
2. SAT soli(sa + um) voices and room-music (set version) (flute — gut-strung guitar(P) · steel-strung guitar · mandolin(ukulele) — WXP — strings 1 · 1 · 1 · 0) [Bardic Edition]
3. large room-music (flute — gut-strung guitar(P) · steel-strung guitar · mandolin(ukulele) — W(P)X(P)P — strings 3 · 1 · 2 · 1) or (flute · bassoon — a(E-flat horn) — gut-strung guitar(P) · steel-strung guitar · mandolin(ukulele) — W(P)X(P)P — strings 3 · 1 · 1 · 1) [Bardic Edition]
4. 2 pianos (10 or 11 hands) [Bardic Edition]

Recessional (1905, 1929) [KS18] 3'58"
1. chorus ($s^2a^2t^2\beta^2b^2$) a cappella [Schott]
2. chorus ($s^2a^2t^2\beta^2b^2$) and H(p)+ [Schott]
3. chorus ($s^2a^2t^2\beta^2b^2$) and H(p)P²+ [Schott]

Red Dog (1941) [KS19: 6th mvt of KJBC] 1'11"
    men's voices (t^2b^2) [Schott]

A Reiver's Neck-Verse (1908) 2'16"
    voice and piano [Schott]

The Rhyme of the Three Sealers (1900–1901) [KS] [incomplete]

Ride with an Idle Whip (1899) [KS] 0'20"
    voice and piano [Bardic Edition]

Rimmer and Goldcastle [DFMS3] 0'35"
1. piano solo (1951) [EG] [Bardic Edition]
2. chorus (whereabouts of MS unknown, presumed lost)

The Rival Brothers (*Hjálmar og Agantýr*) (1905, 1931, 1938, 1940, 1943) [FI] 1'15"
1. chorus (smsa²t²b²) and strings 2 · 1 · 1 · 0 [Bardic Edition]
2. piano solo [EG] [Bardic Edition]
3. piano (4 hands) [EG] [Bardic Edition]

Rondo (1897) [YT] 5'20"
    piano (4 hands) [Bardic Edition]

Rufford Park Poachers (1935–7) [3rd mvt of *Lincolnshire Posy*] 4'20"
    wind band (piccolo · 2 · 2 · cor anglais · E-flat clarinet · 3 · alto clarinet · bass clarinet · 2 · double bassoon — $saat\beta b$ — 4 · 3(cornets)(#1 flugelhorn) · 3 · baritone · euphonium · 2 — Tsbc — string bass) [Schott UK; Ludwig Masters USA]

The Running of Shindand (1901–4, 1946) [KS9] 1'41"
1. men's chorus ($t^3\beta b^3$) a cappella [Schott]
2. men's chorus ($t^3\beta b^3$) and 2 double basses [Bardic Edition]
3. 5 cellos [Bardic Edition]

Rustic Dance (1899, 1950) [2nd mvt of *Youthful Suite*] 3'32"
1. orchestra (2 · 2 · 2 · 2 — 4(#3#4) · 1 · 1 · 0 — TP — strings 2 · 1 · 1 · 1) [Schott]
2. small orchestra (2 · 2 · 2 · 2 — 2 · 0 · 0 · 0 — strings 2 · 1 · 1 · 1) [Bardic Edition]

Sailor's Chanty (1901) 3'06"
  1. chorus (um) and piano [Bardic Edition]
  2. male voice and piano [Bardic Edition]

Sailor's Song (1900, 1954) 2'42"
  1. piano solo [Peters Edition]
  2. piano solo (simplified version) [Bardic Edition]
  3. orchestra (ed. Ould) [Bardic Edition] ‡

Saxon Twi-Play (1898) [YT] 2'07"
   piano solo [Bardic Edition]

La Scandinavie (Scandinavian Suite) (1902): 'Swedish Air and Dance' 2'38"; 'A Song of Vermeland' (Swedish) 1'51"; 'Norwegian Polska' 2'47"; 'Danish Melody'* 2'47"; 'Air and Finale on Norwegian Dances' 5'32"
   violoncello and piano [Schott]

La Scandinavie II (Scandinavian Suite II) (c.1902): 'Dalvisa' (Swedish); 'Dance' (Norwegian); 'Folksong & Dance' (Swedish); 'Norsk Dance'; 'Finale' (Polska and Slängdans)
   violoncello and piano (ed. Ould) [Bardic Edition] ‡

Scherzo (1898) [YT] 1'40"
   string orchestra (2 · 1 · 1 · 1) [Bardic Edition]

Scotch Strathspey and Reel (1901–11, c.1937) 7'08"
  1. male chorus (t²b²) and large room-music (piccolo · 1 · 1 · 1 · 1 — 0 · 0 · 0 · 0 — Concertina(H)X — 2 guitars(P) — strings 3 · 2 · 2 · 1) [BFMS28] [Schott]
  2. piano solo [BFMS37] [Schott]

Sea Song (*Grettir the Strong*) (1907, 1922, 1946)
  1. strings (soli 1 · 1 · 1 · 0 + 2 · 2 · 2 · 1) and organ(H) (3 versions) [ed. Stout] 0'19"; 0'24"; 2'59" [Bardic Edition]
  2. string quartet and harmonium(or reed-organ) (ed. Ould) 0'33" [Bardic Edition]
  3. piano solo (sketch) 0'48" [Bardic Edition]

The Sea Wife (1898–1947)[KS] 4'58"
  1. chorus (sat²b²), brass and percussion (4 · 3(cornets)(#3) · 3 · *baritone · *euphonium · 2 — Tc) [KS22] [Schott]
  2. chorus (sat²b²) and single strings (2 · 3 · 2 · 2) or string orchestra (2 · 3 · 2 · 2) + Tc [Schott]
  3. chorus (sat²b²), brass and strings (4 · 3(cornets)(#3) · 3 · *baritone · *euphonium · 2 — Tc — strings 2 · 3 · 2 · 2) [Schott]
  4. chorus (sat²b²) and piano (4 hands) [Schott]
  5. chorus (sat²b²) and piano solo [Schott]
  6. chorus (sat²b²) and brass band (4 horns(#1#2 E-flat tenor horns · #3#4 baritone) · E-flat soprano cornet · 3(cornets) · 3 · 2 euphoniums · E-flat bass · B-flat bass — T) [Bardic Edition]
  7. voice and piano [Bardic Edition]

The Secret of the Sea (1898) 3'30"
   voice and piano [Bardic Edition]

Seven men from all the world (1918) [KS: chorus from *The Ballad of the 'Bolivar'*] 2′02″
piano solo (transcr. from piano roll by Lavender; ed. Thwaites) [Bardic Edition]

Shallow Brown (1910–25) [SCS] 6′04″
1. Male solo voice (singing both solo and chorus) and large room-music (*piccolo · *1 · 0 · 1 · 1 · *double bassoon — 1(a) · 0 · euphonium(horn II or alto saxophone II) — HP — *2 ukuleles · *2 mandolas(*ukuleles) · *2 mandolins · *4 guitars — strings 2 · 2 · 2 · 1) or (P) [Schott]
2. 2 men's voices (1st voice singing solo, 2nd voice singing chorus) and large room-music (*piccolo · *1 · 0 · 1 · 1 · *double bassoon — 1(a) · 0 · euphonium(horn II or alto saxophone II) — HP — *2 ukuleles · *2 mandolas(*ukuleles) · *2 mandolins · *4 guitars — strings 2 · 2 · 2 · 1) or (P) [SCS3] [Schott]
3. women's voice singing solo, male voice singing chorus and large room-music (*piccolo · *1 · 0 · 1 · 1 · *double bassoon — 1(a) · 0 · euphonium(horn II or alto saxophone II) — HP — *2 ukuleles · *2 mandolas(*ukuleles) · *2 mandolins · *4 guitars — strings 2 · 2 · 2 · 1) or (P) [SCS3] [Schott]
4. man's voice singing solo, um singing chorus and large room-music (*piccolo · *1 · 0 · 1 · 1 · *double bassoon — 1(a) · 0 · euphonium(horn II or alto saxophone II) — HP — *2 ukuleles · *2 mandolas(*ukuleles) · *2 mandolins · *4 guitars — strings 2 · 2 · 2 · 1) or (P) [SCS3] [Schott]
5. mixed chorus (uc), uw singing chorus, um singing chorus and large room-music (*piccolo · *1 · 0 · 1 · 1 · *double bassoon — 1(a) · 0 · euphonium(horn II or alto saxophone II) — HP — *2 ukuleles · *2 mandolas(*ukuleles) · *2 mandolins · *4 guitars — strings 2 · 2 · 2 · 1) or (P) [SCS3] [Schott]
6. uw + um chorus and large room-music (0 · 0 · 1 · 0 · double bassoon — 3 · 0 · 1 · 0 — strings 4 · 2 · 2 · 1) [Bardic Edition]

Shenandoah (1907) [SCS] 1′44″
β solo + TTββBB soli + um [Peters Edition]

Shepherd's Hey (1908–9, 1911, 1913, 1918, 1937, 1947, 1949) 2′07″
1. large room-music (1 · 0 · 1 · 0 — 0 · 2 · 1 · 1 — concertina — strings 3 · 2 · 2 · 1) [BFMS3] [Schott]
2. orchestra (piccolo · 2 · 2 · 2 · 2 — 4 · 3 · 3(#3) · 1 — Tsbc2*Δ*G*XA*A*P — strings 2 · 1 · 1 · 1) [BFMS16] [Schott]
3. orchestra (version for Stokowski) (piccolo · 2 · 2 · cor anglais · 2 · bass clarinet · 2 · double bassoon — 4 · 3 · 3 · 1 — TscBXAP — strings 2 · 1 · 1 · 1) [BFMS16] [Schott UK; LM USA]
4. military band (piccolo · 2(#2E-flat clarinet) · 2 · E-flat clarinet · 4 · alto clarinet · bass clarinet · 2 — s(a)atβ — 4 · 3(cornet) · 3 · euphonium · 2 — TsbcΔGXP — string bass) [BFMS21] (ed. Rogers) [Southern Music USA]
5. military band (piccolo · 1 · 2 · E-flat clarinet · 4 · alto clarinet · bass clarinet · 2 — s(a)atβ — 4 · 3(cornet) · 3 · baritone · 2 — TsbcBX*P — string bass) [BFMS21] (ed. Clark/Schmidt) [Carl Fischer USA]
6. violin, violoncello and piano (realised Ould, ed. Thwaites) [BFMS4] [Bardic Edition]
7. piano solo [BFMS4] [Schott]
8. piano (simplified) [BFMS4] [Schott]
9. 2 pianos (4 hands) [BFMS16] [Schott]

The Shoemaker from Jerusalem (1929) [DFMS6] 3'15"
  1. small room-music (flute · trumpet — P^2 — strings 1 · 1 · 1 · 1) (ed. Ould) [Bardic Edition]
  2. violoncello and piano (transcr. Ould) [Bardic Edition]

Sir Eglamore (1904, 1912) [BFMS13] 4'00"
  1. double chorus (biggish chorus $s^2a^2t\beta^2b^2$ + smallish chorus $s^2at\beta^2b^2$) and large room-music (o · o · o · o — st — 9 · 3(cornets) · 2 bugles · 3 · baritone · euphonium · 1 — strings o · 4 · 4 · 4) [Bardic Edition]
  2. double chorus (biggish chorus $s^2a^2t\beta^2b^2$ + smallish chorus $s^2at\beta^2b^2$) and large room-music (o · o · o · o — 6(#5#6) · 4(cornets)(#3 clarinet · #4 clarinet) · 3–5(#3 euphonium · #4 bassoon · #5 bassoon) · 1 — Ts*bc*Δ*A*A — strings 2 · 1 · 1 · 1) [Schott]
  3. double chorus (biggish chorus $s^2a^2t\beta^2b^2$ + smallish chorus $s^2at\beta^2b^2$) and piano [Schott]

Six dukes went a-fishin' (1905–12) [BFMS11] 2'19"
  1. high voice and piano [Schott]
  2. low voice and piano [Schott]
  3. chorus (satb) and flute solo [Bardic Edition]
  4. chorus (satb) a cappella [Bardic Edition]

Skye Boat Song (see also *Songs of the North*) (1900) 1'52"
  1. voice and piano [Bardic Edition]
  2. uc + piano [Bardic Edition]

Soldier, Soldier (1907–8) [KS13] 3'39"
  1. $AT\beta^2b^2$ soli + chorus ($sat^2\beta^2b^2$) a cappella or + harmonium (to support voices) [Schott]
  2. voice and piano (2 settings) [Bardic Edition]

A Song of Autumn (1899) 1'34"
  voice and piano [Schott]

Song of Solomon
  a. Part II (see *Love Verses from the Song of Solomon*)
  b. Part V (see *King Solomon's Espousals*)

A Song of Värmeland (c.1904) 2'51"
  chorus ($s^2a^2t^2\beta b^2$) a cappella [Bardic Edition]

Songs of the North (from *Songs of the North*, ed. MacLeod and Boulton): 'Willie's gane to Melville Castle' 1'45"; 'Weaving Song' 1'50"; 'Skye Boat Song' 1'52"; 'This is no my plaid' 1'25"; 'Turn ye to me' 2'42"; 'Drowned' 3'08"; 'Fair young Mary (Mairi bhan og)' 3'06"; 'Leezie Lindsay' 2'34"; 'The women are a' gane wud' 1'20"; 'My faithful fond one (Mo run geal dileas)' 3'15"; 'Bonnie George Campbell' 0'55"; 'O' er the moor' 2'19"; 'O gin I were where Gadie rins'* 1'43"; 'Mo nighean dubh' [My dark-haired maid]* 4'27"
  voice (*unison chorus) and piano [Bardic Edition]

Spoon River (1919, 1922) [AFMS] 4'00"
1. orchestra (piccolo · 1 · 1 · 1 · 1(t) — 1(a) · 1(s) · 3 · 1 — TsbcGWMSXHP — strings 3 · 1 · 2 · 1) [AFMS2] [Schott]
2. large room-music (piccolo · 1 · 1 · 1 · 1 — 1(E-flat alto horn or a) · 1(s) · *3 · 1) – TsbcG*W*M*S*BXH(p)PPA — single strings 3 · 1 · 2 · 1) [AFMS2] [Schott]
3. †elastic scoring #1 (piano I, piano II, harmonium(pipe-organ) are complete in themselves and may be used in performance without any of the other orchestral instruments. To these may be added any or all of the other orchestral instruments listed in no. 1 above) [AFMS2] [Schott]
4. †elastic scoring #2 (*1·0·*1·0 — *1(*a)·*1(*s) — piano I, *piano II, harmonium(pipe-organ) — single strings 3(#3) · *1 · 2(#1) · 1) [AFMS2] [Schott]
5. †elastic scoring #3 (piano I+, piano II+, H(p)+) to these may be added any or all of the other orchestral instruments as listed in no. 1 above (singly or massed) [AFMS2] [Schott]
6. †elastic scoring (many other possibilities too numerous to list; please consult score for full details)
7. military band (piccolo · 2 · 2 · E-flat clarinet · 4 · alto clarinet · bass clarinet · 2 — saatβb — 4 · 2 · 2 cornets · 3 · euphonium · 1 — TsbchBMWXAP*P) (ed. Carson/Naylor) [Southern Music USA]
8. piano solo [AFMS1] [Schott]
9. 2 pianos (4 hands) [AFMS3] [Schott]

The Sprig of Thyme (1907, 1920) [BFMS24] 2'10"
1. high voice and piano [Schott]
2. low voice and piano [Schott]

Stalt Vesselil (*Proud Vesselil*) (1951) [DFMS] 1'03"
1. piano solo [EG] [Bardic Edition]
2. flute, cor anglais and strings (1 · 2 · 2 · 1) (ed. Tall) [Bardic Edition]
3. voice and piano (ed. Thwaites) [Bardic Edition]

Stormy (Pumping Chanty) (1907) [SCS] 1'19"
    β solo + men's chorus (um + t²b²) ([Peters Edition]

The Sussex Mummers' Christmas Carol (1905–11, 1915) [BFMS] 2'51"
1. chorus and orchestra (incomplete)
2. piano solo [BFMS2] [Schott]
3. violoncello or violin and piano [BFMS17] [Schott]
4. viola and piano (ed. Ould) [BFMS17] [Bardic Edition]
5. organ solo (two versions) (ed. Perna) [Bardic Edition]

The Tents of the Happy Tribes (c.1950–54) [from *The Lonely Desert Man Sees the Tents of the Happy Tribes*] 1'15"
    piano solo [Bardic Edition]

Thanksgiving Song (1945) 14'00"
1. chorus (s²atβb) and large room-music (piccolo · 1 · 0 · 2 · bass clarinet · 1 — a — 1 · 1(cornet) · 0 · 1(b) — sbcwGWMSXH²(R²)P²⁻⁴ — strings 3 · 2 · 2 · 1) (ed. Ould) [Bardic Edition]
    (last movement only complete)
2. 2 pianos (6 hands) [Bardic Edition]

Theme and Variations (1898) [YT] 8′53″
    string quartet (2 · 1 · 1 · 0) [Bardic Edition]

There was a pig went out to dig (1905–10) [BFMS18] 1′57″
    female chorus (s^2a^2) or single voices (S^2A^2) [Schott]

There were three friends (1898–9) [YT] 1′54″
    orchestra (2 · 0 · 2 · 2 — 2 · 0 · 0 · 0 — strings 2 · 1 · 1 · 1) [Bardic Edition]

Thou gracious Power (1952) 2′52″
    chorus ($s^2a^2t^2\beta^2b$) a cappella [Bardic Edition]

Three Burns Songs (c.1898) [YT]: 'Afton Water' 5′58″; 'Evan Banks' 3′14″; 'Yon wild mossy mountains' 3′51″
    voice and piano [Bardic Edition]

Three Scottish Folk Songs (1954) (see also under title for different versions): 'O gin I were where Gadie rins' 1′22″; 'Will ye gang to the hielands, Leezie Lindsay?' 1′05″; 'Mo nighean dubh' 1′47″
    piano solo [Peters Edition]

The Three Ravens (1902, 1942–3, 1950) [BFMS41] 4′02″
1. β solo + $S^2A^2T\beta$ soli, chorus ($sa^2t^2\beta b$), flute and 4 clarinets (or harmonium) [Schott]
2. β solo + $S^2A^2T\beta$ soli, chorus ($sa^2t^2\beta b$) and 5 clarinets (or harmonium) [Schott]
3. β solo + $S^2A^2T\beta$ soli, chorus ($sa^2t^2\beta b$) and elastic wind quintet (ed. Ould) [Bardic Edition]

Tiger, Tiger (1898–1905, 1912, 1939, 1946) [KS4: 9th mvt of KJBC] 1′40″
1. men's chorus (t^2b^2) (1898 setting) [Bardic Edition]
2. *Tenor solo(or lots of tenors + lots of baritones) and men's chorus ($t^2\beta^2b^2$) [Schott]
3. brass ensemble (0 · 2 · 3 · baritone · 1) [Bardic Edition]
4. 5 cellos [Bardic Edition]
5. recorder ensemble (3 descant, 1 treble, 1 tenor) [Bardic Edition]
6. piano solo [EG] [Bardic Edition]
7. organ or harmonium (4 hands) [EG] [Bardic Edition]

To a Nordic Princess (Bridal Song) (1927–8) 12′31″
1. orchestra (piccolo · 2 · 2 · cor anglais · 2 · bass clarinet · 2 — 4 · 3 · 3 · euphonium · 1 — TcGM³SBC(D)A+P+H²(p²)+O — strings 2 · 1 · 1 · 1) [Schott]
2. piano solo (excerpt) [Schott]

To Wolcott Balestier (1901–2) [KS]
    men's chorus ($at^2\beta b^2$) + organ pedals (incomplete)

Train Music (1901–7, 1957)
1. orchestra (piccolo · 3 · 3 · cor anglais · 3 · bass clarinet · 3 · double bassoon — 4 · 3 · 3 · 0 — strings 2 · 1 · 1 · 1) (ed. Rathburn) 1′35″ [Bardic Edition]
2. piano solo (excerpt) 0′36″ [Bardic Edition]

Tribute to Foster (1913–31) (see also *Lullaby*) 11′15″
1. SATβB soli, chorus ($s^2at^2b^2$) and orchestra (piccolo · 2 · 2 · 2 · 2 — 4 · 2 · 3 · 1 — Tsbctw*M²*W²*SC(D) + 2 rattles · *bowed metal marimba · musical glasses — strings 2 · 1 · 1 · 1) [Oxford University Press]

2. SATβB soli, chorus (s²at²b²) and 2 pianos (4 hands) [Oxford University Press]

The Twa Corbies (1903–9) 3′27″
1. voice and single strings (2 · 2 · 2 · 1) [Schott]
2. voice and piano [Schott]
3. (uc, um or uw) and string orchestra (2 · 2 · 2 · 1) [Bardic Edition]
4. (uc, um or uw) and piano [Bardic Edition]

The Two Sisters (1925–6) 2′30″
1. violin (or viola or violoncello) and harmonium (pipe-organ) [Bardic Edition]
2. violin, violoncello and pipe-organ [Bardic Edition]

Two Musical Relics of my Mother (1905–12) 3′03″ (see under separate titles): 'As Sally Sat a-Weeping'; 'Hermunder Illi'

Under en Bro (*Under a Bridge*) (1945–6) [DFMS12] 3′44″
1. mSβ soli(uw + um) and room-music (flute(violin I) · *clarinet — trumpet(viola I) — W²M(V)²S³XP² — strings (*violin II · *violin III · *violin IV · *viola II · *2 violoncellos · *double bass)) [Bardic Edition]
2. mSβ soli(uw + um) and piano [Bardic Edition]

Up-Country Song (1932) 1′03″
piano solo [EG] [Bardic Edition]

Variations on Handel's 'The Harmonious Blacksmith' (see also *Handel in the Strand*) (1911) 1′28″
1. voice and piano [Bardic Edition]
2. violoncello and piano [Bardic Edition]

Walking Tune (1900–1912, 1932, 1939–40) [RMTB3] 4′00″
1. wind quintet (flute ·oboe · clarinet · bassoon — horn) [Schott]
2. symphonic wind (piccolo · 2 · 2 · cor anglais · 2 · bass clarinet · 2 · double bassoon — 4 · 3 · 3 · 1 — strings 0 · 0 · 0 · 1) (ed. Perna) [Bardic Edition]
3. piano solo [Schott]
4. piano solo (simplified version) [EG] [Bardic Edition]
5. piano duet (2 versions — short and long) [EG] [Bardic Edition]
6. organ or harmonium duet [EG] [Bardic Edition]

The Warriors (Music to an Imaginary Ballet) (1913–16, 1922) 19′00″
1. orchestra (piccolo · 2 · 2 · cor anglais · *bass oboe(heckelphone) · 2 · bass clarinet · 2 · double bassoon — 6 · 4 · 3 · 1 — TsbcgkwtGX*W*M*B*S*(*barpiano)*DCPPP+AA — strings 2 · 1 · 1 · 1) [Schott]
2. 2 pianos (6 hands) with or without brass ensemble (2 · 0 · 2 · 1) [Schott]

Warriors A (1918)
1. piano solo (only available on piano roll in Grainger Museum)
2. piano solo (transcr. as *Bridal Lullaby Ramble*, ed. Lavender/Thwaites) 6′47″ [Bardic Edition]

Warriors B (1918)
piano solo (only available on piano roll in Grainger Museum)

The Warriors II (1919–20, 1929) 12′30″
1. large room-music (sketches survive) [Bardic Edition] ‡
2. 2 pianos (4 hands) (ed. Lavender, Ould, Thwaites) [Bardic Edition]

We be three poor mariners (1901) [OEPM]
  β solo + um and orchestra (o · 4 · 2 cor anglais · o · 2 · double bassoon — 2 · o · o · o — strings o · 2 · 12 · 6) [Bardic Edition] ‡

We have fed our sea for a thousand years (1900, 1904–11) [KS2] 3′14″
1. boy's chorus (sa) and men's chorus (t²β³b³), 3 horns and strings (o · o · 12 · 6) [Bardic Edition]
2. chorus (sa²t²βbb²) , brass and strings (o · o · o · o — 4 · 3(cornets)(#3) · 3 · euphonium · 1 — strings o · *1 · *1 · *1) or brass alone (4 · 3(cornets)(#3) · 3 · euphonium · 1) (brass may be doubled at will) [Schott]

We were dreamers (1898–9) [YT] 3′49″
1. chorus (satb) a cappella [Bardic Edition] ‡
2. orchestra (2 · 2 · 2 · 2 — 4 · o · o · o — strings 2 · 1 · 1 · 1) [Bardic Edition]

When Highland Shotterty (Shorterte) (1893) [YT] 1′30″
  voice and piano [Bardic Edition]

When the World was Young (1910–11, 1950, 1959) [S2] 3′47″
  2 pianos (4 hands) [Bardic Edition]

The Whistling Rider (*Der pfeifende Reiter*) (1898, 1959) 1′45″
  piano (6 hands) [Bardic Edition]

The Widow's Party (1901) (1st setting; different from version below) [KS]
  T solo + men's chorus (t²β²b²) and room-music (o · o · 6 · 2 — 2 · o · bugle · o · o — strings o · 3 · 3 · 1) (ed. Perna) [Bardic Edition]

The Widow's Party (1906–29) [KS7] 3′59″
1. men's chorus (t²b²) and orchestra (piccolo · 2 · 2 · 2 · 2 · double bassoon — 4 · 2 · 3 · 1 — TsbcXH*P*P — strings 2 · 1 · 1 · 1) [Schott]
2. men's chorus (t²b²) and large room-music (*piccolo 1 · o · 1 · 1 — 1 · 2 · 1 · o — Tsb*XHP*P — strings 2 · 1 · 1 · 1) [Schott]
3. men's chorus (t²b²) and piano (4 hands) [Schott]
4. men's chorus (t²b²) and military band (piccolo · 2 · *E-flat clarinet · 3 · bass clarinet · 2 · double bassoon — *s*a*t*β — 4 · 3(cornet) · 3 · euphonium · 2(E-flat bass and B-flat bass) — Tsbc) (all wind/brass parts can be doubled or trebled) [Bardic Edition]
5. men's chorus (t²b²) and orchestra (piccolo · 2 · *E-flat clarinet · 3 · bass clarinet · 2 · double bassoon — *s*a*t*β — 4 · 3(cornet) · 3 · euphonium · 2(E-flat bass and B-flat bass) — Tsbc — strings 2 · 1 · 1 · 1) [Bardic Edition]
6. voice and piano (4 hands) [Schott]
7. piano (4 hands) [EG] [Bardic Edition]
8. piano solo [EG] [Bardic Edition]

The Widow's Party March (1905–8) 4′14″
  2 pianos (6 hands) [Bardic Edition]

Willow Willow (1902–11) [OEPM1] 4′18″
1. voice and piano (early setting) [Bardic Edition]
2. voice and piano [Schott]
3. solo voice (uc or um or uw) and room-music (guitar(A) — strings 1 · 1 · 2 · 0 or 2 · 1 · 1 · 1) [Schott]

The Wraith of Odin (1903–48) 6′45″
1. double chorus (s²a²t³β²b² + male altos + sa²tb²) and orchestra (2 piccolo · 2 · 0 · 6 · 2 alto clarinet · 2 bass clarinet · 2 · 2 double bassoon — 6 · 2 · 4 bugelhorns · 2 · 2 euphoniums · 0 — strings 2 · 2 · 2 · 2) [Bardic Edition]
2. double chorus (s²a²t³β²b² + male altos + sa²tb²) and piano [Bardic Edition]
3. 2 pianos (4 hands) [Bardic Edition]

Ye banks and braes o' bonnie Doon (1902, 1932–7, 1953–7) [BFMS] 2′55″
1. unison women, men's chorus (t²b²), whistlers and harmonium [BFMS30] [Schott]
2. orchestra (piccolo · 1 · 1 · E-flat clarinet · 3 · bass clarinet · 2 — satβ — 2 · 2 · 2 · 2(euphonium and tuba) · 1 — H(p) — strings 4 · 2 · 4 · 1) [BFMS31][Schott]
3. †elastic scoring (many possibilities — consult score for full details) [BFMS31] [Schott]
4. wind band (piccolo · 3(#3) · 2 · *cor anglais · *E-flat clarinet · 4 · alto clarinet · 2 bass clarinets(*1) · 2 · *double bassoon — *saat*tβ*βb — 4(E-flat horns) · 3 cornets · *2 flugelhorns · *2 trumpets · 3 · euphonium · B-flat bass · E-flat bass · 1 — *H(*p) — string bass) [BFMS32] [Schott]
5. wind choirs (consult full score for many different possibilties too numerous to list here) [Bardic Edition]
6. clarinet choir (E-flat clarinet · 3 · alto clarinet · 2 bass clarinet) + *H(*p) [Bardic Edition]
7. saxophone choir (saattββb) + *H(*p) [Bardic Edition]
8. piano (4 hands) [EG] [Bardic Edition]
9. piano (6 hands) [EG] [Bardic Edition]

The Young British Soldier (1899) [KS] 7′17″
voice and piano [Bardic Edition]

Youthful Rapture (1901, 1929) [RMTB] 5′11″
1. violoncello solo and piano [Schott]
2. violoncello and large room-music (1 · 0 · 0 · 0 — 1(a) · 1(s/clarinet) · 0 · 0 — GHPA — strings 2 · 1 · 2 · 1) [Schott]
3. †elastic scoring (violoncello, piano and harmonium + any of the instruments listed in no. 2 above) [Schott]

Youthful Suite (see under separate titles for full scoring details): 'Northern March' 6′36″; 'Rustic Dance' 3′32″; 'Norse Dirge' 8′56″; 'Eastern Intermezzo' 1′51″; 'English Waltz' 4′23″
orchestra [Schott]

Zanzibar Boat Song (1902) [RMTB6] 4′08″
1. 1 piano (6 hands) [Schott]
2. percussion ensemble (incomplete)

Arrangements by Grainger

Unless otherwise stated, all titles are published or are in the process of being published by Bardic Edition.

ADDINSELL, RICHARD

Festival (arr. 2 pianos, 4 hands) 1954 c.5'10" [Keith Prowse]
Warsaw Concerto (arr. 2 pianos, 4 hands) 1942, 1946 c.9'10" [Keith Prowse]

ALFORD, KENNETH

Colonel Bogey (see Arnold, *Bridge on the River Kwai Marches*)

ANONYMOUS

Ad cantum laetitiae (arr. voices + winds or strings) (EGM)
Alleluia Psallat
    (arr. 3 unmixed or 6 mixed voices + optional accompaniment (organ and/or strings and/or winds)) 1943–52 (EGM)
    (arr. brass, clarinet or saxophone trio or choir) (EGM) (CGW)
    (arr. 3 descant recorders) 1947 (EGM)
    (arr. 2 descant and 1 treble recorder) 1947 (EGM)
    (arr. strings) (EGM) (CGS)
    (arr. orchestra) (EGM)
Angelus ad Virginem
    (arr. 3 unmixed or 6 mixed voices + optional accompaniment (organ and/or strings and/or winds)) 1943–52 (EGM) c.4'30"
    (arr. brass, clarinet or saxophone choirs) 1942 (EGM) (CGW)
    (arr. 2 descant and 1 treble recorder) 1947 (EGM)
    (arr. piano solo) 1937 (EGM)
    (arr. wind band) 1942 (EGM) (CGW) c.2'00"
    (arr. strings) 1939, 1942 (EGM) (CGS)
    (arr. orchestra) 1946 (EGM)
Bahariyale V. Palaniyandi (Jalatarangan) (arr. Indian cup bells, harmonium, 3 or 4 hand drums and bass drum) 3'47"
Beata viscera
    (arr. 3 unmixed or 6 mixed voices or single low voice or chorus with optional organ or instruments) 1943 (EGM)
    (arr. clarinet or saxophone choir or woodwind and horn) 1943 (EGM) (CGW)
    (arr. 2 descant and 1 treble recorder) 1947 (EGM)
    (arr. 3 descant recorders or 2 descant and 1 tenor recorder) 1947 (EGM)
Berong Pengètjèt (see *Gamelan Anklung*)
Credo
    (arr. 3 voices and optional woodwind or strings) 1934 (EGM)
    (arr. strings) 1939 (EGM) (CGS)
Edi beo thu
    (arr. 2 voices, wind or strings) 1939 (EGM) c.4'00"
    (arr. wind, clarinet, saxophone, brass duets) 1937 (EGM) (CGW)
    (arr. string duets) 1937 (EGM) (CGS)

(arr. mixed families of instruments in 2 parts) 1937 (EGM)
Fierce Rarotonga I (arr. men's voices) 1909, 1947
Foweles in the frith
   (arr. 2 voices) 1933 (EGM)
   (arr. voice and viola) 1933 (EGM)
Fulget coelestis curia
   (arr. 3 voices, 3 violins and harmonium) 1936, 1950 (EGM) (CGS)
   (arr. 3 women's or 3 men's voices or 6 mixed voices) 1936 (EGM)
Gamelan Anklung (Berong Pengètjèt) (Balinese Ceremonial Music) (arr. room-music (piccolo · flute — Tam-tams^2 · M^2 · h^2(S^2) · *H · P$^{2-4}$ — double bass)) 3'31"
Hac in anni janua
   (arr. 3-part chorus) 1939 (EGM)
   (arr. 6-part strings) 1939 (EGM) (CGS)
Jubilemus omnes una (arr. unison chorus) (EGM)
Mampahory Ny Masoandro Seranin-Javona (Two Madigascar Records, no. 1 only) (arr. 2 voices and strings) 1933
Marionette douce
   (arr. 4-part voices + optional accompaniment (organ and/or strings and/or winds)) 1950 (EGM)
   (arr. strings) 1937 (EGM) (CGS)
Princesse of Youth
   (arr. voices + harmonium, organ or accordion) 1937 (EGM)
   (arr. 3 women's voices or 3 men's voices or 6 mixed voices) 1937 (EGM)
   (arr. strings) 1937 (EGM) (CGS)
Pro Beata Pauli / O praeclara patriae (arr. 4 cellos or string orchestra) 1939 (EGM) (CGS)
Puellare gremium
   (arr. 3 unmixed or 6 mixed voices + optional accompaniment (organ and/or strings and/or winds)) 1950 (EGM) c.2'35
   (arr. orchestra) 1934 (EGM) c.2'35"
   (arr. strings) 1940 (EGM) (CGS)
Quis tibi Christe meritas (arr. 2 violas and cello) 1934 (EGM) (CGS)
Rarotonga I (arr. men's voices) 1909, 1947
Rarotonga II (arr. men's voices) 1909, 1949
Sekar Gadung (Javanese) (arr. SB soli — piccolo — metal marimba(vibraphone)^2, staff bells(tubular chimes or other large toned bells or gongs) , wooden marimba, xylophone) 1933 4'09"
Worcester Sanctus
   (arr. 3 part unmixed or 6 part mixed chorus) [key C] 1939 (EGM)
   (arr. 3 part mixed or 3 part men's chorus (with male alto) [key E-flat] 1939 (EGM)
   (arr. strings) 1939 (EGM) (CGS)

ARNOLD, MALCOLM

Bridge on the River Kwai Marches (arr. 1 piano, 6 hands) 1959 [Grainger Society]

BACH, J. S.

Air in D (arr. strings and optional organ)
Brandenburg Concerto No. 3 (arr. piano and strings) 1946

Fugue in A minor (WTK Book 1 no. 20)
   (arr. 2 pianos, 8 hands (or massed pianos)) 1930 [Schott UK; G. Schirmer USA]
   (arr. piano solo) 1934 c.5′00″
Fugue in C major (WTK Book 1 no. 1) (arr. 2 harmoniums) 1927
Fugue in C-sharp minor (WTK Book 1 no. 4) (arr. 6 saxophones)
Fugue in D-sharp minor (WTK Book 2 no. 8) (arr. 2 pianos, 4 hands) 1928
Fugue in E major (WTK Book 2 no. 9)
   (arr. 4 pianos, octave study) 1928 c.2′15″
   (arr. 2 pianos, 8 hands) 1950 c.2′15″
   (arr. piano solo) c.2′15″
March in D (from *Anna Magdalena Bach Notebook*) (arr. saxophone, clarinet, brass or wind choirs or wind band + percussion) 1946 (CGW) c.1′35″
O Mensch, bewein' dein' Sünde gross (Chorale prelude for organ from *Orgel-Büchlein* no. 24, BWV 622) (arr. saxophone, clarinet, brass or wind choirs or wind band) 1937–42 (CGW) c.3′45″ [R. Smith & Co. UK; Jenson USA]
O praise the Lord, all ye heathen (BWV 230) (arr. SATB chorus a cappella)
Prelude and Fugue V (WTK Book 2 no. 5)
   (arr. strings) [keys D and E] 1927 (CGW)
   (arr. 4 saxophones) 1943 (CGW)
Seht, was die Liebe tut (Tenor aria from Cantata no. 85) (arr. harp and wind band) [keys E-flat and D-flat] 1937 (CGW) c.3′10″
Toccata in F (BWV 540) (arr. 3 pianos (6 hands) or massed pianos) 1939 c.8′15″ [Schott UK; G. Schirmer USA]
Toccata and Fugue in D minor (BWV 565) (arr. piano solo from transcriptions by Busoni and Tausig) 1950 c.9′00″

BALAKIREV, MILY

Tamara (arr. 2 pianos, 8 hands) [MS lost]

BIRD, GEORGE

Melody (harmonised by Grainger) [sketch] 1945

BRADE, WILLIAM

Allemande (arr. for strings)

BRAHMS, JOHANNES

Cradle Song (transcribed for piano) 1923 (FS1) c.3′45″ [Schott UK; G. Schirmer USA]
Variation 12 [from *Paganini Variations*, Op. 35 no. 2] (transcribed for piano — concert and simplified versions) 1957 c.1′10″

BROCKWAY, HOWARD

Kentucky Rhapsody (miscellaneous sketches for 2 pianos, 4 hands, of folksongs from Kentucky) 1945

BULL, OLE

The Dairymaid's Lament (arr. 2 violas and 2 violoncellos) 1940

BYRD, WILLIAM

The Carman's Whistle (arr. piano solo) 1942–7 c.4'30"

CABEZÓN, ANTONIO DE

Prelude in the Dorian Mode
   (arr. 2 violas, 2 violoncellos) 1934 (CGS)
   (arr. string orchestra) 1939 (CGS)
   (arr. wind band) 1941 (CGW) c.4'30" [R. Smith & Co. UK; Jenson USA]
   (arr. saxophone choir) 1943 (CGW)
   (arr. string quartet or string orchestra) 1957 (CGS)

CHEATHAM, KITTY

Harvest Song (arr. 4 part mixed voices, violin, harp (or piano), organ (or piano)) [?USA]

CHOPIN, FREDERIC

Study Op. 10 no. 7 (arr. as a note-repetition study for 2 pianos, 6 hands; 2nd pianist's part only, single-stave part)

CORTECCIA, FRANCESCO

O begli anni dell'oro (*O Glorious Golden Age*)
   (arr. tenor voice, 2 violas, 2 violoncellos) 1934
   (arr. voice and piano (harmonium)) 1934 c.1'45"

COWELL, HENRY

Caoine (arr. sopranino sarrusophone, baritone saxophone and harmonium) c.0'35"

CURTIS-BURLIN, NATALIE (COLLECTOR)

Lenten Chant (see *Sangre de Cristo*)
Matachina (from *Memories of New Mexico*) (arr. large room-music (1 · 1 · 1 · 1 — 1 · 0 · 0 · 0 — APP — strings 2 · 2 · 2 · 1)) 1925
Negro Lullaby
   (arr. mixed voices + optional strings) 1934
   (arr. string orchestra) 1934 (CGS)
Sangre de Cristo (Lenten Chant) (from *Memories of New Mexico*) (arr. large room-music (piccolo · 1 · 1 · 1 · 1 — 1 · 0 · 0 · 0 — MSBAP²*P²H — strings 2 · 2 · 2 · 1)) 1925
Zulu Love Songs: 'Igáma lo Tándo' I & II (Zulu), 'Lúmbo lgo Lúdo' (Chindaú) (from *Songs and Tales of the Dark Continent*) (arr. mixed voices) [Grainger Society]

DAMETT, THOMAS

Salve Porta Paradisi (arr. 5 part mixed chorus) (EGM)

DEBUSSY, CLAUDE

Bruyères (*Heather Bells*) (arr. flute · oboe · bass oboe(cor anglais) · 2 clarinets · alto clarinet(bass clarinet) · bassoon · alto saxophone · horn · harmonium) 1918 c.3'15"
Pagodes (from *Estampes*) (arr. tuneful percussion (gGW³M³BCDX³H(R)PPP*P) and harmonium and four pianos) 1928 c.6'00"

DELIUS, FREDERICK

Air and Dance (arr. piano) c.4'35"
Dance Rhapsody no. I (arr. 2 pianos, 4 hands) 1923 c.12'00"
Song of the High Hills (arr. 2 pianos, 4 hands) 1923
Hassan (part of the 'General Dance' completed by PG) [Boosey & Hawkes]

DOWLAND, JOHN

Now, O now, I needs must part
   (arr. piano solo, concert version) 1937 (FS3 UK / FS5 USA) c.4'30" [Schott UK; G. Schirmer USA]
   (arr. piano solo, simplified version) 1937 (FS4 UK / FS6 USA) c.4'30" [Schott UK; G. Schirmer USA]

DUFAY, GUILLAUME

Le jour s'endort
   (arr. voice, 2 violins, viola and violoncello or violin and 2 violoncellos) 1934
   (arr. voice and piano) 1934
   (arr. string orchestra) (CGS)

DUNSTABLE, JOHN

O rosa bella
   (arr. 4 mixed voices and 2 instruments or 6 mixed voices and optional accompaniment) 1953 (EGM)
   (arr. strings) 1939, 1955
Regina coeli (unfinished) (EGM)
Veni Sancte Spiritus
   (transcribed for 4 mixed voices or 4 women's voices + optional percussion and keyboard) 1939 (EGM)
   (arr. strings) 1946 (EGM)
   (arr. orchestra) 1939 (EGM)

ELGAR, EDWARD

Nimrod (transcr. piano) 1953 c.4'00"

FAURÉ, GABRIEL

Après un rêve Op. 7 no. 1 (arr. piano) 1940 (FS7) c.3'00" [Schott UK; G. Schirmer USA]
Funerary Chant (arr. brass ensemble, incomplete) 1937 [Grainger Society]
Piano Quartet no. 2 in G minor Op. 45 (arr. 2 pianos, 4 hands, first movement only)
Nell Op. 18 no. 1 (arr. piano) 1925 (FS3) c.2'35" [Schott UK; G. Schirmer USA]
Tuscan Serenade Op. 3 no. 2 (arr. piano and wind band) c.3'00" [R. Smith & Co. UK; Jenson USA]

FERRABOSCO, ALFONSO II

The Four Note Pavan
   (arr. strings) 1944 (DC1; CGS) c.3'15" [G. Schirmer USA]
   (arr. wind, brass or saxophone choir) 1940 (CGW) c.3'15"
   (arr. wind band) 1940 (CGW) c.3'15"

FINCK, HEINRICH

O schönes Weib (arr. tenor voice and string trio) 1934–40 (CGS)

FRANCK, CESAR

Chorale no. 2 (arr. for wind band) 1942 (CGW) c.12'00" [R. Smith & Co. UK; Jenson USA]

GARDINER, BALFOUR

English Dance (arr. 2 pianos, 4 hands) 1925 [Forsyth]
Flowing Melody (sketches) 1946–51 [Grainger Society]
Gardineriana Rhapsody
   (arr. piano and orchestra (sketches survive)) 1947 5'30" [Grainger Society]
   (arr. piano solo (realised Stevenson 1984)) 1947 5'30"
Joyful Homecoming (sketches) 1946 [Grainger Society]
London Bridge (arr. 2 pianos, harmonium and tuneful percussion) 1935 c.2'35" [Grainger Society]
Movement for Strings in C minor (elastic setting) 1949 [Schott]
Prelude 'De Profundis' (edited for piano) 1905–27 (GV1) [Forsyth]

GERSHWIN, GEORGE

Embraceable You (arr. 1 piano, 4 hands, from Maurice C. Whitney's piano solo paraphrase) 1951 c.1'30"
Fantasy on Themes from 'Porgy and Bess' (arr. 2 pianos, 4 hands) 1951 c.19'30" [Gershwin Publishing Co. USA]
Love Walked In (arr. piano) 1945 c.3'45" [Gershwin Publishing Co. USA]
The Man I Love (concert adaptation of Gershwin's own piano transcription) 1944 c.3'45" [Harms Inc. USA]
O Lord I'm on My Way (from *Porgy and Bess*) (arr. 2 pianos, 4 hands) 1950 [Grainger Society]
Oh, I Can't Sit Down (from *Porgy and Bess*) (arr. 1 piano, 6 hands) 1950

GOOSSENS, EUGENE

Folk-Tune Op. 38 no. 1 (arr. wind band) 1942 (CGW) c.2'35" [Grainger Society]

GRAINGER, ELLA

Bigelow March of 1949 (arr. piano) c.2'15"
Crying for the Moon
   (arr. contralto voice and tuneful percussion) 1946 c.1'35"
   (arr. contralto voice and piano) 1946 c.1'35"
Farewell to an Atoll
   (arr. voice and piano) 1944 c.1'45"
   (arr. soprano voice, optional mixed chorus, and orchestra) 1945 c.1'45"
Honey-Pot Bee
   (arr. mezzo-soprano and room-music) 1947 c.1'30"
   (arr. voice and piano) 1948 c.1'35"
Love at first sight
   (arr. soprano, women's chorus + optional baritone solo) 1946 c.1'50" [G. Schirmer USA]
   (arr. soprano, mixed chorus) 1946 c.1'50" [G. Schirmer USA]
   (arr. voice and piano (organ)) c.1'50"
The Mermaid

(arr. mezzo-soprano and alto saxophone) 1947
(arr. voice and piano) 1947

Playing on Heart Strings (arr. contralto and tenor solos, mixed chorus or women's chorus) 1950

To Echo
(arr. voice and 7 instruments) 1945–6 c.1′45″
(arr. voice and piano) 1945–6 c.1′45″

GRIEG, EDWARD

Knut Lurasen's Halling II (arr. 2 pianos, 4 hands) 1921 c.2′15″

Norwegian Bridal Procession Op. 19 no. 2 (edited and fingered by Grainger) 1920 [Theodore Presser USA]

Piano Concerto in A minor Op. 16
(edited by Grainger for 2 pianos, 4 hands, with orchestra transcribed for piano 2) 1920 c.28′15″ [G. Schirmer USA]
(piano transcription of main themes and episodes of 1st movement) 1945 c.4′00″ (CT) [G. Schirmer USA]

Symphony in E minor (sketch orchestration of first 9 bars of sonata in E minor, Op. 7) 1944 [Grainger Society]

Three Lyric Pieces, Book I Op. 12 nos. 2, 4 and 5 (arr. orchestra) 1898

HANDEL, GEORGE FRIDERIC

Harmonious Blacksmith (sketch variations for voice or violoncello and piano) 1911 (see also *Variations* in list of original compositions) c.1′30″

Hornpipe (freely arranged for piano) 1923–6 (FS2) c.1′45″ [Schott UK; G. Schirmer USA]

HARRIS, CHARLES K.

After the Ball Was Over (sketch for whistlers and strings) 1901 [Grainger Society]

HERBERT, VICTOR

March: 'The Finest' (arr. 2 pianos, 4 hands) 1928 [Grainger Society]

HOWARD, JOSEPH E.

The 'Rag-Time' Girl (Hello, ma baby) (chorus only)
(arr. piano solo) 0′46″
(arr. voice and piano) 0′46″

HUGHES, CEIRIOG

Dafydd Y Gareg Wen (*David of the White Rock*) (arr. voice and piano) 1954 2′08″ [Schott]

JAPART, JEAN

Nenciozza mia
(arr. 2 violas, 2 violoncellos) [low key F] 1934, 1939 (CGS)
(arr. 4 violins or 2 violas, 2 violoncellos) [high key G] 1934, 1939 (CGS)

JENKINS, JOHN

Fantasy no. 8

 (arr. 3 recorders)
 (arr. violin, viola and cello)
Five Part Fantasy no. 1
 (arr. strings) 1944 (DC2; CGS) *c*.3'20"
 (arr. brass, clarinet or saxophone choir or wind band) 1933, 1937, 1941, 1953 (CGW) *c*.3.20"
 (arr. piano solo) 1934

JOSQUIN DES PREZ

La Bernardina
 (arr. violin, viola and violoncello) 1934 (CGS)
 (arr. 3 violins) 1934 (CGS)
 (brass or clarinet trio) 1943 (CGW)
 (arr. brass, wind ensembles or wind band) 1943 (CGW) *c*.1'20"
A l'heure que je vous
 (arr. 2 violins, viola and violoncello) 1934 (CGS)
 (arr. string ensemble) 1939 (CGS)
Royal Fanfare (arr. brass choir) 1937 (CGW)

LAWES, WILLIAM

Six Part Fantasy and Air
 (arr. strings) 1944 (DC3; CGS) [G. Schirmer USA]
 (arr. brass, clarinet or saxophone choir or wind band) 1932, 1937, 1944 (CGW)
 (arr. 2 pianos, 4 hands) 1932

LE JEUNE, CLAUDE

La bel' aronde (*Pretty Swallow*)
 (arr. 6 mixed voices)
 (arr. brass, clarinet, saxophone and wind choirs) 1942 (CGW)
 (arr. 2 harmoniums) 1932 *c*.1'45"
 (arr. 1 piano, 4 hands) 1932 *c*.1'35"
 (arr. strings) 1932 (CGS)
 (arr. piano solo) 1932

LEMCHE, PETER

Little Ole with His Umbrella (arr. and harmonised for voice and piano with English words by Percy and Ella Grainger) *c*.2'35"

LINEVA, EUGENIE

The flowers that bloomed in the field (edited for 4 mixed voices or choir) 1934
Kindling Wood (edited for 3 women's voices (ssa) or choir (ssa)) 1934

LISZT, FRANZ

Fantasy on Hungarian Folk-Songs (arr. piano and wind band) 1950 *c*.16'45"

MACHAUT, GUILLAME DE

Ballade no. 2: Helas! tant ay dolour (arr. 2 voices)

Ballade no. 17: Sans cuer m'en vois
   (arr. 3 voices) 1934
   (arr. strings) 1934 (CGS)
   (arr. brass, clarinet, saxophone and wind choir or wind band) 1940–42 (CGW) c.2′15″
Rondeau no. 14: Ma fin est mon commencement (arr. 6 strings + optional tenor solo) 1935 (CGS)

MASON, DANIEL GREGORY

Free and Easy Five Step (arr. Simmons for band) [sketch score]

MOHR, HALSEY K.

Liberty Bell (It's time to ring again) (arr. Briegel for wind band and chorus, + optional parts for bells, brass and voices by Grainger) 1937 [Grainger Society]

MORLEY, THOMAS

O Mistress Mine (arr. chorus (s²a²tβb) a cappella) (1903) 1′40″

OLSEN, SPAARE

Mountain Norway
   (arr. mixed chorus and optional piano) 1931/32/34 [Grainger Society]
   (arr. mixed chorus and orchestra) 1932 [Grainger Society]
   (arr. strings and piano) 1932 [Grainger Society]
When Yuletide Comes
   (arr. soprano, alto and men's voice) 1937 [Grainger Society]
   (arr. 3 saxophones) 1943 [Grainger Society]

PALESTRINA, GIOVANNI PIERLUIGI DA

Mori quasi il mio core (arr. 2 harmoniums)

PARKER, KATHERINE

Down Longford Way (arr. elastic scoring from 3 instruments up to full orchestra) 1936 c.2′10″

PISADOR, DIEGO

Paseabase, the Moorish King
   (arr. voice, lute and 3 plucked strings with ad lib. piano) 1934 (CGS)
   (arr. voice and small orchestra) 1934

POWER, LYONEL

Anima mea liquefacta est (arr. voice and 3 strings) 1935 (EGM) (CGS)
Sanctus
   (arr. voice and 3 strings) 1934 (EGM)
   (arr. 3 mixed voices or mixed chorus + optional strings and/or winds and /or keyboard) 1936, 1950 (EGM)

PURCELL, HENRY

Four Part Fantasy no. 8 (arr. strings and harmonium or massed pianos and harmonium)

RACHMANINOV, SERGEI

Laud ye the name of the Lord (arr. voices and harmonium — incomplete parts) [Grainger Society]

Piano Concerto no. 2 (transcription for piano solo of main themes and episodes of finale) 1946 (CT) c.5'20" [G. Schirmer USA]

RAVEL, MAURICE

La Vallée des cloches (*The Valley of the Bells*) (from *Miroirs*) (arr. tuneful percussion and strings (gWM²(V²)SBAP²*CD(P or A) — strings *1 · 1 · 1 · 1)) 1944 c.5'30"

ROSS, ORVIS

Away in a manger (arr. cello and piano) [Grainger Society]

SANDBY, HERMAN

Chant (The Page's Song) (arr. room-music) 1925 [Grainger Society]
Elfhill (song sketch) 1937 [Grainger Society]
Intermezzo (arr. wind band) 1937
Love Song (arr. strings and harmonium) 1939 (CGS) [Grainger Society]

SCARLATTI, DOMENICO

The Quiet Brook (Sonata in B minor, L. 33)
    (arr. string quartet) 1930 (CGS)
    (arr. clarinet choir) 1942 (CGW)
    (arr. string orchestra 4 and 10 part) (CGS)

SCHUMANN, ROBERT

Piano Concerto (transcription for piano solo of main themes and episodes from 1st mvt) 1947 (CT) c.9'00" [G. Schirmer USA]

SCOTT, CYRIL

Handelian Rhapsody (transcription for piano solo of material from Scott's Piano Sonata) 1909 c.6'30" [Elkin]
Solemn Dance (arr. strings, harmonium, piano and percussion) 1933 [Grainger Society]
Three Symphonic Dances (arr. 2 pianos, 4 hands) 1922 c.18'00" [Schott]

STANFORD, CHARLES VILLIERS

Four Irish Dances Op. 89 (arr. piano solo) 1916: no. 1 'A March Jig (Maguire's Kick)' c.3'25"; no. 2 'A Slow Dance' c.4'35"; no. 3 'The Leprechaun's Dance' c.3'00"; no. 4 'A Reel' c.4'10"

STRAUSS, RICHARD

Ramble on the Last Love-Duet from 'Der Rosenkavalier' (arr. piano solo) 1928 (FS4) 6'50" [Boosey and Hawkes UK; Schott Europe]

STOKEM, JOHANNES

Harraytre Amours (arr. violin, viola and cello) 1934 (CGS)

TCHAIKOVSKY, PYOTR ILYICH

Paraphrase on Tchaikovsky's Flower Waltz (*The Nutcracker*) (piano solo) 1905–16 c.6'35" [Schott]

Piano Concerto no. 1 (transcription for piano solo of 1st mvt) 1943 (CT) c.3'30" [G. Schirmer USA]

WAGNER, RICHARD

Wach' Auf! (from Act III of *Die Meistersinger*) (arr. 5 cellos)

WILLAERT, ADRIAN

O salutaris hostia
  (arr. 2 voices and 4 instruments) 1941 (CGW)
  (arr. brass, clarinet choir with or without voices) 1941 (CGW)
  (arr. chorus (at) and 4 or 5 brass instruments 0 · 2 · 2 · 1) 1937
  (arr. strings) 1934 (CGS)

Main Grainger Contacts

GRAINGER MUSEUM
The University of Melbourne
VIC 3010
Australia
tel.: +61 (0)3 8344 5270
fax: +61 (0)3 8344 5221
grainger@unimelb.edu.au

INTERNATIONAL PERCY GRAINGER SOCIETY
7 Cromwell Place
White Plains, NY 10601
USA
tel.: +1 (914) 582 1237
      +1 (914) 816 1137
casowa@aol.com

BARDIC EDITION and THE PERCY GRAINGER SOCIETY
2 George Street
Huntly, Aberdeenshire AB54 8BT
UK
tel.: +44 (0)1466 799555
info@percygrainger.org.uk

SCHOTT MUSIC
48 Great Marlborough Street
London W1 7BB
UK
tel.: +44 (0)207 292 6090
londonshop@schott-music.com

254 West 31st Street, Floor 15
New York, NY 10001
USA
tel.: +1 (212) 461 6940
ny@schott-music.com

The publishers below are best contacted via the internet for up-to-date contact details

    Boosey & Hawkes
    C. F. Barnhouse
    Elkin & Co.
    Carl Fischer Inc.
    Faber Music Ltd
    Faber Music USA & Canada
    Forsyth Brothers
    G. & R. Brand / R. Smith
    G. Schirmer
    Gershwin Publishing Co.
    Harms Inc.
    Keith Prowse
    Ludwig Masters
    Oxford University Press
    Peters Edition Ltd
    Southern Music Inc.
    Theodore Presser
    To the Fore Publishers
    TRN Music Inc.
    Universal Edition

Index

Page numbers referring to figures are in *italics*; those to the Discography are in **boldface**. The Catalogue of Works and the Bibliography have not been indexed.

Aarhus 92; Aarhus Municipal Orchestra 71, 120, **232**, **236**; concert programme *105*; recording **232**, **236**
ABC Classic FM Radio 93
Adams, Francis 124
Addinsell, Richard: *Festival; see* Arrangements *under* Grainger
Adelaide xix, xxii, 92, 94, 123, 133–5, 187, 216, 218–20; plate 26; Chamber Singers 93, *106*; Grainger Festival 16–17, 92–4, 109; String Quartet 134; Symphony Orchestra 92–3, *106*; Town Hall *106*, 187
Aeolian (Recording) Company 235; plate 2
Aeolian Hall xxi, 47
African music; *see* World Music
Afro-American music; *see* World music
Agnew, Roy 146
Ainsley, John Mark **247**
Albéniz, Isaac: *Triana* 95
Aldis, A. E. 158
Aldridge: origin of name 131
Aldridge, Athalie [cousin] 187
Aldridge, Cara [cousin]; *see* Ham, Cara
Aldridge, Clara Jane [aunt] 135, 209, 211, 220; *Auntie Clara's Aldridge History* 209
Aldridge, Emma Elizabeth [aunt] 135, 211, 220
Aldridge, Frank Herbert [uncle] 135, 211, 220
Aldridge, George Sydney [cousin] 188, 211, 219
Aldridge, George [grandfather] 135, 209, 211, 219
Aldridge, James [cousin] 187
Aldridge, James Henry [uncle] 188, 211, 219, 220; plate 26
Aldridge, Rosa Annie; *see* Grainger, Rose
Aldridge family 135, 139, 188, 217–20; family tree 211; 'Penelope Thwaites meets Cara Ham' 135
Aldridge's Horse Repository 131, 135; plate 15
Alger, H. Raynard *104*
Alger, K. *104*

Allison, Brian 149–51
America, United States of xxi–xxii, 3–4, 10, 34, 63, 75, 81, 85, 107, 128, 140–43, 166, 168, 172, 175, 182, 183, 202, 203
American Bandmasters Association, Convention 24
American Communist Party 183
American music [Native American, African-American]; *see* World music
Ancelet, Capt. Treg **244**
Andersen, Hans Christian xix, 137, 149, 152
Anglo-Saxon Chronicle 159
Armstrong, Louis 170
Arndt, Felix: *Nola* **231**
Atkinson, Fred 37
Auckland Public Library 134
Auer, Leopold 186
Augener: *Minstrelsy of England* 46
Austin, Frederic 173, 175; *Symphony* 171, 172
Australian Broadcasting Commission (Corporation) 142, 190, 208

Bach, Johann Sebastian xix, xx, 2, 9, 27, 65, 68, 78, 88, 95, 114, 163, 179, 200, **228**, **237**
Air in D major 103
Brandenburg Concerto No. 3; see Arrangements *under* Grainger
Fantasia and Fugue in G minor 119, **228**, **235**
Fantasia and Fugue in A minor **229**, **237**
Gigue from first Partita **228**
March; see Arrangements *under* Grainger
O Mensch, bewein' dein' Sünde gross; see Arrangements *under* Grainger
Prelude and Fugue in A minor **235**
St Matthew Passion 42
See what His love can do; see Arrangements *under* Grainger
Toccata and Fugue in D minor; see Arrangements *under* Grainger
Balinese music; *see* World music

· 295 ·

Balough, Teresa **x**, 30, 39, 107, 189–96
Bardic Edition [music publisher] 2, 65, 108, 112, 113, 293
Barry, Raymond 125
Barrymore, Lionel 166
Bartók, Béla 88, 170, 174
Bashford, Rodney 28
Bauer, Harold 42
Bauer, Moritz 176
Bauld, Alison 89
Bax, Arnold 175
BBC: 'Grainger's Only Appearance on Television' 186; Radiophonic Workshop 147
Beauchamp, David 133
Bechstein Hall (later Wigmore Hall) 173
Beecham, Sir Thomas 112, 145
Beethoven, Ludwig van 149; *Symphony in F (Pastoral)* 127
Benjamin, Arthur 89, 146
Bennett, Tom **243**
Beowulf 159
Berliner Phonogramm-Archiv 80
Bernhardt, Sarah 127
Berntsen, Anton 160, 161
Bird, John 3, 47, 116, 120, 147, 182 , **227**
Bizet, Georges 203; *Carmen* 126
Black, Amy; *see* Chalk
Blacking, John 73, 83, 84, 158, 191; *A Commonsense View of All Music* 73, 191
Blanche, Jacques-Émile 153
Bloch, Ernst 163
Blom, Philipp 158
Bly, Nelly 166
Boosey & Hawkes [instrument maker] 184
Border Watch Newspaper: 'Great Reception for Visiting Artist' 186
Børner, Walter **232**
Bostock, Douglas 172, 180
Boswell, Rita 209
Boulton, Harold 178
Brabbins, Martyn 172
Brade, William: *Allemande*; *see* Arrangements *under* Grainger
Bradford, Vera 186; plate 12
Brahms, Johannes 88, *104*, 114, **228**, **235**, **237**
  Cradle Song; *see* Arrangements *under* Grainger
  Paganini Variations [No. 12]; *see* Arrangements *under* Grainger
  Piano Sonata in F minor 118, **228**
  Waltz in A-flat 118, **228**
Brigg, Lincolnshire xx, 37, 98; Musical Competition Festival 3, 37

Briggs, Asa 123, 124, 125
Brighton, Melbourne xix, 124, 135
Brimer, Michael *100*, *101*
Brion, Keith, **242**, **243**; new edition of *Marching Song of Democracy* 24
Brisbane, Katherine 126, *127*, 128
Britten, Benjamin xxii, 116, 120, 168; *Salute to Percy Grainger* 88, 107
Broadwood, Lucy 3, 37, 46, 47
Brown, Sarah Jane 135, 211
Bryant, Stephen 89
Bunny, Rupert 153
Burns, Robert 49
Burt, Warren 93
Busoni, Ferruccio xx, 65, 117, 119, 183–4, **228**, **235**
Butterworth, George 22
Byrd, William 30; *The Carman's Whistle*; *see* Arrangements *under* Grainger

Cabezón, Antonio de 78, *104*, **243**
Cameron, Basil xxi, 145
Cameron, Colin 186
Cannon, Michael 128, 129
Carley, Lionel 173
Carlyle, Thomas 149
Carroll, Mark 34
Cave, George 133
Cecchi, Pietro 145
Chalk, Amy (née Black) 130
Chamberlain, Stewart 164
Chandos [record company] 2, 53, 108, 172, 176, **239–44**
Chaplin, Nesta 182
Chappell, William: *Old English Popular Music* 32, 46
Chester, J. & W. [music publisher] 107
Chicago Civic Opera House 89; plate 12
Chicago Musical College, Grainger's classes xxi, 187
China, traditional music; *see* World music
Chopin, Frédéric 88, *104*, 114, 116, **228**, **230**, **235**
Clarke, Robert 92
Classico [record company] 172
Clifford, May *100*
Clifford, Phil 171, 176
Clunies Ross, Bruce 1, 21, 36, 148, 157–65
Coast Artillery, 15th Band 24, **230**
Code, Percy 208
Coldstream Guards Band 24
Collings, David 178
Columbia [record company] 116, **228**
Comettant, Oscar 125

Conan Doyle, Sir Arthur 51
Coperario, John 75
Copland, Aaron 170
Corperon, Eugene Milgiaro **244**
Corteccia, Francesco 78, 79, **247**
Counihan, Noel 153
Covell, Roger 140–48, 193
Covent Garden; *see* Royal Opera House, Covent Garden
Cowell, Henry 82, 168, 176, 179, **231**
   The Aeolian Harp **231**
   Celtic Set 29
   The Lilt of the Reel **231**
Cowell, Mrs (Henry Cowell's mother) 196
Cowen, Sir Frederic Hymen 126–7, 186; *Minna-Waltz* 126–7
Cox, G. W. 159
Crabtree, Libby **247**
Cramer: *Songs of the North* 46
Crawford, John 93
Croce, Benedetto 189
Cromwell, David 166, 168
Cromwell Place; *see* White Plains
Cross, Burnett xxii, 3, 138, 148, 156, 193, 194
Crossin, Carl 93
Crossley, Ada xx, 141
Curtis-Burlin, Natalie 80, 81, 84, 85

Daily Telegraph 34, 123
Damett, Thomas 79
Davis, Andrew 248
Deas, Stewart 180
Debussy, Claude xx, 9, 91, 95, 114, 228
   Claire de Lune 228
   Estampes 91, 230
   Gollywog's Cake Walk 228, **235**
   Jardins sous la pluie 230
   Pagodes; *see* Arrangements *under* Grainger
   Toccata from *Pour le Piano* 114, **227**, 228, 230
Decca [record company] **232**
Deering, Richard 75
Delius, Frederick xx, xxi, 9, 88, 92, 97, 140, 174, 176, 178, 179, **237**; plate 28
   Air and Dance; *see* Arrangements *under* Grainger
   Brigg Fair 178
   Dance Rhapsody [No. 1]; *see* Arrangements *under* Grainger
   Florida Suite 153
   In a Summer Garden 106
   North Country Sketches xxi
   Piano Concerto **234**
   Song of the High Hills xxi, 68, 162, 192

Delius Edition 111
Delius, Jelka: plate 28
Denmark xx–xxii, 3, 14, 34, 51, 87, 88, 92, 105, 160, 161, 171; 'Percy Grainger and Denmark: a Love Story', concert programme 88; *Danish Folk-Music Suite*; *see* Works *under* Grainger; *see also* Kristensen, Evald Tang
Denton, Co. Durham 131, 212; Chapel 131; plate 39
Des Prez, Josquin 78, *104*, **244**
Dett, [Robert] Nathaniel 179, 190, **230**
   Juba Dance 188, **228**, **230**
   Prelude [*Night*] **230**
Dickens, Charles xix, 37, 149
Dillon, Fannie Charles 92; *In a Mission Garden* 103
D'Indy, Vincent 203
Dobson, John 131
Dolmetsch family xxi; Arnold 73, 74, 77, 169; Mabel 74; Nathalie 74, 75; Dolmetsch Collection 74–5, 76; Dolmetsch Consort 74; Dolmetsch Festival 74
Dowland, John: *Now, O now, I needs must part*; *see* Arrangements *under* Grainger
Downes, Olin 189, 192, 193
Dreier, Per 105, **232**, **236**
Dreyfus, Kay 3, 34, 43, 107, 138, 141, 144, 145, 151, 153–6, 165, 172
Dubal, David 115, 116
Dufay, Guillaume 78
Dulwich Picture Gallery 89
Dunstable, John 78
Duo-Art Co [piano roll company] 115

Easte, Michael 75
Eastman Wind Ensemble 180
Eastwood, Jill 125
Eckhart, Meister 189
Eden, I. J. 133
Edison Bell phonograph xx, xxi, 14, 34, 39, 53, 54, 80–82, 178; plate 30
Egypt, traditional music; *see* World music
Elder, Sir Thomas 134
Elgar, Sir Edward xx–xxi, **237**, **240**; *Cockaigne Overture* 29
Ellington, Duke 163, 179, 207; *Creole Love Call* 162
Elwes, Gervase 37, 47
Elwes, Lady Winefride 37, 47
Engel, Carl 74
English Folk Dance and Song Society; *see* English Folk-Song Society

English Folk-Song Society 3, 34, 39, 47, 54, 143, 178

Fairfax, Bryan 171
Fairlight Computer Musical Instrument 147
Falconer, Winifred 130, 132, 134, 137
Farren-Price, Ronald 100
Fauré, Gabriel 9, 285
  Après une Rêve; see Arrangements *under* Grainger
  Nell; see Arrangements *under* Grainger
  Tuscan Serenade; see Arrangements *under* Grainger
Fenby, Eric 167
Fennell, Frederick 22, 180; 'An Interpretative Analysis' 22
Ferrabosco, Alfonso II 75, 77, 78, **244**
Ficino, Marsilio 189
Fickenscher, Arthur 179, 207
Finck, Heinrich 78
Flannery, Tim 123, 124, 125
Florrimell, Rosemary 154
Floyd, James Michael 83
Folk-Song Society; see English Folk-Song Society
Folktrax Archive 37
Foreman, Lewis ix, 142, 171–80
Foster, Stephen: *Camptown Races* 34
Fowler, Richard Hindle 130, 130
Franck, César 285; *Chorale*; see Arrangements *under* Grainger
Frankfurt gang xix, xxi, 141, 158, 169, 174, 181, 187; plate 24
Frolova-Walker, Marina 163

Ganz, Rudolph 186; plate 12
Garafalo, Robert: *Folk Songs & Dances in Wind Band Classics* 22
Gardiner, Henry Balfour xix, 88, 95, 97, 172, 174, 175, 176, 179, 181, 182, 187, 286; Balfour Gardiner Concerts xxi, 175
Gardiner, John Eliot 102, 116, **247**
Gardner, John 135
Gentry, Gerald 187
George, Stefan 182
German, Sir Edward 7
Gershwin, George 114, 162
  Embraceable You; see Arrangements *under* Grainger
  Love Walked In; see Arrangements *under* Grainger
  The Man I Love; see Arrangements *under* Grainger

Porgy and Bess; see Arrangements *under* Grainger
Gilchrist, James 98
Gillespie, Rhondda 99, **238**
Gillies, Malcolm 1, 21, 34, 36, 127, 136, 140, 141, 144, 145, 157, 163, 164
Gimson, Ernest 153
Glanville-Hicks, Peggy 146
Gluck, Christoph Willibald **228**
Goethe, Johann 149, 189
Goldman, Edwin Franko 22
Goldman, Richard Franko 77, 169, 179, **232**
Goldmark, Carl 92
Goossens, Eugene 179, **244**
Gouldthorpe, George 47, 48; plate 29
Grainger: origin of name 131
Grainger, Annie [aunt] 131, 133, 210, 215
Grainger, Arthur Walter [uncle] 132, 210, 217
Grainger, Elizabeth [aunt] 132, 210, 216
Grainger, Ella Viola (née Ström) [wife] xxi, 4, 10, 51, 107, 139, 149, 162, 167, 168, 169, 170, 181, 185, 188, 211; plates 4–7
  Bigelow March; see Arrangements *under* Grainger
  Crying for the Moon; see Arrangements *under* Grainger
  Farewell to an Atoll; see Arrangements *under* Grainger
  Honey-Pot Bee; see Arrangements *under* Grainger
  Love at First Sight; see Arrangements *under* Grainger
  To Echo; see Arrangements *under* Grainger
Grainger, Frederick [uncle] 132, 210, 216
Grainger, Henrietta Louisa [aunt] 132, 210, 217
Grainger, Henry Charles [uncle] 132, 133, 210, 216
Grainger, Herodias [aunt] 132, 210, 215
Grainger, Jacob [great-uncle] 210, 213; plate 40
Grainger, Jacob [great-grandfather] 2, 131, 209, 210, 212; plate 38
Grainger, Jane [aunt] 131, 210, 215
Grainger, John [grandfather] 132, 210, 213, 214
Grainger, John Harry [father] xix, xxi, 123, 125, 172, 209, 210, 216; plates 17, 18
  alcoholism 136
  architectural achievements 124, 134; plate 20
  design awards: Paris Exposition 132–3
  early life 131–4
  musical interests 133, 135
  rift with father 136

Roman Catholic beliefs 132
syphilis, effects of 137
Grainger, Mary Ann [aunt] 132, 133, 210, 216

Grainger, Percy Aldridge (b. George Percy):
aleatoric methods ix, 12, 35; *see also* Works: *Random Round under* Grainger
American citizen xxi
Army enlistment xxi, 10, 140; plate 1
'Art for all' 84, 190, 191
Australasian tours xx–xxii, 80, 95–6, 141–2, 172, 187
Australian background 123–9, 140–48
birthplace: plate 19
broadcast talks 73, 82, 83, 92, 142, 162, 189, 190, 208
'Butterfly piano': plate 35
cancer xxii, 140, 183
childhood education 137, 159
chronology xix–xxii
compositional milestones xix–xxii; plates 13, 22
concert programmes about 97–102, 106
concert programmes by 95, 96, 103 [wedding programme], 104, 105
death and burial xxii
debuts as pianist: Melbourne xix; London xx; New York xxi
democracy in music 30, 73, 84, 157, 158, 189
Denmark; *see separate entry*
Discography **227–48**
early music, interests in ix, 27, 70, 73–9; *see also* English Gothic music
elastic scoring ix, 10–16, 19, 27, 37, 47, 52, 58, 72, 76, 84, 89, 199–200
'Electric Eye Music Machine' 93
English Gothic music xxii, 74, 75–6, 77
ethnicity in music 157, 158, 163
flagellation 138
folk song ix, 3, 7, 16, 37, 87; collecting xx, xxi, 37, 39, 46, 54, 143, 150, 190; plates 29, 30; settings xx, 34, 47–8, 89, 112–13, 173–4, 178–9, 184
Frankfurt, studies at Hoch Conservatorium xix, xx, 3, 7, 30–31, 137, 138, 141, 150, 158, 176; plates 24, 25
Free Music; *see* Works *under* Grainger
'Free music' concept 3, 30, 31, 84, 148, 153, 156, 162, 169, 171, 176, 179, 193, 194, 195, 207, 208; plate 33
'kangaroo pouch Free Music machine' 148, 150

language interests and skills x, 159, 161
marriage xxi, 4, 10, 92, 103, 139, 140, 162, 211; plate 4
Marxism 183
Museum; *see* Grainger Museum
New York University lectures xxii
Nordic music 157–65, 172
orchestral experimentation 200–201
origins 2, 131–2, 209–20
percussion, orchestral use of 7–8, 11, 15–17, 21, 26–7, 32, 71, 81, 83, 93, 202–3
philosophy of life and art 189–96
photographs: frontispiece, 97; plates 1, 2, 4–9, 11, 12, 14, 16, 21, 24–6, 28, 31, 37
piano playing, approach to 1, 58–62, 114–20
piano rolls 115, 119, **233–6**
primitive music, love of 36
Promenade Concerts 115; appearance at xxii
private life, writing about 2, 162, 164
racial attitudes 2, 157–65, 190, 192
recordings by Grainger **227–36**; performances by others **237–48**; *Grainger Plays Grainger* 26, 115, 119; home recordings 168, 169
'Reed-Box Tone-Tool' 156
residence in White Plains, New York xxi, xxii, 3, 89, 107, 166–70; plates 3–5, 14, 27, 30
'roller desk': plate 10
saxophones, orchestral use of 196, 203–4
St Olav Medal xxii
teaching xxi, xxii, 68, 73, 75, 80, 138, 142, 156, 157, 158, 161, 162, 164, 186, 190, 208; plate 9
World music, exploration of; *see* World music

Original Works and Folk Settings

Afterword 9, 112, **241**, **245**, **247**
Afton Water 56 , **246**
Agincourt Song **246**
Always Merry and Bright 59, 68, 69, **238**
Anchor Song 50, 56, 98, **241**, **245**, **246**
Andante con moto 58, 67, **237**, **238**
Arrival Platform Humlet; *see In a Nutshell*
At Twilight xix, 67, **238**, **246**, **247**
Australian Marching Song 32; *see also Marching Song of Democracy*
Australian Up-Country Song 43, 102, **239**, **243**, **244**, **246**, **247**
The Beaches of Lukannon; *see Jungle Book Cycle*

Beautiful Fresh Flower 16, 18, 58, 66, 80, 84, 163, 186, **237**, **240**, **242**
Bell Piece 27, 67
Birthday Gift (Childhood Works) xix, 137; plate 22
Blithe Bells 2, 18, 27, 65, 68, **101**, **228**, **237**, **238**, **239**, **240**, **242**, **243**, **248**
Bold William Taylor 47, 47, 48, 57, 59, 98, **246**, **247**, **248**
Bonnie George Campbell; see *Songs of the North*
A Bridal Lullaby 9, 58, 59, 60, 65, 71, 106, 108, **237**, **239**
Bridal Lullaby Ramble 10, 65, 69, 91, 110, **234**, **239**
The Bridegroom Grat **246**, **247**
The Bride's Tragedy 34, 45, **247**, **248**
Brigg Fair 37, 38, 45, 52, 98, 102, 107, 178, **241**, **245**, **247**, **248**
The Brisk Young Sailor; see *Lincolnshire Posy*
British Folk-Music Settings 36–45, 57
British Waterside 56, 98, **246**
Children's March: Over the Hills and Far Away 18, 24, 26, 29, 59, 66, 67, 68, 69, 101, 104, 184, **232**, **234**, **237**, **238**, **239**, **242**, **243**, **244**
Choosing the Bride; see *Danish Folk-Music Suite*
Colleen Dhas (The valley lay smiling) 16, 18, 113, **241**, **242**, **245**
Colonial Song 10, 18, 21, 24, 26, 45, 59, 65, 66, 72, 90, 106, 111, 145, 147, 175, 178, 179, **228**, **230**, **234**, **237**, **239**, **240**, **241**, **242**, **243**, **244**, **248**
Country Gardens xxi, 9, 18, 28, 65, 67, 68, 69, 71, 90, 99, 106, 142, 171, 185, **228**, **230**, **231**, **232**, **234**, **236**, **238**, **240**, **241**, **242**, **243**, **244**, **248**
County Derry Air; see *Irish Tune from County Derry*
Creeping Jane 37, 54, 54, 56, **246**, **248**
The Crew of the Long Serpent 19, 67, 68, 159, **238**, **242**, **246**
Dalvisa **241**, **245**, **247**
Danish Folk-Music Suite 7, 9, 12, 14, 57, 63, 64, 71, 91, 92, 105, 179, **232**, **236**, **239**, **242**, **246**
   'Jutish Medley 14, 63, 64, 69, 91, 99, 119, 180, **228**, **234**, **237**, **238**, **239**, **242**
   'Choosing the Bride' 14
   'The Dragoon's Farewell' 14, 119
   'Husband and Wife (Hubby and Wifey)' 14, 51, 57, 90, 98, 112, **246**, **247**
   'The Shoemaker from Jerusalem' 14, **247**, **248**

'Lord Peter's Stable Boy' 14, 64, 112, 180, **228**, **242**, **247**
'The Nightingale and The Two Sisters' 14, 61, 61, 63, 64, 180, **237**, **242**, **247**, **248**
'The Power of Love' 10, 45, 51, 57, 61, 62, 63, 64, 89, 90, 98, 180, **241**, **242**, **245**, **246**, **247**
Danny Deever 42, 43, 44, 45, 91, **241**, **245**, **247**
Dedication 46, 50, 51, 57, 98, **246**
Died for Love 18, 56, 65, 98, **237**, **239**, **241**, **244**, **245**, **246**, **247**, **248**
Dollar and a Half a Day 40, 41, 45, **241**, **245**, **247**
Dragoon's Farewell; see *Danish Folk-Music Suite*
Dreamery 10, 18, 112, **240**, **242**, **245**
Drowned; see *Songs of the North*
Duke of Marlborough Fanfare 18, 21, 24, 29, 68, **234**, **238**, **240**, **243**
Early one morning 16, 18, 57, **231**, **236**, **238**, **240**, **241**, **244**, **245**, **246**, **247**
Eastern Intermezzo; see *Youthful Suite*
English Dance xxi, 9, 10, 69, 111, 171, 175, **237**, **238**, **240**, **241**
English Waltz; see *Youthful Suite*
Evan Banks 56, **246**
Faeroe Island Dance (Let's Dance Gay in Green Meadow) 26, 27, 67, 68, 90, 175, **235**, **238**, **242**, **243**, **244**
Fair young Mary; see *Songs of the North*
The Fall of the Stone; see *Jungle Book Cycle*
Father and Daughter 34, 45, 91, 102, 175, **241**, **245**, **247**
The First Chanty 51, 57, **246**
Fisher's Boarding House 18, **240**
Free Music No. 1 xix, xxii, 90, 193, 194, **247**
Ganges Pilot 50, 53, 57, 98, **246**
Gay but Wistful; see *In a Nutshell*
Gigue in C (Childhood Works) 58, 67; plate 22
Grainger Suite for solo piano and orchestra 9, 71, 106
Green Bushes x, 69, 70, 99, 106, 111, 171, 175, **238**, **240**, **241**, **242**, **244**
'The Gum-Suckers' March'; see *In a Nutshell*
The Gypsy's Wedding Day 45, **246**, **247**, **248**
Handel in the Strand 9, 18, 52, 63, 65, 68, 69, 70, 71, 90, 106, 142, 171, 186, **230**, **231**, **236**, **237**, **238**, **240**, **241**, **243**, **244**, **245**, **248**
Hard-hearted Barb'ra (H)Ellen 46, 54–5, 57, 90, 98, **234**, **237**, **239**, **246**
Harvest Hymn 9, 18, 66, 67, 69, 90, 99, **237**, **238**, **239**, **240**, **241**, **244**, **245**, **247**, **248**
Hermunder Illi; see *Two Musical Relics*

INDEX

Hill-Song I and *II*: xx, 14–15, 18, 20, 21, 29, 68, 69, 102, 160, 171, 175, 179, 184, 194, **238**, **241**, **242**, **243**, **244**; *Hill-Song I* rescored as *Room-music for 22-some* 15

Horkstow Grange; *see Lincolnshire Posy*

The Hunter in his Career 32, 43, 65, **230**, **237**, **239**, **240**, 248

The Hunting Song of the Seeonee Pack; *see Jungle Book Cycle*

Husband and Wife; *see Danish Folk-Music Suite*

The Immovable Do 9, 18, 24, 26, 27, 29, 66, 89, 104, 106, **237**, **241**, **242**, **243**, **244**, 245

I'm Seventeen Come Sunday 37, 43, 102, **241**, **244**, **245**, **247**, 248

In a Nutshell (Suite) xxi, 7, 8, 16, 26, 57, 68, 69, 71, 83, 91, 93, 106, 171, 179, 181, 187, **235**, **236**, **238**, **240**, **242**
  'Arrival Platform Humlet' 9, 16, 63,.64, 90, **237**, **239**, 248
  'Gay but Wistful' 9, 17, 63, 64, **237**, **239**
  '"The Gum-Suckers" March' 9, 17, 24, 26, 29, 63, 64, 179, **228**, **230**, **234**, **237**, **239**, **240**, **242**, **243**, **244**, **245**
  'Pastoral' 9, 17, 63, 64, 91, 99, **237**, **239**

In Bristol Town 67, **237**, **238**, **239**, **246**

In Dahomey 58, 63, 64, 108, 163, **237**, **239**, **240**

The Inuit; *see Jungle Book Cycle*

Irish Tune from County Derry x, 9, 15, 18, 26, 27, 29, 29, 36, 45, 66, 67, 102, 104, 106, 175, **228**, **230**, **236**, **237**, **239**, **240**, **241**, **242**, **243**, **244**, **245**, **246**, **247**, **248**

Jungle Book Cycle xx, xxii, 40, 42, 43, 52, 102, 194, 195, **247**
  'The Beaches of Lukannon' 42, 46, 50, 57, **246**
  'The Fall of the Stone' 42
  'The Hunting Song of the Seeonee Pack' 42, **246**
  'The Inuit' 42, 175
  'Morning Song in the Jungle' 42, 43, 45
  'Mowgli's Song Against People' 40, 68, 105, **232**, **238**
  'Night Song in the Jungle' 42, **246**
  'The Only Son' 40, 42, 52, 90, 98, **246**, **247**
  'The Peora Hunt' 32, 42
  'Red Dog' 42
  'Tiger, Tiger' 42, 67, 175, **238**, **239**, **241**, **245**, **246**

Jutish Medley; *see Danish Folk-Music Suite*

The Keel Row 45, 99, 110, **238**

King Solomon's Espousals 31, 248

Klavierstücke 58, 66, 67, 110, **237**

Kleine Variationen-form 19, **241**, **246**

Knight and Shepherd's Daughter 58, 66, **235**, **237**, **239**

The Lads of Wamphray March 24, 25, 32, 43, **242**, **243**, **244**, **245**

The Land o' the Leal 56, **246**, **247**

Leezie Lindsay; *see Songs of the North*

Let's Dance Gay in Green Meadow; *see Faeroe Island Dance*

Lincolnshire Posy xxii, 20, 21, 28, 53, 58, 68, 69, 91, 104, 131, 180, 185, **238**, **242**, **243**, **244**
  'The Brisk Young Sailor' 22, 53, 67, 68, **237**, **239**
  'Horkstow Grange' 22, 68, **239**, **248**
  'Lisbon (Dublin Bay)' 22, 29, 67, 68, **234**, **237**, **239**, **247**, **248**
  'Lord Melbourne' 22, 68, 69, 70, **248**
  'The Lost Lady Found' 22, 37, 43, 46, 53, 56, 68, 102, 106, **241**, **245**, **246**, **247**, **248**
  'Rufford Park Poachers' 22, 23, 68, 69, **248**

Lisbon (Dublin Bay); *see Lincolnshire Posy*

The Lonely Desert-Man Sees the Tents of the Happy Tribes 35, 45, 52, 67, 98, 112, **238**, **239**, **241**, **245**, **246**, **248**

Lord Maxwell's Goodnight 56, 98, 112, **241**, **245**, **246**, **247**

Lord Melbourne; *see Lincolnshire Posy*

Lord Peter's Stable Boy; *see Danish Folk-Music Suite*

The Lost Lady Found; *see Lincolnshire Posy*

The Love Song of Har Dyal 43, 57, 98, **241**, **245**, **246**, **247**

Love Verses from the 'Song of Solomon' xx, 31, 45, 105, 109, 109, 193, **232**, **241**, **245**, **247**

The Maiden and the Frog 248

March of the Men of Harlech 43

Marching Song of Democracy xxi, 20, 21, 22, 24, 31–2, 33, 83, 192, 195, **242**, **248**

Marching Tune 43, 106, **241**, **245**

Mary Thompson **246**, **247**

The Men of the Sea 50, 56, **246**

Merciful Town 50, 56, 98, **246**

The Merry King 18, 26, 27, 29, 65, 106, **237**, **239**, **240**, **241**, **242**, **243**, **244**, **245**

The Merry Wedding 34, 45, 101, **241**, **245**, **247**

Mo Nighean Dubh 45, **237**, **246**, **247**

Mock Morris 18, 59, 60, 63, 64, 66, 67, 72, 90, 101, 142, 175, **228**, **231**, **236**, **237**, **239**, **240**, **241**, **243**, **245**, **248**

Molly on the Shore 18, 28, 29, 58, 65, 68,. 88, 90, 101, 102, 142, 171, **229**, **230**, **231**, **234**,

Molly on the Shore (cont.) 235, 236, 237, 238, 239, 240, 241, 242, 243, 244, 245, 247, 248
Morning Song in the Jungle; see Jungle Book Cycle
Mowgli's Song Against People; see Jungle Book Cycle
My faithful fond one; see Songs of the North
My Love's in Germanie 113, **246**, 247
My Robin is to the Greenwood Gone 65, 72, 90, 113, 171, 184, **231**, 237, **241**, 242, **245**, 248
Near Woodstock Town 56, 66, 237, 239, **246**, 247
Night Song in the Jungle; see Jungle Book Cycle
The Nightingale and The Two Sisters; see Danish Folk-Music Suite
Norse Dirge; see Youthful Suite
Northern Ballad 40, 50, 56, **246**
Northern March; see Youthful Suite
O'er the moor; see Songs of the North
O gin I were where Gadie rins; see Songs of the North
The Old Woman at the Christening 90, 112, **247**
One More Day, My John 39, 58, 61, 66, 67, **229**, **230**, **231**, **234**, 237, 239
The Only Son; see Jungle Book Cycle
Over the Hills and Far Away; see Children's March
Pastoral; see In a Nutshell
Peace 58, 66, **237**, **238**
The Peora Hunt; see Jungle Book Cycle
The Power of Love; see Danish Folk-Music Suite
The Power of Rome and the Christian Heart 9, 10, 20, 21, 24, 89, **241**, **242**, **243**
Preludes (Childhood Works) 58, 67
The Pretty Maid Milking Her Cow 56, 113, **246**
Pritteling, Prattleing, Pretty Poll Parrot 58, 68, **238**
Proud Vesselil; see Stalt Vesselil
Random Round 45, 69, 70, 81, 90, 93, 99, 112, 163, 171, 194, **238**, **241**, **245**
Recessional 43, **246**
Red Dog; see Jungle Book Cycle
A Reiver's Neck-Verse 52, 57, **246**
Ride with an Idle Whip 50, 56, 98, **246**
Rimmer and Goldcastle 237
The Rival Brothers 67, 68, **235**, 237, **238**, 239, **241**, **245**, 247
Rondo 67, 68, **238**
Room-music for 22-some; see Hill-Song I

Rufford Park Poachers; see Lincolnshire Posy
The Running of Shindand 241, 247
Rustic Dance; see Youthful Suite
Sailor's Chanty 51, 57, **246**
Sailor's Song 66, 67, **237**, 239
Saxon Twi-Play 58, 66, 67, **237**, **238**
La Scandinavie xx, 90, 173, **248**
Scherzo **241**, **245**
Scotch Strathspey and Reel 38–9, 45, 63, 64, 91, 102, 106, 171, **229**, 237, 239, 240, **241**, 243, **245**, 247
Sea Song 59, **239**, 247
The Sea Wife 40, 56, 105, **232**, **241**, **245**, **246**
The Secret of the Sea 51, 57, **246**
Seven Men from All the World **234**, **235**, 239
Shallow Brown 40, 43, 45, 50, 52, 57, 91, 98, 102, 116, **241**, **245**, **246**, 247
Shenandoah (Two Sea Chanties) 40, 45, 108, **241**, **244**, **245**, 247
Shepherd's Hey 18, 28, 29, 58, 65, 67, 68, 142, 171, 202, **228**, **229**, **230**, **234**, 235, 236, 237, **238**, 239, 240, **241**, 242, **243**, **244**, **245**, 248
The Shoemaker from Jerusalem; see Danish Folk-Music Suite
Sir Eglamore 32, 248
Six dukes went a-fishin' 43, 48, 56, **241**, 243, **244**, **245**, **246**, 247
Skye Boat Song 56, 98, **241**, **245**, **246**
Soldier, Soldier 40, 42, 45, 56, **246**, 247
A Song of Autumn 46, 56, 98, **246**
The Song of Solomon; see Love Verses from the 'Song of Solomon'
A Song of Värmeland 44, **241**, **245**, 247
Songs of the North 48, 49, 184
 'Bonnie George Campbell' 56, **246**
 'Drowned' 49, 56, **246**
 'Fair young Mary' 56, **246**
 'Leezie Lindsay' 56, 56, **237**, **246**
 'My faithful fond one' 46, 49, 56, 98
 'O'er the moor' 49, 56
 'O gin I were where Gadie rins' **237**, **241**, **245**
 'The women are a' gane wud' 49, 56, **246**
 'This is no my plaid' 56, **246**
 'Turn ye to me' 56, 98, **246**
 'Weaving Song' 53, 56, **246**
 'Willie's gane to Melville Castle' 49, 53, 56, 98, **246**
Spoon River 10, 65, 68, 69, 102, **229**, **234**, 237, **238**, 239, **241**, **243**, **245**, **246**, 247, 248
The Sprig of Thyme 52, 56, 98
Stalt Vesselil (Proud Vesselil) 51, 56, **237**, **241**, **245**, **246**

Stormy (Two Sea Chanties) 40, 45, 102, 108, 241, 245, 247
The Sussex Mummers' Christmas Carol 66, 67, 72, 90, **234**, **237**, **239**, **243**, **244**, 247, **248**
Thanksgiving Song 9, 17, 71, 94, 106, 109, 111, 112, **248**
Theme and Variations **248**
There was a pig went out to dig 37, 45, **241**, **244**
There were three friends 18, **240**
The women are a'gane wud; see Songs of the North
This is no my plaid; see Songs of the North
Thou Gracious Power **241**, **245**
The Three Ravens 36, 43, **241**, **245**, 247
Three Scottish Folksongs 66, 108, **239**
Tiger, Tiger; see Jungle Book Cycle
To a Nordic Princess 7, 9, 10, 65, 71, 89, 91, 101, 103, 106, 171, **237**, **239**, **241**, **242**, **245**
Train music 59, 184, **237**, **239**, **242**
Tribute to Foster 17, 34, 35, 43, 63, 64, 71, 91, 93, 101, 106, **237**, **239**, **240**, 247, **248**
Turn ye to me; see Songs of the North
The Twa Corbies 46, 53, 57, **246**, 247
Two Musical Relics of my Mother 58, 68, 69, **234**, **238**
    Hermunder Illi 102
Two Sea Chanties; see Shenandoah; Stormy
Under a Bridge (Under en bro) 52, 90, 98, 112, **242**, **246**, **248**
Up-Country Song **237**
Variations on Handel's 'The Harmonious Blacksmith' 79, 247
Walking Tune 18, 66, 67, **234**, **237**, **238**, **239**, **240**, **243**, 247
The Warriors x, xxi, 7, 10, 11–12, 13, 14, 20, 35, 58, 68, 69, 71, 83, 89, 99, 101, 103, 109, 110, 112, 151, 168, 171, 184, **234**, **238**, **240**, **242**, **243**, **244**; plates 12, 13
We have fed our sea 175, **241**, **245**
We were dreamers 18, 42, **240**
Weaving Song; see Songs of the North
When the World was Young 58, 68, 69, **238**
The Widow's Party 42, 43, 45, 50, 57, 58, 66, 67, 69, 98, 99, **237**, **238**, **239**, **241**, **245**, **246**
Willie's gane to Melville Castle; see Songs of the North
Willow Willow 43, 46, 56, **246**, 247
The Wraith of Odin 32, 68, 110, 159, **238**
Ye banks and braes o'bonnie Doon 18, 26, 27, 45, 67, 69, 70, 99, **237**, **238**, **241**, **242**, **243**, **244**, **245**, 247
Yon Wild Mossy Mountains 57, **246**

The Young British Soldier 42, 50, 57, 90, 194, **246**
The Young Pianist's Grainger 67
Youthful Rapture 18, 90, 181, **241**, **245**, **248**
Youthful Suite xx, 7, 8
    'Eastern Intermezzo' 7, 8, 65, 68, 86, **230**, **237**, **238**, **241**, **243**, **248**
    'English Waltz' 7, 63, 64, 67, 68, **237**, **238**, **244**
    'Norse Dirge' 7, 159
    'Northern March' 7
    'Rustic Dance' 7, 102
Zanzibar Boat Song 42, 58, 69, 70, 99, **234**, **238**

Arrangements and Transcriptions

Air and Dance [Delius] **237**, **240**
Alleluia Psallat [anon.] 70
Allemande [Brade] 78
Angelus ad Virginem [anon.] 43, 70, **237**, **244**
Après un rêve [Fauré] 65, 66, **237**, **240**
Bahariyale V Palaniyandi [anon.] 80, 82, **248**
Ballade no. 2 'Helas! tant ay dolour' [Machaut] 79, **244**
Beata viscera [anon.] 77
Bell Piece [Dowland] 27, 79, **242**, **243**
La Bernadina [Josquin] **244**
Berong Pengètjèt; see Gamelan Anklung
The Bigelow March [Ella Grainger] **237**
Brandenburg Concerto no. 3 [J. S. Bach] 79, 103, 204, 205
The Carman's Whistle [Byrd] 78, **235**, **236**, **240**
Chorale [Franck] **243**
Chosen Gems for Strings 78
Chosen Gems for Winds 78
Cradle Song [Brahms] 96, 104, **228**, **237**
Crying for the Moon [Ella Grainger] 52, **246**, **248**
Dance Rhapsody [No. 1] [Delius] 68, 69, **238**
David of the White Rock (Dafydd y Gareg Wen) [Hughes] 51, 56, 98, **246**
Down Longford Way [Parker] 147, **243**, **244**
Embraceable You [Gershwin] 67, 68, 286, **238**, **240**
Fantasy and Air no. 1 [Lawes] 74, 77, 78, 79
Fantasy on Themes from 'Porgy and Bess' [Gershwin] 68, 69, 91, **238**
Farewell to an Atoll [Ella Grainger] 52, **246**
Festival [Addinsell] 68, **238**
Fierce Rarotonga 1 [anon.] 81, 86
Five Part Fantasy [Jenkins] **244**
Folk Tune [Goossens] **244**
Four Irish Dances [Stanford] 63
The Four Note Pavan [Ferrabosco] **244**

Four Part Fantasy no 8 [Purcell] 79, *103*
Fugues [J. S. Bach] 79
Gamelan Anklung (Berong Pengètjèt) [anon.] 80, 82, **248**
Good-bye to Love (Bridal Lullaby) [Gibbs] **247**
Handelian Rhapsody [Scott] **240**
Honey-Pot Bee [Ella Grainger] 52, **246**
Hornpipe [Handel] **237**, **240**
Hungarian Fantasy [Liszt] **244**
Knut Lurasen's Halling II [Grieg] 68, **238**, 287
La bel' aronde [le Jeune] 68, 79, **238**
Lenten Chant; see Sangre de Cristo
Little Ole with his Umbrella [Lemche] **247**
London Bridge [Gardiner] **248**
Love at First Sight [Ella Grainger] 52, 98, **248**
Love Walked In [Gershwin] 65, 66, *104*, **231**, **237**, **240**
Mampahory Ny Masoandro Seranin-Javona (Two Madagascar Records no. 1) [anon.] 80, 82, 83
The Man I Love [Gershwin] 65, 66, 179, **231**, **237**, **240**
March [J. S. Bach] **243**, **244**
Marionette douce [anon.] 70
'Matachina' Dance [Curtis-Burlin] 80, 81
Die Meistersinger [Wagner] 112
Mori quasi il mio core [Palestrina] 79
Negro Lullaby [Curtis-Burlin] 80
Nell [Fauré] 65, 66, **233**, **237**, **239**, **240**
Norwegian Bridal Procession [Grieg] **229**
Now, O now, I needs must part [Dowland] 65–6, 67, 79, 98, **237**, **239**, **240**
O begli anni dell'oro (O Glorious Golden Era) [Corteccia] 79, **247**
O Mensch, bewein' dein' Sünde gross [J. S. Bach] **243**, **244**
O mistress mine [Morley] **246**, **247**
O praise the Lord, all ye heathen [J. S. Bach] 79
O rosa bella [Dunstable] 70
O salutaris hostia [Willaert] 79
Paganini Variations [Brahms, No. 12] **238**
Pagodes [Debussy] 15, 18, 80, 83, 86, **242**, **248**
Paraphrase on Tchaikovsky's Flower Waltz 58, 63, **229**, **237**, **239**, **240**
Porgy and Bess; see Fantasy on Themes from 'Porgy and Bess'
Prelude in the Dorian Mode [Cabezon] **243**, **244**
Puellare gremium [anon.] 70
The Quiet Brook [Scarlatti: Sonata in B minor] 78, 205
The Rag-Time Girl [Howard] 87
Ramble on the Last Love-Duet from 'Der Rosenkavalier' [R. Strauss] 58, 61, 63, **229**, **232**, **234**, **236**, **237**, **239**, **240**
Rarotonga I and II [anon.] 81, 86
Salve porta paradisi [Damett] 79
Sangre de Cristo (Lenten Chant) [Curtis-Burlin] 80, 81, 82
See what His love can do [J. S. Bach] **244**
Sekar Gadung [Javanese] 80, 81, 90, **248**
Song of the High Hills [Delius] 68
Songs of Love (Zulu Love Songs) [Curtis-Burlin] 84
Three Symphonic Dances [Cyril Scott] 68, 69, 183, **238**
Toccata and Fugue in D minor [J S Bach] 79, 119, **228**, **235**, **237**, **240**
To Echo [Ella Grainger] 52, **239**, **246**
Tuscan Serenade [Fauré] **243**, **244**
Two Madagascar [sic] *Records; see Mampahory Ny Masoandro Seranin-Javona*
La Vallée des cloches [Ravel] 15, 80, 83, 86, **242**, **248**

Writings

'The Aldridge-Grainger-Ström Saga' 189, 195
'Arnold Dolmetsch: Musical Confucius' 73
'Can Music Become a Universal Language?' 73
'Characteristics of Nordic Music' 162
'Collecting with the Phonograph' 53, 54, 82
'The Completion of the Percussion Family in the Orchestra' 81
'The Compositional Life of Percy Aldridge Grainger' xix, 192
'The Culturizing Possibilities of the Instrumentally Supplemented *A Cappella* Choir' 30, 191
'Democracy in Music' 73
Foreword to 'The Band's Music' by Richard Franko Goldman 77
'Free Music' 207–8
'The Fun that Lies in Making Music' 191
'A General Study of the Manifold Nature of Music' 73, 158, 191
'The Gregarious Art of Music: Australia Needs the Get-Together Spirit' 76, 196
'Grieg: Nationalist and Cosmopolitan' 194
'Guide to Virtuosity' 1
'Hints to Performers' (*Lost Lady Found*) 37
'The Impress of Personality in Unwritten Music' 36, 163, 191
Introduction to *Bold William Taylor* 47, 48
'The Love-Life of Helen and Paris' 162, 164
'Melody versus Rhythm' 174

'Music: A Commonsense View of All Types' 73, 83, 142, 190, 193
'Nordic Characteristics in Music' 161, 162
'Percy Grainger's Fighting Creed: His Guiding Principles as a Composer' 191
Preface to *Jutish Medley* 83
Programme notes for *Marching Song of Democracy* 31–2
'Rare Music of Early English Age Restored' 190
'Richard Strauss: Seer and Idealist' 196
'The Saxophone's Business in the Band' 196
'To Bandmasters' 25
'To Conductors' 199–205
'The Unique Value of Natalie Curtis' Notations of American Folksongs' 81
'Why "My Wretched Tone-Life"?' 34, 165, 195

Grainger, Richard 131
Grainger, Rose [mother] née Rosa Annie Aldridge xix, xxi, 92, 123, 124, 125, 134–9, 144, 152, 181–2, 189, 195, 211, 216, 220; plates 16, 24, 36
  as pianist 69, 144
  break-up of marriage 124, 128
  characteristics 135, 137, 138, 177
  cultural motivation 127, 189, 195
  discipline, ideas on 137
  educational approach 137
  homes in London and New York 166–8, 173
  illness 137, 138
  in the Grainger Museum 153, 155, 156
  suicide 14, 51, 152
  support for Grainger's career 141
  treatment by commentators 137
Grainger, T. [distant cousin] 130
Grainger, Thomas [great-uncle] 210, 212; plate 38
Grainger family 130–39, 212–17; family tree 210–11
Grainger festivals: Adelaide 17, 92–4; London 171
Grainger Museum, Melbourne xxii, 4, 35, 73, 86, 107–8, 113, 130, 136, 138, 142–4, 149–56, 161, 168, 172, 176, 181, 293; plates 32–7
  archive 108
  classification system for museum holdings 154–5
  Grainger's collection of music by other composers 171–6
  history and refurbishment ix, xxii, 2, 4, 149–51, 155
  treasures 151–3
Grainger website 167
Grant, Madison 164
Gray, Antony 99, **238**
Green, Eddie **243**
Green, W. K. 133
Greene, Graham: *Our Man in Havana* 148
Grettir the Strong xix, 159–60, 165
Grieg, Edvard xx, 88, 91, 97, 105, 114, 170, 179, 194, **229**, **230**, **234**, **235**, **236**, **237**; plate 27
  Evening in the High Hills 192
  Knut Lurasen's Halling II; see Arrangements *under* Grainger
  Lost in the Hills 192
  Lyric Piece 115
  Nineteen Norwegian Folk Songs 173
  Norwegian Bridal Procession; see Arrangements *under* Grainger
  Norwegian Peasant Dances 88, 173, **230**
  Peer Gynt Suite 91, 105, 117
  Piano Concerto in A minor xx, 29, 92, 93, 105, 106, 115, 120, **227**, **231**, **232**, **235**, **236**, **237**; plate 10
  To the Spring **229**, **230**
  Wedding Day at Troldhaugen **229**
Grofé, Ferde 203
Guion, David **229**
Gupta, Rolf **234**

Ham, Cara Aldridge 135, 187
Hamelin, Marc-André **239–40**
Hammershaimb, V. U.: *Færøsk Antologi* 34
Handel, George Frideric 79, **229**, **230**, **237**, 287; *Hornpipe*; see Arrangements *under* Grainger; *Largo* 127
Hansen, H. P. 14
Hanson, Howard 92
Harris, Charles K. 287
Harris, Mabel 176
Harris, Roy: *American Creed* 192
Harrogate Festival xxi, 175
Hart, Fritz 89, 146
Hawthorne, Melbourne 124
Heidelberg School 129, 144; plate 23
Heifetz, Jascha 187
Heighington village 212, 213; plate 41
Heinze, Sir Bernard 145, 146
Herrmann, Bernard 93
Hersée, Rose 126
Hickox, Richard 45, 108, **240**, **241**, **245**, **246**
Hill, Alfred 146

INDEX

Hill, Martyn 53, **246**, **247**
Hindemith, Paul 207
HMV (His Master's Voice, record company) 114
Holbrooke, Josef 176
Hollywood Bowl xxi, **232**, **235**, **236**; concert programme 103
Holst, Gustav 20, 174, 175; *Dargason* 27; *First Suite in E-flat* 24
Holtan, Lt. Col. Timothy **244**
Holten, Karen xx, 9, 136, 159, 165, 178
Hopkins, John 35, *100*, *101*, 112
Horn, Charles Edward: *Cherry Ripe* **230**
Hornbostel, Erich Moritz von 80
Hornby, James 53
Hough, Lotta Mills 26
Houghton College Band, concert programme 104
Howard, Joseph E.: *The Rag-Time Girl*; see Arrangements *under* Grainger
Howard, Leslie: corrections to *Lincolnshire Posy* 69
Howards End [film] 9, 65, 108
Hughes, Ceirioc 287
Hughes, Dom Anselm (Humphrey Vaughan) xxii, 75–9, *104*, 169
Humble, Keith 147

Iceland, sagas 194
Indian music; *see* World music
Indonesian music; *see* World music
Interlochen International Music Camp, Michigan xxii, 77; plate 9
International Musical Society 191
International Percy Grainger Society 108, 170, 232, 293; website 167
Ives, Charles 35, 176, 179
Ivory, James: *Howards End* 9, 108

Jackson, Paul 30–45
Japan, traditional music; *see* World music
Japart, Jean 78
Java, traditional music; *see* World music
Jenkins, John 74, 75, 77, 78, **244–5**
John, Augustus 153
Jones, Della 53, 98, **246**, **247**
Jones, E. H. 159
Jones, Martin 110, **237–8**
Jordan, Albert 176
Jørgensen, Jesper Grove **241**
Josquin; *see* Des Prez
Jost, Mack 100
Judd, James 7, 9, 16–17, 92, 94, 106

Junkin, Jerry **244**

Kasshau, Frank **229**
Kellerman, Karen; *see* Holten, Karen
Kelly, Ned 125
Kendall, William 102
Kensington & Norwood Brass Band 93
Kingston Brass 89
Kipling, Rudyard 30, 40, 42, 43, 50, 87, 124, 134; *Barrack Room Ballads* 42, 50; *Jungle Book*; *see* Works *under* Grainger
Klavier Records [record company] 183
Klimsch, Eugen 177
Klimsch, Karl Ferdinand xix, 30, 176, 177, 178; radical view on composition, 178
Kneller Hall 28
Knorr, Iwan (Ivan) xix, 30, 176
Knox, Garth 89
Kodály, Zoltán 174
Koehne, James 9, 92–4
Kosei Wind Orchestra; *see* Tokyo Kosei Wind Orchestra
Krautschneider, Astrid Britt 151–3
Kreines, Joseph 24
Kristensen, Evald Tang xxi, 14, 92, 160, 178; plate 31
Kwast, James xix

Lane, Piers **240**
Langfield, Valerie 175
Lavender, John **68**, 89, 99, 109, **234**, **238**
Laver, Professor W. A. 186
Lawes, William: *Fantasy and Air*; *see* Arrangements *under* Grainger
Lawson, Henry 129
Lawson, Malcolm 178
Lawson, Rex **234**, **235**
Layton, Stephen **247**
Leaning, Joseph 47
Leighton, Lord 149
Le Jeune, Claude 68, 79
Lemche, Peter **247**
Leopold, Ralph **229**, **234**
Library of Congress: Archive of American Folk Song 74
Lichnovsky, Michael **248**
Liddell, Nona 102
Lindsay, Norman 153
Link, Antonietta 127
Liszt, Franz 114, 152, **229**, **230**; plates 33, 34
Hungarian Fantasy; *see* Arrangements *under* Grainger
Hungarian Rhapsody [No. 2] **229**

Hungarian Rhapsody [No. 12] 114, 127, **227**
Hungarian Rhapsody [No. 15] **230**
Lloyd, A. L. 48; *Folk Song in England* 48
Longfellow, Henry Wadsworth 51; *Saga of King Olaf* 32
Lorenzen, Poul 14
Lovell, Chen 150
Ludwig [instrument maker and music publisher] 22

McCubbin, Frederick xix, 144
MacDowell, Edward: *To a Water-Lily* **229**
Machaut, Guillame de 78, 79; *see* Arrangements *under* Grainger
McLachlan, Murray 114–20
Macleod, A. C. 178
McMahon, Richard **237**
Macquarie Dictionary 143
Madagascan music; *see* World music
Mangeot, Andre 204
Manning, Jane 89
Manville, Stewart 3, 107, 166–70
Maori music; *see* World music
Marshall, Wayne 99, **238**
Marshall-Hall, G. W. 146, 151; plate 23
Martin, Benjamin 106
Martin, Philip **237**
Medley, Sir John 155
Melba, Nellie 141, 145
Melbourne 3, 23, 123–9, 144–6
    Albert Street Conservatorium 146
    Centennial International Exhibition 126, 127, 128
    Concert Hall 100
    Conservatorium of Music 186
    Masonic Hall xix, 134
    Philharmonic Society 101, 125
    Prince of Wales Opera House 127
    Princes Bridge xix, 134, 145; plate 20
    Symphony Orchestra 100, 101
    University ix, 125, 143, 155, 149; Baillieu Library 150
Melchior, Harriet 152
Mellers, Wilfrid 145, 174
Mendelssohn, Felix 184; *Violin Concerto* 127
Meng, L. Kong 128
Menpes, Mortimer 153
Merchant, Ismail: *Howards End* 9, 108
Merriam-Webster Dictionary 143
Mitchell, David 145
Mitchell, Dugald, ed.: *Book of Highland Verse* 49
Mitchell, Helen Porter; *see* Melba, Nellie

Monteverdi Choir 102, 116
Morley, Thomas 79
Morris, William 160
Morrish, Bill [cousin] 188
Morrish, Jack [cousin] 188
Morse, Richard A. **232**
Munro, Ian 147
Museum; *see* Grainger Museum
Music Hall, British 169
Musik des Orients, 78-rpm records 80
Musikkens Verden ['World of Music'] 157, 165, 189

National Music Camp, Michigan; *see* Interlochen International Music Camp
New Mexico 81
New York xxi; College of Music 186; University xxii, 73, 74, 75, 92, 158, 191
New Zealand xx, 95, 86, 141; *see also* Maori
Newman, John Henry 132
Niles, John Jacob 74
Norway xx, xxii, 88, 157, 160–62, 170, 173, 178; St Olav Medal xxii
Novello [music publisher] 107
Nygaard, K. K. [Grainger's doctor] 138, 183

Olsen, Sparre 160, 179
O'Neill, Norman xix, 97, 175, 179
Ould, Barry Peter 17, 70, 94, 107–13, 227, **238**

Pabst, Louis xix, 144
Padmore, Mark **241**, **245**, **246**
Painter, Karen 163
Palestrina, Giovanni Pierluigi da 79; *Mori quasi il mio core*; *see* Arrangements *under* Grainger
Pappajohn, Frank, arrangement of *The Warriors* 20
Paris Exhibition xx, 14
Parker, D. C. 180, 192
Parker, Katharine: *Down Longford Way*; *see* Arrangements *under* Grainger
Parsons, Mary Ann [grandmother] 132, 210
Paterson, Banjo 129
Patti, Adelina xx
Payne, Dorothy 168
Pear, David 34, 127, 136, 141, 144, 145
Pears, Sir Peter 168
Percy Grainger Society [UK] 107, 113, 138, 293
Perring, John 39, 50, 52, 91
Persia, traditional music; *see* World music
Perth Town Hall 134
Peters Edition [music publisher] 67, 108

Piano rolls **233–6**
Pickard, John 9, 28
Pierson, Martin 75
Piggot, Harry 39
Pisador, Diego de 78
Pitt, William 124
Plainsong and Medieval Music Society 75
Polynesian music; see World music
Power, Lionel 78
Purcell, Henry 91; *Fantasias* 192, 204; *Four Part Fantasy*; see Arrangements *under* Grainger
Purcell Room, London 97, 179

Queen's Hall 132, 175
Quilter, Roger xix, 48, 88, 97, 172, 173, 175, 179, 182, 187; *I arise from dreams of thee* 175, *Children's Overture* 175

Raab, Alexander 187
Rachmaninov, Sergei 65, 170, **236**, 237
Ragtime 163, 179
Ramona [Mrs Helfer] 168
Rarotongan music; see World music
Rathbone, William Gair 152
Rattle, Sir Simon **242**
Ravel, Maurice: *Le Gibet* 95; *La Vallée des cloches*; see Arrangements *under* Grainger
Reese, Gustave 75
Reményi, Eduard 127
Resta, Rocco 24
Reynish, Timothy 20–29, **242**
Roberton Publications [music publisher] 108
Roberts, Tom 153; plate 23
Rogers, Charles, ed.: *Modern Scottish Minstrel* 49
Romanel, Phineas 133
Röntgen, Julius 173
Rosher, Charles 39
Rossini, Gioachino: *William Tell Overture* 104
Royal Liverpool Philharmonic Orchestra 172
Royal Opera House, Covent Garden 9
Royal Victorian Institute of Architects 133, 134
Rubinstein, Anton 144
Rundell, Clarke **242**, **244**
Russell, Dr Robert Hamilton 144
Russell, Ken: *Song of Summer* 178

St James's Hall, Piccadilly 133
Sala, George Augustus 123
Sandby, Herman xix, xx, 14, 72, 92, 158, 172, 173, 176, 178, 179; *Sea Mood* 192

Sargent, John Singer 153
Sawyer, Antonia 166, 172
Scarlatti, Domenico: *Quiet Brook*; see Arrangements *under* Grainger
Scharwenka, Franz Xaver 114, *Polish Dance in E flat minor* **229**
Schering, Arnold: *History of Music in Examples* 75
Schirmer [music publisher] 74, 112, 115, 116, 205
Schoenberg, Arnold xx, 163, 207; *First Chamber Symphony* 179; *Five Orchestral Pieces* 179
Schofield, Margaret 100, 101
Schopenhauer, Arthur 189, 194
Schott & Co., now Schott Music [music publisher] xx–xxi, 2, 63, 67, 113, 175, 180, 185, 293
Schrader, Herman 133
Schubert, Franz 104; *Marche Militaire* **230**
Schumann, Robert 88, 95, 114, **229**, 237
Études Symphoniques 119, **229**, **234**, **235**
Piano Concerto 237
Romance in F-sharp 118, **229**, **230**, **234**
Scott, Cyril xix, xx, 88, 43, 97, 140, 141, 158, 168, 172, 173, 175, 176, 179, 181, 182, 187, 195, 204, 207, **230**, **234**; plate 25
Danse Nègre **230**
First Symphony 171, 172, 176
Handelian Rhapsody; see Arrangements *under* Grainger
Pierrot Triste **230**
Third Symphony 171, 172
Three Symphonic Dances; see Arrangements *under* Grainger
Scott, Desmond [Cyril Scott's son] 176, 181–3
Scott, Sir Walter xix, 137; *Minstrelsy of the Scottish Border* 32
Sculthorpe, Peter viii, 16, 18, 186
Seeger, Ruth Crawford 183
Semmens, John 156
Servadei, Alessandro 12, 222, 224
Sharp, Cecil 37, 47, 141
Shaw, George Bernard ix
Shostakovich, Dmitri 184
Siam (Thailand); see World music
Silver, Frank: *Yes, We Have No Bananas* 188
Simon, Geoffrey 7, 9, 10–16, 36, 89, **242**
Sinding, Christian 114; *The Rustle of Spring* **229**
Sisley, Thomas xix, 144
Slattery, Thomas C. 3, 28, 42, 179
Smalley, Roger 140

Sousa, John Philip 169
Southern [music publisher] 24
Smith, John Stafford: *Musica Antiqua* 32
Stanford, Sir Charles Villiers 64, 290; *Four Irish Dances* 65, 114, **227**, **230**, **234**, **236**, **239**
Stanhope, David 147
State Heritage Council, register of historic buildings 155
Steffens, Max 186, 194
Steiner, Rudolph 189, 190, 194, 195
Stephen, Pamela Helen **241**, **245**
Stevenson, Robert Louis 49
Stevenson, Ronald 108, 115, 179, 183–5
    Corroboree for Percy Grainger 184
    The Young Pianist's Grainger 63
Stewart, Rev A. 49
Stoddard, Lothrop 164
Stokem, Johannes 78
Stokowski, Leopold 179, **231**, **235**, **236**, **240**
Strahan, Frank 153
Strauss, Richard 64, 180, 203
    Ramble on the Last Love-Duet from 'Der Rosenkavalier'; see Arrangements under Grainger
    Till Eulenspiegel **234**
Stravinsky, Igor xx, 174, 207; *L'Histoire du soldat* 179; *Piano Concerto* 179
Strecker, Willy 175
Ström, Ella Viola; see Grainger, Ella [wife]
Sutherland, Margaret 88–9, 146
Swinburne, Algernon 30, 32, 34
Sydney Bulletin 123
Sydney Symphony Orchestra 112, 188

Tait, J. and N. 95, 96
Tall, David 107
Taylor, Joseph 37, 47, 52, 131
Tchaikovsky, Pyotr Ilyich 64, 114, 176, **237**
    Nutcracker Suite 58, 95, 119, **229**, **233**, **234**
    Paraphrase on Flower Waltz; see Arrangements under Grainger
    Piano Concerto No. 1 xx, 92, 104, 115, **237**, **239**
    Romeo and Juliet Fantasy Overture **234**
Testro, Ron 126
Theremin 208, **248**
Thornton, Donald 100, 101
Threlfall, Robert 112
Thuren, Hjalmar 34; *Folksong in the Faeroe Islands* 34
Thwaites, Penelope 1–4, 7–10, 58–72, 87–92, 93, 97, 98, 99, 108, 109, 110, 130–39, 209, **234**, **238**, **239**, **241**, **245**, **246**
Tibbits, George 132, 155
Todhunter, Mabel 136
Tokyo Kosei Wind Orchestra 180
Tompkins, Thomas 75
Trinity College of Music 186
Trollope, Anthony 123
Tunisia; see World music
Tunley, David 175, 176
Twopeny, R. E. N. 124, 125, 126

Urso, Camilla 127

Varcoe, Stephen 46–57, 98, **241**, **245**, **246**, **247**
Vaughan, Humphrey; see Hughes, Dom Anselm
Vaughan Williams, Ralph xx, 20, 47, 48, 146, 173, 174, 175, 204
    Pastoral Symphony 192, 194
    Songs of Travel 49
Verney, Helen 89
Viola da Gamba Society 75

Wagner, Richard 7, 149, 163, 185
    Lohengrin 127
    Die Meistersinger 112, 177
    Rienzi 127
    Tannhaüser 127
Walker, David 123–9
Warlock, Peter 204
Watts, George Frederick 149
Wawn, Andrew 159
Weelkes, Thomas 75
Weill, Kurt 170
Weir, Kenneth 100, 101
Wells, H. G. 143, 174
West Point Military Academy xxii, 29; band members: plates 8, 11
Whirlwind Music Publications [music publishers] 22
White Plains, New York xxi, 3, 89, 107, 108, 166–70; plates 3, 4, 5, 27
Whiteman, Paul 203
Whitman, Walt 30, 192, 194, 195
Wigmore Hall 89
Wilde, Oscar 168
Willaert, Adrian 79; *O salutaris hostia*; see Arrangements under Grainger
Willis, Jane [great-grandmother] 131, 210, 212
Wilson, William 133
Wilson-Johnson, David **247**
Wood, Francis Derwent 153

Wood, Sir Henry J.: Promenade Concerts 115
Woods, W. Creary: plate 2
Woolgar, Alan 185–6
World music ix, xx, 3, 7, 73, 79–86, 152, 186,
    190–93
  Africa 73, 79, 80, 83, 84, 188
  Afro-American 163
  Americas 18, 81, 84–5
  Australasian 73, 80–81
  Bali 73, 80, 82, 85, 94, 192
  China 16, 19, 80, 84, 85, 188
  Egypt 14, 80
  India 79, 80, 81–3, 85
  Indonesia xx, 73, 79, 81–3, 85
  Japan 80, 188
  Java 73, 80, 85, 188
  Madagascar 80–83, 86
  Maori 80, 81, 86, 146, 157, 158
  Oriental 86
  Persia 80
  Polynesia xx, 12, 39, 73, 79, 81, 73, 157, 188
  Rarotonga 35, 80, 81, 86, 163, 193
  Thailand 73, 80
  Tunisia 80
  record collection *Musik des Orients* 80

Yasser, Joseph 84
Yeung, Roland **243–4**
Young, Timothy 238

Zelman, Alberto 127

www.ingramcontent.com/pod-product-compliance
Lightning Source LLC
Chambersburg PA
CBHW052056300426
44117CB00013B/2152